D0274807

Derek Gibson

17·12-16

Interests and Obsessions

BY THE SAME AUTHOR

POLITICIANS AND THE SLUMP

ENGLISH PROGRESSIVE SCHOOLS

OSWALD MOSLEY

JOHN MAYNARD KEYNES:
Hopes Betrayed 1883–1920

JOHN MAYNARD KEYNES:
The Economist As Saviour 1920–1937

EDITED BY THE SAME AUTHOR

THE END OF THE KEYNESIAN ERA

THATCHERISM

with Vernon Bogdanor
THE AGE OF AFFLUENCE

with Michael Holroyd
WILLIAM GERHARDIE'S GOD'S FIFTH COLUMN

Interests and Obsessions

SELECTED ESSAYS

Robert Skidelsky

MACMILLAN

LONDON

First published 1993 by Macmillan London Limited

a division of Pan Macmillan Publishers Limited
Cavaye Place London SW10 9PG
and Basingstoke

Associated companies throughout the world

ISBN 0-333-60457-1

This collection copyright © Robert Skidelsky 1993

The right of Robert Skidelsky to be identified as the
author of this work has been asserted by him in accordance
with the Copyright, Designs and Patents Act 1988.

All rights reserved. No reproduction, copy or transmission
of this publication may be made without written permission.
No paragraph of this publication may be reproduced, copied or
transmitted save with written permission or in accordance with
the provisions of the Copyright Act 1956 (as amended). Any
person who does any unauthorized act in relation to
this publication may be liable to criminal prosecution
and civil claims for damages.

1 3 5 7 9 8 6 4 2

A CIP catalogue record for this book is available from
the British Library

Typeset by Cambridge Composing (UK) Limited, Cambridge
Printed by Mackays of Chatham PLC, Chatham, Kent

Contents

PART TWO

THE INTER-WAR YEARS

PART THREE

THE ERA OF WARS

PART FOUR

COMMONWEALTH AND EUROPE

PART FIVE

THE USES OF HISTORY

Introduction

Most scholars remain captive to their first adult piece of research. This is certainly true of me. I did my doctoral dissertation on 'The Labour Government of 1929–1931 and the Unemployment Problem', published in 1967 as *Politicians and the Slump*. This set all my historical work in a certain frame. Its period was late nineteenth-century British history onwards; its field of interest, the interplay between politics, economics, and ideas.

The choice of my dissertation topic was not accidental; but nor did it arise from any history I had done as an undergraduate. Between 1958 and 1961, I read Modern History at Jesus College, Oxford. British history was supposed to go up to 1914. However, the main passion of John Walsh, my College tutor, an exact scholar and delightful man, was Methodism. This meant that, in practice, we failed to progress much beyond the Napoleonic wars. John Hale, a noted scholar of Renaissance Italy, taught me the earlier British period, with much charm, but without much engagement. What I liked best was my foreign period – the late Roman Empire – in which I had tutorials with that remarkable and inspiring man, Peter Brown of All Souls. I remember his excessively shabby clothes, and his habit, when seized with an idea, of darting round his room, and jumping like a cat into an armchair, in which he would curl up. Such nineteenth- and twentieth-century British history as I ever learnt, I learnt on my own – working on my dissertation, and reading up for the teaching I myself did as a Student, later Research Fellow, of Nuffield College, Oxford.

For history, there were no classes, and lectures played a small part in my tuition. I have forgotten them all, except a course given by the Regius Professor of Ecclesiastical History, Canon Claude Jenkins of Christ Church, on the Paston Letters, which I attended in my first year. A dozen undergraduates came to his first lecture; by week three, I was the only one. This did not put the Canon off his stride. '*Some* of you *may* recall from last week . . .' he started, with evident disbelief in any such possibility, raising his eyes to glare at me. He, too, had a remarkably unkempt appearance, his face full of tufts of hair left over from perfunctory shaving. The selvedges of his gown, it later transpired, were stuffed full of old bits of food. He had a resonant voice, in which he denounced 'the tobacco habit' and the presence of women at the university. I must have been his last student, since he died shortly after he completed his lectures.

This obliviousness of the dons of that period to their surroundings never ceased to delight me. In the mid-1960s I arrived at the Examination Schools to give a lecture on the Suez Crisis (of which the printed version is reproduced in this volume). There must have been two or three hundred students in the room. To my consternation, I found the podium occupied by a Fellow who had already started on some deeply obscure aspect of medieval theology. I was soon able to persuade him that he was in the wrong room, but it had evidently never occurred to him to wonder why his regular audience had swelled by a factor of ten.

If I go back much earlier, my passion for history was first aroused by my father, who gave me a history of the world when I was eight. I graduated to Hendrik van Loon's *The Story of Mankind*, illustrated with his own inimitable pictures, which I later read to my own children. It starts more memorably than it continues: 'High up in the North in the land called Svithjod, there stands a rock. It is a hundred miles high and a hundred miles wide. Once every thousand years a little bird comes to this rock to sharpen its beak. When the rock has thus been worn away, then a single day of eternity will have gone by.' Serious history started for me with *The Outline History of the World: A Record of World Events from the Earliest Historical Times to the Present Day*, edited by Sir J. A. Hammerton, and full of dates. At one time I virtually knew that book by heart; by the age of ten I had written my third history of the world. After that I renounced the broad sweep for the monograph. My earliest interest was ancient history. By thirteen I had progressed to the Anglo-Saxons. In adult life I have continued to read about all periods in a spasmodic way, but the amount of time it has taken me to write my own books, especially the Keynes biography, has drastically curtailed the time left for pleasurable reading of history outside my 'period'.

I believe *Politicians and the Slump* has been an influential book. It certainly influenced the way I started to think about recent British history, and the politics of my own time. (But perhaps I already thought about them in that way, and that is why I wrote my first book the way I did?) I took the view that the British unemployment problem of the inter-war years could not be effectively tackled within the framework of a political struggle between the Conservative and Labour Parties, between Capitalism and Socialism. It was wrong politics, not wrong economics, that prevented a British 'New Deal'. Thereafter I always hankered for a 'Middle Way'.

Perhaps the explanation for this is autobiographical. My family were victims of both Communism and Capitalism. My father's family fled from Russia in 1917, but managed to escape with an enormous amount of cash – $30 million. Most of this was lost in the Stock Market crash of 1929, ten years before I was born. What remained of the family fortune – the largest private coal-mine in Manchuria – was finally lost in 1949. I certainly had no reason to sympathize with Communism, but *laissez-faire* capitalism had done my family little good either.

The Labour Party fared worse in my first book than did the Conservatives or Liberals. I blamed the feebleness of Ramsay Mac-Donald's Labour government in face of the great slump on its 'utopian socialism'; its failure to recognize, or unwillingness to believe, that capitalism could be 'managed' in the interests of progress. Ever since then I felt that the Labour Party would be a hopeless instrument of government, torn between its head and its heart, though for many years I remained a lukewarm supporter of the Party. I partially retracted the analysis of my book in an essay written in the early 1970s, here published for the first time. This switches the emphasis to those elements of the Victorian culture which Labour *shared* with its political opponents. Keynes had put the matter much better than I did when he said that the Victorians divided into two camps: those who believed classical economics was true, but beneficial, and those who believed it was true, but intolerable.

From the stem of my dissertation on the Labour Government of 1929–31 grew my biographies of Oswald Mosley and Maynard Keynes. They were the joint heroes of *Politicians and the Slump*: Mosley, the Minister who resigned when his 'New Deal' was turned down; Keynes, the Adviser, whose advice was rejected. Mosley was a false trail for me, though traces of him still linger in the way I think about things. He was an obvious influence on the history I wrote in the 1970s, as the reader will become aware. My biography of him, published in 1975, was emotionally centred on the years covered by my dissertation – 1929 to 1931 – but most of the controversy which that book aroused had to do with my unduly benign treatment of his later Fascist phase, with which I never had the slightest political sympathy, and regarded as a tragic aberration. I admired three things about Mosley as I still do: his passion for ideas – so rare in an Englishman, and so amazing in one of his background – his courage, and the fact that he cared so much about the decline of his country. I was loath to admit that he had a dark side.

Keynes is a healthier obsession, and I have spent most of the last fifteen years writing a biography about him – the third volume is yet to come. I no longer believe, in any simple way, that Keynes was 'right' and his opponents wrong. We have lived through the breakdown of Keynesian economics, and though I feel sure in my own mind that Keynes himself would not have succumbed to the hubris of the post-war Keynesians, there was something, after all, in his theories which fed their belief in the omni-competence of governments. Still, he was by far the most exciting person one could hope to meet as a biographical subject, and my fascination with him is undimmed. Perhaps it will be said of my biography, as Lytton Strachey remarked of Froude's life of Carlyle, that Froude's admiration for Carlyle was so total that 'it shrank with horror from the notion of omitting a single wart from the portrait'.

Writing *Politicians and the Slump* not only confirmed a bias towards 'Middle Way' thinking in politics, but also led me to disproportionate admiration for those politicians who had what the late Henry Fairlie called 'cross-party minds'. I accepted far too readily the 'Locust Years' theory of the inter-war period, with its corollary that the mediocrities in charge of the party machines kept the great and talented 'in the wilderness', to the great detriment of the country. My historical sympathies were lavished on the 'outsiders', partly because I identified with them: men like Joseph Chamberlain, Lloyd George, Mosley himself, Churchill. The great merit of such Outsiders, in my eyes, was that they were not only outsize in personality, but they straddled the ground between Right and Left. I was much more ambivalent about Churchill than the others, partly because he had nothing of great interest to say on economic and social problems, partly because I thought he liked war too much. The vileness of Nazism seemed to vindicate Churchill. Yet it must always remain questionable whether going to war with Germany in 1939 was the best policy for a declining, overstretched world empire.

It was the start of my work on Keynes which reawakened my interest in the late Victorians. It was not so much the history of late Victorian England which concerned me as the psychological worlds which the late Victorians inhabited. This is best brought out in my essays on Henry Sidgwick and the Fabians. I am afraid I still tend to regard the great Fabians – Sidney and Beatrice Webb, Bernard Shaw – as period pieces, with comic rather than horrific potential, but the infirmities of

Henry Sidgwick, poised between belief and unbelief, struck a much more responsive chord. Sidgwick believed it was not possible to keep morality going without religion, and it was impossible to believe in religion. The Keynes generation cheerfully embraced atheism, and thought that unaided reason could give morality all the support it needed. I have come increasingly to see this 'solution' as an evasion. I feel that Sidgwick stated the problem correctly, though he had no answer to it. I no longer believe that to hold beliefs which cannot be rationally justified is to be in a state of unpardonable delusion. Beliefs which keep people good are much to be preferred to moral anarchy.

My work on Keynes has taken me away from straight history, and I doubt if I shall ever return to it. I have used history and biography as vehicles for political, economic and moral argument. But I feel that my increasing interest in ideas is about to break through the historical frame. I get increasingly impatient with shaping narrative, marshalling evidence – the historian's necessary tools. I want to address the world directly, not shelter behind the past. Others will see this as a sign of senility; I see myself as having reached the age of wisdom. The future will tell which of us is right.

Most of the pieces which appear in this book have been published as articles, chapters, or reviews. The exceptions are 'J. A. Hobson', a lecture I gave at Lincoln College in 1978; 'The Labour Party and Keynes', a paper given in 1972; 'Fascism and Expansion', the development of a talk at Reading University in 1976, which I gave at the invitation of my friend Adrian Lyttleton; 'A Critique of the Ageing Hypothesis', which I wrote in 1982; and 'Psychohistory', a lecture I gave in 1977.

At various times in my life I have done a great deal of reviewing. Reviewing is not conspicuously well paid. Its main benefit is that it forces one to read books, and think about what one has read. In my experience successful reviewing depends on the relationship between the reviewer and commissioning editor. The editor has to like what the reviewer writes and feed him books suitable to his talents. The three literary editors with whom I felt the greatest rapport were Hilary Spurling and Peter Ackroyd, both of *The Spectator*, and Tony Gould, of *New Society*, later the *New Statesman*. Many of the reviews which appear here were done for them. Between 1968 and 1986 I wrote half a dozen articles and review articles for *Encounter*, three of which I reproduce here. I have the fondest memories of Melvin Laski, its redoubtable editor, who was ostracized by most British intellectuals for supporting the Cold War against Soviet communism. How right he was, and how silly they now seem.

The point in republishing these particular pieces, some substantial, others fugitive, is that they form part of patterns of interest and obsession, more apparent to me now than when I wrote them. Since they are about history I have not ordered them by when they were written, but by the conventional period to which they refer, starting with the late Victorians and early Edwardians and continuing up to the post-war years. In some instances I have given the original rather than the published – and cut – version of a review; and occasionally I have omitted or altered a phrase on stylistic grounds. Otherwise they appear as they were published.

I wish I had written more on European history. But, despite my cosmopolitan origins, I share with most of my fellow-countrymen the handicap of being frightfully bad at languages. I have often dreamt of remedying this, but like many of my dreams, this one is now unlikely to be fulfilled.

Sources

Places and dates of the published pieces are given below:

PART ONE
VICTORIANS AND EDWARDIANS

'Henry Sidgwick: Between Reason and Duty', *Times Higher Educational Supplement*, 26 August 1988. This was based on an address given on 31 May 1988 at the dinner at Newnham College, Cambridge to mark the 150th anniversary of the birth of Henry Sidgwick, founder of Newnham College.

'Leslie Stephen', *New Society*, 17 January 1985.

'The Fabian Ethic' in Michael Holroyd (ed.), *The Genius of Shaw*, 1979.

'The Letters of Sidney and Beatrice Webb', *The Spectator*, 30 May 1978.

'Beatrice Webb's Diary', *New Society*, 11 October 1985.

'Victorian Wives', *Sunday Times*, 20 November 1986.

'J. G. Frazer', *Sunday Telegraph*, 13 December 1987.

'Bertrand Russell', *Sunday Telegraph*, 3 July 1988.

'Keynes and His Parents' in Stephen R. Graubard (ed.), *Generations*, 1979.

'William Beveridge', *New Society*, 10 November 1977.

'Liberals and Progressives', *New Society*, 11 January 1979.

'Europe Transformed', *New Society*, 14 April 1983.

'Cecil Rhodes', *The Spectator*, 3 July 1976.

'Chamberlain's Squalid Argument', *New Statesman*, 22 October 1976.

'Joseph Chamberlain and Enoch Powell', *The Spectator*, 12 November 1977.

'Julian Grenfell', *The Spectator*, 24 April 1976.

PART TWO
THE INTER-WAR YEARS

'Our Age', *New Statesman*, 3 October 1990.

'Oxford in the 1920s', *The Spectator*, 12 June 1976.

'Vera Brittain', *Sunday Telegraph*, 23 August 1987.

'Stanley Baldwin', *The Listener*, 19 February 1970.

'The Taming of Labour', *Guardian*, 22 April 1971.

'Baldwin Revisited', *Sunday Telegraph*, 1 March 1987.

'Ramsay MacDonald', *The Spectator*, 12 March 1977.

'Lloyd George', *The Spectator*, 7 February 1976.

'Life with Sylvester', *The Spectator*, 7 June 1975.

'Life with Pussy', *The Spectator*, 11 October 1975.

'Rhodes James's Churchill', *Guardian*, 14 May 1970.

'Martin Gilbert's Churchill', *The Spectator*, 30 October 1976.

'Oswald Mosley', *Encounter*, September 1969.

'British Fascism' in S. J. Woolf (ed.), *Fascism in Europe*, 1981.

'Nicholas Mosley on his Father', *Times Literary Supplement*, 22 October 1982, 11 November 1983.

PART THREE
THE ERA OF WARS

'War and Change', *New Society*, 16 June 1977.

'The Diplomatic Diaries of Oliver Harvey', *The Spectator*, 25 July 1970.

'The Impact of Hitler', *The Spectator*, 26 July 1975.

'Going to War with Germany', *Encounter*, July 1972.

'The Meaning of the Polish Guarantee', *Books and Bookmen*, March 1977.

'Adam von Trott', *Sunday Telegraph*, 3 April 1988.

'The Cambridge Communists', *Encounter*, June 1980.

'The Science of Treason', *Sunday Times*, 22 January 1986.

'War Correspondents', *The Spectator*, 22 November 1975.

'Churchill's War', *The Spectator*, 31 July 1976.

'The Resistance', *The Spectator*, 18 December 1976.

'The Road to 1945', *The Spectator*, 25 October 1975.

PART FOUR
COMMONWEALTH AND EUROPE

'The Commonwealth Experience', *The Spectator*, 7 March 1969.

'Suez', in V. Bogdanor and R. Skidelsky (eds), *The Age of Affluence*, 1970.

'Anthony Eden', *Sunday Times*, 12 October 1985.

'Harold Macmillan', *Sunday Times*, 18 June 1989.

'The Choice for Europe', *The Spectator*, 23 May 1970.

'Britain and Europe' in D. P. Calleo and P. H. Gordon (eds), *From the Atlantic to the Urals*, 1992. This was first given as a talk in Washington in May 1991.

PART FIVE
THE USES OF HISTORY

'The Economic Decline of Britain', *Time and Tide*, Autumn 1985.

'Rhodes James's British Revolution', *The Spectator*, 25 September 1976.

'Our Finest Hour?' *Times Literary Supplement*, 21 March 1986.

'Hugh Dalton', *New Society*, 21 March 1985.

'Nye Bevan', *Sunday Times*, 29 March 1987.

'The Misuse of History', *Times Educational Supplement*, 3 June 1977.

'A. J. P. Taylor', written 1987, published in the *Independent*, 8 September 1990.

PART ONE

Victorians
and Edwardians

CHAPTER ONE

Henry Sidgwick: Between Reason and Duty

[1988]

WITHIN a few years of his death, the nineteenth-century Cambridge philosopher Henry Sidgwick was already being dismissed as a Victorian period piece. In 1906 Maynard Keynes, after reading the *Memoir* to Sidgwick compiled by his widow and brother, wrote to his friend Bernard Swithinbank: 'He never did anything but wonder whether Christianity was true and prove that it wasn't and hope that it was.' Of course, Sidgwick *did* much more than that. He founded Newnham College, championed university reform, wrote books. But Keynes's remark does capture with wicked accuracy Sidgwick's state of mind. Sidgwick feared above all that loss of Christian belief would under-mine morality; and this in turn would undermine the social order. To young twentieth-century Cambridge, secure in its belief that atheism was part of progress, and that morals needed no supernatural support, Sidgwick's doubts seemed absurd. Today we are not so sure. His problems now seem to be true enough; it is our truths which seem problematic.

Sidgwick's life, which lasted from 1838 to 1900, spans the Victorian age – the passage of its thought from belief to doubt; and of much of its propertied classes from Liberalism to Conservatism. In these respects, Sidgwick was a typical Victorian intellectual. What made him untypical was his intellectual fastidiousness. His reason undermined his faith, but he refused the late Victorian escape routes into mysticism, evolutionism, imperialism. He described himself as a 'monu-ment . . . to Protean vacillation'. Shortly before he died of cancer, he composed his own carefully qualified epitaph: 'Let us commend to the love of God with silent prayer the soul of a sinful man who partly tried to do his duty.' Duty always weighed heavily with Sidgwick. His clergyman father died when he was three. From then on the dominant male influence in the Sidgwick household was his cousin, Edward White Benson, a future Archbishop of Canterbury. Three years at Rugby, still heavily Arnoldian in atmosphere, completed Sidgwick's apprenticeship

3

to duty. At seventeen, he went up to Trinity College, Cambridge, intending on graduation to take holy orders. He secured a double first in Classics and Mathematics, and in 1859 was elected a Fellow of Trinity College.

It was at Cambridge that Sidgwick's lifelong crisis started. Darwin's *Origin of Species* appeared in the year of his fellowship election. Shortly after this Sidgwick succumbed to the influence of John Stuart Mill. He swallowed Mill's Utilitarianism and lost his faith. Reason became his watchword: 'I have taken service with reason and have no intention of deserting,' he proudly declared. His problem was that the Reason to which he gave allegiance could not justify the Duty in which he had been bred. In 1862 he wrote to his friend Graham Dakyns: 'I cannot persuade myself, except by trusting intuition, that Christian self-sacrifice is really a happier life than classical insouciance.' And in 1880 he repeated, in a letter to an old Rugby schoolfriend, that belief in God was necessary to his other beliefs. 'Duty is to me as real a thing as the physical world, though it is not apprehended in the same way; but all my apparent knowledge of duty falls into chaos if my belief in the moral government of the world is conceived to be withdrawn ... Therefore I sometimes say to myself "I believe in God"; while sometimes again I can say no more than "I *hope* this belief is true, and I must and will act as if it was." '

Something must be said about these two words in Sidgwick's moral lexicon – Reason and Duty. For Bentham there was no conflict between them. Individuals were psychologically driven to pursue pleasure and avoid pain. The state of affairs to be aimed at was one in which the greatest number were happiest. For Bentham duty was only a particular kind of pleasure: the pleasure the enlightened person gets in helping the human race achieve universal felicity. Benthamism does not, therefore, require a rational motive for the thinking person to do his duty: he is so constructed that doing it will give him pleasure. Sidgwick, like John Stuart Mill, discovered, on the contrary, that doing his duty made him ill. Morality, he concluded, could not be derived from the facts of psychology as Bentham supposed. It needed arguments capable of convincing.

For Sidgwick duty was associated with pain, not pleasure, and this was, on the whole, true for the Victorian academic class. Duty for this class had a particular association with celibacy and childlessness. After Lytton Strachey read Keynes's obituary of Alfred Marshall, Sidgwick's

4

great Cambridge contemporary, he wrote to its author (in 1924): 'What a world it opens up! What strange people were the married monks of the nineteenth century.' Sidgwick was one of these married monks. His marriage in 1874 to Eleanor (Nora) Balfour, sister of the politician Arthur Balfour, was described by Nora Sidgwick's biographer as 'a joining of forces towards the same ends'. It was childless. Sidgwick's overpowering sense of duty probably made him impotent; it certainly made him unhappy. Friends noted what his portrait also show: a sadness and wistfulness underlying handsome looks and surface playfulness. So Sidgwick questioned the justification for making oneself unhappy for the sake of promoting the universal happiness.

Sidgwick's crisis was partly that of a peculiarly situated Victorian. To the married monks of his day duty appeared almost entirely a matter of self-sacrifice, because they denied themselves the family life (and more generally the circle of affections) which could have linked up self-love with love of others. Their life-styles and dispositions made the opposition between what Sidgwick called Rational Egoism and Rational Benevolence seem more radical than it need have been. Part of Sidgwick's dilemma also arose from the peculiar meaning he attached to reason. He equated it with science; rational argument was one capable of empirical proof. It seemed to Sidgwick that it was only in one's rational self-interest to do one's duty if doing so would make one happy – in this life or the next. But then one came up with the problem of the 'proof' of God's existence. However, having said all this, there remains a problem which survives Sidgwick's own time. We have gone to the opposite extreme in believing that self-expression, even self-indulgence, somehow 'adds up' to the 'greatest happiness of the greatest number'. Much of official philosophy today is simply vulgar Benthamism – the pursuit of trivial pleasure, without attention being paid to the nourishing of the benevolent dispositions which the best of the Utilitarians like Mill saw as necessary to make Benthamism morally reputable.

If Sidgwick failed to discover adequate reasons for people to do their duty, he had no doubt where the duty of people like him lay. It was to improve the conditions of human happiness. 'What we aimed at from a social point of view', Sidgwick recalled of his early years in Cambridge, 'was a complete revision of human relations, political, moral, and economic, in the light of science directed by comprehensive and impartial sympathy; and an unsparing reform of whatever, in the judgment of science, was pronounced to be not conducive to the general happiness'. This was the Utilitarian programme, which inspired many of the great Victorian reforms. In some moods, at least, Sidgwick hankered for an active public life – one that took him beyond Cambridge, which he typically described as a 'comfortable hospital for maimed intellects and *carrières manquées*'. The chance for a break came in 1869 when, after half a decade of hesitation, he resigned his Trinity Fellowship, on the ground that he could no longer accept the 'dogmatic obligations' of the Apostles' Creed attached to Cambridge fellowships at the time. He remained at Cambridge as a lecturer in Moral Sciences; but freed, temporarily, from 'egoistic' absorption in his doubts, he plunged wholeheartedly in to the movement for university reform, itself one of the main objects of Gladstone's Liberal government of 1868–74. The causes which he promoted without any of his usual hesitations included the abolition of the so-called 'idle fellowships', the scrapping of the celibacy requirements and religious tests for fellowships, the abolition of Greek and Latin for university entrance, the abolition of the Poll or Ordinary degree, and access to Higher Education for women.

Sidgwick's most notable achievement in this period was the foundation of Newnham College. In 1871 he started financing a hostel where women could live in Cambridge while attending special lectures by sympathetic Cambridge dons in preparation for the Higher Local Examinations (something like the present 'A' levels). It was decided to erect a permanent hall of residence, and in October 1875 Newnham Hall was ready to accept a Principal, assistant lecturer, and thirty students. Sidgwick was not the only college builder: Emily Davies had built Girton, three miles outside Cambridge, in 1873. There was strong disagreement between the two reformers, Emily Davies claiming a right of equal treatment for women, whereas for Sidgwick the issue was the right of women to knowledge as part of the general Utilitarian programme. In 1874 Mary Paley and Anne Bulley, living at the Newnham hostel in Regent Street, became the first women to take the Moral Sciences Tripos. The occasion is a well-established part of Cambridge legend. They were not allowed to sit the Tripos formally, so they were examined informally in the drawing room of Dr Kennedy's house in Bateman Street. The Tripos papers came by 'runners' who collected them from Senate House. These runners were Sidgwick, Marshall, Venn and Sedley Taylor. Keynes, who tells the story in his memoir of Mary Paley Marshall, recalls them 'as familiar figures of my youth. Apart from

6

Marshall, they were all very short, and had long, flowing beards ... I see them as the wise, kind dwarfs hurrying with their magical prescriptions which were to awaken the princesses from their slumbers into the full wakefulness of masculine mankind.'

Sidgwick's enthusiasm for reform dwindled the older he got. He noted in 1885 that he had been re-reading Comte and Spencer with all his old amazement at their 'fatuous self-confidence. It does not seem to me that either of them knows what self-criticism is.' The seeds of later disillusionment can plainly be seen in the unwarranted optimism of the young Sidgwick's reforming programme quoted above. Even if the 'greatest happiness' principle is accepted, Utilitarianism cannot tell the social reformer what needs to be done, since the consequences of his acts – the quantities of pleasure and pain which they will produce – cannot be accurately calculated. The Utilitarian reformer is forced back onto experience as a guide to probable consequences; but acceptance of experience was bound to rob Utilitarianism of its radical cutting edge. Thus we have the paradox that a philosophy which promised to sweep away all traces of superstition in political and social arrangements ended up in the hands of its most sophisticated practitioners like Sidgwick praising Queen Victoria, the British Constitution and conventional morality.

In the 1880s and 1890s Sidgwick produced vast cheerless tomes on politics and economics, whose reformist aspirations simply collapsed under the weight of their qualifications and uncertainties. ('Decidedly', he noted in 1886 after being appointed Knighbridge Professor of Moral Philosophy, 'nature intended me to read books and not write them; I wish the former function was regarded as sufficient fulfilment of Professorial duty.') They are monuments to inconclusive reasoning. Take, for example, Sidgwick's discussion of the principles of punishment in his *Elements of Politics* (1891):

It is a difficult matter to determine satisfactorily the right degree of punishment for any given offence. It is easy to say, with Bentham, that it ought to be sufficient to deter, and not more than sufficient. But our general knowledge of the variations in human circumstances and impulses would suggest what experience amply confirms – that no punishment whatever can be relied on to be adequately deterrent in all cases. Murder and manslaughter, burglary and larceny, have continued to harass

7

society through all changes in the allotment of punishment; and no change is likely to put an end to them. Now, impulsive crimes we cannot hope to prevent by any intensification of punishment until human nature is fundamentally altered; but crimes planned in cold blood are matters of calculation, and it does not seem impossible that it should be made unmistakably a man's interest, on a cool calculation of chances, not to commit a crime. Since, however, the attainment of this result depends not only on the amount of punishment, but also on the chances that the criminal (1) will be caught, and (2) will be condemned if caught, it may easily happen that in a community where the police is ill organised, and the judges liable to be corrupt or inefficient, the required adjustment of interests cannot be effected: the uncertain chance of the maximum punishment which humanity admits may not be enough to outweigh the prospective profit of the crime. For the same reason, in societies where similar governmental defects exist to a less degree, an increase in the efficiency of police and judicature will often enable intensity of punishment to be reduced without increasing crime.

The key phrase, which runs like a leitmotiv through Sidgwick's life, is the difficulty of effecting 'the required adjustment of interests' between egoism and benevolence; in this case, the egoism of the wrongdoer and the benevolence of society.

The political distance Sidgwick had travelled by the end of his life is evident from his last essay 'The Relation of Ethics to Sociology':

In criticising this 'evolutionary optimism', as we may call it, I ought to explain that I am not opposing optimism as a philosophical doctrine. I am not myself an optimist; but I have great respect for the belief that, in spite of appearances to the contrary, the world now in process of evolution is ultimately destined to reveal itself as perfectly free from evil and the best possible world. What I would urge is that, in the present state of our knowledge, this belief should be kept as a theological doctrine, or, if you like, a philosophical postulate, and that it should not be allowed to mix itself with the process of scientific inference to the future from the past.

In other words, by the end of his life Sidgwick had come to regard belief in progress as a kind of intellectual bet which he expected to lose but hoped to win.

And this became his underlying attitude to the question of belief in God. In his main work, *The Methods of Ethics* (1874), Sidgwick set himself the problem of providing a rational justification for a person to do his duty; he could solve it only by means of an even more ominous bet. He accepted Bentham's 'greatest happiness' principle as self-evident: the sole end of conduct is to maximize human happiness. The problem was to bring the two main methods for achieving this aim, which Sidgwick calls Rational Egoism and Rational Benevolence, into harmony with each other; and this, he thought, required the 'postulate' of God's existence, since Divine Sanctions 'would . . . suffice to make it always in everyone's interest to promote universal happiness'. This 'bet' was needed to close Sidgwick's ethical system.

Having established life after death as a necessary condition of a coherent ethics, Sidgwick spent much of the remainder of his life trying to discover empirical evidence of it. He attempted to get in touch with the dead, accepting the presidency of the Society for Psychical Research when it was founded in 1882. Unfortunately, the main result of these researches was 'a considerable enlargement of my conceptions of the possibilities of human credulity'. These efforts are likely to cause the modern reader to rub his eyes, but Sidgwick was simply being faithful to the tenets of rational enquiry as he conceived them. After all, the search for empirical evidence for life after death did not seem absurd to a generation whose initial belief in God had been destroyed by the 'scientific' demonstration that God did not create the world in seven days, that it was more than four thousand years old, and that the order of evolution was different from the order of creation as told in the Bible.

For Sidgwick the Victorian age ended in gloom. All his hopes came to rest on 'postulates' in which he could neither believe nor bring himself to disbelieve. The great search of the twentieth century has been to find grounds for cheerfulness. These it has discovered by simply evading Sidgwick's dilemmas. Economics seemed to solve the problem of how to reconcile Rational Egoism with Rational Benevolence. Individuals, it was assumed, would behave selfishly; the duty of Rational Benevolence (or 'caring') was simply transferred to the state. Now Mrs Thatcher wants to cut down on the state's benevolence, and seeks to remind us of our Christian duty as individuals. But we are a hundred years on from

Sidgwick's day, and duty no longer weighs so heavily with us. It is not likely that a few quotations from the New Testament will induce us to believe what Sidgwick failed to prove in 800 pages – that it is rational to care for others *at the expense* of our own happiness; which, in a consumption-oriented society, has come to depend increasingly on self-gratifying consumption. The family, which was the main traditional agent in reconciling selfishness to altruism is in course of dissolution; all attachments have become conditional on their 'not getting in our way'. Sidgwick found no answers; but his questions do not go away, and sooner or later we will have to come back to them.

CHAPTER TWO

Leslie Stephen

Noel Annan, *Leslie Stephen – the Godless Victorian*
[Weidenfeld & Nicolson, 1985]

SIR LESLIE STEPHEN is a virtually forgotten Eminent Victorian. He was a prolific essayist. His literary criticisms were much feared. He wrote prodigiously on the history of thought. He was the first editor of the *Dictionary of National Biography*. He died, as they say, loaded with honours. Today he is known, if at all, as the father of Virginia Woolf; immortalized, not by his own words, but by his daughter's unflattering portrait of Mr Ramsay in her novel, *To the Lighthouse*. Mr Ramsay is the killjoy patriarch who demands that his family sacrifice themselves to his genius; but they are, in fact, merely victims of his bad temper. Leslie Stephen's trouble was that he lacked genius. His mind was penetrating; his erudition wide; his style vigorous, even humorous; his analysis often subtle. But there is a pedestrian quality about his arguments and judgments. This has to do, I think, with his belief that morals are in the end more important than truth or imagination. Leslie Stephen was basically in the business of moral uplift; and nothing wears so badly.

In Noel Annan he has found an ideal biographer. Wisely Annan does not pitch the claims of Stephen too high, though he puts in a good word for his *magnum opus*, *The History of English Thought in the Eighteenth Century*, praising not only Stephen's close attention to actual arguments, but his sensitivity to the relation between thought and the circumstances which produced it. What Annan does is to treat Stephen as a representative intellectual of his time: someone whose life and work were dominated by the Victorian crisis of religious faith. Much of the moralism which limits Stephen's achievement can be explained by his determination 'to live and die a Christian gentleman' in a world in which belief in a Christian God (or any kind of God) could, it seemed, no longer be rationally entertained. So much of what we find unsympathetic about Eminent Victorians – their cheerless work ethic, their philistinism, their mistrust of the emotions – seems to spring from fear of the abyss which the passing of faith opened up. Their sense of sin remained powerful even as their conception of the good became attenuated. Morals elbowed out ethics. The negative attitude to life, the self-disgust almost, which made Leslie Stephen so trying to his children, limits his appeal to us.

Annan is perfectly equipped to guide us through the traumas of Stephen's world. There is enough in him of the Arnoldian schoolmaster to empathize with Stephen's 'muscular Christianity' – the absurd ambition of the intellectual Cambridge don to turn himself into the boon companion of the 'manly affectionate fellows' by leading them to victorious exploits on the river. Indeed, one rubs one's eyes at Annan's glowing account of Stephen's achievements as a rowing coach; and Annan's accompanying disquisition on the moral value of rowing – not to mention other body-pushing pursuits – as an antidote to the poisonous passions. Despite such backsliding, Annan's allegiance is to the mind rather than the body. Having got the biographical details over in the first third of the book he devotes the remainder to setting Stephen's intellectual cargo afloat in the cross-currents of the age. So deftly, and with such assured learning, does Annan move between the different worlds of thought in the main European countries as they have developed and interweaved over the last 150 years that Stephen's own contributions tend to get lost – which is perhaps as it should be.

Nothing in Annan's book reveals the vanished world of our Victorian ancestors more vividly than the controversy in the 1890s on the Gadarene Swine. The leading scientist of the day, Thomas Huxley, tried to impale the Christians on the horns of a dilemma: either the Evangelists were making up the story of Jesus casting out devils and permitting them to enter a herd of swine or Jesus had wantonly destroyed other men's property. Roused by the suggestion that

Christ may have overlooked the sanctity of private property, the former Prime Minister Gladstone replied with an analysis of Mosaic law showing that Jews were not allowed to keep pigs. Huxley rejoined with additional evidence about property rights in Galilee; the argument raged furiously in the learned journals. Stephen entered into such religious disputes with gusto, on the rationalist, agnostic side. His work was part of the great current of disbelief undermining the faiths of the Victorians. But just because faith was waning he was more than ever determined to keep up standards. Despite interesting ambiguities, to which Annan does full justice, Stephen's work in biography and literary criticism was that of a 'hanging judge'. Since nothing is so tiresome to the next generation as the voice of the moralist of the previous one, Stephen's judgements remain curios in the history of ideas.

But the questions he asked are not dead, nor have they been answered. Why should we behave decently? Can the standards in which we are still brought up be made acceptable to reason, or do they require the support of a religion – secular or supernatural? The answers of Stephen and his 'godless' generation – evolutionary ethics, Auguste Comte's 'religion of humanity' – have been rejected. But much of the intellectual endeavour of our day still goes into the search for justifications of 'behaviour which makes for righteousness'. Annan's enthralling biography puts beyond doubt Stephen's claim to a large footnote in the history of this enterprise.

CHAPTER THREE

The Fabian Ethic

[1979]

EACH age invents its own historical heroes. From the past it selects for special admiration those thinkers, artists, public persons, who seem psychologically closest to it, to be fighting its own battles. For example, John Stuart Mill has recently found favour as a pioneer of the feminist movement. Edward Carpenter has been revived as a precursor of Gay Liberation. Others fall into disfavour, and must sometimes languish there for decades, even centuries, until a new age once more finds them sympathetic, or relevant. The original Fabians fall into the second category – notably Beatrice and Sidney Webb and George Bernard Shaw. (Graham Wallas and Sydney Olivier, while important, were less distinctive; H. G. Wells's later involvement in the Society was brief and tempestuous.) My concern here is with their ethic, or attitude to life. I shall try to show how it developed out of Victorian moralism, and determined both their political ideas and life-styles.

The heart of the Fabian ethic was an overwhelming sense of public duty. The Victorians believed that the individual was accountable to God for how he lived his life. The Fabians believed he was accountable to Humanity. In neither case was life to be lived for its own sake – for the enjoyment, or experience, it might intrinsically afford. It must show some result. In 1934, Beatrice Webb wrote to the Bloomsbury novelist, E. M. Forster: 'Why don't you write another great novel giving the essence of the current conflict between those who aim at exquisite relationships within the closed circle of the "elect" and those who aim at hygienic and scientific improvement of the whole race?' Neither the Webbs nor Shaw had time for 'exquisite relationships'. Huge tasks of world construction beckoned; it was these which gave purpose and meaning to human existence. It is easy to see that their admiration for Soviet Russia was no senile aberration. Beatrice Webb saw the Communist Party as a 'puritanical religious order' dedicated to the scientific construction of Utopia. Bernard Shaw saw Soviet Russia as the first Fabian state.

It is precisely this *selfless* ideal which makes the Fabians seem remote from us. Monasticism, even of the secular variety, is out of fashion. The most striking revolution in the West has not been the socialist revolution which the Fabians wanted, but the sexual revolution they feared. This in turn has been part of a wider liberation of self from the Puritan restraints of the nineteenth century. The Fabians wanted to redirect the Puritan instincts from the service of God to the service of Humanity. We have been engaged in abolishing them altogether. The Fabian ethic was exemplified in life-style. The most striking feature of the lives of the Webbs and Shaw is the great outpouring of impersonal energy. Shaw's John Tanner wanted to be 'used for a purpose recognized by yourself as a mighty one'. Both Shaw and the Webbs trained themselves to become efficient instruments of social progress. They also determined to train their friends. People were objects to be animated (or permeated) with the collectivist spirit; no wonder they tended to fall away exhausted.

By contrast, the great attempt of our time has been to carve out an autonomous place for love, friendship, art. We like to enjoy relationships and experiences, for their own sake, not for the good they will do the world. This doesn't altogether exclude involvement in public affairs. But political categories, as Richard Sennett has remarked, are increasingly translated into psychological categories. 'Caring' for others is considered psychologically admirable; but the great impersonal causes to which Shaw and the Webbs devoted their lives are likely to be interpreted as projections of neurotic fantasies. Even before the First World War, Beatrice Webb was complaining that the young Cambridge Fabians were more interested in sexual questions than in social reconstruction. Freud was to have more impact on the twentieth-century West than Auguste Comte.

The clear Fabian line of division between private and public concerns took some time to establish itself. The pre-history of the Fabian Society presents a more complex psychological picture. In the early 1880s, Sheila Rowbotham and Jeffrey Weeks have observed, 'the boundaries between [the] moral, aesthetic and political revolt were still fluid'. The Fabian Society had its origins in the Fellowship of the New Life founded in 1882 by the Scottish philosopher, Thomas Davidson, an enthusiastic student of religious communities. His aim was to promote social improvement through individual ethical perfection. Individuals should aim to realize their own highest possibilities; their example would infect others. Among those associated with the Fellowship, Edward Carpenter represents the most sustained attempt to combine socialism with self-culture.

Carpenter's philosophy rested on two fundamental principles. Man must try to perfect his own possibilities; and all social improvement rested on individual improvement. It seemed a neat way of combining the private and the public. However, there were two snags. Shaw remarked that the ideal society 'would have to wait an unreasonably long time' if it depended on all its individuals reaching perfection. The other problem was that Carpenter defined self-realization in ethical terms. This ignored the conflict between instinctual drives and ethical imperatives. In time, the programme of self-development would become divorced both from social reconstruction and from the moral under-pinnings which Carpenter gave it.

14

As with all reformers, the date of his birth is important in understanding Carpenter's ideas. He was born in 1844, over a decade ahead of the leading Fabians. His crisis of identity took place before the economic convulsions which produced the socialist revival: he resigned his Cambridge fellowship and curacy in 1874. On the other hand, like the Fabians, he was victim and product of what G. M. Young has called the 'moralizing society' created by Evangelicalism. His own upbringing, and the fact that he had to live, work, and publish in Victorian England combined to give his quest for self-expression its characteristically moralizing tone; it had to be fitted into a scheme of improved living which appealed to the moral susceptibilities of his time. What made Carpenter a rebel was his homosexuality. This was probably denied physical expression till middle age: he was fifty before he 'came out' with George Merill. So his revolt against conventional morality had to take indirect forms. What he did was to attack the uselessness and dishonesty of upper-class life. In appealing to wealthy despoilers to 'simplify' their lives, he was asking the Victorians to live up to their moral ideals, not just pay them lip service. This 'simplified life', he hoped, would provide the ethical basis of socialism. The homosexual element was idealized in a vision of a world united by the 'love of comrades', a theme derived from Walt Whitman. In 1883, Carpenter took a seven-acre small holding at Millthorpe in Derbyshire, cultivating it as a market gardener.

What was his vision of self-development? Three interconnected themes, heavily derived from Ruskin, Whitman, and Thoreau, run through his writings: the duty and dignity of manual labour; the drastic reduction of possessions; and the maintenance of vital health. Manual labour was important for several reasons. It renewed contact between man and Nature. It was the only genuine title to property: the upper classes must become producers, not just consumers, of wealth. It would also reunite the classes in a common experience: like Tocqueville, Carpenter believed that it was industrial specialization which sundered society by separating life-styles.

Reduction of possessions also had a dual object: to remove the parasitic element in private property, and to free the individual from being a slave to them. Carpenter believed that possessions over and above those that a person created by his own labour (for direct use or exchange) represented, in Marxist terms, surplus value extracted from the unpaid labour of others. More directly, great houses and estates could be maintained only by others' labour: one important aim of simplifying life was to get rid of servants. But the stately mansion was also a prison of the soul – it tied the individual to artificial manners, clothes, respectability. Carpenter painted a grim picture of great houses with 'books rotting by hundreds on the library shelves', 'boudoirs and bedrooms seldom opened, with fusty smelling furniture', 'forgotten dresses lying in the deeps of unexplored wardrobes', 'accumulations of money, of certificates and securities, of jewels and plate, hoarded away in safes and strongboxes . . .'

Vital health was the third element in the simple life. Carpenter was convinced that the upper classes suffered more than others from bad health. Vigorous manual work would partly remedy this; but it also needed a most careful attention to clothes and diet. Carpenter painted a harrowing picture of upper-class attire: 'the pure human heart grown feeble and weary in its isolation and imprisonment, the sexual parts degenerated and ashamed of themselves, the liver diseased, and the lungs straitened down to mere sighs and conventional disconsolate sounds beneath their cerements'. In his writings at least he attached more importance to liberating the feet than the sexual parts. He was the great apostle of sandals, and spent much of his time at Millthorpe making them. For the rest of the body, he recommended suits of handspun, unlined wool, with outside pockets. As for food, Carpenter rejected meat as an 'artificial stimulant'. The main meal of the day should consist of a 'central dish' such as a 'vast vegetable pie', round which would circle 'satellite platters' of oatmeal cakes and fresh fruit. Though strict moderation was to be the rule, Carpenter did not exclude the 'occasional orgy' to restore moral tone and prevent a lapse into 'pharisaism'.

In these ways the improved life of the individual could become the basis and the means of the improved life of the race: for the voluntary simplification of the lives of the rich automatically entailed a redistribution of wealth to the poor. However, Carpenter's attempt to base socialism on individual perfection proved unsuccessful. Those interested in pursuing the New Life lost interest in its bearing on social reform; while those who wanted to transform society favoured a more direct approach. This split became clear when a group of New Lifers headed by Edward Pease and Hubert Bland broke off to found the Fabian Society in 1884. The same year, William Morris and some anarchist New Lifers left the Marxist Social Democratic Federation to pursue a more hedonistic ideal in the Socialist League.

The Fellowship's vision of the 'simplified life' continued to exert its attractions. One offshoot was the progressive movement in education: both Reddie, the founder of Abbotsholme (where Lytton Strachey spent some hardy, if miserable, months), and Badley, the founder of Bedales, were strongly influenced by Carpenter. The Arts and Crafts movement owes something to his example; as does the 'garden suburb'. Middle-class intellectuals earnestly simplified their lives by acquiring labourers' cottages in Surrey, where they grew food, made sandals, and communed with Nature: Shaw has left a memorable account of a weekend spent with Henry and Kate Salt at Tilford, near Farnham, during which his woollen clothes shrank every time they had to be dried out after exhausting rambles in the pouring rain.

As the connection between the New Life and institutional change faded, so sexual radicalism became a more prominent feature of the former. The Anarchists in the Socialist League, inspired by the example of Eleanor Marx and Edward Aveling, started to 'live out' their companionate sexual ideals, regardless of the effect on orthodox schemes of social reform. We see here the start of the 'privatization' of radical politics: politics became the direct, not sublimated, expression of psychological drives. Carpenter's own sexual radicalism became more explicit when he set up house with Merill in 1896 and published *Love's Coming of Age* in 1896, and *The Intermediate Sex* in 1908. Lowes Dickinson and E. M. Forster took this aspect of the New Life back with them to Cambridge after visits to Millthorpe; the latter after having had his bottom traumatically pinched by Merill. Carpenter also seems to have influenced D. H. Lawrence through their mutual friends, William and Sally Hopkins and Alice Dax of the Eastwood set near Nottingham; and Havelock Ellis, another New Lifer, and a pioneer of sexual psychology.

The practical Socialist case against the Fellowship's philosophy is obvious. The abolition of poverty could not wait till every man had divested himself voluntarily of his possessions. Moreover, for a socialist movement trying to win a mass following, these middle-class experiments in new styles of living were not only irrelevant but counter-productive. After a visit to the Salts at Tilford, the frock-coated Hyndman wrote to Shaw: 'I do not want the movement to become a depository of old cranks, humanitarians, vegetarians, anti-vivisectionists and anti-vaccinationists, arty-crafties and all the rest of them. We are scientific socialists and have no room for sentimentalists. They confuse the issue.'

More importantly, the ideal of self-culture for its own sake was unacceptable to moralists. Here was the weakness in the Fellowship's position. What was self-improvement for? It was no longer possible to answer 'for the service of God'. The inability of the twentieth century to give a satisfactory answer to this question meant, inevitably, that the ideal of self-development would be transformed into one of self-expression. But nineteenth-century moralists, capable only of sublimated pleasures, needed an ideal of service. And this the Fellowship, with its emphasis on individual perfection, failed to provide. A question from Sidney Webb clarifies the point at issue. He is criticizing Goethe for being 'horribly self-willed'. 'We have no *right*', he goes on, 'to live our own lives. What shall it profit a man to save his own soul, if thereby even one jot less good is done to the world.' Goethe was 'a great deserter in the army of humanity'. Webb concluded that individuals were 'parts of a whole, the well-being of which *may* be inimical to our fullest development'. Certainly the time he and Beatrice gave to socialism left little over for the arts. To Sidney's timid wish to 'carve out a little time together for pictures and poetry and music . . . bye and bye', Beatrice sternly replied, 'it will be difficult'.

The feminist movement of the time, an important element in political socialism, was also opposed to any hint of 'anarchy in sexual relations'. In its view, it was the sexual relationship which tied the woman to the home and motherhood. Thus the feminist ideal was that of the celibate woman: as Beatrice Webb put it: 'it would not have been practicable to unite the life of love with the life of reason.' The feminist campaign concentrated on securing women such things as the right to a career and to better education. When feminists offered themselves in marriage, they often did so in forbidding fashion. 'What does a poet think', wrote Kate Conway to Bruce Glasier, 'of a woman with ink on her finger and a hole in her stocking? What would he say to two thick ankles? What would he say to a woman who would sooner eat bread and butter and drink milk or buy fruit for dinner than cook it . . .?' It was only with the development of efficient contraception and the lessening of guilt about the body that the feminist movement would be weaned from the sexless ideal.

Nevertheless, the quest for a New Life left its mark on the leading Fabians. Both Shaw and the Webbs renounced the ideal of self-development for its own sake but they embraced certain aspects of new living, such as the simplification of domestic arrangements, and the

18

maintenance of health through the right clothes and diet, as the key to personal efficiency in social reconstruction. Personal fulfilment was to be had in submerging the self in great causes; but for this the New Life could provide an appropriate mental and bodily hygiene.

To understand the Fabian shift from individual perfectionism to social reconstruction, dates are again important. Beatrice Potter was born in 1858, Sidney Webb in 1859, Bernard Shaw in 1856. They discovered their purposes in life at precisely the moment when public events had started to acquire an ominous aspect: as Beatrice Webb noted in her diary in 1884, 'social questions are the vital questions of today: they take the place of religion'. In the last decades of the nineteenth century the feeling was growing that society was in a state of crisis; that big changes in social organization were needed if external decline and domestic convulsions were to be avoided.

Here, then, is the objective reason for the shift in attention. But, equally, involvement in public affairs arises from inner needs. Late-Victorian middle-class reformers were people whose upbringing had given them a great sense of sin. With the loss of religious faith, this sense of personal sin became fused with a sense of social guilt; the service of God was transferred to the service of Humanity. A little later the energies liberated from the service of God would go into the expression of self. But this required a very different upbringing, one in which the child would start to be treated as an end or value in itself, not as a sinful creature to be beaten into righteousness. It was the combination of social crisis and spare moral energy which created the middle-class Victorian reform movement and gave it its particular character. Puritanism turned the social question into a moral question.

Consciousness of social crisis dates from the last quarter of the nineteenth century. Before that most people had thought that *laissez-faire*, plus a modicum of private philanthropy, was making things steadily better and would go on doing so. Then came a cluster of unpleasant, interrelated events: the collapse of the mid-nineteenth-century boom, followed by twenty years of violent economic oscillations; the emergence of new great industrial powers which threatened Britain's economic supremacy and the security of its Empire; and the parallel rise of democracy and industrial militancy, through the two suffrage acts and the start of the 'new unionism'. Much of Shaw's writing is an index of the concerns created by these happenings: the heightened awareness of the competitive struggle, the premonitions of international and domestic anarchy, the lack of faith in the capacity of democratic politicians, the fear that the degraded masses will take horrible revenge on their oppressors. The last was given a new immediacy by the revelation of widespread 'poverty in the midst of plenty'. In the 1880s, Charles Booth started his mammoth survey of poverty in London. It revealed that 30 per cent of the inhabitants of the richest city in the world lived at or beneath the poverty line. This scale of destitution emphasized the irrelevance of private philanthropy, the waste of human resources, the potential threat to the stability of the state.

That economic fluctuations and widespread poverty revealed grave imperfections in social organization is undeniable. The way they were interpreted, however, owes a good deal to the intellectual and moral consciousness of the age. On the one side, Britain's economic problems were fitted into a Darwinian view of life. The contemporary phase in history was widely seen as a struggle between great empires in which success would go to those which were more efficiently organized. Thus Beatrice Webb thought that the Japanese victory in the Russo-Japanese war of 1904–5 would

> alter not merely the balance of power, but the balance of ideas – it will tell against Christianity as the one religion, against materialistic individualism, against autocracy, against luxury, in favour of organisation, collective regulation, scientific education, physical and mental training – but on the whole *not* in favour of democracy. They have suddenly raised the standard of international efficiency . . .

Here was one very important root of Fabian collectivism, the chief weapon in the Fabian armoury of permeation. The survival of Britain as a world power required the building of a healthy race – healthy in mind, body, and morals. This required both social and eugenic 'drainage', particularly to get rid of poverty.

But it was the moral interpretation of Britain's crisis which best explains the character of the Fabian attack and the nature of the Fabian remedies. Britain's economic failure was blamed on the moral failure of capitalist civilization; particularly its growing tendency to separate wealth from work. The Fabians inherited the moral critique of the New Lifers. The economic failures of the late nineteenth century enabled them

20

to attack the weakest point of the Victorian compromise: the anomaly of great possessions in the moral scheme of life.

The pursuit of self-enrichment had always been hard to reconcile with the moral notions of the Victorians: hence the flight of the bourgeoisie from money-making to imperial and social service. The way the Victorians had combined the two was to justify private riches as a reward for moral virtue (abstinence) and, in Fabian language, as a 'rent' which society paid to outstanding individuals for the hire of their wealth-producing, or other, capacities. But the emergence of a large and expanding class of wealthy *rentiers* living off past accumulations rather than present efforts, as well as a new group of ostentatiously wealthy South African millionaires, broke the moral link between wealth and virtue. It was the moral resentment felt by the first Fabians against this parasitic and luxurious class which led them to question its economic justification. Basically, what the Fabians argued was that private capital no longer justified its 'rent'. Increments of wealth were being collectively produced, but privately appropriated. The existence of a large class of unproductive *rentiers* was a 'tax' on the rest of the community; a tax which explained poverty. The community should reverse the process: it should tax the wealthy out of existence, using the proceeds to establish minimum conditions of life for all. As private production became increasingly unprofitable the municipalities, representing associations of consumers, should take it over. In this way, the lives of the rich would be compulsorily 'simplified' without having to wait for their individual ethical perfection.

In Fabian eyes, the chief offence of capitalism was to create loafers and idlers at each end of the social scale. According to Shaw, the real competition in the modern world was not between Bombay and Manchester but 'the competition of Regent Street with the Rue de Rivoli, of Brighton and the South Coast with the Riviera . . .' In socialist morality, the 'burden of labour' would be a 'debt of honour' which the individual owed society. Capitalism aimed to support a small group of rich in unproductive idleness; socialism would impose 'compulsory industrial and civil service' on the poor as well as the rich.

The dedication to work, the hatred of idleness, lies deep in the Victorian moral outlook. But one cannot fully understand the political expression it took with Beatrice Webb and Bernard Shaw without considering their personal and social circumstances. A certain character-type is inevitably associated with any widely held morality: the same psychological traits are to be found, in some degree, in all the eminent Victorians. Nevertheless, the personal ethics of Beatrice Webb and Bernard Shaw reflect some desperate and unusual features in their own early circumstances.

Both Beatrice and Shaw were neglected children. Beatrice's father was affectionate and easygoing, but had to spread his love round nine daughters, and Beatrice was not his favourite. Her puritanical mother, on the other hand, positively resented her. This neglect, only partly offset by the usual saintly Victorian nanny, resulted in a 'morbid and at times near-suicidal childhood', punctuated by 'chronic psychosomatic illnesses'. Shaw, too, had a miserable childhood. His father was nicknamed 'the Hermit' by his children; his mother, a stern puritan, lavished on him, in Michael Holroyd's words, 'the full force of maternal indifference'. He seems to have had no important relationship with his two sisters. Both children thus grew up unloved. The self-hatred that resulted dominated their lives. Theirs was a despair reconciled to life through work and service.

Both families had the virtues of their vices: they starved the affections, but provided, by way of compensation, marvellous food for the intellect and imagination. Beatrice's mind was nourished in the family library, by a circle of family friends which included Herbert Spencer, T. H. Huxley, and J. A. Froude, and by an atmosphere of complete intellectual freedom. Shaw's house was full of music; his mind was peopled by the heroes and heroines of grand opera, most of whose arias he could hum or whistle by the time he was twelve; he spent many hours in Dublin's art galleries, starving, as he put it, on 'imaginary feasts'.* Moreover, the adults in their lives, precisely because they were so remote and forbidding, could provide models for emulation. Beatrice's neglectful mother was a model of the intellectual woman; the philosopher, Herbert Spencer, a close family friend, provided an ideal of unselfish devotion to truth and social betterment. Lucinda Shaw was a complete failure as a mother; but Shaw could worship her on the opera stage, where she performed with an agreeable mezzo-soprano voice. Her singing teacher, George 'Vandeleur' Lee, who moved to the Shaw home

---

* C. E. M. Joad has acutely remarked that throughout his life Shaw tended to 'find in music what men who live out more fully and variously to the full scope and range of their senses normally find in nature, in sexual relations, in the athletic pleasures of the body and the sensations of the palate'. (Joad, *Shaw*, 1949, p. 59)

to form an apparently harmonious trio, provided with his 'Method' of vocal training an example of systematic dedication to his craft. In their later indifference to personal relationships and surroundings and their dedication to things of the mind and spirit, both children reflected the balance of their upbringings.

Their social circumstances were, of course, very different. Beatrice came from a well-connected, upper-class, English family; Shaw from an Irish family of 'feudal downstarts', linked by history, kinship, and aspiration with the Protestant Irish gentry, but by actual circumstances with Dublin's petty bourgeois Bohemia. But both found similar difficulties in realizing their exceptional talents in a world which reserved its choicest prizes for wealthy and well-born males. Educational opportunities both for women and for 'aspiring intellectual proletarians' (the phrase is Norman MacKenzie's) were still severely restricted; the best careers were the preserve of those who went to public schools and the still-male ancient universities.

For Beatrice, there beckoned the conventional life of the upper-class woman: to flirt and to marry; to be adored from afar while her husband hunted and shot and dabbled in politics; to be accomplished, but never serious; to produce children, but not look after them; to preside over a household of servants; in short, to be decorative, but useless. All this she rejected with open eyes: 'it will be necessary for women with strong natures to remain celibate', she noted in her diary. Inevitably, the renunciation involved left a strong sense of bitterness. She came to believe that the 'nice girl' was an 'insidious parasite'; her resentment came to focus on the whole class of 'useless' women and men. What the world offered to someone with Shaw's background was the modest career of the clerk on the proverbial stool. He worked as one for almost five miserable years in a Dublin estate agency. Moving to London in 1876 in his twentieth year he determined to make himself into a writer, at whatever cost. And the costs were heavy. For years he lived off his mother while he wrote five unsuccessful novels. He slowly acquired self-confidence by studying books on etiquette at the British Museum, speaking at debating societies, deliberately cultivating the over-confident, paradoxical style which would force the world to take notice of him. 'Nothing is more difficult', he later wrote, 'than to realise a superiority which the world has always treated as an inferiority.' His early plays were fierce and brilliant attacks on the artificial system of conventional morality which crushes human vitality. He came to see this conventional morality as a product of a parasitic, functionless class. In this mood, he was attracted by Henry George's doctrine that an idle class of landlords had creamed off collectively-produced wealth for their own enjoyment. With the help of Ricardo, Marx, and Jevons, he and his fellow Fabian musketeers worked out an economic justification for dispossessing the wealthy of their crippling gains. But this was to be done not to put the idle poor in power. As an unrecognized genius with squirarchical pretensions, Shaw felt very strongly that the new state should be run by the best: he felt himself to be an aristocratic revolutionary. Thus the artist became a socialist; the pen would be at the service of the cause; the plays would get the 'bluebooks over the footlights'. Shaw's plays were much more than the sermons he sometimes made them out to be: that is why they survive. But, as with Beatrice Webb, the moral climate as well as the actual conditions of the times conspired with personal circumstances to force genius into the service of humanity.

The life-styles of Beatrice Webb and Bernard Shaw were inseparable from their creeds. Idleness was as much a hell to them as it was a disaster for society. Nevertheless, a distinction must be made between Shaw's and Beatrice's attitudes to work. Shaw worked to realize himself as an artist as much as to change society. Beatrice, who had a low opinion of her abilities, worked entirely in the service of humanity. Sidney Webb provided her with an economic justification for a moral compulsion. *Rentiers* had a duty to render unpaid social labour. 'Unless each individual', he wrote, 'does work in utility equal to the utility of the commodities he consumes, he is a dead loss to the world.' They lived up to their principles. Their work schedules were forbidding. For a decade from 1885, Shaw worked eighteen hours a day, seven days a week. He exercised his faculties on socialist pamphleteering, journalism, public speaking, service on the St Pancras Vestry, writing novels and plays, and carrying on a gigantic correspondence. He believed he owed his genius to his will to work. 'Anyone', he wrote, 'can get my skill for the same price, and a good many people could probably get it cheaper.' Early in their partnership the Webbs, too, devised a punishing work plan to which they more or less kept for the remainder of their active lives.

There were many relapses, particularly by Beatrice, but on the whole they thrived on it. After several weeks of non-stop work, Shaw wrote to Beatrice in 1898: 'By this time I was in an almost superhuman condition – fleshless, bloodless, vaporous, ethereal and stupendous in literary efficiency . . .' Ten years later Beatrice could report that Sidney and she were 'living at the highest pressure of brainwork' on the most 'hygienic basis – up at 6.30, cold bath and quick walk or ride, work from 7.30 to 1 o'clock, bread and cheese lunch, short rest, another walk, then tea and work until 6 or 6.30'. She could hardly sleep from 'brain excitement'.

The main challenge to their programme, as to any monastic deal, was posed by what Beatrice called 'human nature'. Her own sexual renunciation was not easily achieved. She was a beautiful and passionate woman; in her mid-twenties she had fallen for Joseph Chamberlain. But she was not prepared to sacrifice her ideals for the conventional marriage to the Liberal statesman which was probably on offer; and decided on a sexless life of social investigation. Personal happiness for her became an 'utterly remote thing'. It was in this mood that she married Sidney in 1892. The winning of Beatrice was Sidney's greatest success in Fabian permeation. She did not love him, but he won her by persistently parading his character defects, which excited her 'mother's pity', and by stressing the advantages to socialism which would follow from pooling their talents. Their marriage was undertaken in the Fabian spirit of self-sacrifice. She told Sidney that she was marrying his 'head only'; the experience convinced her that it was safe for a 'brain-working woman to marry – if only she can find her Sidney'. Certainly their union ushered in years of intellectual and administrative fecundity. When, in the mid 1900s, H. G. Wells, an uncomfortable Fabian at the best of times, raised the challenge of 'free love' (on the ground that it would extend knowledge of human nature), Beatrice was strongly disapproving. 'That way madness lies,' she commented, and wondered, in Shavian fashion, whether man would

> only evolve upwards by the subordination of his physical desires . . . I suggested to Sidney for consideration whether our philosophy was not tending to the restriction of all physical desires to the maintenance of health in the individual and the race – meaning by health, the longest continued and greatest intensity of mental activity – and to the continuance of the species at its highest level of quality.

With Shaw the problem of 'human nature' seems to have been solved more easily, at any rate as he described it. Although Beatrice disapproved of his 'philandering' with actresses, it was, as Michael Holroyd says, little more than an 'ejaculation of words' on Shaw's part. Virtue, Shaw wrote, consists not in 'abstaining from vice, but in not desiring it'. Like his Julius Caesar, he came to feel he had no unhealthy passions to control. He described himself a 'voluptuary rather than an ascetic . . . I . . . never deny myself a Beethoven symphony . . .' On the other hand, he remained a virgin till he was twenty-nine. He did not apparently feel any great sense of loss, remarking briskly 'I am too busy and preoccupied to make opportunities for myself'. Bertha Newcombe, looking back in 1928 on her affair with Shaw, thought him a 'passionless man'. To Ellen Terry, Shaw wrote 'I am fond of women . . . but I am in earnest about quite other things . . . I require whole populations and historical epochs to engage my interests seriously.' His marriage to Charlotte Payne-Townshend in 1898 was in the Fabian tradition. She took down his dictation, nursed him, and had plenty of money to service the writing machine. To Beatrice Webb he wrote: 'The thing being cleared thus of all such illusions as love interest, happiness interest, and all the rest of the vulgarity of marriage, I . . . hopped down to the Registrar.'

Friendship for its own sake had little place in the Fabian scheme of life. Nevertheless, the Webbs and Shaw had a different attitude to relationships. For the Webbs, friends were mainly 'instruments' for advancing the cause. They gathered the great to their house, giving them less food and drink than they wanted, and more collectivism than they could stand. Beatrice was far from being insensitive to human character. She felt the 'peculiar charm' of Bertrand Russell; she clearly liked Balfour for his own sake, and was drawn to the elegant living and clever chatter of the Souls. She felt uneasy about manipulating people, though Sidney revelled in it. Yet the half-submerged wish to form human attachments ran up against her renunciation of self for the cause. 'I do not wish to forgo the society of my own class,' she wrote, 'and yet to enjoy means wasted energy.' As she approached middle age she conceded that she had become 'too utilitarian to make new friends'.

Shaw, too, had a manipulative view of human beings. But he saw them less as instruments of social plotting than as outlets for his insatiable reforming zeal. In his letters, he poured out an endless stream of advice and exhortation, parodying the manner of an improving schoolmaster. He breezily told the drama critic William Archer to 'take more exercise and earlier hours'. To the actress Florence Farr he confessed an 'extraordinary desire to make the most of you – to make effective and visible *all* your artistic potentialities'. He urged Janet Achurch to take more Shaw and less morphine. To Golding Bright he wrote, 'Make attainment of EFFICIENCY your sole object for the next fifteen years'. The famous Fabian quartet – Webb, Shaw, Olivier and Wallas – had succeeded, Shaw felt, because they were on 'quite ruthless terms with each other'. The Fabian family found their friendships in work, not play. The contrast is with Bloomsbury whose members played with each other, but worked on their own.

What is striking about Shaw's relationships, as revealed by his correspondence, is that they were quite impersonal. His advice was only slightly individuated. It was not based on personal needs, as they might strike a sensitive onlooker, but on general principles which Shaw had worked out for his own case. As he put it to Alice Lockett, his first girlfriend, his exhortation was directed at the nine-tenths of her personality which was exactly like his; the tenth of individual differences was of no importance. It was very much this attitude which informed his relationship with his public. Shaw was a great artist, who deliberately renounced an artistic creed. When Henry James sent him his play, *The Saloon*, based on his story *Owen Wingate*, Shaw told him that 'it is a really damnable sin to draw with such consummate art a household of rubbish. . . . People don't want works of art from you: they want help . . . above all, encouragement'. To this Henry James replied that 'all *direct* "encouragement" . . . is more likely than not to be shallow and misleading, and to make [a man] turn on you with a vengeance for offering him some scheme that takes account of but a tenth of his attributes'. This difference between the two men on the function of art turns directly on their different philosophies of life. For Shaw the world consisted of a Life Force only slightly differentiated into individual human beings. A sermon could directly activate the universal energy in everyone. For James, the world was peopled with individuals, who share common experiences, but who have completely different needs. Shaw's was closer to the traditional religious outlook, James's to the contemporary disintegration of common values. Beatrice's attitude was the same as Shaw's. She could not get on terms with Virginia Woolf: 'Her men and women do not interest me . . . no predominant aims . . . one state of mind follows another without any particular reason.'

True to their principles, the great Fabians treated their bodies as machines to be kept in the highest state of efficiency. Shaw was a lifelong follower of the 'sanitary woollen system' devised by Dr Gustav Jaeger, who denounced the evil effects of cotton and linen. His views on diet were even more stringent than Carpenter's. Man should eat 'good bread and fruit and nothing else'. Beatrice, too, had an obsession about overeating and overdrinking. It would be pleasant to think that it was their 'training' which kept them at work for so long. Productive to the end, Shaw died at ninety-four, soon after falling off a tree he was pruning. Beatrice lived to be eighty-five; Sidney till eighty-eight. Their huge, if unreadable, volumes on Soviet Russia were written when both were in their late seventies. To the last, they remained true to their creeds.

What I have tried to do is to explain the Fabian response to the crisis of their age in terms of its psychological compulsions. These compulsions produced a moral energy which issued in both a creed and a life-style. It is because our own psychological conditions are so different that we no longer accept either.

The moral revulsion against idleness, so central to the Fabian outlook, has diminished. Steep progressive taxation has decimated the class of idle *rentiers*, thus restoring the connection between wealth and work. In that sense, Fabianism has triumphed. The 'involuntary' idleness which Victorian conventions imposed on upper- and middle-class women is also largely a thing of the past. But more fundamentally, there has been a marked decline in the puritan work ethic in all classes. An affluent, technically advanced society both requires less effort from its members and provides many more varieties of pleasure. It thus breaks down the psychological compulsion to work. Probably the hardest workers today are the millionaires: they need to be. It is a joke Shaw would have appreciated.

The decline in the sense of sin, in part the result of the growing ease of life, has also lessened our need for a secular creed. Both Shaw and the Webbs tried to overcome the 'death of God' by establishing new Gods. They failed mainly because we no longer feel the need for them. The purely philosophical criticisms of Shaw's Life Force, his God-substitute, while valid in their own terms, overlook the weakening of the compulsion to seek what T. H. Huxley called 'something, not ourselves, which makes for righteousness'. The collapse of these drives has destroyed the Fabian attempt to establish an 'ethic' based on self-sacrificing service to an impersonal cause. According to Shaw, the individual should seek his gratification in serving the Life Force; for the Webbs, it was in the service of Humanity. This type of ethic has long been in decay. This is not to say that intellect is now less of a passion for clever people than it was in Shaw's day. But increasingly 'thought' is pursued for its own sake, as one of the many manifestations of the 'monstrous self' which Beatrice tried to batten down, rather than as a duty to the evolutionary process. Also today's outlook is much more hedonistic than it was in Shaw's day. To what extent acceptance of pleasure as a desirable end will lessen the will to achievement is not clear.

It is thus their psychological remoteness which has caused the first Fabians to lose favour. When her full diaries are published Beatrice Webb may yet find her true historical place as a writer and social observer of genius. Shaw's plays will surely live on as plays. But it is their joint *messages* which are, for the moment, stone dead. Whether or not we ever again take Beatrice Webb and Shaw seriously on their own terms depends very much on what happens to our hedonistic civilization. If we can continue to play without disaster, their creeds will remain museum pieces. If life forces a new religion on us, they may yet find themselves among its prophets.

CHAPTER FOUR

The Letters of Sidney and Beatrice Webb

Norman Mackenzie (ed.), *The Letters of Sidney and Beatrice Webb*:
vol. 1, *Apprenticeship*; vol. 2, *Partnership 1893–1912*;
vol. 3, *Pilgrimage 1912–1947*
[Cambridge University Press, 1978]

FROM today's perspective, the Webbs are likely to seem repellent, admirable, comic. Repellent is their monomaniacal obsession with what they called 'sane collectivism'; their inhuman quest for human betterment. Admirable is their total integrity. They knew what they were about; they made their choices with open eyes; their lives were of a piece with their ideals. Those lives are a rich subject for comedy: what Lytton Strachey would have done with them! The things they wrote to each other, or which Beatrice confided to her *Diaries*, seem incredibly funny, because in our day, with all public causes more or less discredited, we can no longer take such high seriousness seriously.

In their ideas and compulsions, they were very much Late Victorians. Moralists, who repudiated both God and Mammon, they had little psychological option except to put their moralism at the service of humanity. By the time Bloomsbury arrived on the scene, aesthetic and sexual experiences would fill the void left in middle-class lives by the 'death of God'. But this was not open to the Webbs' generation. They were dated in other ways. To them the horrors of capitalism were vivid, the horrors of collectivism still to come. Beatrice could write, in 1915, that 'the conditions under which people live are infinitely more important than millions of premature deaths'. Thirty years later, no civilized person could have made such a life-denying remark; and by that time, few civilized people would have experienced the kind of childhood and adolescence which prompted Beatrice to make it. Also, although the Webbs were first generation British socialists, they were the last generation of pre-democratic reformers: the last who could ignore and despise the masses who were supposed to benefit from their plans. 'Permeation', the Fabian Tracts, the London School of Economics, the *New Statesman*, were all stratagems of a pre-democratic world, designed to culminate in the rule of experts. They had little to do with democratic politics.

A reassessment of this remarkable couple is long overdue. I'm not sure that 1000 odd pages of their letters is the best way to do it. As in Verdi's *Il Trovatore*, most of the action takes place off stage – in Professor Mackenzie's copious and illuminating programme notes which tell you what is actually happening. Nor is one even left with the consolation of divine melody. The Webbs were not good letter writers. With their guns trained on capitalism, they had little inclination for gossip; and lacked the linguistic vivacity which makes tolerable Shaw's massive boringness. Beatrice is much better than Sidney. She makes sharp remarks about human character under different social circumstances. She might have been a superb novelist. But her best writing is kept for her Diaries, still largely unpublished. One wishes Mackenzie had sacrificed Sidney's perfunctory notes to Edward Pease and other epistolatory debris to make space for the incoming letters of Wells, Shaw, Keynes, Leonard Woolf, etc., which are to be published separately in two further volumes. Tedium would have been reduced, and understanding increased.

The great gain, and it is considerable, is the light thrown by the letters on the famous partnership, particularly Sidney's place in it. The first volume is mainly concerned with their sixteen-month courtship, if such a word can be used to describe their discussion of the benefits of pooled intellectual effort. In 1890 Sidney and Beatrice were both over thirty. Sidney, a humbly-born clerk at the Colonial Office, and already a leading Fabian, was looking for class and moral backbone. He firmly believed that the coupling of two compatible minds would multiply achievement. Beatrice, clever, imaginative, heart-broken by her unrequited passion for Joseph Chamberlain, had decided on a celibate life of social investigation. Guilt-ridden over her advantages, and rejecting the domestic ideals which had destroyed her mother, Beatrice had come to believe that those with private means must perform unpaid social duty, spending only enough money to keep body and mind in full working efficiency. Prone to depression and inertia, she too needed a co-worker to help her with the books she planned.

When the two met in 1890 they quickly agreed to form a friendship for work. The winning of Beatrice was Sidney's greatest success in Fabian permeation. For he rapidly found himself overcome by a 'hurricane of feeling'. Beatrice attempted to divert the hurricane onto the safer ground of sanitary provision, but Sidney discovered a winning tactic. Beatrice was never one to shirk the challenge of a character defect. Sidney had many. He must not talk so openly about manipulating other people, Beatrice told him. Sidney seized the opportunity. 'Yes – you are quite right in your criticism of my egotistical loquacity – Now tell me of other faults'. Beatrice was eager to do so. He must brush his coat, mind his accent, and not talk of 'when I am Prime Minister, as it jars on sensitive ears'. Sidney was the soul of contrition. He was eager to be improved. And Beatrice, too, needed a secretary to 'seize your ideas, arrange your materials'. But how could he help her when he was leading the life of a 'London cabhorse'? Beatrice's defences were slowly penetrated. Soon she was admitting to a 'Mother's pity'. She tried to withdraw: 'But I do not love you ... I cannot love you' she wrote in December. They must not think of love, but of Socialism, Sidney replied. In May 1891, Beatrice capitulated in an 'act of renunciation of self'.

Sidney, for his part, promised not to press 'la vie intime' to the point of injuring 'our common usefulness . . . your fullest efficacy'. Soon, they were happily 'working away undermining the Individualism of the British race, with intervals of "human nature" '. But Beatrice's surrender was far from unconditional. When Sidney sent her his portrait, she wrote back 'No, dear, I do not even look at it. It is too hideous for anything. Do be done in a gray suit by Elliott and Fry and let me have your *head only* – it is the head only I am marrying.'

The pattern of their partnership justified Sidney's Malthusian theory of intellectual and administrative fecundity. The second volume covers their years of maximum activity. After ten years of marriage 'your devoted wifsey' was writing to Sidney that their union had proved 'far more fruitful in output of thought and action than either one of us expected'. After sixteen years, Beatrice could congratulate herself on how well they had been able to 'think out plans for making life happier and nobler for the rest of our poor kind'. Much 'sustained work' remained to be done. But fortunately 'one's body becomes less and less of an incubus as the years roll on'.

Although Shaw reported them 'spooning' over their card indexes, the body was kept firmly in place, perhaps to Sidney's regret. Instead of children, they produced books: huge and turgid tomes on trade unions and local government. Without Sidney's speed in writing, and 'gutting' official reports, his capacity to organize material and remember everything, they could not have been written. These, too, were the years when Beatrice's aptitude for what Mackenzie calls 'salon politics' joined with Sidney's belief in permeation to win them the friendship of Haldane, Rosebery, Balfour. Balfour appointed Beatrice to the Royal Commission on the Poor Law: her Minority Report was a bold administrative blueprint for the abolition of destitution through the concept of an 'enforced minimum'. All the while, she drove Sidney to prodigies of independent achievement: through his chairmanship of the Technical Education Board of the LCC, he dominated the politics of London education; he ran the Fabian Society; he founded the London School of Economics and the *New Statesman*; he was brilliant in getting money out of rich patrons. She stopped him from overeating, and forced him to take long walks.

Yet how much did they actually achieve? Sidney's institutions proved durable; but in their larger aims they were much less successful. In the Edwardian age they already seemed out of touch. At a time when class alignment was growing as the basis of politics, they tried to permeate all parties impartially, or even found a 'collectivist' party above class. Worse, they pinned their hopes on Rosebery and Balfour at the precise moment when these fascinating, but ambiguous, personalities were losing out to the new mood of Liberal Radicalism. They not only 'misread the emerging pattern of British politics' as Mackenzie says, but misjudged the content or 'nourishment' which British politics needed. The ruthless collectivism which they represented was very far from the easygoing, pragmatic British attitude to reform. Their stern moralism which demanded improvement in working-class conduct in return for 'treatment' of working-class ills, was remote from the 'ninepence for fourpence' of Lloyd George's populist social insurance schemes. As they entered their fifties, they became increasingly isolated moralists in a new age of hedonism, disapproving alike of Wells's experiments in free love, and the 'ideal of anarchic ways in sexual questions' which they discovered among the young Cambridge Fabians.

It was these symptoms of the 'decay of capitalist civilisation' that drew them, in their declining years, to Soviet Communism. This is the most interesting part of the third volume. At first, they disapproved of the Soviet experiment. 'The sinister aspect', Beatrice wrote to H. G. Wells in 1920, 'is the military caste based on creed and supported by millions of peasants incapable of democracy'. 'Creed autocracy' she was writing to Wells in 1928, results from the breakdown of religious beliefs. In Britain, she thought, 'we have a great measure of common consent as to what is desirable and an authoritative outlook on life'. Yet it was precisely this that was collapsing. 'The important thing' Sidney wrote to the French historian Halévy in 1926 'is that the people in general, in all classes, seem to have lost practically all their "taboos" in such matters as sex relations . . .' For the Webbs, whose whole achievement had been built on the repression of the body, this came as a personal threat. The economic collapse of 1931 completed their disillusion. In 1931, Beatrice wrote to Sidney of 'world movements which are growing to bring about a far deeper cleavage between the '*Haves* and the '*Have-Nots* . . . than we have yet experienced'. With capitalist civilization bankrupt both morally and economically, the Webbs turned for consolation to the 'puritanical religious order' being created in Russia. Their conversion to the 'new civilisation' had taken place: their visit to the Soviet Union in 1932 only confirmed what Beatrice, in particular, needed to believe.

In the last years, it was her will-power alone which kept the partnership going. By the 1920s, Sidney had become incapable of more than 'routine work'. In 1938 he had a stroke. 'The inevitable has come – one of the partners has fallen on the way – we shall never again march together in work and recreation' wrote Beatrice in her diary. 'Uncomfortable by day, and sleepless by night' she drifted to her death in April 1943. Sidney lingered on for four more years. To the last, they remained true to their obsolescence.

CHAPTER FIVE

Beatrice Webb's Diary

Norman and Jeanne MacKenzie (eds), *The Diary of Beatrice Webb*: vol. 4, *The Wheel of Life*
[Virago, 1985]

THE FOURTH volume of Beatrice Webb's diary concludes a magnificent literary and historical, editorial and publishing enterprise. The only English twentieth-century diary to equal it is that of Virginia Woolf. The two formidable ladies were not unknown to each other, and they matched each other's comments, meeting for meeting.

'Mrs W is far less ornamental than of old,' wrote Virginia Woolf on 3 February 1927 after thirty-six exhausting hours at Liphook, 'wispy untidy drab, with a stain on her skirt & a key on her watch chain; as if she had cleared the decks & rolled her sleeves & was waiting for the end, but working.' Mrs Webb responded on 6 February: 'she is, though still beautiful, a spare self-contained ascetic looking creature . . . tall, stooping figure, exquisite profile, refined, an almost narrow and hard intellectuality of expression.' To Mrs Webb, Mrs Woolf was a 'clever artist in personal psychology', but her 'men and women do not interest me . . . no predominant aims . . . one state of mind follows another without particular reason.' And to Mrs Woolf, the Webbs seemed to be 'perfectly adjusted machinery: but talk by machinery does not charm, or suggest: it cuts the grass of the mind close at the roots.'

The artist promises more than the social engineer; yet though both were great diarists, Beatrice Webb is the more satisfying. This is because her range is greater. She relates her experiences to history, whereas

Virginia Woolf chronicles fleeting impressions, passing emotions. Thus Beatrice Webb's diary is a biography of the time; Virginia Woolf's a biography of moments of time. But the achievement depends on balance. Although Beatrice Webb tends to group her characters into social, racial and even animal types ('English are mostly dogs and birds – less often horses, cats and apes, but still fewer pigs'), they are never just types. She has the artist's eye for individuality combined with the social scientist's urge to classify.

Giving power to her observation and unity to her mood is a strong sense of the link between private and public qualities. In case after case we are treated to the spectacle of public virtue being undermined by private vices – vanity, loose living, luxurious habits, social climbing, intellectual frivolity – until we are half persuaded by her picture of a governing class incapable of solving the problems which confront it. Her cast of characters are actors in the great historical drama she unfolds for us: the spiritual and material decay of capitalist civilization and the search for a faith and creed capable of restoring progress by harmonizing the moral with the scientific; a search which led her to Soviet communism.

Before coming directly to this, the main theme of her fourth volume, it is worth considering the place of the diary in her life. The clue is given in *My Apprenticeship*, where she describes the transformation of the beautiful, passionate Beatrice Potter, lover of Joseph Chamberlain, into Mrs Sidney Webb, the scientific investigator, instrument of permeation, and servicer of the human computer who became her husband. The personality of Mrs Webb was built on a denial of the sexual and religious nature of Beatrice Potter: the 'self' was too painful for her to live with and had to be *obliterated*. The psychology of this transformation is as baffling as it is fascinating. But accomplished it was, and resulted in the 'firm of Webb' producing one huge volume after another on local government and trade unionism; leading the Fabian Society and founding the London School of Economics; beavering away, as Beatrice Webb put it, to 'undermine the individualism of the British race', or, as Virginia Woolf saw it, to 'destroy everything one likes and loves'. The diary was Mrs Webb's receptacle for the suppressed Beatrice.

Her diary rather than her marriage was the real waste-paper basket of her emotions. Night after sleepless night she poured her 'self' into it. And in it we get a picture of her that is unrecognizable from the mainly disobliging contemporary comments on Mrs Webb, with her clear-cut opinions, her hydraulic vocabulary, her card-index conversation. We see someone who fights by night the doubts and terrors which she conquers by day. So the reader comes to mock but stays to admire – even to love – her for her honesty, her disinterestedness, her devotion to the 'other one', ultimately for her fortitude in the face of mounting physical infirmities. 'Courage, old woman, courage: be game to the end. And don't give way to the egotism of old age; live up to what old age *ought to be*, the impersonal beneficence of the Ancient unmoved by the opinion of the world he or she is about to leave.' She wins us over in her diary as she could never do in her life.

Three things set her on the road to Moscow: her own need for a religion to replace Christianity; her belief that 'the game is up for profit-making enterprise'; and old age – she was 70 in 1928. Her conversion to Stalinist communism *was* senile infatuation (rather than the infantile disorder it was for bright Cambridge undergraduates), in the sense that the catastrophe of the Great Depression found her in a state of spiritual and mental exhaustion.

Beatrice Webb had staked her life on faith in secular salvation to be brought about by near-celibate experts. The trouble with this 'solution' to religious doubts was that it failed to satisfy either her spiritual or ethical needs. It offered neither the mysticism of a religion nor the discipline of a religious order with its 'communion of the faithful, with its religious rites and . . . above all its definite code of conduct'. There was nothing in her creed to feed her emotions. She herself recognized this: 'the concrete questions which I have investigated – trade unionism, local government, cooperation, political organisation, no longer interest me', she wrote in 1924. 'I dislike reading about them, thinking about them, talking or writing about them.' This sense of spiritual loss undoubtedly grew with age. It was reinforced by her sense of growing moral anarchy. She reverts time and again to the 'unrestrained animal impulses' of the young; their 'mania for the sub-human in art, literature, music and manners – Epstein, D. H. Lawrence, Aldous Huxley, Jazz music': their lack of any 'fixed scale of values'. Her favourite nephew Malcolm Muggeridge, Kingsley Martin, even her old friend William Beveridge exhibit these distempers. Their cause, Beatrice Webb feels, lies in 'this terrible doctrine of relativity, latent in all modern science'. Instead of producing the 'holy order' dedicated to human betterment, capitalism was turning out a generation of lascivious monks. 'I prefer the hard hygienic view of sex and the conscious subordination of sexuality to the task of "building up socialism" characteristic of Soviet Russia', she wrote in 1932.

The Great Depression of 1929–32 was the catalyst, but the reader has already been prepared for her repudiation of parliamentary democracy. The diary entries in the 1920s are full of her growing disillusion with the Labour Party as an instrument of government and reform. This culminated in her reactions to the crisis of August 1931. Within a few weeks of it, write Norman and Jeanne MacKenzie, 'Beatrice had concluded that the future could and should lie with communism, and that for all its shortcomings the Soviet Union was the exemplar.' Sidney Webb was a cabinet minister in both the Labour governments of 1924 and 1929–31, so Beatrice Webb had a ringside view of the circus. What she saw was the corruption of Labour's leadership by the aristocratic embrace. We glimpse Ramsay MacDonald at the 1926 party conference surrounded by 'lithe and beauteous forms – leaders of fashion or ladies of the stage attended by six-feet-tall and well groomed men.' We see Ethel Snowden 'climbing, climbing, climbing, night and day'; Philip Snowden 'romancing about the royal family'; Jimmy Thomas boozing with the captains of industry; Harold Laski 'just a trifle too smart for a professor of socialist opinions'. Even her oldest friend, Bernard Shaw, was entangled in a smart set and luxurious habits, so that he reminded her of a 'Nonconformist minister concocting his Sunday sermon in the intervals of gambling in a low public house'.

Beatrice Webb was also fascinated by the reappearance of the nineteenth-century governing class in the ranks of Labour. Her profound insight into the English machinery of co-option – and its success in preventing social and economic renewal – sprang from self-recognition. Beatrice Potter was as susceptible to the attention of the old governing class as Mrs Webb was repelled by the social climbing of the proletarian leaders and their wives. She relished physical beauty and charm in men and women, artistry in personality and manners. She found Oswald and Cynthia Mosley 'delightful to look at and listen to'. MacDonald was the 'supreme artist' in British politics: 'his figure, features, colouring, gestures and voice "make up" splendidly.' Bernard Shaw was always the 'great charmer'. Not surprisingly Mrs Webb found the equalitarian atmosphere of the Sokolnikovs more to her taste on a visit to the Soviet embassy in 1930: 'It was impossible to distinguish the ambassador, his wife and staff from those serving them in what is here called a "menial" capacity – ideas, manners and mutual relations being the same all through.'

By 1932 Beatrice Webb was not as mentally alert or inquiring as she had been fifty years earlier. She realized that the Fabians had failed to foresee the growing problem of unemployment and the decay of capitalism, British-style ('brainworkers ... inferior in training, the manual workers ... ca'canny ... [with] too high a standard of leisure and pleasure; the nation as a whole ... slipping down the slope of casual and sloppy thinking ...'). But she was too old to work on the problem afresh, simply concluding that the new situation required even more state control, and quicker, than she had thought.

It was the Beatrice Webb generation Keynes had in mind when he talked of state socialism as 'little better than a dusty survival of a plan to meet the problems of 50 years ago', and complained of the Labour Cabinet of 1931 that 'they have been totally out of sympathy with those who have had new notions of what is economically sound.' Beatrice Webb's comments on Keynes are among the shrewdest in her diary: 'the imaginative forecaster of events and speculator in ideas'. But she could not believe that Keynes was 'serious' – 'he plays a game of chess with [economics] in his leisure hours.' She was misled, partly because she did not understand what Keynes was saying – she does not try to reproduce any of the economic talk she had with him – partly because he did not conform to her conception of a serious social investigator. 'The only serious cult with him is aesthetics', she wrote. She was equally dismissive of the unemployment plans of the proto-Keynesians. Oswald Mosley's schemes for the 'state organisation of credit ... are as impracticable as they would be mischievous if carried out'; Lloyd George's proposals, 'though brilliantly conceived and advocated, are always unsound and turn out terribly expensive'. Without the energy to rethink her own position and with a strong Victorian disapproval of the character-types of those propounding a 'middle way', Beatrice Webb had nothing to fall back on except Soviet Russia's 'benevolent experiment in organising production and consumption for the common good'.

The aged Webbs sailed for the Soviet Union in May 1932 and duly discovered in that alien civilization the sermons they had brought with them, which they worked up into a famous, two-volume book. Having found her church and religion Beatrice Potter protected them from the cold eye of Mrs Webb with all the passion of the fulfilled mother and lover. In the nightmare world of Hitler and war, Soviet Russia increasingly beckoned to her as a beacon of light and hope. In dreadful agony from a 'rotting' kidney, she slipped away on 30 April 1943, knowing that her child was safe. In her last confused moments the world she had sought all her life seemed to become strangely fused with the world she was going to – a world in which there would be no more pain or hurt because no one would exist.

CHAPTER SIX

Victorian Wives

Barbara Caine, *Destined to be Wives: The Sisters of Beatrice Webb*
[Clarendon Press, Oxford, 1986];
Pat Jalland, *Women, Marriage, and Politics 1860–1914*
[Clarendon Press, Oxford, 1986]

THE CASE for women's history is that women have been subject to special kinds of experience because they are women. The trouble with it is that it tends to attribute to male domination oppressive states of affairs for women which were the result of more general conditions applying to both men and women. Family life in Victorian England is particularly hard to get right, partly because the weight of convention pressed so heavily on both sexes; partly because we find it difficult to interpret the language in which the Victorians discussed their feelings, having invented new languages like psychoanalysis which were unknown to them. For example, areas of feeling and behaviour we would now want to call homosexual were not then identified as such; and perhaps we are wrong to do so. Similarly, situations which seem to us oppressive to women may not have been thought so then, or may have been thought oppressive in different ways, because the system of consolations was different then from what it is now.

To negotiate a pathway through this particular foreign country requires exceptional historical tact and sensitivity; both of which are displayed in these two fine books by Australian-based scholars. There is no strident feminism here; rather a compelling examination of the ways groups of middle- and upper-class women coped with, manipulated, and occasionally transcended the conventions which required them to be wives and mothers, with varying degrees of grace and gracelessness, fulfilment and despair. Barbara Caine's account is more satisfying, because more focused. She concentrates on a single family – the Potters – and takes us through the life-cycles of nine remarkable sisters, one of whom was the formidable Beatrice Webb. Their experiences of education, courtship, childbirth and old age, together with their marital strategies are carefully nuanced, and each of them comes to life as an individual, most notably Rosie, the *Traviata* of the clan, whose extra-marital love affairs caused the sisters to threaten her with the lunatic asylum, chiefly to protect their own reputations and the marriage prospects of their daughters. The smallness of the sample, however, prevents any safe generalization. Most of the sisters experienced loveless, or progressively loveless, marriages (one of them, Blanche Cripps, hanged herself) and miserable old ages. But as Barbara Caine notes 'few of the Potter sisters exhibited any capacity for expressing warmth or affection'. They would have been better off today, where their administrative and intellectual abilities would have had scope outside family life.

On the other hand, Pat Jalland's book makes clear that disappointing marriages and alienated children were not the upper-class Victorian norm. Her sample of women is drawn from a diffuse collection of fifty or more families, ranging from the Cecils to the Ramsay MacDonalds, linked together only by the fact that they were married to politicans or came from political families; a principle of selection which has little relation to the subject-matter of her study which, like Barbara Caine's, has to do with the life cycles of upper- and middle-class wives and mothers. The range of situations and strategies is greater – there is an interesting chapter on the Victorian spinster – but the only woman who comes alive is that flirtatious 'Soul', Laura Tennant, whose life was cut short in childbirth. This is the penalty for using lives to illustrate themes.

More than Barbara Caine Ms Jalland has set out to argue a thesis: that there were satisfactions and power to be got out of the Victorian situation provided women played their cards right, which most of them did. 'Actual reality' as evidenced in these family records diverged considerably from legal and fictional stereotypes. For example, although married women were not allowed to own property till the Acts of 1870 and 1882, the financial settlements which accompanied most of these marriages were designed to give the wife an independent income through trusts. So far from such wives being decorative and useless, the management of large households 'was comparable to running a substantial business'. The norm of married life was 'loving, close, and fulfilling'. Victorian women were characteristically resilient and resourceful in face of ill health or bereavement, unlike the Darwin aunt described in Gwen Raverat's delightful *Period Piece* who went to bed at eighteen and never got up again for sixty years. Their childbirth practices, with home deliveries, husband in attendance, and breast-feeding 'might have been applauded by the modern movement for natural childbirth'. Ms Jalland makes the point that most upper-class women were hostile to the women's suffrage because they felt they already had all the influence they needed; understandably, since as Beatrice Webb noted, they all came from families who gave orders and did not take them. The legal, economic and social emancipation of women this century benefited mainly women from the lower middle and working classes: Beatrice Webb 'never experienced the disabilities assumed to arise from my sex'.

Other stereotypes are effectively knocked by both authors. The Victorians are generally held to have been both reticent and starry-eyed about feelings. But it turns out to have been much more a matter of styles of frankness. There are no Kinsey Reports to tell us how often Victorian husbands and wives made love on average. But the Victorians were explicit in ways which would now be considered bad taste. Marriage manuals suggested that women should be three to seven years younger than their husbands because they aged faster; and there is nothing starry-eyed in Mary Gladstone's contention that 'a great love conquered all, whilst moderate affection required material comforts and social status', or Lady Selborne's advice to her son that judgment should precede love in the choice of a partner.

In other ways Victorian reticence *is* a barrier to knowledge. One of the striking things about the second half of the nineteenth century was the fall in the birth-rate, contrary to Malthus's expectation that people had more children the richer they became. The average number of children for twenty years of marriage fell from 6.16 live births in the 1860s to 2.43 by 1915. But we still do not understand the mechanism by which this was accomplished. In 1914 Keynes complained of the conspiracy of silence surrounding contraception. 'The present position appears to be that a practice actually followed by enormous numbers of the most respectable persons is publicly branded as the height of immorality.' Was it women who mainly used contraceptives or men? Margot Asquith told Cynthia Mosley: 'Henry always withdrew in time, such a noble man.' But neither the Potter sisters nor their husbands seem to have made any effort to control their fertility. Perhaps it was the postponement of marriage among the wealthy, rather than the use of contraception, which constituted the main 'artificial check' on their fecundity? We don't really know. Again, we don't fully understand the demographic and economic patterns which produced nearly 2 million 'redundant women' in Victorian England – the root of the hysterical or invalid spinster problem, and one of the main sources of feminism.

In the end it is difficult to say which sex got the worst deal from the Victorian division of labour. There is ample testimony from both books of the horrors of home education for girls: 'For more than ten years I was bored to death all the time,' wrote Molly Trevelyan. But how often has that remark been echoed by exceptional men looking back on their public school life? And if the 'accomplishments' girls were taught are considered a travesty of education, what about the mechanical and threadbare classical education to which generation of schoolboys were subjected? Barbara Caine records the appalling brutality of the young Lawrence Holt to his sister Betty; but at least girls were spared the systematic bullying at boarding school which was considered an appropriate preparation for upper-class masculine life. Women were vulnerable to death in childbirth, largely due to the absence of antibiotics; men were killed off in wars. It is often forgotten that both sexes suffered from lack of career opportunities, on account both of the pancity, and low status, of most professional jobs. And so one can go on. The truth is that the moral price for the maintenance of social and economic privilege went up for both men and women during the Victorian era; and by the end of it neither the daughters nor the sons of the families portrayed in these studies were prepared to go on paying it.

CHAPTER SEVEN

J. G. Frazer

Robert Ackerman, *J. G. Frazer: His Life and Work*
[Cambridge, 1987]

J. G. FRAZER'S *The Golden Bough* was one of the seminal books of the early years of this century. One can see why. Frazer discovered a language for talking about man's religious beliefs, and primitive origins, which gave confidence in progress, and comfort to the the agnostics, without offending the Christians. The book's success owed as much to the archaic charm of its writing and the skilfulness of Frazer's story-telling as to its philosophy. Frazer was no Grimm, or Freud, reminding his readers of irrational forces seething below the crust of civilization, but a respectable Cambridge don, with an optimistic outlook, and a Romantic turn of phrase. Today Frazer has been consigned to his own anthropological grave. His faith in the triumph of reason is now seen to be a delusion as gross as any he attributed to the priests of Nemi; his conjectures are discounted, his style no longer appeals.

In writing about him, Robert Ackerman, an American literary historian, has had to overcome a formidable biographical problem; namely, the radical disjunction between the materials of Frazer's work and those of his life. Frazer's riotous imagination left almost no imprint on his pattern of existence, which was that of a reclusive gentleman-scholar, who worked in his library seven days a week. Basically, his life was passed in writing *The Golden Bough*, seventeen volumes altogether, spread over three editions. When he was not writing that, he was writing other books, chiefly his six-volume commentary on Pausanias, a Greek geographer of the second century AD, with an equally unbridled anthropological curiosity. He corresponded with his intellectual peers, with his publisher George Macmillan, who had to suffer the repeated postponements and uncontrollable growth of his books, and with Edmund Gosse, who several times baled him out of financial difficulties. In middle age, he briefly took time off from scholarship to marry a French widow, Lilly Grove, who tirelessly and tiresomely promoted her husband's interests. They spent a surprisingly peripatetic old age together, before dying, she deaf and he blind, on the same day. The

Cambridge joke was that she would not leave him even a few hours' peace to himself. Ackerman extracts the maximum interest and amusement from this curious tale. But the psychological conditions which produced Frazer's notably Victorian ability to flirt with savagery at a safe distance somehow eludes us. Even allowing for sublimation, we expect a greater interplay between the inner and outer life than Frazer exhibits.

Ackerman triumphantly succeeds in re-creating the mental atmosphere of the late-Victorian world, suspended between religion and science. Frazer was anti-Christian, but not fiercely so. He treated religious beliefs as logical mistakes: his task was not to condemn them, but to explain their origins. The clear inference of his book was that Christianity belonged to the family of superstitions, superseded by the march of science. But he was too tactful to say so. And like most sensible Victorians he was prepared to concede that these superstitions could have evolutionary value, particularly in regulating the sexual instinct and establishing the rights of private property. This was part of his technique for fitting the 'savage mind' into the progressive scheme of things. In an uncharacteristic lecture delivered in Liverpool in 1907 he came close to acknowledging something else – the social function of religion in controlling forces of chaos which reason might never be able to touch. In a prophetic image he likened Western Europe to a volcano about to erupt. Perhaps this was merely the effect Liverpool had on him. But it was the nearest his evolutionary faith came to faltering.

Ackerman guides us through the intellectual and publishing complexities of Frazer's great book with scholarly assurance and literary grace. *The Golden Bough* rested on the simple idea that the scientific outlook is the culmination, but not the starting point, of rationality. Rationality starts with magic, regresses to religion when magic is seen to fail, and then both give way to science. Frazer sets up this three-stage progression by asking us to imagine how a powerful 'savage mind' (an unsung Aristotle or Einstein) would set about tackling the problem of maximizing his tribe's food-supply and fertility. Primitive rites and customs provide the 'evidences' of the solutions adopted. Frazer takes the fact that similar customs occur in communities widely separated by time and place to confirm his hypothesis of underlying systems of rational, though mistaken, thought.

It is easy to mock this rationalist view of the origins of culture. Wittgenstein wrote: 'All that Frazer does is to make this practice [the killing of the priest-king] plausible to people who think as he does.' And Ackerman observes: 'With his propensity for planning and taking long views [Frazer's] kangaroo-man would have been at home in the Fabian Society of 1898.' Anthropologists disown Frazer's interpretations; and his own disciple, Malinowski, broke with his comparative method. But the questions Frazer raised – Is man a problem-solving or a playful animal? What is the relationship between magic and science? What part do outstanding individuals play in the birth and life of cultures? – are not dead. As long as educated people discuss them, Frazer cannot be written off as an anthropological specimen. And people interested in them will love this book.

CHAPTER EIGHT

Bertrand Russell

Alan Ryan, *Bertrand Russell: A Political Life*
[Viking, 1988]

A SCHOOLMASTER once told the 16-year-old Alan Ryan that Bertrand Russell was an 'old fool'. This was just about the time when the 85-year-old Russell was starting his last crusade as head of the Campaign for Nuclear Disarmament! After reading Ryan's *Bertrand Russell: A Political Life*, I would say: not foolish, but often over simple to the point of dishonesty.

A. J. P. Taylor once said to me that he tried to tell the truth in his history, but would lie through his teeth to stop the world blowing itself up. Russell seems to have made the same distinction between his philosophical work and his political advocacy. He saw it as his mission to save the world from destruction, and did not hesitate to blacken the characters and motives of those whom he conceived to stand in the way. Churchmen, he wrote, 'value morals as affording a legitimate outlet for their desire to inflict pain'; Macmillan was 'much more wicked than Hitler' for equipping Britain with the hydrogen bomb. The Big Lies here are not less gross for containing small particles of sense.

Alan Ryan's defence of Russell is that he 'woke up the middle-aged and encouraged the rebellious young'. I think this defence stands. Russell still delights with his lucidity, wit, irreverence. He helped make people less anxious and afraid, and by entertaining them certainly added to the sum of human happiness, if, perhaps, not quite in the way he intended. Ryan suggests that Russell would have given up pure philosophy even had the First World War not happened. I think this is true, and not just because Wittgenstein had persuaded him that he had reached an intellectual dead-end. He had much of the temperament of the preacher; he also admits to experiencing 'unendurable loneliness' which could be overcome only by identifying himself with the cause of suffering humanity. But it was the war which pushed him into the political pulpit. It convinced him that folly and wickedness were rampant in the world and only the most drastic reforms of attitudes and institutions would avert total destruction. This was really the message he preached for the rest of his life.

But his persuasive style owed a great deal to two other factors. Russell always had to earn his living from his pen. Like Shaw, Wells, Koestler and other intellectual gad-flies of our time he was in the business of writing pot-boilers for an audience which now included the half- and the self-educated, and wanted to be instructed with a light touch. Secondly, Russell was sublimely indifferent to politics in the narrow sense of winning power and working out policies. The institutional route from damnation to salvation never received more than his sketchiest attention.

If Russell's passionate lucidity was unique to him, neither in content nor intellectual method was there anything very original in his political ideas. He did not coin, he used, the progressive currency of the day – and inherited most of its problems. The chief one was this. Russell and his upper-class Cambridge friends 'shared the liberal belief that economic and social reform should free the poor and control the capitalist without intruding on the private and personal freedoms they so much prized'. The trouble is that liberty and social justice may conflict. If they do, which should come first? This is the basic divide between liberalism and socialism, and there have been many ingenious attempts to bridge it. The dilemma was particularly acute for the Russell generation since, unlike us, they believed they knew – or that social science could tell them – how to maximize happiness by collective action. From this point of view, institutions which protected freedom, including private property, could come to be seen as obstacles to the attainment of universal felicity.

From some forms of the collectivist temptation Russell was always immune. He hated Bolshevism, and never accepted the case for state ownership of the productive instruments, preferring to disperse power through guild socialism. However, his liberalism grew notably less ardent as a result of the First World War. Between the wars we have a Russell so alarmed by the danger of war and social strife that he is prepared to accept a great deal of indoctrination and thought control, as well as endowing a world government with tyrannical powers, in order to avert these horrors. The crux of the matter was that his belief in freedom faded with his belief in the rationality of man. If people's desires – conditioned as he came to believe they were by a life-hating conspiracy of 'capitalists, militarists, and ecclesiastics' – could no longer be relied on to maintain peace and progress, it would be necessary to 'alter men's characters and desires in such a way as to minimize occasions for conflict'. In such moods Russell was prepared to advocate the tranquil hell of a *Brave New World* as preferable to continuing with the distempers of the actual world.

The same line of thought led Russell on several occasions to advocate world domination by a single power. In 1936 he argued that a Europe run by Nazi Germany was preferable to another war. In 1948 he championed a pre-emptive nuclear strike by the United States against the Soviet Union if the latter refused to abandon the right to manufacture the atom bomb. At the end of his life he took up the cause of a neutralist Europe, shorn of its nuclear defences. All these positions represent a *reductio ad absurdum* of the early Russell's acceptance of British imperialism as a utility-maximizing principle of international order. The proposition that being red is less unpleasant than being dead seems incontestable. What is odd, as Ryan notes, is Russell's refusal to take the deterrence argument seriously. But this was part and parcel of his refusal or inability to see any middle way between heaven and hell. As Ryan writes: 'It was noticeable that he hardly considered the possibility that things might go on in much the same way, a good deal sub-paradisaical, but a good deal super-infernal . . .' Without minimizing his faults, Ryan has written an intelligent and compassionate book about his old hero, which is also a very good read.

CHAPTER NINE

Keynes and His Parents

[1979]

MAYNARD KEYNES'S break with the values of his parents needs to be put into its proper cultural setting, as part of a wider reaction against Victorianism.

The Victorians were activists. Their allegiance was given to making money, saving souls, and improving the world. Theirs was a religious age, but it was not the kind of religion which encouraged withdrawal from the world. Rather, it spurred men to pile up money and achievements for the greater glory of God and the security of their immortal souls. Morality was a matter of right conduct: acting rightly was deemed more important than thinking rightly or feeling rightly. In the standard utilitarian ethics of the time, actions were supposed to be judged by consequences. In practice, Victorian morality was largely conventional, a matter of good form, rather than ratiocination.

The high achievements of the Victorian age were purchased at a price. One casualty was the arts. In Matthew Arnold's view, the Victorians sacrificed culture to machinery; the cultivation of what is 'beautiful, graceful and becoming' to the 'machinery of business, chapels, tea-meetings and addresses . . .' The other loss was in the area of personal development and personal relationships. Both were sacrificed to the extreme consciousness of sin, which repressed both sexuality and affection, and to the doctrine of work, which condemned what was not *useful* as a waste of time and energy. If there was any single principle of Victorian life it was the sacrifice of the present to the future. It was a society geared to saving, both economically and psychologically.

It was to a group of Cambridge undergraduates, of whom Keynes was one, brought up in this tradition, that G. E. Moore's *Principia Ethica* came, in 1903, as a revelation. What is of greatest interest to philosophers in this book is Moore's argument that 'good' is indefinable. But what chiefly interested his young Cambridge friends was his distinction between good as a means and good as an end. Moore argued that the life of action, with its associated virtues, has no intrinsic value. It is valuable only as a means to the good, and, moreover, a pretty incalcula-

48

ble one, since 'we can never be sure that any action will produce the greatest value possible.' Ethics had been largely concerned with commending certain actions, to the neglect of what was intrinsically valuable. The things, says Moore, which are good in themselves are not virtuous actions, but certain states of mind which are sought for their own sake. These were 'the pleasures of human intercourse and the enjoyment of beautiful objects'. By making this central distinction between means and ends, and by wrongly accusing ethics of having concentrated on the former at the expense of the latter, Moore in effect devalued the whole Victorian scheme of life – conventional morality, the life of action, dedication to public causes. Over thirty years later, Keynes called the *Principia Ethica* 'the beginning of a new renaissance, the opening of a new heaven on earth' whose effect 'dominated, and perhaps still dominates, everything else'.

Moore's influence can be seen in the work of two leading members of Bloomsbury, Lytton Strachey and Clive Bell. Strachey's *Eminent Victorians*, published in 1918, is the dramatization of the conflict between good actions and good states of mind. His four eminent Victorians were all relentless activists, always wanting, like Florence Nightingale, to be 'doing something'. Their values were worldly; they were ambitious for honour and power, or wanted to do good. Strachey sets out to show how such lives of action are incompatible with what is intrinsically good, and also how action is quite likely to be futile, even destructive. Cardinal Manning tramples on Newman, the unworldly hero of the first essay; Florence Nightingale, in 'doing good', drives Sidney Herbert to his death. The consequences of Arnold's actions turn out to be quite contrary to his intentions: 'The earnest enthusiast who strove to make his pupils Christian gentlemen . . . thus proved to be the founder of the worship of athletics and the worship of good form.' The one character for whom Strachey feels sympathy is General Gordon, whose actions were dotty. His state of mind was not as bad as the others'.

Clive Bell asks the question: what is meant by civilization? Civilization, he says, in a book with that title, published in 1928, is not a belief in private property, chastity, patriotism, or God, since all these beliefs exist in savage societies, and many societies regarded as civilized did not have them. Nor does it consist in being fittest for survival, democratic, or technologically advanced. Civilization is the direct means to good states of mind. Its defining characteristic is respect for art and thought. Civilized people dislike the 'life of action'. Some activities, it is true, may be means to the good. But since life is already full of immediate means to good, civilized persons are less concerned to promote indirect means. Action is a disease for those who cannot find satisfaction in love, friendship, conversation, creation, or contemplation of beauty, pursuit of truth and knowledge, gratification of the senses. It is the vice of those 'inapt for civilized pleasures . . .' A civilized society, Bell feels, is one which contains groups of highly civilized men and women, living off the labour of others, and large enough to influence the whole tone of life. He was far from feeling that England met these requirements. In fact, English civilization was so 'grossly Philistine' that any English boy 'born with a fine sensibility, a peculiar feeling for art, or an absolutely first-rate intelligence' was bound to find himself 'at loggerheads with the world in which he is to live', bound to become 'an outlaw'.

Now, the point about Keynes was that he was *never* an outlaw. He jettisoned much of what we think of as Victorianism, but not, on the whole, the values of his family, school and university. The seeming contradiction is easily explained. Keynes's background was by no means typical of middle-class Victorian England. His family milieu was much more scholarly than was normal. At Eton and at King's College, Cambridge, he stepped into an intellectual tradition: in fact, Moore's *Principia Ethica*, while rejecting Victorian morality, embodied much of what was best in the Cambridge tradition. Thus Keynes was brought up in a society sufficiently civilized not to force him into the rebellion which Clive Bell thought inevitable for anyone of his temperament. In their own lives, Keynes and his Cambridge circle broadened that civilization to include other 'goods'. They had no cause to repudiate it.

Keynes's parents, John Neville and Florence Ada Keynes, emerge from Sir Roy Harrod's biography as rather shadowy figures. John Neville was a fellow of Pembroke College, Cambridge, a logician and economist. He seems to have been a kind, modest, considerate, retiring man, honourable and punctilious, with a fondness for ceremonial and a weakness for Royalty. Florence Ada was the more forceful, active character. One of the first graduates of Newnham, the new women's college, she was heavily involved in good works, particularly as a member of the Charity Organisation Society. Through this, she became active in local politics, ending up as Mayor of Cambridge. 'When is [your mother] not busy?' John Neville once asked Maynard, writing on another occasion, 'What a devoted woman she is! If there is anything in heredity, her children certainly ought to have a sense of duty.' Their marriage was, by his account, ideally happy.

In one crucial respect, they were also ideal parents for someone of Maynard Keynes's exceptional gifts. Very early on (he was born in 1883) they appeared to recognize that their eldest son had the makings of a genius. According to Maynard's school reports, he was showing 'talent' at arithmetic at six, 'power' at seven. At nine he was 'decidedly the brightest boy in his division' at St Faith's preparatory school; at eleven, the senior wrangler who taught him reported him doing 'really brilliant' work in mathematics. His classics, too, were 'full of promise'. (He was to win an open scholarship in both to King's College, Cambridge.) His parents, particularly his father, provided the strongest possible support, intellectual and moral, for Maynard's mental development. Not only was he encouraged to take part in adult conversations with such visitors as W. E. Johnson, Alfred Marshall, and Henry Sidgwick, but John Neville appointed himself, in effect, his director of studies.

As Maynard's mentor, his father probably found an increasingly satisfying intellectual outlet. His second, and last, book, *The Scope and Method of Political Economy*, appeared when he was thirty-seven, and Maynard seven. Thereafter, although he became a university administrator of legendary good sense, he wrote nothing of importance. Perhaps he felt that, with nothing original to say himself, his time was best spent encouraging his son's originality. Father and son worked together in John Neville's study, in a relationship which recalls that of James Mill and John Stuart Mill. There was another motive. Although Maynard's parents were comfortably off, they were not wealthy. They wanted Maynard to go to Eton; but this depended on his getting a scholarship; and his educational programme was geared to that end. Maynard duly became a King's Scholar at Eton in the autumn of 1897. Among the many advantages which his background gave him, conspicuous financial advantage was not one. He was a 'scholarship' boy.

This strenuous intellectual regime was, on the whole, perfectly suited to Maynard's quick, active, incisive mind. But there were signs of stress. Up to the age of sixteen or so he was subject to frequent, and rather mysterious, illnesses. They were so habitual, in fact, that they were known in the family as his 'periodicals'. He was also subject to stammering. In 1896 his father wrote in his diary, 'Maynard's holiday task was some four or five hundred lines of Homer and as there has certainly been an increase in stammering lately – indicating a need for entire rest – I wrote to ask that he might be excused this.' His headmaster, Goodchild, agreed, replying '[Maynard] seemed so bright all round that I did not connect the increased hesitation in speaking with his work.' Maynard's mysterious fevers and 'liver attacks' may well have been 'migraine', which, like his stammering, suggests that he was under considerable strain.

As an Eton 'Colleger', Maynard found himself in a highly stimulating, competitive intellectual environment. Weekly letters of encouragement and exhortation, which included detailed advice on examination strategy, poured in from his father. But undoubtedly the main stimulus was provided by the school itself. To a remarkable extent, Eton had managed to escape the Arnoldian blight; at College, the scholars' house, Maynard sharpened his wits against those of some of the cleverest boys in the country. Athletics reigned, but they did not reign supreme. Intellectual accomplishment was highly valued; and there was enough privacy, and sufficient numbers of able and dedicated masters, to make the most of a boy's intellectual talents. In this atmosphere, there was little enough reason for Maynad to rebel, as did so many outstanding boys at more philistine boarding schools. In fact, his was a triumphant progress, punctuated only by illness. He won forty-nine prizes, and became a member of 'Pop'. What struck his tutor, Gurney Lubbock, was the entire absence in him of the 'mercenary, mark-getting feeling which so often spoils excellent scholars'. For him work was 'worth doing for its own sake'.

I have indicated one of the great strengths of Maynard's upbringing – the encouragement of his intellectual growth. But there were at least two important weaknesses. The first was a certain coldness in family relationships, the product of a bourgeois suspicion of emotional experience. The conventions of Maynard's upbringing did seem to exclude the expression of feelings. Remarkable in the dense correspondence between Maynard and his parents is the absence of any clue to the emotions of the letter-writers. The only exceptions are his parents' expressions of pride in his accomplishments and worry about his state of health. There is no sense, for example, that either Maynard or his parents missed each other in his years of boarding. Even as an adult, when any youthful embarrassment at the expression of such sentiments may have been expected to fade, Maynard never discusses in his letters to his father or mother his feelings about himself, or his friends, or about them. Making every allowance for the conventions of the time, this does suggest a rather constricted relationship. Maynard's younger brother, Sir Geoffrey Keynes, uses the word 'neutral' to describe his home, and perhaps this quality permeated the home environment. (Maynard was not close to Geoffrey, four years his junior, though he was more intimate with his sister Margaret.) The evidence suggests that they were a 'happy' family – but perhaps happiness was achieved only by transferring out of the family anything awkward or sensitive.

From a certain point of view, family life was indeed ideal. There was much tolerance: Maynard, in particular, seems to have established a remarkably independent life-style from a quite early age, successfully claiming the un-puritan right to sleep late in the mornings (and to get breakfast served long after the others). Family members were linked together by a large number of hobbies and activities. There was a collectively produced family newspaper, which ran intermittently, under different names, for many years. There were long family summer holidays, visits to the grandparents at Bedford (Florence Ada's father was an eminent Congregational divine, author of a standard life of Bunyan), occasional trips abroad. Maynard's father managed to involve the others in his passion for stamp-collecting, chess, and golf. In fact, golf, which he took up, together with university adminstration, when he abandoned serious scholarship, seems to have been the one thing which caused John Neville real agonies of mind. He struggled with his recalcitrant swing in much the same spirit as Gladstone wrestled with sin, and apparently equally unavailingly. After his earliest years, it was his relationship with his father which was central to Maynard's childhood.

Maynard did not, on the whole, break through these emotional barriers at Eton. A clue to why this may have been so is provided by his confession to Lytton Strachey in 1906 that 'I have always suffered and I suppose always will from an unalterable obsession that I am ... physically repulsive ... The idea is so fixed and constant that I don't think anything – certainly no argument – could ever shake it.' That this was the most powerful barrier to the open expression of feeling can readily be imgined, especially in a school, and even university, world dominated by a supercilious physical aristocracy. At Eton, Maynard's friendships were with other amusing, intellectual boys of his own age.

His public demeanour was high-minded, even priggish; his feelings were veiled by clever and amused gossip.

Although the Keynes family paid great respect to thought, art was at a severe discount, retaining, in Noel Annan's words, its status as the 'temptress which they had to control by inadequate theories'. On their marriage in 1882, Maynard's parents moved into a bleak, double-fronted house at 6 Harvey Road, part of a new 'development' for married dons. Here Maynard grew up. 'The furnishings', writes Sir Geoffrey Keynes, 'were undistinguished, but comfortable. The pictures were conventional specimens of period taste ... Our home surroundings afforded no aesthetic stimulus.' The literature, too, was conventional, with popular writers like Anthony Hope in the ascendant. There was no music. The theatre was one of John Neville's great hobbies, and visits to plays in London were the special treat of Maynard's schooldays. But what they saw were conventional comedies, musicals and melodramas, with titles like 'The Rose of Passion'. We find no mention of Ibsen, or even of Pinero and Wilde. In this respect, the Keynes family merely mirrored Cambridge's parochialism. Maynard's own aesthetic emotions remained largely dormant, the exceptions being a certain dandyish delight in smart clothes and a passion for putting fine bindings on the book prizes which he received in such abundance. His buying of second-hand books, which started when he was at Eton, is more properly considered as an example of the collecting urge, a family trait which he shared with Geoffrey.

Keynes was liberated from this constricted world of high-minded academic and civic values by his post-school experiences in Cambridge and London. One should not make exaggerated claims. His new interests, tastes and feelings were, in a sense, simply part of growing up. He came in 1902 to King's College, Cambridge, intellectually precocious, but emotionally undeveloped. Relieved from the pressure of continuous examinations, he could develop other sides of his personality. Nor should it be imagined that Keynes 'dropped out'. He worked hard enough to become twelfth wrangler in the mathematics tripos, a result which Harrod calls 'respectable, but not triumphant'. He became president of the Cambridge Union. In fact, his extraordinary energy and quickness enabled him to do many things well. Nevertheless, there occurred a permanent shift in values. Intellect retained its high place. He found it a 'much more comfortable passion' than some others he had started to experience. By the end of 1905 he was finding economics 'increasingly satisfactory', and commented, 'I think I am rather good at it. I want to manage a railway or organise a Trust or at least swindle the investing public. It is so easy and fascinating to master the principles of these things.' However, his order of priorities had changed. To Strachey he wrote in 1906 'I don't wonder Aristotle put this intellectual activity first. Still, I don't agree with him. Love first, Philosophy second, Poetics third, and Politics fourth.' And over thirty years later he recalled that 'our prime objects in life were love, the creation and enjoyment of aesthetic experience and the pursuit of knowledge. Of these love came a long way first.' This was not the language of his parents, much less of the Victorian age as a whole. Neither was it characteristic of his generation. About the same time, the 22-year-old C. P. Trevelyan was writing to his parents, 'I should never mar my prospects of doing good to the people for the sake of any love for woman.' This was the authentic note of upper-class Victorianism.

One needs to place this 'transvaluation of values' in its proper setting. Sir Roy Harrod has rightly emphasized that Maynard's new departure depended on 'the security and good order of the British Empire ... Within the framework of a secure society thus kept in being, it was possible and desirable to make new experiments and to set one's eyes fixedly upon certain ideals, too long neglected.' We can be more precise. The Edwardian era was an interlude of prosperous calm between the economic troubles of the 1880s and 1890s, and the First World War. As Keynes wrote after the war, 'The projects and politics of militarism and imperialism, of racial and cultural rivalries, of monopolies, restriction, and exclusion, which were to play serpent to this paradise, were little more than the amusements of [the] daily newspaper, and appeared to exercise almost no influence at all on the ordinary course of social and economic life ...' And if England was a paradise, Cambridge was a paradise within a paradise, even more remote from the world of practical affairs. The other important factor is the general breakdown of Victorian morality. 'I know I believe in nothing ... but I do not less believe in morality,' wrote Leslie Stephen. But the Victorian moral code could not long survive the loss of its religious supports. This was the setting in which a leisured class could experiment in new styles of living. Both its situation and its morality were transitional. The Bloomsbury group, as

Roger Fry claimed, were the last of the Victorians. They were also the first sexual and aesthetic radicals.

In the formation of Keynes's personal 'ethic', three names stand out: G. E. Moore, Lytton Strachey and Duncan Grant. The first two he got to know in an exclusive Cambridge discussion society, the 'Apostles', to which he was elected in his second term at Cambridge. According to the mid-nineteenth-century Apostle Henry Sidgwick, the Society was animated by 'the spirit of the pursuit of truth with absolute devotion and unreserve by a group of intimate friends'. In Keynes's day, the dominating influence was G. E. Moore, and discussion revolved to a great extent round those ethical and aesthetic questions which made up the subject-matter of the *Principia Ethica*.

We have already referred to Moore's distinction between good actions and good states of mind, and, in summary fashion, to his ideal of personal affection and aesthetic enjoyments. But an equally important part of his appeal lay in what Keynes and his friends called Moore's 'method', by which they meant his technique for ranking states of mind in order of value. Its centre-piece was his theory of 'organic unities'. Moore held that the good was a complex whole which did not equal the sum of the value of its parts. A whole formed of one good part and one indifferent or bad part might have far greater value than the good part itself possessed. For example, the most valuable aesthetic enjoyments were made up of an appropriate emotion, a cognition of beautiful qualities, and the true belief that the object of appreciation possessed those qualities. But which was more valuable: an inadequate appreciation of a superior object, or a true appreciation of an inferior object? It is easy to see what scope for intellectual games such questions provided. Keynes later gave examples of the games he and his friends played: 'If A was in love with B under a misapprehension as to B's qualities, was this better or worse than not being in love at all? If A was in love with B because A's spectacles were not strong enough to see B's complexion, did this altogether, or partly, destroy the value of A's state of mind?' The point about Moore's ideal and method was that they gave young intellectual puritans an approach to the feelings: emotions themselves became the subject-matter of intellectual and moral analysis. It may seem a remarkably indirect way of coming to terms with basic things; but many basic things were excluded by the Victorian scheme of life. It was 'not done' for middle-class Victorian males to attach high, much less supreme, value to intimacy and beauty. Clever young people, brought up in moral Victorian homes, could only approach these, initially, by indirect paths. That is why Moore's highly abstruse 'method' was seen as a liberation. What is, perhaps, more surprising is that early Edwardian Cambridge remained completely untouched by parallel movements of revolt against the nineteenth century, in Britain and abroad. (It could not be expected to know about Freud, whose work was as yet untranslated.) For example, Keynes wrote to Strachey after having seen Shaw's *John Bull's Other Island*, 'Is it monomania – this colossal moral superiority that we feel? I get the feeling that most of the rest never see anything at all – too stupid or too wicked.' Although Moore's revolution in ethics can be seen as part of a wider movement, it was a very home-grown affair, tailor-made to the needs of repressed young Cambridge intellectuals, whose striving for greater intimacy and joy in life had to be justified by a new moral philosophy.

Moore's ideal had a lasting influence on Keynes. But after the initial sense of liberation, his 'method' proved too restrictive. By 1904–5, Maynard was looking for a more direct expression of sexual emotion, one which would, at the same time, free the intellect for analysing more substantial questions than whether A's defective vision lessened the value of his state of mind. Basically, he was fed up with endlessly intellectualizing the problem of forbidden love. He complained that Moore's 'method' had made him too 'idealistic', without realizing that this was the effect, not of Moore, but of his moral upbringing. In his quest for psychological liberation, Strachey was his companion and confidant. To Strachey he wrote on 6 November 1905, 'I foresee no remedy without a new method. There *must* be a new method: something that will bring ease, that will allow a half and halfdom when there are ten, and the whole hog when there are two.' On 15 November 1905, he wrote to Strachey, more realistically, 'Of course, everyone would be a hedonist if he could, in practice. Certainly you and I would. The disease is that we can't. Will we have to give up the Grand Life?' But the remedy was to come not through a new method, but through the move to London. Strachey was strongly encouraging. 'It would surely be mad', he wrote, 'to be a Cambridge economist. Come to London, go to the Treasury, and set up house with me. The parties we'd give!' Keynes, who felt reasonably sure of getting employment in Cambridge if he wanted it, took the plunge, sat for the Civil Service Examination, and went to the India Office. It was in London, between 1906 and 1908, that he discovered a satisfying personal identity. By doing so, he freed himself to return to Cambridge – and home. But only partly: he never left London entirely, and Bloomsbury was to become his second family, giving him the things which his own family, and Cambridge, could not.

It was Maynard's friendship with the painter Duncan Grant, whom he met in London in 1906, which made the arts an integral part of his life. Duncan was the cousin and (at the time) the lover of Lytton Strachey. He had studied painting at the Westminster School of Art and in Paris under Jacques Emile Blanche. Duncan Grant recalled the holiday he and Maynard spent in the Orkneys in the autumn of 1908:

> Naturally I took my paint box, brushes, etc., and he his writing books, pens, etc. I don't think either of us doubted that we should be each employed in doing regular work of our own. Maynard with his writing board was a good subject, so when he was immersed in the *Theory of Probability* ... I was immersed in trying to figure out the shape of his face. The result of this, I think, was that Maynard gradually accepted the fact that painting had its difficulties, without me having to point it out, that the painter had a serious job in hand. I may be quite wrong but I think that from this time on, he became very much aware of the part the arts might play in life. I am thinking ahead now, of the great part he played in the formation of the Arts Council and after his marriage to Lydia Lopokova of his passionate interest in the Ballet and the Theatre.

In these ways, Maynard continued, added to, and rearranged, the values he had grown up with. His upbringing, at home and school, was never sufficiently philistine to make him a rebel or 'outlaw' in Clive Bell's sense. Yet it left out sufficient of what Keynes came to regard as valuable to make him a reformer. We are left with a final question. What influence did his 'ethic' have on his work as an economist? There are a number of suggestive leads which are worth following up.

Moore's distinction between 'good as means' and 'good as end' was clearly relevant. Economics was a 'science of means'. It was valuable only as a means to the good. This meant that it must above all be practical, relevant, useful. Keynes's complaint against economics in the *General Theory* was that it had lost its 'practical influence'. Having no practical use was a luxury reserved for those things which were intrinsically valuable, not those whose only value was to promote good results. He determined to remedy this. A second influence stemmed from the nature of Moore's ideal itself. Political goals such as justice or equality had no place in Moore's utopia and Keynes's economics were not geared to achieving them – he was never a socialist. He saw economics, rather, as a means to make life beautiful, intelligent, loving. Wasted resources, he wrote in the depth of the Great Depression, could have been used to make Britain's cities 'the greatest works of man in the world', rather than being degraded slums which shut out art and culture. The third influence is more speculative. If the kernel of Keynesian theory be translated into Mooreite language, it amounts to this: that saving or abstinence, which is undoubtedly good as a means under some circumstances, had come to be mistaken as good in itself. As Keynes himself put it in the *Economic Consequences of the Peace*, through saving, 'the cake increased; but to what end was not clearly contemplated . . . the virtue of the cake was that it was never to be consumed.' Keynes believed that the time had come to consume the cake. Standing in the way was the utilitarian psychology of puritanism which, as Moore wrote, tended to hold that 'what is here and now never has any value in itself.' *Principia Ethica* set out, among other things, to destroy this belief in moral philosophy. Keynes set out to destroy it in economics. In succeeding in doing so, he fulfilled his parents' expectations, and helped undermine their world.

CHAPTER TEN

J. A. Hobson

Lecture given on the Quincentary of the Foundation
of Lincoln College, Oxford, 1978

To be asked to talk on J. A. Hobson is a challenging task. Before indicating the nature of the challenge, I should say a word about Hobson's association with Lincoln College, and Oxford University. It will be brief, because the association was brief, and uneventful. Hobson was born in Derby in 1858, of middling middle-class parents, and came to Lincoln College from Derby School as a classical scholar in 1877.

This, it appears, was the high point of his academic career. As an undergraduate he made little or no mark, except at the high jump. He obtained a third-class Honours degree in Greats, at which point his connection with the university came to an end. Whether this failure was because the subject, the surroundings, or the tuition was insufficiently stimulating I have no means of judging. The *Derbyshire and North Staffordshire Advertiser* produced a different explanation: the examiners, it felt, had been 'working for some years on the wrong lines'.[1] Perhaps this was what Hobson reported. The newspaper was owned by his father.

To talk about Hobson's life as a whole would also produce a very short lecture. Hobson lived to be eighty-one. For most of that time he simply sat at home and wrote articles and books. He did venture out, but here we come to a curious situation. His expeditions had surprisingly little impact. For fifty years he had some kind of contact with practically everyone of importance on the British Left. But when one looks for Hobson in this throng, one generally finds an empty space. His name, to be sure, appears regularly in memoirs, biographies, general history. Usually it is in the middle of a list; few of the writers have paused long enough to give any impression of the man. And when they occasionally do so, they may well be muddling him up with someone else. G. K. Chesterton surely takes the prize when he recorded, in 1937, his antipathy to the 'late J. A. Hobson, not to be confounded with the S. J. Hobson whose excellent economic studies still enlighten our debates'. The fact that neither of the gentlemen in question was dead, and both wrote about economic subjects, makes the task of identification rather difficult.[2] How many people today have the faintest idea what Hobson looked like? How many people even know that his name was John Atkinson Hobson?

Hobson, of course, was a thinker, not a man of action. But the prospect of giving an account of his thought is even more daunting. He is one of those annoying people who believed firmly in the interconnectedness of all knowledge; and proceeded to put his theory into practice by writing fifty books and several hundred articles about practically everything. This immense output has, after a considerable time-lag, started to provide intellectual employment for an increasing number of scholars. What they have generally done has been to break up Humpty-Dumpty into small fragments, and discuss them more or less in isolation from each other – a process which Hobson himself would have abhorred, and which would have confirmed all his worst suspicions about academics. Nevertheless, as a result of these efforts, a certain picture of Hobson's place in the history of social thought does emerge. He was the Great Anticipator. His theory of underconsumption anticipated Keynes. His theory of imperialism anticipated, and influenced, Lenin. He has been hailed as one of the founding fathers of sociology, as a 'visionary prophet of social welfare'. He is an honoured name in the history of growth economics and of the economics of imperfect competition. He has been seen as a pioneer of the idea of international government. Some of his strictures on the Jews may be said to have anticipated Hitler.

Recently, in the work of Peter Clarke, Alan Lee, and Michael Freeden* a more sensible attempt has been made to consider Hobson's ideas in relation to each other, and also in the context of his age. The characteristic conclusion of this approach is to see him as one of the architects of the New Liberalism, of a doctrine and method of social reform which testifies to the vitality of Liberalism in its period of supposed decay. Three defects of this re-evaluation may be noticed. First, it tends to exaggerate the coherence of Hobson's thought, a coherence which he himself finally denied when he referred to his life work as 'a composition of successive heresies ... defective when regarded as a whole'.[3] Secondly, it exaggerates the influence of New Liberalism on the social thought and action of the twentieth century. Michael Freeden is surely going much too far when he claims that Hobson's mixture of Idealism and Organicism 'has received the accolade of public consensus in Western democracies'.[4] Finally, by emphasizing the common ground which Hobson shared with other thinkers of this day like L. T. Hobhouse, Ritchie, the Fabians, etc., the new approach minimizes Hobson's own distinctive contribution – his 'oversaving' or underconsumptionist theory, which remained a heresy even in his New Liberal circle.

What I will attempt is to try to throw light on why Hobson remained a 'heretic'. For this assessment of himself is just. He said interesting and important things about most of the social and political questions which have exercised our era. Yet in no area was his influence decisive. He was often present at the start, and sometimes at the finish,

---

* Peter Clarke, *Liberals and Social Democrats* (1978); A. J. Lee, 'The Social and Economic Thought of J. A. Hobson (Ph. D. dissertation, University of London, 1970); Michael Freeden, *The New Liberalism* (1978).

but he never carried off the prize. Why is this? Hobson himself believed that part of the answer lay in his exclusion from the university world. At the age of eighty he wrote:

> I have sometimes felt regret that I was never able to pursue my economic studies in the quiet atmosphere of an academic life where I could have developed in a more orderly way my humanist theory, and tested it by lectures and discussions among serious-minded students. But I never had this opportunity. Though I spent most of my time in early middle life as a University Extension Lecturer, I was never invited to apply for any professorship in an English university . . . Though I was in friendly contact with the founders of the London School of Economics, it was never suggested that I should go upon the staff. Though I once allowed my name to be put forward for membership of the Political Economy Club, I heard no more of the proposal, and I have never written for the Economic Journal, though I have been for many years a member of the Society. My exclusion from organized academic economics has, therefore, been complete.[5]

This exclusion he regarded as an 'inevitable consequence' of his earliest 'heresy': 'I hardly realized that in appearing to question the virtue of unlimited thrift I had committed the unpardonable sin.'[6] Hobson was forced to earn his living as a journalist and writer of more or less popular books. Although he found in the London community of New Liberals a substitute 'common room', it contained no academic economists. He was forced to work out his ideas on his own.

The story of Hobson's relationship with the academic community is more complicated than this account would suggest. Certainly, his early books received pretty shabby treatment at the hands of academic reviewers. Edgeworth attacked the 'paradoxical' opinions contained in *The Physiology of Industry* (1889) – Hobson's first book written with A. F. Mummery, in which the 'oversaving' heresy was first proclaimed.[7] It was after this book was published that Hobson was barred from lecturing for the Oxford Delegacy in London, but was left free to address provincial audiences: a nice distinction. The argument of *The Problem of the Unemployed* [1896] was dismissed by Edwin Cannan as a 'complete delusion'. Cannan proceeded to deliver himself of the following remarkable judgment: ' "Unemployment" was at its maximum before the expulsion of Adam and Eve from Paradise, and it has been diminishing ever since.'[8] A. W. Flux was less severe on the *Economics of Distribution* (1900), in which Hobson first tried to work out his theory of the 'unproductive surplus', but found himself bemused by the way in which Hobson 'with premises in many respects of the soundest . . . finds himself at variance with . . . many of the results of the soundest thinkers'.[9] Here was a more serious point, to be echoed by Keynes when he reviewed Hobson's *Gold, Prices and Wages* (1913). He found it a 'very bad [book], made worse than a really stupid book could be, by exactly those characteristics of cleverness and intermittent reasonableness which have borne good fruit in the past . . . Mr Hobson has given us the Mythology of Money – intellectualised, brought up to journalistic date, most subtly interlarded . . . with temporary concessions to reason'.[10] Later, in his own *General Theory,* Keynes praised Hobson as one of 'the brave army of heretics . . . who, following their intuitions, have preferred to see the truth obscurely and imperfectly rather than to maintain error, reached indeed with clearness and consistency and by easy logic but on hypotheses inappropriate to the facts'.[11] But in 1913 he asked to be excused from reviewing any more of Hobson's books.

What bothered economists about Hobson's work was not that it questioned the moral value of thrift, but that it failed to meet their professional standards. He never gave a satisfactory explanation of how 'oversaving' could occur because, as Keynes said, he accepted the orthodox theory of the rate of interest. Conceivably he might have been able to crack the problem had he stuck with it; but as time went on Hobson's view of what the study of economics was about took him further away from rigorous analysis, and therefore from the development of economics as a discipline. By 1896 he was attacking the use of mathematical methods as inducing 'a sequence of thought antagonistic to the grasp of living and moral unity'.[12] The study of economic motives as a separate discipline was misconceived; society must be treated holistically. Hobson was not being entirely consistent here; at the end of his life he accused Ruskin of failing 'to recognise that political economy was capable of being made a study distinct from the wider study of the art of life . . .'[13] But he himself gravitated more and more to Ruskin's position.

In particular, he increasingly linked his oversaving theory to a critique of a system which allowed private appropriation of a socially produced 'surplus'. In books like *The Industrial System* (1909), he took great pains to establish the existence of an 'unproductive surplus' consisting of the 'whole of the economic rent of land, and such payments made to capital, ability, or labour, in the shape of high interests, profits, salaries, or wages, as do not tend to evoke a fuller or better productivity of these factors'.[14] This 'unproductive surplus' represented reward without effort, a kind of tribute exacted by superior market power. This surplus is unproductive in the sense that it is invested in productive facilities which turn out more consumer goods than the remaining income for consumption can absorb at prices sufficient to recover the investment. Hence over-production, slumps and unemployment. Thus economic injustice led to economic waste. What Hobson was trying to do, we can now see, was to destroy the logical distinction between the allocative function of the market, and the distribution of rewards as determined by social institutions. Economists insisted that the first was 'efficient', but the second could, and perhaps should, be modified by the taxation system. Hobson took the view that unjust distribution caused allocative inefficiency, but he never clinched the logic of the connection.

The increasingly holistic development of Hobson's thinking put him increasingly at odds with the contemporary attempt to establish economics as a profession, with its own body of knowledge, methodology, language, and professional credentials. At this time a considerable gap had grown up between the demand of the universities for specialized knowledge and the demand of an educated public for large social theories capable of filling the void left by the collapse of religious belief. It was one of the few periods in British history when there was an appetite for general ideas, which produced its supply of popular philosophers – H. G. Wells, Bernard Shaw, Bertrand Russell, a little later. The temper of the times, as well as Hobson's own position as an intellectual at large, drove him increasingly to fulfilling this demand, rather than the academic demand for professional excellence.

We must add to this the specific demands made on Hobson by journalism. Journalism, as Hobson himself put it, is 'fragmentary thought and feeling'.[15] Not only does a journalist have no time or space to develop a sustained argument; but the subject-matter of his writing is constantly changing as different problems capture the public's attention. Certain characteristic Hobson themes – such as underconsumption and imperialism – disappear for years at a time, and are replaced by quite different, even contrary, ideas. This has led to much scholarly debate about what Hobson really meant. But the mystery is not so great if one remembers that as a journalist Hobson addressed himself to the great questions of the day, and that these questions took on different aspects at different times. For example, underconsumption emerged as a dominant theme in the 1880s and 1890s, more or less disappeared from view in the years leading up to the First World War, and re-emerged again in the early 1920s. A glance at the business-cycle provides the explanation. In this sense, Keynes was luckier than Hobson. He was a man of a single period – that of mass unemployment. He could stick with the problem long enough to 'solve' it, because the problem was permanent. Conditions over Hobson's lifetime were much more variable; and journalism exaggerated the variability.

I have said that Hobson's interest slowly shifted from the narrow problem of explaining business depression to the larger task of constructing a 'humanist economics'. As time went on, he became increasingly obsessed with developing a unified system of thought which would offer the legislator a single standard of social welfare against which to judge proposals for social action. This attempt, repeating Bentham's, was doomed to failure; even at the time, it seemed to many economists old-fashioned. Hobson's contemporary, Pareto, was demonstrating with great clarity the difficulty of moving from a concept of individual (or subjective) utility to one of 'utility of the species'. What, Pareto asked, is a 'healthy' society? Is it one in which the greatest number enjoy material well-being? Or is it one which covers itself with military glory? 'There is no criterion', Pareto wrote, 'which I could apply to determine which of us is right and which wrong.' Yet Hobson attempted to supply just such a criterion of social health; and he did so by assuming that the community had a 'social personality' with standard, ascertainable needs – material, ethical, psychological.

Hobson's defects were those of his time. The last quarter of the nineteenth century produced the twofold demand that the social sciences be moralized; and morals be made scientific. We may see the first as arising, in part at least, from growing economic fluctuations, and the revelation of widespread urban poverty, which increased dissatisfaction with orthodox political economy; the second, from the loss of religious faith which not only transferred moral energy from the service of God to that of humanity, but brought to a head the demand for an alternative guarantee that the good would triumph. These demands were partly satisfied by Idealism, whose brief dominance over English philosophy occurred at this time. In place of the picture of the individual governed by a calculus of pain and pleasure, Idealism offered a picture of the individual striving for moral perfection. In place of freedom to pursue one's self-interest in the market, it offered the 'higher' freedom of self-realization as part of a whole. It also secularized the religious idea of salvation by offering a view of history in which the ideal is implicit in the actual, which grows towards it.

Most of Hobson's ideas were developed within this system of thought. It was from Ruskin rather than T. H. Green that he derived his belief in the need for an ethical basis for the social sciences: Ruskin's distinction between 'wealth' and 'illth' is echoed by his own between 'property' and 'improperty'. From Muirhead and Bosanquet, leaders of the London Ethical Society, Hobson got the idea of a 'rational conception of moral welfare'. But he was too eclectic to be a consistent Idealist, lacking the intellectual ruthlessness and detachment from practical problems necessary for successful Idealist system-building. Into his Idealist framework he inserted elements of both Darwinism and Utilitarianism. In evolutionary theory he found a 'biological proof of the progress of Reason in the concrete world'. He tried to develop a precise concept of 'social utility', holding that it is maximized when all reward is exactly proportioned to effort.

I don't want to spend time picking holes in all this. His key concepts – 'unproductive surplus' and 'social utility' – cannot be made precise, and therefore offer no criterion for legislation. They are metaphysical ideas decked out in biological and utilitarian language. Nor do I want to linger on the problems which the Idealist approach posed for Hobson's liberalism. Perhaps he only remained a liberal because his flaw was stronger than his logic. The main point I wish to make is that the energy Hobson invested in this 'holistic' effort, while yielding a string of fascinating, and fertile, insights, precluded him from making a decisive contribution in any single field.

I turn now to the question of his failure to make a decisive political impact. Here considerations of a different kind arise. Why did Hobson's theory of oversaving or underconsumption remain a heresy even within the Labour Party? Why was it Lenin's, rather than Hobson's, theory of imperialism which was read by revolutionary leaders? One answer is obvious: Hobson was no Lenin. It does wonders for the influence of one's ideas if one has led a successful revolution and established monopoly rights for their propagation. The diffusion of ideas depends, to some extent, on being able to create an appropriate power base. Why was Hobson so politically ineffective? On the face of it this is somewhat surprising. At different times he was quite active in the politics of radical Liberalism and Labour. He was on the executive committee of the Union of Democratic Control; he was appointed to the Whitley Council; he was a friend of Herbert Samuel; he was consulted by MacDonald; he even stood for Parliament in 1918. None of this added up to much; he remained a name on a list.

One reason is that, like many other New Liberals, he seems to have suffered from constant ill health, though Nevinson was surely exaggerating – in more ways than one – when he wrote that 'for forty years at least the stupefying sword of death has been hovering over him like a cobweb'.[16] The tubercular condition of his American wife, Florence Edgar, daughter of an American attorney, who provided a welcome supplement to his income, drove him first to the high ground of Hampstead, later to the Surrey village of Limpsfield, where he lived from 1899 onwards, presiding over a society of 'Limpsfield Socialists and Seekers'. Nevinson commented on Hobson's 'ghostly' appearance. Mary Agnes Hamilton remembered him as 'tall, emaciated, pale as parchment'. By temperament he was a recluse: Margaret Gladstone, who married Ramsay MacDonald, described him in 1896, as a 'quiet bookwormy sort of person'.[17] Brailsford, in his Hobhouse Memorial Lecture of 1947, recalled Hobson's gift for friendship: 'friendship was his recreation; he had no other distraction'. Clearly he was happiest in intimate circles of high-minded persons.

Impressions of the public Hobson differ. He lectured extensively – early on as a University Extension Lecturer, regularly to the South Place Ethical Society, occasionally in America and Scandinavia. But he was far from being a showman in the style of Shaw or Laski, holding his audiences by clarity and irony, both of which overcame a slight stammer. To Virginia Woolf, who came to know him in the First World War, he was already 'Old Hobson', 'shrewd, judicious and kindly', but unmistakably associated with the pre-war generation of 'clean, decorous, uncompromising and high-minded old ladies and old gentlemen'.[18] He had a sardonic humour, and could throw out ironic shafts of light in committee or discussion; but this comes out much too rarely in his writing. There is little passion either. A rare exception is when he wrote of the War Loan in the First World War: 'The men of property proudly surrender their own sons to the call of their country, but for the money which the country equally requires they extract the utmost farthing . . .' Brailsford notes that he 'would express himself at times with a blunt violence that was not wholly humorous'. But perhaps the most telling vignette of Hobson's ineffectiveness comes out in A. J. P. Taylor's memory of him emerging from seclusion in 1931 for the winding-up meeting of the 1917 Club. He made a passionate protest at the state of the accounts, stormed out of the room, and fell down the stairs.

Temperamentally, then, Hobson was quite unfitted for the life of politics. But this does not entirely explain the failure of his ideas to make more of a political impact. The nearest Hobsonian underconsumption theory came to being the basis of a political programme was in 1925–6, when elements of his analysis were adopted in the ILP's 'Living Wage' proposals and in the Mosley/Strachey pamphlet, 'Revolution by Reason'. The political failure of Hobsonianism at this time can be explained by the failure of these groups to capture the Labour Party. In particular, had Mosley been able to build up a stronger power base in the Labour Party, there might have been an attempt to apply a mixture of Hobsonian and Keynesian remedies for the slump of 1929–31.

But the failure of Hobson's 'heretical' economics to have a deeper political impact can also be explained by the general failure of economic radicalism between the wars. The nature of the two-party system did not allow an easy injection of Hobsonian economics into the political process. Hobson himself joined the Labour Party in 1924, and underconsumption became a kind of slogan on the Left, to be trotted out in periods of bad trade to reinforce a moral argument. But generally the programme of income redistribution which followed from the oversaving analysis of slumps was seen as an alternative to socialism, not a support for it. Although Hobson insisted that the ownership of property must be judged by social utility, he maintained that, by this test, most industry must be allowed to remain in private hands. In short, like Keynes, he stood for a system of reformed capitalism.

Nor could his theory serve as a rallying point for business radicalism. This approach had been briefly opened up by his association with the remarkable but forgotten businessman A. F. Mummery, who inspired as well as co-authored his first book *The Physiology of Industry*. Mummery, who was in the tannery trade, first started discussing economics with Hobson in the 1880s. The only other fact known about him is that he was a mountaineer, who was killed on 23 August 1894 trying to climb Nanga Parbat in the Himalayas. Hobson quite specifically attributes to Mummery the 'oversaving' heresy. And the argument in *The Physiology of Industry* is much clearer, the focus more precise, than Hobson, alone, ever achieved in his later books.

The quality of that book deserves to be recalled. Mummery and Hobson were the first to draw attention to the 'paradox of thrift': that saving reduces the immediate demand for consumption goods without necessarily increasing the demand for consumption goods in the future, and that 'any undue exercise of this habit must, therefore, cause an accumulation of Capital in excess of that which is required for use, and this excess will exist in the form of general over-production'. In a striking intuition they asserted that the 'effective love of money' might cause effective demand to fall short of supply, leading to depression and unemployment.[19] It was humanist economics, with its particular stress on getting the *purpose* of economic activity right, which opened up this insight into the causes of economic malfunction.

The important point to make, in the present context, is the book's endorsement of Protection as a remedy for unemployment.[20] There is no mention of income maldistribution or 'superior bargaining power' as a systemic cause of oversaving or unemployment: it results from the defective psychology of the wealthy. Hobson's later insistence on income maldistribution as the cause of slumps, his fervent commitment to free trade, his advocacy of nationalization, all made him ineligible as a spokesman for business radicalism.

We still haven't reached the heart of the problem of the political failure of Hobsonianism. We must look more closely at the period when it was first developed. Hobson's various 'heresies' all sprang from the circumstances of their day. The unemployment problem in Hobson's formative years was very different from the unemployment problem between the wars. The late nineteenth-century problem was essentially cyclical. It is hard to tell from the figures whether one should regard the 'normal' state of employment as high or low. But it was cetainly possible to take the former view, which was also backed by the whole weight of economic authority, and this was confirmed by the years of good trade which led up to the First World War. The attention of Hobson and Mummery, whose book was conceived in the four years of bad trade in the mid-1880s, naturally focused on the forces which tended to bring the boom to an end. They were able to assume that recovery was automatic, as indeed it appeared to be: something always 'turned up'.

Thus they spent little or no attention analysing why an economy stayed stuck in a slump. During the inter-war years, 'bad trade' became more or less permanent. Keynes's theory, attempting to explain the apparent existence of a high unemployment equilibrium, was more relevant. The *General Theory* devotes only a few pages to the trade cycle, after the static model had been set up.

The circumstances of the gestation of the Hobson–Mummery 'heresy' thus had two consequences. First, the unemployment problem was never sufficiently persistent before the First World War to call for any reorientation of thinking or policy. People protested against the plight of the unemployed in periods of bad trade. But as soon as a revival started their attention shifted to other things. The political effect of interrupted trade before 1914 was rather to give rise to the notion of protecting workers from 'interrupted' earnings through a system of social insurance. This was the general trend in Europe from the late nineteenth century onwards. There is a second sense in which a Hobsonian analysis rooted in the cyclical problem of the late nineteenth century appeared irrelevant to the inter-war problem. In Hobson's model, the oversaving, and consequent overproduction, took place in the upswing of the trade cycle. It was at this point that the political programme for taxing the 'surplus' could most plausibly be applied: as indeed it was, to a limited extent, in the Lloyd George budget of 1909, whose passage was considerably eased by the prosperity of that year. But the inter-war years were years of bad trade and even Hobson found it difficult to make the case for steeper taxation in this period.

In one important respect Hobson did pay attention to the recovery mechanism, for that is the basis of his theory of imperialism. In 1896 we find the first important mention of the notion of a 'foreign vent' for surplus savings:

> ... it is clear that no absolute limit is set at any given time to the 'savings' of a single nation, other than the total field of investment in the industrialised world. It would therefore follow that not only is there no theoretic limit to the proportion of his income which any Englishman might legitimately save, but that no limit could be placed upon the proportion of the national income which can be saved, provided that the surplus savings beyond what can find useful occupation in home trade dispose themselves in foreign countries.[21]

The implication of the argument is that the crucial recovery mechanism is the diversion of national saving from home to foreign investment. Within a year or so Hobson had made the link between the recovery mechanism from slump and the 'new imperialism' in Africa. He spent 1899 as the *Manchester Guardian*'s correspondent in South Africa during the Boer War. In his famous book, *Imperialism* [1902], he gives on page 17 a list of territorial acquisitions by Britain between 1874 and 1900, mainly in Africa; on page 52 a table showing the growth of income from foreign and colonial investments from £33.8 million in 1873 to £63.8 million in 1903; and on page 62 another list showing the growth of foreign investment from £144 million to £1698 million between 1862 and 1893. He comments on the second list: 'From this table it appears that the period of energetic imperialism coincided with a remarkable growth in the income from foreign investments', leaving the reader to draw the obvious, but wrong, conclusion.[22] What he omits to say is that the vast bulk of the new investment was outside the newly acquired territories, so that their acquisition could not possibly have been the direct cause of successive waves of foreign investment in the last quarter century. There is one exception to this: the foreign investment upsurge starting in 1894 does seem to be linked to the boom in South African mining shares that year.

Hobson's theory of imperialism is best seen as a daring generalization from the single case he knew best: the events leading up to and including the Boer War. But his general proposition that in the late nineteenth century the recovery mechanism from slumps was provided by foreign investment is much more securely based. In the careful words of Professor Cairncross, 'an increase in activity abroad, generally associated with an increase in foreign investment by Britain, pulled the country out of pre-1914 slumps by improving the prospects of the export industries'.[23] Here, too, was a feature of the situation which, for various reasons, had disappeared by the 1920s.

Hobson was essentially a thinker of the 1880s and 1890s, whose preoccupations were those which exercised those decades. The framework within which he developed his ideas and tried to link them to each other itself soon became dated. That is why his insights remained 'heresies'. Even if he failed to bequeath a coherent legacy his many books are full of intuitions which should not be allowed to perish from neglect. Specifically, his argument for increasing the propensity to consume as societies become richer, restated in Keynesian terms, remains powerful;

his idea of a 'foreign vent' for investment to get capitalist economies out of slumps continues to be suggestive. It is good to see some of his classical works being reprinted; it is surely time to bring out an 'Essential Hobson', incorporating his most important ideas between two covers. It is appropriate to end with a quotation taken from his *Evolution of Modern Capitalism* (1894), which expresses a recurring theme in Hobson's writing:

> The Trade Union movement and the various growths of Industrial Partnership, valuable as they are from many points of view, furnish no remedies against the chief forms of economic monopoly and economic waste; they can only change the personality and expand the number of monopolies and alter the character, not the quantity, of economic waste. Society has an ever deeper and more vital interest in the economical management of the machinery of transport, and this interest is in no whit more secure if the practical control of railways and docks were in the hands of the Dockers' Union or the Amalgamated Society of Railway Servants, or of a combined board of directors and trade union officials, than it is under present circumstances. On the contrary, an effective organisation of capital and labour in an industry would be more likely to pursue a policy opposed to the interests of the wider public than now, because such a policy would be far more likely to succeed.[24]

As on so many occasions, Hobson posed a problem which our generation has yet to solve.

NOTES

1   A. J. Lee, 'A Study of the Social and Economic Thought of J. A. Hobson' (Ph.D. 1970), p. 27.

2   G. K. Chesterton, *Autobiography* (1937), p. 270.

3   J. A. Hobson, *Confessions of an Economic Heretic* (1938), p. 90.

4   M. Freeden, 'J. A. Hobson as a New Liberal Theorist', *Journal of the History of Ideas*, 34 (1973), p. 422.

5   Hobson, *Confessions*, pp. 83–4.

6   Ibid., p. 31.

7   In the *Journal of Education* (1890), p. 194.

8   *Economic Journal* (1897), p. 88.

9   Ibid. (1900), pp. 380–85.

10 ibid. (1913), pp. 393–8.

11 J. M. Keynes, *The General Theory of Employment, Interest, and Money* (1936), p. 371.

12 Hobson, *The Evolution of Modern Capitalism* (1894), p. 8; quoted in Lee, p. 189.

13 Hobson, *Confessions*, p. 40.

14 Hobson, *The Industrial System* (1909), p. viii.

15 Hobson, *Confessions*, p. 87.

16 H. W. Nevinson, *Fire of Life* (1935), p. 214; quoted in Lee, p. 25.

17 Quoted in David Marquand, *Ramsay MacDonald* (1975), p. 48.

18 N. Nicolson (ed.), *Letters of Virginia Woolf*, vol. 2 (1976), p. 286; Anne Olivier Bell (ed.), *Diary of Virginia Woolf*, vol. 1 (1977), p. 83.

19 A. F. Mummery and J. A. Hobson, *The Physiology of Industry* (1889), p. iii–vi, 10n.

20 Ibid. ch. 8.

21 Hobson, *The Problem of the Unemployed* (1896), pp. 86–7.

22 Hobson, *Imperialism* (1902; 2nd edn 1938), p. 53. See also D. K. Fieldhouse, 'Imperialism: an historiographical revision', *Economic History Review*, 2nd ser., XIV: (1961), p. 190.

23 A. K. Cairncross, *Home and Foreign Investment 1870–1913* (1953), p. 196.

24 Hobson, *The Evolution of Modern Capitalism*, p. 409.

CHAPTER ELEVEN

William Beveridge

José Harris, *William Beveridge: A Biography*
[Oxford University Press, 1977]

IN THE transformation of Britain from a *laissez-faire* into a social economy, two names stand out – John Maynard Keynes and William Henry Beveridge. Keynes was the founder of 'managed' capitalism; Beveridge the architect of the Welfare State. Neither man's achievement has been properly set in the context of his time. For Beveridge, the omission is now remedied in this outstanding biography based on the Beveridge papers.

José Harris goes beyond the 'conventional biographical questions' to consider the assumptions of Beveridge's social philosophy, the changing historical context in which it evolved, and Beveridge's role in the growth of the state and the history of social policy. It is an ambitious project, requiring not just historical and biographical skills, but also the ability to tackle the main intellectual issues involved – the question of method in the social sciences, the causes of poverty and unemployment, the fate of freedom in a collectivist age, the debate between different forms of social organization.

In nearly all respects Harris succeeds triumphantly. There are quibbles, of course. She does not fully explain what it was about Beveridge which caused his services to be so frequently declined by the men in power. His conceit and rudeness obviously did not help. But there was more to it than that. Beveridge was a new type of public man, neither politician, civil servant, academic, nor entrepreneur, but a mixture of all; a product of that semi-official world of public bodies and technocratic skills which has grown so luxuriantly this century, but which was then unfamiliar, and therefore suspected. Nor am I convinced that Beveridge's oscillations between planning and *laissez-faire* have quite the intellectual or emotional importance that Harris gives them, preferring to see them largely as responses to the different circumstances of war and peace. The points at issue between Beveridge and Keynes on the causes of unemployment and the type of intervention required to meet it are not as sharply defined as they might be.

Beveridge's background, like that of so many social reformers, was Anglo-Indian. Harris sees him as 'heir . . . to the administrative ideals of the Indian Civil Service'. Born in 1879, his schooldays at Charterhouse were unhappy, and he came to Oxford intellectually precocious, emotionally insecure, and aesthetically undeveloped, a state of affairs that was to persist all his life. His feelings, it seems, were briefly expanded by a fellow Balliol undergraduate, Arthur Collings Carré, with whom he fell in love, who introduced him to poetry, and who died of opium poisoning. It is a romantic tale, but the awakening was momentary only. Beveridge remained a Very Superior Person, preferring books which were 'socially informative and morally uplifting'. He was an obsessive worker and 'broad-minded Philistine' all his life. Harris is not as frank as one would have wished about his relationship with Mrs Jessy Mair, his lifelong confidante and *éminence grise*, whom he married in his sixties, after the death of her presumably long-complaisant husband,

David Mair. One imagines it to have been a mental and spiritual – rather than a physical – companionship, on the model of the Webbs who, with Tawney, were to be his best friends.

Beveridge was not interested in people, but in society. Social problems appealed alike to his scientific interests, his organizing genius, and his need for a cause. In 1903, having gained a First after switching from Mathematics to Greats, he became subwarden of Toynbee Hall, the universities' settlement in east London, founded by a group of dons and clergymen in 1884. He quickly rejected the prevalent 'do-gooding' approach to social work in favour of impersonal schemes of social reform. Beveridge, Harris explains, felt no personal sympathy for the victims of poverty – he could not abide the poor, derelict and sick. In this switch from missionary to legislative action, he was very much in tune with the Edwardian temper. Out of the Boer War had come the movement for national efficiency. Poverty was a hindrance to the survival of the imperial state. The government's first duty was to secure the 'future of the race'. This required the planned conquest of poverty and unemployment, the encouragement of better stocks, and the elimination or segregation of the work-shy and unfit: a programme of regeneration which would have made Beveridge a respected sage in Hitler's Germany. It was to be carried out by a powerful state assisted by experts, to which all individual and sectional interests were to be subordinated.

In this mood, Beveridge, writing on social problems for the *Morning Post*, proclaimed himself a 'Labour Imperialist' and a 'tremendously revolutionary conservative'. He was never able to define his political position more satisfactorily. He remained, like Keynes, rooted in the Edwardian tradition of reform 'above class' through the agency of a benevolent state serviced by a technocratic elite. The chance to try out his theories on a national scale came in 1908 when Churchill brought him to the Board of Trade. Beveridge came with the reputation of an expert on unemployment: his book. *Unemployment: A Problem of Industry*, was published in 1909. He attributed unemployment mainly to imperfections in the labour market. His remedy was its better organization, through a system of labour exchanges, plus compulsory unemployment insurance against 'interruptions' in employment. These ideas found legislative expression in the Labour Exchanges Act, 1909, and the National Insurance Act, 1911. The latter embodied Beveridge's favourite principles of flat-rate (as opposed to need, or means, related) benefits, and insurance contributions as opposed to provision through general taxation: principles which were to dominate British social services policy for the next fifty years.

Beveridge's analysis of unemployment reveals the flaw in his method of social inquiry. He hoped to extract the causes of unemployment from empirical data. (Late in life he spent years trying to link unemployment to variations in the price of wheat, in which he was assisted by a young Oxford don, Harold Wilson.) But, in fact, the assumptions of his inquiry were governed by his adherence to Say's Law of Markets, which claimed there could never be prolonged unemployment through insufficient demand. Thus his attention was directed by his premises to the structure of labour markets. It was a useful, but not then the most useful, perspective. Both Joseph Chamberlain and J. A. Hobson, two contemporary Edwardians, did better. Beveridge was a social organizer of genius, but a poor social theorist. His lifelong focus on the inefficiencies of labour markets makes his oscillations between central planning and market economics less significant than Harris believes and less radical theoretically than the alternative Keynesian approach. Markets and central planning are simply alternative means of allocating resources, depending on whether the purpose is to satisfy individual, or collective, wants. In war, Beveridge tended to favour central planning; in peace, markets. There is nothing inconsistent, or particularly radical, in this. The theoretically interesting breakthrough was the argument that modern unemployment was not a problem of supply, but of demand; and this Beveridge failed to grasp. Many of his fears about the future of freedom in a planned society would have receded had he realized there was an alternative route to full employment and prosperity.

In the First World War, Beveridge planned manpower under Lloyd George at the Ministry of Munitions; and food supplies under Lord Rhondda at the Ministry of Food. His zeal for efficiency made him favour complete state control over labour. Even in its final watered-down version, the Munitions of War Act, drafted by Beveridge and Llewellyn Smith, imposed compulsory arbitration, prohibited strikes and lock-outs, forbade workers to leave their jobs, suspended restrictive practices, and set up a scheme of industrial 'enlistment' under a quasi-military regime. Not surprisingly, Lloyd George found him too rigid, and the trade union leaders thought him insufferable. Yet though Beveridge wanted to retain statutory controls over industrial relations after the war (in the interests of market efficiency), he was quite prepared to make a bonfire of the other controls, the most sophisticated experiments in which, he wrote, were the 'farthest removed from any possible task of peace'. Harris attributes this revulsion against administrative centralization to his sense of personal failure during the war; but, as I have suggested, the move back to the 'laws of the market' is not as surprising as it seems.

Beveridge's long reign as Director of the London School of Economics from 1919 to 1937, reveals a familiar mixture of qualities. He was brilliant at raising money, acquiring buildings, organizing expansion and new academic programmes, building up London University; but bad at human relations and administrative routine. Robbins wrote of him (in a passage not quoted by Harris): 'I doubt if it ever occurred to him to regard the great men of those days as his equals, let alone, what some of them certainly were from the academic point of view, his superiors.' His last years at LSE were bitter and unhappy. This was partly due to attacks on the unpopular Jessy Mair, whom Beveridge had made Dean. But there were also conflicts between the 'theoretical' and 'empirical' approaches to the social sciences, and between 'market' and 'collectivist' remedies for the Depression.

Although Beveridge endorsed the 'Free market' theories of the LSE economists Robbins and Hayek in the early 1930s, he gradually swung back to his planning and technocratic ideas. This was a response to the continuing Depression. He aspired to expound a new Liberal *via media*, but his ideas were hopelessly confused. Harris provides a fascinating glimpse of his discussions with the Webbs, then on their spiritual odyssey to Moscow. In reply to Beveridge's 'there is no alternative to capitalist enterprise', Beatrice Webb writes characteristically: 'What about the scientific materialism of Karl Marx tempered by the religion of humanity of Auguste Comte?' But Beveridge couldn't stomach the Soviet suppression of 'liberty of thought and speech'. In his ideal system, parliaments and dictators would alike be succeeded by 'enlightened professional administrators who would control the psychological and physical environment.' But Beveridge was no more able than before to resolve the contradiction between freedom and planning. Harris argues on several occasions that he favoured a corporate structure in which the individual, voluntary organizations, and the state were harmonized and integrated. But Beveridge seems to have been temperamentally incapable of living with such organizational messiness, reverting in practice to administrative or market solutions to economic and social problems.

Harris traces the famous Beveridge Report of 1942 back to two inter-war developments in Beveridge's thought. In 1923 he advocated an 'all in' insurance scheme – a single stamp to insure against sickness, unemployment, old age and industrial injury, the different contingencies linked together by the concept of 'interruption of earnings'. In 1924, he was converted by Eleanor Rathbone to family allowances, realizing that the wage system took no account of the size of families. (An additional motive was his fear of falling population and rising wage costs.) What made the Beveridge Report one of the two pillars of the post-war consensus, the other being the Keynesian commitment to full employment, was Beveridge's genius for administrative innovation, his flair for publicity, and the radical temper of the times. The report itself was not specially advanced. It unified all the existing benefit schemes, and included everyone in them, on the old basis of compulsory insurance and flat-rate benefits. But the proposal to insure everyone against life's hazards from cradle to grave, at a subsistence standard, proved overwhelmingly popular.

Poverty and insecurity through interruption of earnings had been the greatest hazards of twentieth-century industrial life. Now Keynes attacked the problem on one side, Beveridge on the other. Moreover, their approaches were at last complementary. Social service spending could be seen as an additional instrument of demand management: while Beveridge was persuaded by Nicholas Kaldor of the validity of Keynesian techniques for maintaining full employment, on which the financial viability of the insurance scheme rested. Harris does well to remind us of the loose ends of this post-war consensus. The main one arising from the Beveridge Report was Beveridge's attempt to square the concept of subsistence needs, which may vary, with uniform benefits available to all. The present British Welfare State thus lacks a secure intellectual basis. On the other side, Beveridge's *Full Employment in a Free Society*, in which he expounded the new Keynesian wisdom, left unsolved the problem of how to combine full employment and price stability, thus leaving the Keynesian state in an equally shaky intellectual condition.

In old age, on a world cruise, Beveridge 'overwhelmed' his fellow passengers by his 'amazing vitality', relentlessly filling idle moments with organizing debates on the 'conditions of world peace'. He died in 1963. José Harris has brought the man and his ideas memorably to life.

CHAPTER TWELVE

Liberals and Progressives

Peter Clarke, *Liberals and Social Democrats*
[Cambridge University Press, 1979]

PETER CLARKE has written an infuriating book; infuriating not just because this reviewer has had to work so hard to extract meaning from it, but because it could have been so much more important had Clarke tackled his subject more rigorously. The subject itself is certainly important. It is about the attempt of a small group of progressive, turn-of-the-century, English intellectuals to adapt liberalism to the politics of mass democracy and social reform. The result of their efforts was the New Liberalism; its supposed legislative embodiment is the Welfare State, started by the Liberal government of 1906–15.

There were a number of ways of approaching such a project. One would have been simply to discuss New Liberal ideas. This has already been done by Michael Freeden, whose book, *The New Liberalism*, appeared last year (see *New Society*, 26 January 1978). A second would have been to attempt a group biography. Or, and this would have been best, one could have written about the relationship between ideas and politics, theory and practice, at a crucial transitional point in English history, asking the question: to what extent had New Liberalism established itself, by 1914, as an effective ideology of social reform?

Unfortunately, Clarke tries to do all three. He does none of them very well, partly because they get in each other's way. The discussion of Hobson's ideas, itself pretty elusive, is rendered more so by its interruption with details of Mrs Hammond's tubercular problems. The attempt at group biography – of Graham Wallas, L. T. Hobhouse, J. A. Hobson, and the Hammonds – was probably misconceived. The trouble is that the New Liberals weren't really a 'family' like the Philosophical Radicals

79

or the Fabians. There were a few semi-institutionalized centres of activity – the *Nation* lunches, the Rainbow Circle, various Ethical Societies – but mainly they communicated with each other through their writings. So one gets little sense of group dynamics. Moreover, the biographical approach means carrying the book through to the 1960s, forty years after the progressives had shot their bolt. Finally, though Clarke implies that New Liberal ideas were important, he does not seriously try to evaluate their influence.

What was the progressive doctrine? Clarke never tries to summarize it, but three elements seem crucial. The first was the attempt to insert ethics into politics. The purpose of economic and social arrangements should be to improve the moral quality of individual life and not just increase the quantity of goods or national power. Secondly, there was the assumption that moral failure is not just, or mainly, due to character defects, but results from a diseased social environment; from which it follows that the state has a responsibility for providing a social environment conducive to moral growth. Thirdly, the New Liberals, with Fabian help, worked out a fiscal theory to justify collective provision of incomes and services. This was the famous theory of the 'unearned increment', the vital link between socialist and New Liberal economics, which postulated a taxable 'surplus' which could be gradually applied to social welfare without diminishing the sum available for accumulation. In Hobson's view, such redistribution would stabilize the economic system. In these ways, the New Liberalism sought a middle way between the old liberalism of *laissez-faire* and self-help, and 'confiscatory' socialism of the marxist type.

How should a historian write about a doctrine of this kind? In his prologue, Clarke has some interesting, but inconclusive, suggestions. First, a historian can see the doctrine as serving the spiritual, or social, needs of those who invent it. Secondly, he can ask questions about its logical status. Thirdly, he can ask questions about its relevance to actual problems. Fourthly, he can ask questions about its influence. And fifthly, if he finds it is influential, he can try to account for its diffusion. Unfortunately, though Clarke says, or implies, he is about to do all these things, he does none of them, or none of them systematically. Did New Liberal ideas influence the Liberal programmes of 1906–14? Clarke suggests they did, but does not argue the case. For example, it is often claimed that Lloyd George got his ideas not from the New Liberals but from Bismarck's social insurance scheme in Germany.

Certainly the fact that between 1883 and 1914 all industrialized European countries adopted some form of compulsory social insurance suggests that influences were at work in England other than those stemming from the mind of T. H. Green. But even assuming that Lloyd George and, more plausibly, Winston Churchill got their reforming ideas from the New Liberals, there is still the question of why they found it politically useful to take them up: an obvious question, which perhaps only Clarke's animus against the 'Peterhouse school' prevents him from asking.

Clarke says, rightly, that it is important to ask of progressive reforming ideas whether they were 'compatible with the evidence'. But he does not do so. To start with, he does not provide the evidence. What were the evils which progressive reforms were designed to remedy? The basic problem was widespread poverty. For example, 30 per cent of Londoners lived at or beneath the poverty line. Poverty was caused by low wages and/or interruptions to employment – either through the operation of the trade cycle, or through sickness, for both of which the only provision was the Poor Law. Assuming that state intervention was needed to remedy this, there were two possible strategies. The first was to go for a high wage, full employment, economy. The second was to try to secure a minimum income for workers regardless of the state of the job market. These two strategies were not logically, or practically, incompatible, as Keynes and Beveridge were later to show. But in England in the 1900s they emerged as political alternatives. Chamberlain's tariff reform campaign was based on the view that a British capitalist system protected against foreign competition could solve the poverty problem. New Liberals and socialists took Chiozza Money's view that 'work is irregular, but pay must be regular.' Which was more relevant – the attempt to raise output on the basis of protection, or the attempt to redistribute existing output on the basis of free trade? It's a complicated question, but at least Clarke should have had a bash at answering it.

Clarke insists that one must ask of progressive ideas whether they were 'true', 'rational', 'logical': an ambitious task. He is good on the Hammonds as historians. Even more enterprising is his lucid account of the differences between Hobsonian and Keynesian economics. But he never really comes to grips with the basic problem of New Liberal thought: its eclecticism. Hobhouse is the most ambitious of the New Liberal system-builders, with his attempt to combine utilitarianism and

Idealism, individualism and socialism, biology and ethics. But his system is pretty shaky. For example, he attempts to ground the argument for social co-operation in an Idealist interpretation of Darwinism: evolution is the progress of mind or reason in social affairs. But is this to be taken as individual or collective mind? Hobhouse rejects the idea of a collective mind, or good, apart from individual volition. But what then is the relationship between individual and social good? Again an Idealist formula comes to the rescue: the individual 'realizes' himself as part of a greater whole. But how does this justify the state in taking away some of his property against his will to provide old age pensions for others? Here Hobhouse falls back on a different kind of argument: part of that property is 'socially' not 'individually' earned. The community has a right to take back the socially earned part for communal purposes. But how is this 'social' part to be calculated? Hobhouse doesn't know.

Into such tangles did New Liberalism get in its elaborate attempt to update the old liberalism. Keynes's reformulation of liberalism thirty years later was more successful in avoiding conceptual quagmires. Maurice Cranston, in a recent essay, sees much more clearly than Clarke that Keynes 'stands apart from the endeavour to modernise liberalism by transforming its philosophy'. His great strength was that he stuck to the 'simple liberalism' of Locke, on to which he superimposed a theory of market manipulation which left individuals with actual, and not just 'rational', liberty.

When confronted with a doctrine whose logical status is so slight, one must ask: what non-logical purposes did it serve? The essence of progressivism was its moralism: social reform was to be undertaken for ethical reasons, and given an ethical character. There is a problem here. Michael Freeden claims that 'the search for a general ethical conception of society was dictated . . . by the enormity of the social problems facing English society at the time.' This is not so. No general ethical conception was required to justify health, or even unemployment, insurance. They could be justified, and often were, even by progressives, on grounds of efficiency and/or social stability. But even the most practical New Liberals, like Hobson, insisted that 'both concrete reforms, and methods of attaining them, must strengthen the moral character of individuals . . .' Why all this stress on moralism? It arose, I think, for two main reasons.

In its broadest sense, the moralization of liberalism was the result of the religious, particularly evangelical, character of Victorian society. But more particularly, it reflected a transfer of moral energy from the service of God to the service of humanity. Clarke writes, 'The intellectual collapse of the Christian world-picture was distressing because its social and psychological functions were left unfulfilled.' But he doesn't develop the insight. Late Victorian middle-class reformers were people whose upbringing had given them a great sense of sin: three of the four main progressives in this book had clergymen for fathers. With the loss of religious faith, this sense of sin became increasingly fused with a sense of social guilt. To this must be added the sense of moral outrage aroused in this high-minded group by the new class of Edwardian *nouveaux riches*. Its moralism fixes the limit of New Liberalism's appeal. It was essentially a transitional phenomenon, because its psychological underpinnings were soon to disappear.

But New Liberalism's moralism also served a social function. One had to talk about morals if one wasn't prepared to talk about class. The sons and daughters of clergymen genuinely wanted to redistribute some wealth from Riviera idlers and South African millionaires to the deserving poor and hardworking shopkeepers – but on condition that the rest of the social order remained unchanged. They certainly did not want redistribution to be effected by working-class power. Hence they were driven to pose the question of social reform in an ideal moral context: as a matter of reciprocal moral duties rather than class relations. The technocratic emphasis on 'enlightened' leadership had the same function of removing class relations from the agenda of reform. Here I would question the force of Clarke's distinction between the 'moral reformism' of the New Liberals and the 'mechanical reformism' of the Fabians. *Both* groups looked to middle-class 'brains' and 'morals' to enlighten, and control, working-class brawn.

In the upshot, this moral vocabulary proved entirely inadequate. It did not persuade the rich voluntarily to give up their 'unearned' possessions, though it may have weakened their resistance to doing so. Nor was it able to head off, as it was intended to do, the creation of a powerful, independent, working-class movement. What in fact happened was that the workers took the money and ignored the New Liberal sermons. After the Second World War, ageing New Liberals, deprived of their domestic servants, were loud in their complaints about the 'nastiness' of trade unions, about the vast sums which workers were spending on 'tobacco, drink, gambling and amusements' despite all the opportunities New Liberals had provided for their moral perfectibility. Such is the sad, but inevitable, fate of self-deception.

CHAPTER THIRTEEN

Europe Transformed

Norman Stone, *Europe Transformed 1878–1919*
[Fontana History of Europe, 1983]

IN 1934, George Dangerfield wrote a famous book, *The Strange Death of Liberal England*, which claimed that the days of British liberalism were numbered even before the First World War. Norman Stone, Fellow of Trinity College, Cambridge, and scourge of E. H. Carr, has now applied the Dangerfield thesis to the whole of Europe. His theme is the developing social crisis which preceded, and in some sense, produced, the First World War.

The Great Depression of the late 1870s and early 1880s expanded the towns, ruined the countryside, and destroyed the 'rule of the notables' which had depended on the historic balance between the two. It ushered in an era of mass politics in which traditional Conservative and Liberal parties competed with the new 'machines' of social Catholics and Socialists for control of the mass mind on rival platforms of imperialism, nationalism, social reform, anti-semitism and class war. After 1909 European societies became ungovernable. Everywhere irresistible forces ran up against immovable objects. The result was political paralysis and fiscal crisis. The Left could not get a majority behind taxes for social reform; the Right's imperialism and tariff policy brought greater costs than revenue. Stone argues that the only available solution implied war: 'The right would vote for graduated income taxes provided they were spent on arms; and the left would accept arms, provided they came with a a graduated income tax ... almost everywhere ... large armies went together with large taxes ... By 1913, all of Europe was committed to an arms race; and after 1911, the war had already broken out in people's minds'. But the actual war which broke out in 1914 solved nothing. It merely replaced political stalemate by military stalemate. In 1917–18 the forces of movement at last got their chance.

Revolution triumphed in Russia, the most rigid of the *ancien régimes*, though the rest of Europe was spared the 'Red Dawn'.

Such, in brief, is Stone's thesis, and it is argued with great verve and brilliance. He brings to his task enviable gifts: a sharp eye for comic detail, a blind eye to narrow specialisms, a superb memory for facts, a mastery of several languages, and a generalizing flair which never gets out of control. The book is full of good things. Stone argues plausibly that political events moved in parallel with the trade cycle, and with each other, since 'the increasing integration of the European economy meant that economic ups and downs now tended to affect all countries at roughly the same time'. The 1880s were a sorting out period when the classical Liberals deserted to their old enemies on the Right. The early 1890s were a period of Liberal rule, the later 1890s 'an orgy of nationalism and imperialism'. 1905, 'the ghost of 1848', was followed by Liberal and 'technocratic' government offering efficiency and reform. This is fairly convincing, despite the occasional inconvenient fact which upsets all beautiful historical hypotheses. There is a superb chapter explaining the causes of the military stalemate from 1914 to 1918, and an excellent one on culture, though Stone is unusually respectful of custom in sticking it at the end, as in all those Oxford histories. Indeed, the structure of the book is not wholly successful. The device of starting with nine chapters of general survey, followed by a further five dealing with individual countries in the same period makes for a good deal of repetition. In compensation, the individual country chapters are brilliant, though England for some reason ceases to count as part of Europe at this point, rejoining it for the First World War. I particularly liked the one on Russia, in which Stone effectively contrasts the *opéra bouffe* atmosphere of the Tsar's court, where Nicholas II appointed the manager of his stud farm Minister of the Interior, with Stolypin's 'technocratic' attempt to reform the feudal system of land tenure, and the strains of too rapid industrialization.

The thesis that the First World War was the vent for social conflict is not new, but is it true? Stone accepts the 'primacy of internal politics': the view that what happens inside societies determines international relations. But it may be the other way round; or it may vary from epoch to epoch; or, most probably, the relationship is reciprocal. Whether external or internal solutions to conflicts come about depends largely on what part of the system gives easiest. For most of the nineteenth century the international system was fairly sticky while domestic societies were fairly fluid. This encouraged *laissez-faire* and free trade. Between 1890 and 1945 the international situation seemed changeable, domestic situations fixed: hence, perhaps, the two World Wars. Since 1945 both domestic and international environments have been rigid: what has 'given' is the price level. Any complete investigation of, say, the origins of the First World War requires an account of what was happening in both areas. But Stone devotes only five pages out of 400 to international relations.

One can ask a different question. Were the domestic situations of the main European countries really as fraught as Stone says? He seems to have taken to heart Geoffrey Barraclough's dictum that the historian should concentrate on the world being born, not the world which was dying. This can be a valuable corrective to traditional history, but it can give a lopsided picture of an age. Racial, social, and political strife, unemployment, inflation, militarism, 'social problems' – all the horrors of the twentieth century dominate Stone's pre-1914 world. Yet Keynes, looking back at it in 1919, dismissed these things as the 'amusements of the daily newspaper', which 'appeared to exercise no influence at all on the ordinary course of social and economic life'. His pre-war Europe was an 'economic Eldorado', peopled by citizens reasonably content with their lot, in which there existed 'an almost absolute security of property and person'. Which gives the truer picture? Did Europe go to war in 1914 because societies were being torn apart by social conflict? Or was it because Europeans were bored with prosperity?

CHAPTER FOURTEEN

Cecil Rhodes

John Flint, *Cecil Rhodes*
[Hutchinson, 1976]

TODAY one is praised for giving up empires, not founding them. Once Cecil Rhodes was a popular hero. Millions applauded his deeds in southern Africa. His plans for a world empire ruled by an Anglo-Saxon élite fascinated some of the cleverest men of his time. Today he is more likely to be castigated as a wicked racialist and exploiter; while a

86

psychologist would probably view his dreams of power as the fantasies of the impotent and immature. Professor Flint's new biography of Rhodes has two great merits. Helped by an excellent map, it offers the best historical introduction yet to the problems of southern Africa today. Secondly, it takes a cool, unsentimental look at the Rhodes legend, avoiding both eulogy and denigration.

Born in 1853, the son of an Anglican parson burdened with ten other surviving children, Rhodes lacked the birth, money, or intellectual bent to succeed in Victorian England. Like many others similarly placed, he was shipped off to the colonies, landing at Durban in 1870. He came at the moment when the discovery of diamonds at Kimberley, soon to be followed by that of gold at Witwatersrand, was starting to transform south Africa from a collection of autonomous rural communities, white and black, into a unitary capitalist state based on black labour and white supremacy. The young Rhodes quickly made £10,000 to finance a BA pass degree at Oxford which, with interruptions, took him eight years. It was at Oxford that he developed his vision. God's purpose, he felt, was revealed in the Darwinian scheme of evolution. Historical evolution was synonymous with the progress of the Anglo-Saxon race. In the 'bringing of the whole uncivilised world under British rule' Rhodes would be fulfilling the Divine plan. Rhodes dreamt of promoting this ambitious aim through a secret society modelled on the Jesuits and Freemasons. These were the lunatic origins of the vastly respectable Rhodes Scholarships.

In practical matters, Rhodes was far from lunatic. He took the sensible view that it was no use having big ideas, if one didn't have the cash to carry them out. So his first priority was to make a fortune, and quickly, since an early heart attack convinced him (rightly) that he would not live long. In the diamond business he was almost from the start an aspiring monopolist. By 1880 he had acquired control over De Beers mine. In 1888, after a titanic struggle with Barney Barnato, and backed by Albert Beit and Lord Rothschild, Rhodes gained control over the whole of South Africa's diamond output. The financial basis was laid for his political ambitions.

What gave the private empire builder his chance was British government policy. Mr Flint gives a very clear account of the forces behind the 'new imperialism'. Rhodes, he rightly points out, was a colonialist rather than an imperialist. He believed in the spread of self-governing British communities, not rule from Whitehall. The economic motives behind expansion in southern Africa were likewise locally, not centrally, generated. Britain's aims were political: to keep the two breakaway Boer Republics north of Cape Colony isolated and thus politically impotent. This meant preventing them from joining forces with European powers encroaching on the area, particularly Germany. However, for reasons of economy, no British government wanted the expense of an active foreign policy in this area. This suggested leasing out government functions to private institutions. Rhodes's aim of keeping a broad corridor open for northern expansion coincided with the Colonial Office's aim of preventing the Boer Republics pushing westwards to link up with the Germans. The instrument for achieving both was the chartered company.

This was an ideal instrument of imperial expansion on the cheap. Rhodes's ambition to found a new empire in what later became Rhodesia drew together idealists, colonists and gold speculators. It depended on tricking Lobengula, King of the Ndebele, into signing away his sovereignty under cover of a mining concession; and then using this as a lever to get a royal charter to run a vast territory. Rhodes's ruthless destruction of the tribal societies which stood in his way is part of the tragedy that overwhelmed black Africa in this period. For the London side of his campaign he relied on his financial standing and on his power base in the Cape Colony, where an alliance with the Boer Bond led by Hofmeyr brought him the premiership between 1890 and 1895. A little judicious bribery and much charm were added ingredients. By 1889 Rhodes had triumphed alike over rival concession hunters and the humanitarian lobby which wanted to protect native rights. A royal charter of 29 October 1889 gave the British South Africa Company the right to colonize, exploit and govern an almost undefined area of south-central Africa.

There followed the heroic years when the Company struck out in all directions. Rhodes's reckless designs on Katanga and Portuguese East Africa, his indifference to methods and consequences, testifies to his growing megalomania. His remaining ambition was to bring the Boer Republics into a federated South Africa. He had conciliated Boer opinion in the Cape Colony by his willingness, in the Glen Gray Act, to settle the 'native question' on racial lines. Standing in the way was Kruger, the stubborn old president of Transvaal, who wanted to retain his state as a fossilized monument to unreformed Dutch Calvinism, despite the massive influx of gold-seeking Uitlanders. In 1894, Rhodes decided to overthrow him by force. As Mr Flint puts it, 'his economic interests in the Transvaal ... now merged with the dream of South African confederation and his morbid preoccupation with death and history to suggest a bold stroke.' The stroke was to co-ordinate an uprising by Johannesburg's politically deprived Uitlanders with an invasion by the British South Africa Company's police force led by Rhodes's old associate, Leander Jameson. The new colonial secretary Joseph Chamberlain helped the plan along by ceding a strip of Bechuanaland to the Company so as to give it a common border with Transvaal. Jameson's Raid of 28 December 1895 was a complete fiasco. Rhodes was only saved from its full consequences by the Kaiser's foolish telegram of support for Kruger; Chamberlain was saved by an elaborate cover-up. Rhodes remained a great imperial figure, but his political career as well as the possibility of uniting southern Africa under Anglo-Saxon leadership was finished. He died in 1902, his last years spent trying to evade the attentions of that cosmopolitan adventuress, Princess Radziwill.

As the British empire crumbled, so did Rhodes's legacy. Spengler saw him as the forerunner of a new Caesarism, 'midway between Napoleon and the fact men of the next century'. In fact he came at the tail-end of the great European expansion. Retreat was not long in setting in. Today white Rhodesia is the last monument to Rhodes's dream of Anglo-Saxon empire.

CHAPTER FIFTEEN

Chamberlain's Squalid Argument

[1976]

ON 9 September 1903, Joseph Chamberlain resigned as Colonial Secretary in Balfour's Conservative Government to launch his public campaign for tariff reform. That autumn, he toured northern Britain, putting his arguments and plans to vast audiences, mainly working-class. He was challenged and pursued by Asquith, the Liberal champion of free trade. The battle between the two was followed, writes Mr Roy Jenkins, 'with close interest by politically conscious people throughout the country'. It repays attention today, for the issues, economic and moral, then raised and discussed with incomparable breadth and lucidity, have been reactivated by the economic debacle of the last decade.

It was the economic state of the nation which launched Chamberlain on his revolutionary challenge to free trade. He had returned from a tour of South Africa haunted by the contrast between the youthful vigour of Britain overseas and the incipient senility of the Mother Country. When he had last been in Venice, he told his Glasgow audience of 6 October 1903, he had seen the Campanile, rising above the city it had overshadowed for centuries, looking as permanent as Venice itself. 'And yet the other day, in a few minutes, the whole structure fell to the ground. Nothing was left of it but a mass of ruin and rubbish. I do not say to you, gentlemen, that I anticipate any catastrophe so great or so sudden for British trade; but I do say to you that I see the signs of decay . . .' Asquith was to pooh-pooh such forebodings. 'We are more than holding our own,' he declared triumphantly at Cinderford two days later. But it was the trend, Chamberlain insisted, that was alarming; Britain's relative, not absolute, progress that was crucial for the future. 'It is not a question of whether we are richer now than we were fifty years ago or a thousand years ago. It is a question of which of us in the race for existence . . . is progressing more rapidly . . . I say that, although we have shared in the general prosperity, the comparative advance has been much more largely with our competitors.'

Chamberlain's fears were based on two economic trends. Between 1872 and 1902, Britain's exports of manufactured goods to the United States and Europe had dropped from £116 million to £73.5 million per annum. In the same period, manufactured goods imported into Britain from these areas had risen from £63 million to £149 million per annum. His hopes were based, in part, on a third, offsetting, trend. Between 1872 and 1902, Britain's exports of manufactured goods to the colonies had risen by £40 million. It was this third trend which provided the 'squalid argument' for imperial unity. There is no doubt that the Empire was an independent value for Chamberlain – not the Indian Empire which meant so much to Curzon and the Victorian mandarins, but the settler empire of 'Greater Britain'. Chamberlain's ideal was a federal union of the self-governing colonies. But the growing shift of Britain's trade to empire countries gave him the idea of linking the theme of empire union with the other great theme of his campaign, the 'condition of the people', a Disraelian phrase, given an un-Disraelian concreteness by Chamberlain's pledge to 'secure more employment at fair wages for the working men of this country'. Thus his plan for imperial preference was designed both to keep the empire together *and* to expand domestic employment by increasing Britain's manufacturing exports to empire countries.

In return for colonial preferences for British manufactures (some already in existence) he would put duties on foreign foodstuffs from which colonial foodstuffs would be exempted – 7 per cent on corn, 5 per cent on foreign meat, cheese and butter. The proposal to bring back the Corn Laws, repealed in 1846, was predictably denounced by what Chamberlain always called the 'Cobden Club'. They produced a poster showing a huge loaf of bread called 'The Free Trade Loaf', and a tiny one called 'The Zollverein Loaf', to show how much less bread workers' wages would buy if Chamberlain's tax were put on. In reply, Chamberlain produced two loaves of his own, apparently identical in size, at a Birmingham meeting. But this was not the main point. 'The whole object of my policy is not to lessen your loaf; it is to give you more money to buy it with.'

But imperial preference was not enough. Although it was Chamberlain's proposed 'stomach taxes' which attracted the greatest controversy, the centre-piece of his plan was to put a 10 per cent tariff on foreign manufactured goods, the purely Protectionist part of his scheme. The real crisis for Chamberlain was Britain's worsening position *vis-à-vis* America and Europe. As he put it simply to a working-class audience at Preston in 1905: 'You send less, they send more.' Chamberlain had a straightforward, if inelegantly phrased, explanation for the relative decline of Britain's export trade. 'We are losing our foreign markets, because whenever we begin to do a trade the door is slammed in our faces with a whacking tariff.' Asquith denied that the trend was for tariffs to increase. More effective was his rejoinder that since a country's tariffs were aimed equally at Britain and other countries, they could not be the cause of a decline in British exports relative to those countries.

Chamberlain encountered even more difficulty in explaining satisfactorily why Britain was losing its home market to foreign manufactured goods. He started with the notion of dumping. Having got large protected home markets, foreign manufacturers, in a depression, could afford to dispose of their surpluses on the unprotected British market at lower than cost price. In this vein, he described Britain's home market as being 'filched from us, stolen by unfair means'. However, by 1905 he had a better argument. Since the cost of production depended in part on the rate of production, possession of large protected markets had enabled foreign manufacturers to reduce their unit costs to below what British manufacturers could achieve with their penetrated and more specialized markets. The other factor raising the relative costs of British production was social legislation passed to protect the workman. The complaint has often been repeated, but Chamberlain did not provide any evidence to support his assertion that British manufacturers were paying relatively more for their workers' welfare than were their competitors.

Chamberlain also never made it clear whether his 10 per cent tariff was to be a permanent part of the industrial system, or to be used only for retaliation or to secure reciprocity. Asquith denied retaliation could be effective if confined to manufactured goods; and claimed it would be fatal if extended to raw materials. Certainly Chamberlain often argued as though Protection itself made countries successful. Every protected country, he said, 'has progressed more rapidly and in greater proportion than we'. Great Britain's early industrial lead was due to Protection, not free trade. Under free trade, the poor in Britain were worse off than in any other industrial country. Chamberlain vehemently denied that his proposed taxes would raise the living costs of the poor. They would curtail the luxury spending of the rich, while defending the employment and welfare of the worker.

Here we come to the heart of the tariff reform campaign. 'The question of employment, believe me', Chamberlain said in 1905, 'has now become the most important question of our time.' He ridiculed the free trade concentration on cheap food. ' "Cheap food", a higher standard of living, higher wages – all these things, important as they are, are contained in the word employment. If [my] policy will give you more employment, all the others will be added unto you.' He proceeded to draw a distinction, crucial to his argument, between the impact of economic decline on the manufacturer and the worker. The manufacturer 'may lose all his capital. His buildings may be empty; but he will perhaps have something left . . . Yes, the manufacturer may save himself. But it is not for him that I am chiefly concerned. It is for you – the workmen – I say to you that to you the loss of employment means more than the loss of capital to any manufacturer. You cannot live on your investments in a foreign country. You live on the labour of your hands – and if that labour is taken from you, you have no recourse, except, perhaps, to learn French or German.' It was because his labour power was all that the worker had to offer that Chamberlain insisted that it must be the first object of economic policy to 'offer the bulk of our workpeople . . . constant and remunerative employment'.

How could this be done? Chamberlain rejected the argument that constant employment could be secured only by constant adjustment to changing conditions. For Asquith, inefficiency was the problem. Despite his optimism, he recognized in 'defective knowledge, inferior processes, lack of flexibility or versatility, a stubborn industrial conservatism' the 'real enemies of British trade' which 'have done us infinitely more harm than all the tariffs and all the dumping syndicates ever created'. Protection would only freeze inefficiency instead of encouraging the required shifts in resources. Chamberlain's reply was that in an old country, where people had traditional skills of which they were immensely proud, these free trade remedies would not work; rather they would reduce, were already reducing, the economy, like the Campanile, to a heap of ruins. His most eloquent passage is worth quoting:

> I believe that all this is part of the old fallacy about the transfer of employment . . . It is your fault if you do not leave the industry which is falling and join the industry which is rising. Well, sir, it is an admirable theory; it satisfies everything but an empty stomach. Look how easy it is. Your once great trade in sugar refining is gone; all right, try jam. Your iron trade is going; never mind, you can make mousetraps. The cotton trade is threatened; well, what does that matter to you? Suppose you try doll's eyes . . . But how long is this to go on? Why on earth are you to suppose that the same process which ruined the sugar refining will not in the course of time be applied to jam? And when jam is gone? Then you have to find something else. And believe me, that although the industries of this country are very various, you cannot go on for ever. You cannot go on watching with indifference the disappearance of your principal industries.

Asquith thought he had trapped Chamberlain in yet another fallacy. Every import, he said, had to be balanced by an export. Chamberlain had made the unpardonable economic mistake of concentrating on 'visible' trade. But 'by what kind of export is the import balanced?' Chamberlain asked in reply. 'If we import something which is equivalent to a pound of labour, a pound of wages – do we export the equivalent of a pound of wages?' Chamberlain's choice of visible trade was deliberate. It was manufacturing industry which provided the bulk of employment in Britain. No doubt the country might balance its accounts, might even become richer, through increasing its 'invisible' earnings. But where would that leave the bulk of the population? Britain might become richer and richer with less and less employment. Already the rate of emigration was much higher than in Germany. This theme was to become increasingly prominent in the later stages of the tariff reform campaign. 'Whereas at one time England was the greatest manufacturing country, now its people are more and more employed in finance, in distribution, in domestic service, and in other occupations of the same kind. That state of things is consistent with ever-increasing wealth, but it means less men. It may mean more wealth, but it means less welfare.' The distinction between wealth and welfare was a favourite one. Workmen could starve 'in the midst of unprecedented abundance'.

Thinking about what the manufacturer could do to save himself led Chamberlain to an important insight into future British economic development. In a declining Britain 'a great number [of manufacturers], especially those with a large capital, send their works abroad, and wherever they send them they get a double market. If they send them to Germany, they have 50 million of Germans as their customers . . . and they can send to England more cheaply than if they had been in England.' By saving themselves, in fact, big capitalists contributed to the further ruin of British employment. In free imports, Chamberlain saw a philosophy hostile alike to patriotism and trade unionism. The underlying principle of Cobdenism was cosmopolitanism: 'care for all the world, avoiding, and even despising, the special care for which I plead – the care of those who are nearest and dearest to us'. Free imports were also contrary to the principles of trade unionism. Trade unions existed to protect labour; but the products of labour must also be protected. Chamberlain, with only partial truth, maintained that Cobden's Anti-Corn Law League was a manufacturers' ramp, bitterly opposed by the working-class Chartists. He was fond of quoting to working-class audiences Cobden's remark 'Depend on it, nothing can be got by fraternising with the unions. They are founded upon principles of brutal tyranny and monopoly. I would rather live under the Dey [sic] of Algiers than a trades committee.'

In reading through the speeches of both men,* Asquith seems the cleverer, but perhaps Chamberlain was the wiser. He detected the important economic trends, which Asquith missed. He also realized that it is relative, not absolute, performance that matters when you are competing with other countries. One may feel that he failed to give a satisfactory explanation of the growing uncompetitiveness of British industry, but who has succeeded better? Also, one may feel that his Protection plan depended too critically on the existence of 'sheltered' imperial markets to be completely relevant to our own much more exposed position. On the other hand, the down-to-earth 'man of business', as Chamberlain described himself, emerges as more humane than the patrician lawyer Asquith. His message was simple. Whatever the causes of Britain's economic decline, industry had to be protected, because otherwise the community would be destroyed. Chamberlain, unlike other 'men of business', was not prepared to transfer his 'works' or his loyalties abroad, if that meant the ruin of his country. 'I will express my own feelings in two or three words. No one is prouder of England, Scotland, and the United Kingdom than I am. I can never read our past history without a thrill of emotion.' Perhaps this is his message for our time.

CHAPTER SIXTEEN

Joseph Chamberlain and Enoch Powell

Enoch Powell, *Joseph Chamberlain*
[Thames and Hudson, 1977]

IT WAS an intriguing idea to get Enoch Powell to write about Joseph Chamberlain. There are obvious parallels between the two men. Both brought from the Midlands a native strain of provincial radicalism to London politics. Both were highly gifted outsiders challenging the

---

* Charles W. Boyd (ed.), *Mr Chamberlain's Speeches*, vol. 2, (1914), pp. 120–372; *Speeches by the Earl of Oxford and Asquith*, pp. 45–81.

traditional ruling élites; both put cause above party, appealing repeatedly to the people over the heads of their party leaders whom both cordially detested; both became centrally embroiled with Ireland; both denounced mass immigration, though Chamberlain did so at a time when it was still respectable to do so; and both failed in the tasks they set themselves: to stop the rot as they saw it. There is an important book to be written about the great modern British political rebels – men who tried and failed to change the political game to accommodate their vision. It is a story which links together not just Chamberlain and Powell, but both to Mosley, though all three men varied enormously in character and achievement. Instead of adopting the strenuous remedies each advocated, we have preferred to enjoy a mostly agreeable and certainly humane period of national decline.

As one would expect, Enoch Powell's book is both less and more than a work of history. The text is actually quite short, as befits a generously illustrated Thames and Hudson production. Nor has Powell attempted any research beyond the Garvin-Amery *Life*, Hansard, and a few secondary works. His purpose has been political, rather than historical: to establish the proposition that the union of Great Britain and Northern Ireland should be preserved at all costs. So he calls on Chamberlain as his star witness. It was Unionism, according to Powell, that gave meaning to Chamberlain's life: Radical Joe is submerged in Unionist Joe, with 1886 as the great moment of self-awareness. Thus is history refashioned to suit the politician's purpose. This is not altogether satisfactory. The last twenty years of Chamberlain's active life are treated as an epilogue. They are, of course, the imperialist years which Powell now regards as an aberration in British history. But they were also concerned with Chamberlain's attempt, between 1903 and 1906, to provide a secure basis for British employment. Powell's downgrading of the 'bread and butter' issue of tariff reform at the expense of the constitutional issues of Home Rule and Imperial Federation reveals a marked difference in the temperament of author and subject.

There are virtues in Powell's approach which offset his technical deficiencies as a historian. This book is, in a way, the judgment of one man of destiny on another; and with it goes an insight into the psychology of greatness. 'As the drama of politics revolves through its recurrent cycles', Powell writes, 'men recognise by a kind of instinct the scenes in which their own characters have cut them to play the lead.'

This is well put; though the scenes in which Chamberlain and Powell imagined themselves were very different. Interesting, too, is Powell's professional comment on Chamberlain's speech-making: 'his . . . sudden descent into weak endings, often marked by conventional phrases or even bathos'. Also emphasized is Chamberlain's indifference to party connections. It was the cause, not the party, which mattered; the National Education League, which Chamberlain founded, declared in 1873 that it didn't mind whether 'a Tory government sits on the Cabinet bench or a Liberal government passing Tory measures'.

Remarks such as these make one realize that Powell is using Chamberlain to write about himself: in a way one has a double biography for the price of one. Many of Powell's most revealing asides have to do with changing one's political friends. When Chamberlain resigned over Home Rule on 26 March 1886, 'his face, and he knew it, was towards his political enemies, opponents whom he had denounced and detested, but whom he could not now help but place and maintain in power'. Chamberlain and Parnell, Powell suggests, developed that 'cautious respect that grows up between members from widely separated political origins who find themselves fighting on the same side, especially against the feeling of their own parties'. Joe's position after 1886 – 'I shall do nothing to turn out the Government so long as the Government which would take its place is committed to a separatist [for which read, pro-EEC] policy' – is very much Enoch's today. Powell, too, faces what he analyses as Chamberlain's dilemma of the late 1880s: how to support the other side without losing credibility with his previous supporters, and thus his usefulness to his new allies. Powell writes that Chamberlain's secession 'condemned the Liberal Party to eventual extinction at the hands of Labour'. No doubt he feels that a Tory Party deprived of his own services may well be heading for a similar fate. And Powell must have had himself in mind when he wrote of Chamberlain's Birmingham Town Hall speech launching the tariff reform campaign, 'As with many speeches which detonate tremendous political explosions, he said nothing in it that he had not said before, and in public. It was the occasion which was the fulminate.'

As this last quotation suggests, Powell's approach to Chamberlain's career is too simple. The early part of the book is taken up with 'premonitions' of Chamberlain's later stands: for example, it was Chamberlain's co-operation with Conservative Ministers in applying the Artisans' Dwellings Act of 1875 to Birmingham which first suggested to

him the possibility of working with the Tories. Powell next treats
Chamberlain's break with Gladstone over Irish Home Rule in 1886 in a
purely constitutional context. What interests him about the Irish issue of
these years are the various attempts to square the circle of Irish self-
government with continuing British control over foreign policy, defence,
and fiscal policy. Chamberlain opposed Gladstone's first Home Rule Bill
because he said, rightly, that it meant separation. His own counter-
proposal for devolved National Councils to handle specially delegated
matters did not. But general self-government, together with the exclusion
of Irish MPs from Westminster, was bound to destroy Westminster's
supremacy over Ireland. The alternative of keeping Irish MPs at Westminster, which Gladstone proposed in his second Home Rule Bill of
1892, was no better: it would simply add the confusion of double
representation to the initial proposal. A federal solution (Home Rule all
round) was a possible way out, but not practical politics. So the principle
of self-government for Ireland would have to be abandoned if Union
was to be preserved. Thus Powell describes Chamberlain's reasoning.

Powell obviously loves these constitutional questions, and is good
at exposing logical absurdities and insoluble dilemmas. In the course of
this, though, the central question somehow gets lost: why was Chamberlain so hostile to separation in the first place? There is almost nothing on
this; yet this was, to use Powell's phrase, 'the heart of the matter'. What
Powell has done is to transfer to Chamberlain his own obsession with
the purely constitutional implications of great affairs – as witness his
own concentration on the nationality and sovereignty aspects of coloured
immigration and British membership of the EEC. I am not convinced
that Chamberlain thought in those terms. As a mid-Victorian man of
business, he placed more weight on the material and practical aspect of
things; and in the case of Ireland, these no doubt involved both
economics and defence.

It is equally characteristic of Powell to dwell on the federal, rather
than the economic, aspects of Chamberlain's imperialism. As Powell tells
it, Chamberlain pursued the fantasy of imperial federation as a way of
securing that federation of the United Kingdom which might after all
square the circle of Irish self-government and Imperial control. This is
very doubtful. Chamberlain hoped the Irish question would be solved by
economic reform, not by imperial federation. Again, it is significant that
Powell sees 'a customs union or preferential trading block' as an

'attenuated form' of imperial federation. This is clearly not the case with a preferential trading bloc – something quite different from a customs union. The preferential trading bloc created by the Ottawa Trading Agreement of 1932, whatever its economic merits, certainly posed no 'insoluble dilemma' for Britain's imperial relationships. Powell here makes the mistake of thinking of tariff reform simply as federalism by the back door. This entirely ignores Chamberlain's preoccupation with the economic decline of Britain, and growing labour unrest. It was this which prompted his dramatic challenge of 1903. It is only by ignoring its frankly Protectionist appeal that Powell can link tariff reform to the project of imperial federation, and both – by several removes – to the Irish question. Tariff reform was a remedy for economic decline and an alternative to socialism, and it should be treated in that context.

So one must conclude, after all, that the politician's vision, for all its acuteness, has narrowed rather than enlarged our understanding of Chamberlain; which sadly illustrates the fact that writing and making history are two very different kinds of enterprise.

CHAPTER SEVENTEEN

Julian Grenfell

Nicholas Mosley, *Julian Grenfell: His Life and the Times of his Death 1888–1915*
[Weidenfeld & Nicolson, 1976]

'COME and die, it'll be great fun,' urged Rupert Brooke when war broke out in 1914. Upper-class England responded to the call, not dutifully but enthusiastically. In the first months of the war, six peers, sixteen baronets, six knights, 164 companions of orders of chivalry, ninety-five sons of peers, eighty-two sons of baronets, and eighty-four sons of knights were killed. They destroyed themselves eagerly; their parents and friends treated their deaths as the perfection of life, and made a legend out of the Lost Generation. Among this select company was twenty-six-year-old Julian Grenfell, eldest son of Lady Desborough. Soon after the war started he had written to his mother: 'Isn't it luck for me to have been born so as to be just the right age and just in the right place.' When he died, Arthur Balfour wrote to her, 'to live greatly and die soon is a lot which . . . cannot be bettered.'

How did Julian Grenfell and his class come to embrace war so enthusiastically when apparently life had so much to offer them – position, wealth, charm, good looks? Nicholas Mosley's conclusion is that war offered even more – an escape into 'reality' for a functionless aristocracy leading meaningless lives. But this is no sociological treatise. A novelist, Mr Mosley concentrates on personal relationships, notably that between Julian Grenfell and his mother, Ettie Desborough. Indeed, the book is about Julian's effort to escape his mother's suffocating world, his ultimate failure to do so, and the reconciliation of their values in his death. It is a depressing, even macabre, story, reconstructed with great sensitivity and insight from a marvellous collection of family papers. Mr Mosley was no doubt judged a suitable person to read them. He is the grandson of Lord Curzon, one of Ettie's favourite 'Souls'. His first wife, Rosemary, was Ettie's granddaughter. The result is a small masterpiece of social and psychological observation, which is also an important historical essay.

The story starts and finishes with Julian's mother, Ettie. Passionately admired by both men and women ('what a quantity of both flash and stodge are devoted to you', writes a friend in their private slang), she emerges as something of a monster. Her monstrousness has both a personal and social explanation. Descended from two earls, Ettie Fane had grown up with sickness and death. Orphaned at two, she lost an adored brother at eight, a favourite grandmother at thirteen. Forbidden by convention to express grief, Ettie could cope with such losses only through fantasy. On the social plane there was the impact on her character of what Thorsten Veblen called the upper-class woman's 'conspicuous exemption from all useful employment'. Regarded and treated as an ornament, she could fashion her life only from substitute satisfactions – even her babies would probably be breast-fed by wet nurses. It is not difficult to understand Ettie's need for an adoring and dependent circle of men, her manipulative view of human relations, and her habit of romanticizing life and death.

In 1887, at the age of nineteen, she married William Grenfell, a passionate sportsman (he was made Lord Desborough for exiguous political services in 1905). Ettie preferred her games more intellectual. At Taplow, Willie's country house only half an hour from London, she presided over the Souls – a coterie of clever men and beautiful and intelligent women. Including Balfour, Curzon, George Wyndham and Margot Tennant they met at weekends to play games – pencil and paper games, charades, and games with ideas and love. The atmosphere was one of world weariness: life was 'rather depressing apart from ideals'. Ettie was particularly expert at the flirtation game. She kept many men dancing on the end of a string, carefully preserving their epistolary expressions of undying adoration. Love was a game of words and codes, rather than acts, for, as Mr Mosley notes, 'romance and passion, if they were to coexist with ideas of fidelity and duty, had to remain largely in the mind'. Sexual taboo was the psychological basis of female power in a male world. This was what turned women into goddesses and made men feel guilty and distraught about 'hurting' them.

Something which could have done with more exploration is the 'emptiness at the centre of political life' which was the background against which the Souls played their games. The problem was not the actual lack of causes – the great Social Question was starting to rear its head – but the inability of the aristocracy, in its decline, to transcend its narrow rural boundaries. With nothing worthwhile to do in peace, it embraced war as a return to reality.

This, then, was the world in which Julian grew up – women to be worshipped from afar by adoring men who spent most of their time killing animals and birds. He seemed to fall into the pattern. At Eton his beauty drove a master to tears. He became head of his house and a member of Pop. Mr Mosley, an Old Etonian, writes: 'The worst of Eton is that it is its very sophistication that makes growing away from it so difficult. What has been inculcated is charm; and charm is a way of manipulating society. But charm lacks substance; so it is to society that a charming person is tethered, however much he dislikes society.'

It was at Balliol that Julian's battle for independence began. His mother wanted him to be 'affectionate' and 'sociable'. He insisted that he was by nature unsociable. She also attacked his choice of girlfriends. Ettie's technique of dominance was the same as with her lovers: to make him feel guilty. At twenty-one Julian set down his rebellious thoughts on paper. Conventionalism, he wrote, 'turns life into a game, and a bad game at that . . .' It is sustained by the manipulation of ideals like competition and self-sacrifice. In place of these false gods Julian tried to develop an ideal of service. Ettie hated the essays which she (rightly) saw as an attack on her. She may even have tried to stop their publication.

By her disapproval she also contributed to the failure of Julian's love affair with Marjorie Manners. Foiled as author and lover, he had a nervous breakdown and had to leave Oxford.

His actual escape from his mother was through sport. The point of sport, he wrote, was to 'take us back to . . . real things, bringing the elemental barbaric forces in ourselves into touch with . . . nature'. It was not the genteel games of the Souls – golf and tennis – which he loved but boxing, riding, hunting and shooting. Mr Mosley comments that 'he filled in time with violence in order to stop feeling ill', but his own attitude to Julian's 'solution' is ambiguous. Certainly the feeling that Julian and his friends held, that violence was the *only* escape from artificiality, was part of the psychic conditions which drove Europe to war. In any case, Julian's rowdiness is his least attractive side. At Oxford he told his mother how he 'lost all control' with a cabman, and 'tore him down from his seat and shook him till bits started to drop off him'. According to Reginald Pound (in his book *The Lost Generation of 1914*), Julian used to go round Oxford with an 'Australian stockwhip' with which, on one occasion, he 'drove Philip Sassoon out of College, cracking the prodigious lash within inches of Sassoon's sleek head'. This may be exaggerated; but not to discuss the episode at all is odd.

It was, in any case, the triumph of the 'new money' represented by people like the Sassoons, as well as the need to escape from the meaningless rituals of Taplow and Panshanger, his mother's country houses, which determined Julian to get out of England. He joined the Royal Dragoons, went to India, and had a marvellous time pigsticking. In South Africa, he started to find army life incredibly dull, and toyed with politics. The outbreak of war came as a tremendous relief: 'it's all the best fun one ever dreamed of . . .' he wrote from the front. In war he could drop the attractive irony which Ettie so disliked and talk her language.

Why did Julian 'love war'? One reason is that 'for the first time he felt that he had some proper function within a society'. A second is that he felt free for the first time from the conventions of Ettie's society: for someone who was aesthetically, intellectually, politically, and possibly sexually, undeveloped war was 'the one area in which there were standards of excellence other than those of snobbishness, bitchiness or money'. Finally, there was the desire for sacrifice (mother has done so much for me), for heroism (what can I do for her?) and acceptance of death as the highest sacrifice.

On 13 May 1915, Julian Grenfell was wounded by a bit of shell which lodged in his brain. He died on 26 May after two operations. The next day *The Times* published his poem 'Into Battle'. His brother Billy was killed on 30 July. Ettie began to write her family journal 'which was to be her memorial to Julian and Billy; and her assurance to others and herself that in spite of appearances there was still no darkness or sorrow'. In death, Julian became the son she had always wanted.

PART TWO

The Inter-War Years

CHAPTER EIGHTEEN

The Labour Party and Keynes

[1972]

I

WRITING in the aftermath of the 1931 fiasco, Keynes diagnosed the failure of the Labour Party leadership in the following terms: 'The Labour Cabinet was in a hopeless position last August, because most of them conscientiously believed in the Gold Standard and in deflation by economy, and were not prepared to throw these things overboard. Yet at the same time they were equally unprepared to sacrifice the . . . ideal *motifs* in which they had been brought up.' Caught between the obsolete and the Utopian, they had been 'totally unsympathetic with those who have had new notions of what is economically sound'. This had rendered the Labour Party 'exceedingly ineffective for the practical purposes of government'.[1] This quotation is a good starting point from which to analyse the sources of the Labour Party's resistance to Keynesianism. It emphasizes two distinct sources: conventional wisdom and socialism.* The problem, as I hope to show, is actually more complex, since British social democracy was rooted in British conventional wisdom, so that there was a much larger overlap between the obsolete and the Utopian than Keynes appears to recognize – at least in this quotation. The theme of this essay will be the relationship between them; and about the way in which that relationship conditioned Labour's response to the 'new notions of what is economically sound'.

II

To Keynes's charge that the Labour Party was obsolete, A. L. Rowse replied that this was true only of some of its leaders, like MacDonald and Snowden. Since they had been expelled, there was nothing to prevent the fruitful marriage of Keynesianism and socialism.[2] Not only does this ignore the real difficulties which Keynesian thought posed for socialists – difficulties as evident today as then – but it also minimizes the extent

---

* It was a mistake of my book, *Politicians and the Slump*, to concentrate too much on the latter.

of Labour's commitment to the obsolete. As Mosley pointed out, in one of his last parliamentary speeches, the party as a whole had consistently supported Snowden's policies: 'They did not walk out of the Bankers' palace till it fell about their ears.'[3]

These traditional commitments require explanation. No doubt the bankers venerated the gold standard because they saw their profit in it: but how to explain Labour's worship at the same shrine? When we encounter beliefs which may be said to be the property of the whole political system, and not just a segment of it, 'class interest' loses its explanatory power. (What is the Marxist 'false consciousness' other than an attempt to explain why classes do not always act in the way their 'objective' interests dictate?) A broader framework is required. Such a framework, I suggest, is provided by the notion of political culture. I mean by it the intellectual, moral and institutional framework in which public policy is discussed and formulated.* I don't want to suggest that in Britain all politically conscious people agreed on all questions; or that party struggles were fraudulent. Nevertheless, modern British political life has been characterized by an astonishingly high degree of agreement on fundamentals. Two questions arise: how did this consensus come about? And what was socialism's relationship to it?

The British political culture, I suggest, was based first and foremost on an unprecedented set of achievements. This is, of course, true of liberal capitalism in general, which is why it became for a time the dominant world force. But it is especially true of Britain, the pioneering, archetypal, and most successful liberal capitalist state. The hundred years which opened with the loss of the American colonies and the publication of Adam Smith's *Wealth of Nations* (1776), and closed with the onset of the first Great Depression and the passage of the Third Reform Act (1884–5), saw the world triumph of British arms, commerce, industry and ideas. It is not surprising that the political and economic practices associated, substantively or coincidentally, with these great achievements should have acquired the status of fundamental truths; that earlier ideas should have been consigned to the dustbin of

---

* cf. Thomas Kuhn's concept of the paradigm in the physical sciences: 'the entire constellation of beliefs, values, techniques, and so on, shared by members of a given community' (*The Structure of Scientific Revolutions*, 2nd edn, 1970, p. 175). Also Max Nicholson's concept of 'the system' – 'a series of principles, aims, policies, practices and codes of conduct handed down through a group of allied institutions' in his book, *The System: The Misgovernment of Modern Britain*, p. 491.

history. Equally notable in the age of revolutions was the unique stability of the British political system, its success in solving the problem of assimilating new classes into the political order which had brought down all other European regimes. Here were the material foundations of the British 'paradigm'.

What was the relationship of socialism to nineteenth-century British liberalism? The way I would put it is that liberal capitalism posed a particular set of puzzles which increasingly absorbed the attention and energy of its best thinkers. These chiefly had to do with the moral justifications of the existing social order. Liberals advanced claims on behalf of all men to certain fundamental rights which the existing distribution of economic and political power seemed to deny. The nineteenth-century political culture was thus born with a dilemma of its own making: how to reconcile its professed aspirations with its actual practice. Out of the debate on this question grew the case for socialism.*
However, it was a socialism which reflected nineteenth-century moral concerns, not twentieth-century economic problems. Indeed, British socialism by and large assumed that capitalism had solved the economic problem, just as 'parliamentarism' had solved the problem of political action. These were the key links between socialism and liberal capitalism which made both unreceptive to certain types of innovation. But the Socialist Utopia, deriving from the uncompleted agenda of nineteenth-century politics, was similarly ill-equipped to confront a radically different economic reality. The Labour Party was blinkered by its past and by its future.

A further comment may help elucidate the connection between them. The Victorians had an unshakeable belief in what one writer has called 'the institutional momentum' of the nineteenth century, which may be defined as the improvement and generalization of the British achievement. They were convinced that the British way of life was superior to any other and that the whole world would eventually be recast in the British mould: the hubris of those who mistake a unique moment of success for a permanent condition. They believed that the twentieth century would be an improved version of the nineteenth century, not something fundamentally different. Of course, some stressed

---

* As C. Wright Mills remarks, 'The moral bases of his [Marx's] criticism of liberal society are the ideals proclaimed by that society itself – taken seriously and made concrete' (*The Marxists*, 1963, p. 28).

continuity more than improvement, but common to all was a linear view of history and progress. It became very difficult for both conservatives and socialists to change course, because this would mean calling into question not just the nineteenth-century achievement, but the hopes of progress. This helps explain why both conservatives and socialists committed themselves in the 1920s to the 'restoration of normalcy', the former because they wanted to get back there for its own sake, the latter because they wanted to resume socialist progress from the point at which they felt the nineteenth century had started to 'go wrong'.

III

What then was the consensus against which all inter-war Keynesian proposals had to do battle, in the main unsuccessfully? At its most abstract it was the general belief in the efficiency of markets. In the absence of interferences, the market ensures the full and efficient employment of productive resources. The proviso is important. Classical economics, as Keynes noted, rested on a 'theory of liquids'. The system as a whole was self-adjusting providing the various factors of production were allowed to adjust freely to changing conditions. The role of government was limited to creating the conditions for the efficient working of markets. This was the economic philosophy of the Manchester school. However, it would be quite wrong to assume that what economists taught, nations invariably practised. The extent to which these doctrines were acted upon varied enormously from country to country, depending upon circumstances, experiences, social forces, traditions. The particular circumstances of England at the start of the Industrial Revolution fitted, or could be made to fit, the assumptions of the classical model more readily than those of any other country. That is why the doctrines of the classical economists were applied more thoroughly in England than elsewhere, and achieved a higher prestige.

The view that the state should interfere as little as possible with the natural liberty of the individual to pursue his own activities sprang from a particularly British conjunction of circumstances and traditions. In economic life, the vast profits which awaited pioneering British manufacturers, provided they could buy and sell freely, dictated a liberation of markets from the mass of feudal and mercantile regulations which encrusted them. Since existing regulations were often irrational, favouring some groups at the expense of others, it was not difficult to demonstrate that they usually did more harm than good, leading to Adam Smith's sweeping conclusion that 'the sovereign is completely discharged from a duty, in the attempting to perform which he must always be exposed to innumerable delusions, and for the proper performance of which no human wisdom or knowledge would ever be sufficient'.[4] As the wealth of the country multiplied 'without direction, favour or patronage of the state, it is not surprising that it came to be generally agreed that Adam Smith was right'.[5] However, the struggle to eliminate the state from the economic field would never have succeeded so completely had it not been conjoined to other anti-statist forces with even deeper roots: the parliamentary struggle against the Crown (monarchy and state were virtually identical in English constitutional history), the struggle for religious liberty (for the nonconformist business classes, religious and economic freedom went hand in hand). Thus the English tradition of freedom was freedom *from* state interference; the state was associated with tyranny, monopoly, corruption. George Bernard Shaw remarked, only half perversely, in 1933: 'What is the historical function of Parliament in this country? It is to prevent the government from governing ... Bit by bit it broke the feudal monarchy; it broke the Church; and finally it broke even the country gentleman. Then, having broken everything that could govern the country, it left us at the mercy of our private commercial capitalists ... and financiers of all nations and races.'[6]

It is impossible to read through the government papers, the parliamentary debates, the newspaper editorials, the memoirs, of the inter-war years without being struck by the strong antagonism that ran through them to state action. The economic and administrative argument was that government interference would simply 'duplicate' what others – capitalists and municipal authorities – were doing more efficiently. The political argument was that it would lead to dictatorship. Even a hint of it would shatter confidence. The Labour Party's own highly ambivalent attitude to state intervention will be examined later.

The external counterpart of domestic *laissez-faire* was free trade and the international mobility of capital. Here again what we have to bear in mind is not the theory itself, but the conditions which encouraged its application. The key factor was the overseas thrust of British capitalism in near monopoly conditions. From the start of its commercial and industrial revolutions, Britain had locked itself into a system of world economy. Its major growth industries were export industries; an

111

increasing proportion of its savings went abroad; it became progressively more dependent on imported foodstuffs and raw materials. It was under these conditions of actual and increasing interdependence, though initially a British-controlled interdependence, that certain characteristic dogmas took hold. Free trade was invariably to Britain's advantage whatever other nations did, because Britain needed to export more than they did and hence had to maintain a policy of free imports. (The cause and effect was reversed: in reality, Britain needed to import so much because of the huge profits that resulted from the export of goods and capital.) With the proliferation of Britain's business, a stable currency also became a primary economic value. The pound was not devalued once in peacetime between 1719 and 1931, and the gold standard became the proverbial rock on which the City's international financing was built. Interdependence bred a particular sense of responsibility for world order, economic and political, and what Susan Strange has described as the 'belief . . . that the interests of the British economy necessarily always and very closely coincided with that of the international economy'.[7]

The fundamental consequence of this international outlook was an inability to conceive of a solution to economic problems within a national context. Free trade, together with a fixed exchange rate, logically entailed a British economy highly and continually adjustable to changes in world conditions. The strategy of British governments in the 1920s was to restore the world economy by re-establishing the gold standard and then allowing wage-costs to adjust downwards to the restored value of money. In the 1930s, internal deflation was abandoned for 'international reflation' to raise world prices. In both decades, the possibility of an independent British solution was rejected for fear of international repercussions: British exports would be priced out of world markets, others would retaliate, etc. Bernard Shaw put the matter succinctly when he remarked 'If you will not do anything until everyone else does it (although I know that is the British morality in a nutshell) you will never get anything done at all'.

To concentrate on the material context of the British ideology is misleading. The moral context is equally important. Victorians felt an overpowering need to justify their political and economic activities in moral terms. This reflects both the religious temper of Victorian society and the insecurity of the new capitalist order; and accounts for that curious mixture of God and Mammon which runs through Victorian ideas and practices. The psychological cement of Victorian society was puritanism, the meeting-ground of individualistic capitalism and idealistic socialism; of the middle-class businessman and the industrious working-man. Thrift or Saving, not consumption, was the engine of the Victorian economy. It established the moral virtue of capitalism; and provided the upper level of the working class with its main hope of improvement. The economic doctrines we have been discussing owed much of their hold to their identification with virtue. Individualist economics received its most powerful support in the notion of a man's personal accountability for his own actions, e.g. the widespread belief that the unemployed were responsible for their own unemployment.* Free trade would scarcely have survived so long had it been just an economic doctrine, and not believed to be an instrument of world peace and brotherhood. Adherence to the gold standard, too, was viewed as a sign of collective virtue; and the profits which thereby accrued to the City of London were seen as a just reward for collective abstention. Internationalism was rooted not just in the fact of interdependence, but in that evangelical tradition which first campaigned against slavery: the *Pax Britannica* was justified in the name of world improvement. To many in the inter-war years, including Labour leaders bred in the tradition of Wesley and Samuel Smiles, Keynesianism represented a fall from grace. As P. J. Grigg put it in his autobiography, 'I distrust utterly those economists who have with great but deplorable ingenuity taught that it is not only possible but praiseworthy for a country to live . . . on its wits . . . and who have sought to make economics a *vade-mecum* for political spivs.'[8] And across a copy of the Lloyd-George-Keynes public works proposals of 1929, a Treasury official scribbled 'Extravagance, Inflation, Bankruptcy'.[9]

IV

By political culture I mean not just the ideas which people hold, but the social and political systems by which they are transmitted and perpetuated. Many of the beliefs and attitudes mentioned above were the property of that 'intellectual aristocracy' of great liberal families

---

* Even in the inter-war years few were prepared to accept the concept of 'involuntary unemployment'. Workers would always find employment if they were willing to accept an appropriate wage-rate.

described by Noel Annan, with its roots in the evangelical Clapham Sect and its branches spreading through the civil service, the universities, and public life in general. Annan remarks, 'The influence of these families may partly explain a paradox which has puzzled European and American observers of English life: the paradox of an intelligentsia which appears to conform rather than rebel against the rest of society.'[10] This is a fascinating and important subject; but my main concern here is with the role of the political system in perpetuating the conventional wisdom. One of the main arguments against oligopoly is that it drastically curtails choice. Yet a paradox of English political development is that the age of the individual culminated in the triumph of the political combine. The looser and more varied political alliances of earlier times gave way to two disciplined parties who divided up the political market between them. The independent-minded MP, sustained by independent means, was gradually replaced by the good party man, faithfully subscribing to party programmes, dependent on party machines and funds for his election. Dissent came to be equated with disloyalty. The consequence was a catastrophic reduction in what Donald Schon has called 'ideas in good currency'.[11]

The growth of party organization is customarily explained in terms of the need to mobilize the new electorates enfranchised by the nine-teenth-century Reform Acts. However, the emergence of a highly struc-tured, two party system really reflects the division of English society into two classes. Party organization may, in part, be viewed as the capping stone of class organization. For the middle classes, the main organizing agency was the public school system. The anarchic character of the unreformed public schools, which at any rate provided some space for individual growth, was replaced by a highly-articulated social system, aiming to produce a uniform type, loyal to the narrow values of his class and kind, mistrustful of speculation: in short, a good party man who would not dream of 'letting down his side'.* The functional value of these qualities for the instinctive defence of privilege is obvious.†

---

* The role of organized games in inculcating this team spirit is well known. 'A good oar may be dropped from the club if he does not fit in' notes Noel Annan in a rhapsodic passage on the character-building qualities of boating. (*Leslie Stephen*, p. 30) According to Asa Briggs, the public schools mixed the sons of the gentry with the sons of the middle classes in a new social amalgam that helped bridge the divide between landlords and businessmen and fuse their social values (*Victorian People*, pp. 142f).

† At the same time, the tremendous moral emphasis in public school education led some

114

Similarly, the life experience of workers in tightly-knit urban communities and factories found its organizational expression in the trade union, upon which the Labour Party itself was modelled.

The industrial and political structures erected on this primary class division were both competitive *and* complementary. Of the Victorian trade union mentality, Gwyn Williams writes: 'But it was a class consciousness which was essentially corporate, integrated into the system which they [the unions] largely accepted and tried to work for the benefit of their class.'[12] In particular, both political organizations shared a common interest in establishing a 'closed shop' in their sections of the market, which involved a common hostility to ideas and movements which cut across the existing divide. The fact that both Conservative and Labour Parties were subsequently able to continue their struggle in a Keynesian world does not invalidate the statement that in the inter-war years both were afraid that Keynesianism would destroy their distinctive *raisons d'être*. Keynes's own view that 'the historic party questions . . . are as dead as last week's mutton . . . whilst the questions of the future . . . cut across party lines'[13] helped confirm this diagnosis. Keynesianism was thus initially rejected in the name of both capitalism and socialism, owner and worker.

An early example of the institutional nature of the resistance to new ideas is provided by the political reaction to Joseph Chamberlain's campaign for Protection and imperial preference (1903–6) – the first politically significant and, I would claim, relevant, response to the related problems of industrial decline and 'involuntary' unemployment.* The reasons for Chamberlain's defeat are doubtless complex. Here I would only draw attention to the institutional response. Chamberlain's new political combination of imperialism and social reform attacked not only the general belief and vested interest in free trade, but also the validity

---

of its finer products from 'muscular Christianity' to 'Christian socialism' – an important tributary flowing into the Labour Movement.

* Donald Winch (*Economics and Policy*, p. 64) claims that tariff reformers failed to give 'adequate treatment to the connection between foreign trade and unemployment'. This is technically true. On the other hand, Chamberlain saw clearly enough that arguments for the impossibility of involuntary unemployment which rested, *inter alia*, on the assumption of free trade, lost much of their validity in a world of tariff barriers. Chamberlain's challenge – and offence – was his insistence that the 'conditions' of the real world corresponded less and less to the 'assumptions' of the classical economists. This was also Keynes's point of departure – and some would add, his point of arrival.

of existing party divisions. He thus in effect united the parties against him. The Conservative leadership always maintained a reserved attitude to his policy, despite (or perhaps because of) its potential ideological appeal across class lines. More importantly, Chamberlain's 'heresy' was of key importance in bringing about the electoral, and subsequently the parliamentary, alliance between the Liberal and Labour Parties. The Labour Party's role in resisting Chamberlain illustrates a number of points I have been making. First, it demonstrated the Party's attachment to free trade. As L. T. Hobhouse wrote at the time, 'Free Trade finance was to be the basis of social reform. Liberalism and Labour learned to co-operate in resisting delusive promises of remedies for unemployment and in maintaining the right of free international exchange.'[14] Secondly, the Lib–Lab alliance revealed the basic compatibility between the 'new' Liberalism and 'moderate' Socialism, thus defining the *direction* of future social advance from which Chamberlain's programme represented a deviation. Thirdly, we can see a vested institutional hostility to someone who tried to appeal to the people over the heads of their organizations. (The TUC passed a resolution in 1903 condemning as black-legs all workers who supported Chamberlain.) From the start, then, the Labour Party staked out for itself a dual role in the British political culture: as its advance guard, and as intellectual and institutional guarantor of its core values.

Nor did the First World War have the revolutionary impact on political life which is often claimed for it. Arthur Marwick is perfectly right to emphasize the 'unguided forces of social change unleashed by the war'[15] which were bound in the long run to undermine the Victorian culture. But in the public domain, the main proximate effect of the war was to strengthen the hold of conventional ideas and to make their defence increasingly dogmatic. There were two reasons for this. First, the war and its associated consequences were so contrary and damaging to the Victorian map of reality that they were instinctively assigned to the category of aberrations which it was the duty of statesmen to correct. As in 1815, and for very similar reasons, reconstruction was conceived of largely in terms of restoration – of free trade, the gold standard, sound finance, capital exports, 'confidence', etc. Moreover, what had formerly been normal practice, which few questioned, acquired in its restored form the status of doctrine to be defended against heresy. As a result of these ideological blinkers many inter-war policies – the return to the gold standard being a good example – were not only badly

116

conceived, but badly executed. In trying to recover the secret of success, the British post-Victorians merely succeeded in discovering the secret of bad luck. Both Conservative and Labour Parties were committed to restoring 'normalcy', the latter because normalcy was the foundation-stone of its Utopia.

Secondly, by fatally weakening the Liberal Party, the war removed an essential surviving element of flexibility from the political system. The redefinition of the political struggle in terms of capitalism versus Socialism, with its concomitant class cleavage, cut the ground from under the modernizers or 'economic radicals'. The redefinition of post-war politics might not have mattered so much had the distinctive solutions of either party been intellectually or politically viable. But in fact, neither the *laissez-faire* nor socialist dogmas were centrally relevant to the problem of unemployment; while the attempt to put either of them into practice under those circumstances would have shattered the political and social fabric. The lack of congruence between the political struggle and the nature of inter-war economic problems created a vacuum which was filled, on the one side, by the administrative conservatism of the permanent officials, on the other by the MacDonald–Baldwin consensus of decency, dole, traditional values and moral uplift.

V

The Labour Party's pivotal role in sustaining the conventional wisdom is explained by the fact that it viewed the liberal status quo as the only possible basis for further advance. The trouble with Chamberlainism was that it was not just a change of direction but, in progressive eyes, a regression to a more primitive outlook. A socialism incubated in reaction would be disastrous. (This of course is the classic marxist argument for the necessity of a capitalist stage.) The Webbs talked about the 'inevitability of gradualness'. For MacDonald, socialism was the 'completion' of liberalism on its moral side.[16]

With such views, the Labour Party rejected the notion of progress through catastrophe: this is one of the reasons why the experience of 'war socialism' in 1914–18 had so little influence on Labour policy-making in the 1920s. There was, of course, a catastrophic tradition going back to the first half of the nineteenth century when commercial crises were endemic, and which revived in the 1880s and 1890s. For simple evolution, Marx had substituted a violent antagonism between

117

the bourgeois order and the socialist order germinating within it, growing out of the increasing instability of capitalism. He drew a sharp distinction between evolutionary change *within* an epoch, and revolutionary changes *between* epochs. (The idea of historical discontinuity is also very much present in Keynes.) Hobson's 'underconsumptionist' theory also had catastrophic implications, though these were obscured by what Lenin called his 'petit bourgeois reformism'. But it has to be emphasized that these were minority traditions in British socialism. For most British socialists, what on the Continent was called revisionism grew naturally out of the whole British experience.

Indeed, the political significance of the Fabian theory of rent was precisely to deny the theoretical necessity of exploitation under capitalism, and thus establish the possibility of an evolutionary and peaceful transition *pari passu* with continuing capitalist efficiency.[17] What was left after the refutation of the labour theory of value was not a historical necessity, but a historical situation deriving from unequal bargaining power in the market which could be remedied by the 'countervailing' power of trade union pressure and state action.[18] Fabian demolition of the assumptions on which Marx based his catastrophic predictions left only a moral and practical case against capitalism. It was wrong for one class to appropriate the major rewards of socially produced wealth; and this private appropriation created a quite unnecessary 'poverty in the midst of plenty'. The task of socialism, as Shaw defined it in 1888, was to 'transfer . . . the rent from the class which now appropriates it to the whole people . . . not in one lump sum, but by instalments'.[19]

The Fabians envisaged the community gradually buying out a capitalist class caught between the twin pressures of rising wages and steepening taxation. A continuing surplus was a necessary premise of this redistributionist plan. It was necessary also to the socialist strategy of working gradually through parliament, for it was in conditions of prosperity that the capitalists would be most amenable to 'reasonable' redistribution. Indeed socialists had good reason to believe that the capitalists would go at least part of the way with them. At the end of the nineteenth century most enlightened middle-class people combined a pride in the British achievement and moderate optimism about the future with a conscience about poverty and a belief that British society was sufficiently wealthy to be able to afford its poor a decent living without 'killing the goose that laid the golden egg'. 'Let the rich, landowners and capitalists alike, keep their property, but let them ransom the flaw in their titles by compensating other human beings residing in their country for that free use of the material environment which has been withdrawn from them' was the view of the 'semi-socialist'.[20] Evolution towards a 'socialism of a non-revolutionary kind, or a "chivalrous", regulated capitalism', was widely regarded as both inevitable and desirable.[21] There was, of course, an ultimate conflict between taxing part of the surplus, and taxing the capitalist class out of existence. But this conflict was obscured by the gradualist setting of the socialist programme, and the existence of so many intermediate stages at which the redistribution-ist enterprise might halt. In a nutshell, the progressive aim was to moralize success. The idea that a Progressive Government might be called upon to administer a capitalist system 'stuck' in a depression would have struck most socialists as absurd. Yet this is, of course, exactly what happened in the 1920s. There was no 'success' left to moralize. As W. H. B. Court justly remarks, the whole late Victorian debate about the distribution of wealth ignored the fact that wealth was ceasing to expand.[22]

It is from this perspective that we must view the claim that 'on a spectrum running from Marxism to social reform, there was a common repudiation of *laissez-faire* as the guiding precept for the state'.[23] As it stands, this statement is too loose, and obscures, rather than clarifies, the difficulties socialists encountered in coming to grips with the inter-war problem of deficient demand. The argument for *laissez-faire* was that it tended to promote the most effective and economical *production* of wealth. This argument socialists accepted. When historians talk of the repudiation of *laissez-faire* at the end of the nineteenth century they have in mind the growing feeling that the state should do something to alleviate poverty and *redistribute* wealth. But as Henry Sidgwick pointed out, *laissez-faire* never aimed at showing 'that the wealth so produced tends to be distributed among the different classes that have co-operated in producing it in strict accordance with their respective deserts'.[24] Indeed, as Donald Winch argues, 'on questions involving the distribution of income and wealth, the main tradition of British economic thought has always been more consistently radical than on questions that concern . . . the production of wealth'.[25] Thus socialists were perfectly accurate in claiming that their doctrines were firmly grounded in the classical tradition, that there was no conflict between socialism and economic science. The point to remember is that the classical tradition included Say's Law of Markets, which most socialists accepted.

119

The primary function of state action in socialist thought was gradually to distribute a given (and increasing) output in 'accordance with desert' and in the meantime to secure for the poor, the temporarily unemployed, the aged and the sick, such necessaries and amenities as they could not purchase in the market. Such assistance could be – and was – justified on the orthodox ground that 'the poverty and depression of any industrial class is liable to render its members less productive for want of physical vigour . . .'[26] One recalls Sidney Webb's question: 'How can we build up an effective commonwealth – how, even, can we get an efficient army – out of the stunted, anaemic, demoralized denizens of the slum tenements of our great cities?'. In addition, socialists developed two subsidiary arguments for state intervention. Classical theory had always recognized as legitimate government expenditure on certain public utilities which would not be sufficiently profitable to attract private capital, or which it was uneconomic to run on competitive principles. State-aided public works in the 1920s were usually justified in this way; and the Labour Government of 1929 used this 'exception' to *laissez-faire* to expand them. Secondly classical economy admitted the right of the state to break up monopolies* and, more arguably, to impose 'uniformity of action or abstinence' on a whole class of producers where that was required for the most economic production – Sidgwick gives as an example the fishing industry where 'it is clearly in the general interest that the fish should not be caught at certain times, or in certain places, or with certain instruments; because the increase of actual supply obtained by such captures is much overbalanced by the detriment it causes to prospective supply.'[27] Such arguments were much used in the inter-war years to justify legislative sanction for schemes of industrial reorganization. Socialists extended them by arguing that rationalization required nationalization.

These subsidiary forms of state intervention were clearly applicable to inter-war conditions. Explicitly redistributionist intervention was much less so. But neither kind amounted to an attack on the central principles of *laissez-faire*. As long as the Labour Party accepted Say's Law it was tied to the orthodox explanations of post-war unemployment, and the orthodox remedies. And the reason it accepted Say's Law

---

* The socialist case against landlords and capitalists was an application of the classical argument against monopoly.

was not just because, like everyone else, it had grown up with it, but because it was functional to its strategy of gradual social progress. Here then we have an important explanation of why the party of 'state responsibility' espoused *laissez-faire* solutions to inter-war economic problems. The orthodox view, as is well known, was that mass unemployment was caused by the dislocation of markets arising from the war. British wage-costs had got too high; international channels of trade were clogged by political, financial and monetary instability. The centre-piece of the recovery programme was the restoration of the gold standard. For Britain such a step, according to the Chamberlain–Bradbury Committee which examined the whole question in 1924, would bring about an automatic readjustment in costs; internationally, by bringing stability to the exchanges, it would revive confidence in trading and lending and thus make possible tariff reductions. Nothing short of the pre-war parity would achieve both objectives. Unemployment would thus disappear through an initial, moderate readjustment of British costs to world conditions made stable by British initiative.

It is true that the Labour Party's commitment to this version of the 'theory of liquids' was greatly modified by its instinctive resistance to the economists' demand for downward wage flexibility. But domestic rigidities made it even more dedicated in its search for international action: the theory of liquids was transferred abroad. The characteristic note the Labour Party contributed to inter-war economic debates was its faith in international solutions to domestic economic problems. That is why it supported the free-trade/bankers' internationalism of the export industries and the City of London. World growth, secured through the efficient working of markets, remained the indispensable foundation for the world socialist commonwealth which would 'complete' liberalism internationally.

To argue that the Labour Party was captive to a certain vision of economic progress does not sufficiently explain why it remained attached to it when reality had so evidently taken a different turn – had started to do so, in fact, even before the First World War. To explain this we must remember that *laissez-faire* was not just an economic doctrine, but had a deep political, moral and psychological significance. Elie Halévy, puzzling over the fiasco of 1931, concluded that the socialist intellectual's commitment to a strong state had been negatived by the Labour Party's actual roots in municipal, trade union and parliamentary politics:

121

Who are the leaders of the Labour Party in England? Not intellectuals, but trade unionists – a very sympathetic body of men, hard-working, rather timid, very conservative, whose training before they came into Parliament was that of nego-tiators ... with the captains of industry, to extract from them better conditions of work for their clientele ... Their idea was mainly that of a limited monarchy, to control and limit the captains of industry ... They are born parliamentarians. Now, if you go to the root idea of Parliament, the system is not one which wants to make the state strong, but one which wants to keep it weak for the sake of liberty. That is the tragedy. The Labour leaders are men whose doctrine requires them to make the state stronger, and whose good British instinct is to make the state as weak as possible.[28]

My quarrel with this is that, as I have argued, socialist doctrine prior to 1931 did not require a strong state in the Keynesian sense. Only permanent mass unemployment did – an aspect of reality which had not gone into the shaping of the Labour Party. Nevertheless, Halévy is right to draw attention to the immense psychological barrier faced by a trade union party in making the transition to a party of government; right also, to emphasize the similarity between the trade union attitude to the captains of industry and the historic parliamentary attitude to the executive. The trade unions may be called instinctive Keynesians in that they were organized to resist the wage reductions called for by econom-ists and businessmen.* This does not mean that they were ready to accept state Keynesianism, particularly as in the inter-war years this meant great national schemes of public works of the Lloyd George type. Unions feared that workers employed by the state on big national schemes would be used as black-leg labour to depress wages, particularly in the construction industries. As deeply committed as the employers to the languishing industries in which their members worked, they opposed plans which implied providing work outside normal occupations. They relied on industrial reorganization, carried out by the state, to solve the competitive problems of the basic industries. Pending this, they were

---

* This is a neat chicken and egg problem. The classical economist would have argued that it was trade unions which prevented Say's Law from working, and *thereby* made Keynesianism necessary.

prepared to take their chances in the market, relying on superior organization to bring them increasing rewards in good times, and the state to finance unemployment relief out of general taxation in bad times. Collective *laissez-faire* in prosperity and a state dole in adversity not unfairly sums up the union attitude in the 1920s.

There is ample evidence from the 1929–31 period that national public works schemes were rejected not just on grounds of economic theory (the Treasury View) but on the ground that they entailed an illegitimate extension of state power. The Treasury argued that Lloyd George's plan of 1929 implied 'dictatorship'.[29] The Treasury report on the Mosley Memorandum, after enumerating the various difficulties in getting works schemes started, continued, 'If such delays are to be obviated not only the rights of Local Authorities and the whole machinery of local government will have to be overridden, but a very drastic policy would be necessary in dealing with the rights of private individuals.'[30] That this was not the Treasury's view alone is made clear by Mosley's discussion with Ministers just before his resignation:

> 19 May 1930
>
> Mosley answered that money could not be spent if detailed inquiry had to precede the spending. A Napoleon could spend 200 million pounds in three years . . . This, said J. H. T[homas] would bring local government to a standstill.

> 20 May 1930
>
> [Mosley] The alternative was to override municipalities and officials. That, replied J. H. T., meant breaking up local government. Mosley said he could build a machine for a vast programme. Lansbury and Johnston wanted something less revolutionary. Mosley would supersede Departments and officials and put things on a war footing. 'It is a revolution in administrative procedure. I perhaps misunderstood you, when I came into the Labour Party. All these thousands who trusted us should be given a chance of saying what they prefer.'[31]

But what did they prefer? One should not forget the moral context of these debates on unemployment. The psychological core of Keynesianism was the savage attack on thrift, the rejection of that asceticism which sacrifices the present for the future. This is what links the 'new notions of what is economically sound' to the wider revolt against Victorian morality – in sex, aesthetics, philosophy. For the Labour Party, by contrast, the future was to be built on the virtues of the past. In Snowden's words 'moral development must proceed parallel with economic change'.[32] Socialists were always sensitive to their opponents' charge that their higher morality was based on greed, envy and sloth. Hence, Labour leaders, who themselves largely sprang from the virtuous working, or middle, classes, laid great emphasis on the Victorian virtues – work, thrift, self-reliance – which they saw as the only possible psychological foundation for the higher type of man which Socialist faith and subsequently practice would bring into existence. Efforts to win the Labour Party over to a 'reflationary' economic policy were greatly hampered by the puritanism of so many of its leaders. For Snowden deflation rewarded thrift and foresight; inflation penalized it. If virtue went unrewarded and vice unpunished what incentive would remain for people to behave virtuously? Arguments like these united *rentiers* and moralistic socialists in an unholy alliance against spendthrifts.

VI

How far were these attitudes modified by the world depression, the disasters of 1931, and the expulsion of the old guard? How 'Keynesian', in other words, would Labour's policy have been had it taken office in 1935? Would there have been a 'New Deal'? The answers must necessarily be hypothetical, but some indication can be gathered from the various policy statements and party debates of the 1930s. For both major parties, the world depression shattered the optimistic assumptions which had hitherto governed policy-making. The Conservatives reverted to economic nationalism and imperial preference. On the Labour side, the inevitability of gradualness was repudiated by its leading spokesmen, the Webbs. This pessimistic reappraisal produced a much more sympathetic response than before to the croakings of Keynes-Cassandra. But it also made Marxism for the first time a major explicit force in the Labour Party. These two tendencies now divided the allegiance of the party's progressive elements. They produced different analyses of the causes of unemployment, and led to very different conclusions on the plane of struggle and policy. Here we may simply make a general point. For all socialists, the world depression proved not just the moral desirability, but the absolute necessity, for socialism. Thus, while the Keynesian approach gained new adherents, the view that it was merely a palliative was correspondingly strengthened. In the 1920s, it was felt, Keynesianism was no substitute for export recovery. In the 1930s, it was no substitute for socialism. How far it benefited from this shift in emphasis within the Labour Party is not clear.

The Keynesian influence is clearly apparent in the party's new policy statements. The following passage from the NEC document *Socialism and the Condition of the People* (1933) closely follows the argument of Keynes's *Treatise on Money*:

> The national income equals the national expenditure on consumption, plus national savings.
>
> These savings ought to be fully employed in investment . . . This does not happen with any regularity under private capitalism. Because money is forthcoming for investment, not in response to social needs, but only as the expression of the investor's desire to make private profit as quickly and as largely as possible, there is no correspondence between either the amount or the direction of investment, on the one hand, and the benefit to the community on the other.
>
> When savings are not absorbed by the expenditure on capital goods, including additions to stocks, there is less income to spend on their production, and there is a fall in prices and a decline in employment. When the fall in prices occurs, the employer has to meet losses on his stock or the goods that are in process of being produced, and a proportion of the national savings is required to meet these losses. Once this process is started it gets worse and worse. The more savings are diverted into the mere financing of losses the less are available for fresh investment; the less money available for investment the less expenditure there is on capital goods, and the greater is the decline in prices and employment. Then further money has to be diverted for the meeting of still further losses, and so on. This has been the course of events in the present 'slump'.
>
> . . . This alternation of 'boom' and 'slump', 'slump' and 'boom', is the normal and inevitable history of capitalist finance.
>
> The object of the national control of investment is to make investment equal to savings, and to divert investment into socially useful channels.

To reverse the present 'slump' tendency there must be an immediate increase both in consumption and in the expenditure on socially needed capital goods. When there is under-investment on the part of private enterprise, as there is now, the State and Municipal Authorities must fill the gap.

In the NEC's statement, *For Socialism and Peace* (1934), the multiplier justification for public works is clearly stated:

It should not be forgotten that new expenditure on development, not only creates employment, directly and indirectly, in respect of the particular schemes of work put in hand, but creates further employment in an ever widening circle, through the payment of wages to those who are now unemployed, and who, through their increased purchasing power, are enabled to buy additional goods and services.

The Labour Party would set up a National Investment Board,

whose duty it will be to mobilise our financial resources, to guide them into the right channels, and to advise the Government on a financial plan for the full employment of our people. Large schemes of Public Development, including Housing, Electrification, Transport, and the extraction of Oil from Coal will be carried out.[33]

Both analysis and policy proposal point to a Keynesian spending programme. But there are two key omissions which at any rate raise considerable doubt as to whether it would have been carried out on anything like the required scale. The amount of money to be spent, even the approximate sum, is never specified. Nor was it clearly suggested where it would come from. Party statements talked of 'mobilising the national savings' as though there existed an unused surplus of savings, whereas Keynes's point was that an excessive desire to save leads to a destruction of savings through a fall in incomes, making realized savings equal to realized investment. Keynes understood by 1933 that the main way to increase spending was to unbalance the budget. He suggested an additional annual expenditure of £100 million, but made it clear that the amount must be set by the dimension of unemployment at any given time.[34] Perhaps the Labour Party in office would have done this, but there is no specific indication that it would.* Reducing taxation – the simplest way of unbalancing the budget – would have been ideologically difficult. The alternative of increasing spending without raising new taxation was apparently ruled out by the party's insistence on a balanced budget.[35] Of course, these were early days of the new theory, and the Labour Party in power, like Roosevelt, might have thrown its continuing financial orthodoxy to the winds. But in the absence of any clear indication of its willingness to do so, one can only say, as the Liberals did of its 1929 programme, that 'the mere mention in abstract and general terms of one or more forms of work . . . does not constitute a policy'.[36]

Doubts about how far it would have been willing to experiment in a Keynesian direction are reinforced by the existence of a much more traditional 'socialist' explanation of unemployment and depression, which now came to the forefront for the first time, and which certainly exceeded in popularity the newfangled Keynesian one. This was the view that rising unemployment was the inevitable consequence under capitalism of substituting machines for men in the production of goods. Ricardo had raised the possibility that, under certain conditions, the installation of new machinery might render redundant a proportion of the workforce previously employed. On this 'slender foundation', as Schumpeter put it, Marx bases his whole theory of the increasing 'reserve army' of the unemployed. The resulting failure of consumption to rise (since the function of the reserve army, directly and indirectly, is to depress wages), precipitates the familiar marxist 'crises of overproduction'. In this way, the marxist theory of capitalist crisis links up with the more popular and readily understandable 'underconsumptionist' theories, and the whole tradition of instinctive working-class resistance to technical progress. G. D. H. Cole argued in 1930 that capitalist rationalization, in the absence of constantly expanding foreign markets, 'is driven back upon the home market; and there it defeats itself and creates around it a desolation of unemployment and human decay.' This is because the working class 'deprived of its independent source of income ceases to be effective in

---

* A hint of the scale on which the Labour Party might have been prepared to spend money on unemployment is given by Bevin's proposal in 1935 that the Commissioners appointed by the Government for the Depressed Areas should be given £20 million to 'clean them up'. But this, it seems, was to be the total, not annual, amount, and he doesn't say where it is to come from (Trade Union Congress Report, 1935, p. 296).

the market as buyer, and thus defeats the aim of the reduction in costs which has been achieved.'*

Nothing in this analysis is incompatible *per se* with a Keynesian approach. Indeed it pointed to Keynesian spending policies to reabsorb the unemployed created by rationalization. However, this type of reformism had ceased to be fashionable. Under the influence of a pessimistic determinism, as irrational as the previous optimistic one had been, socialists now argued that unemployment was bound to increase under capitalism, perhaps under any economic system. Only socialism could cope with its consequences. A combination of public ownership and socialist planning was required to translate capitalist unemployment 'into new leisure for the people by shortening the working life, by shortening the working week, by shortening the working day'.[37] By raising the school leaving age and lowering the pension age, as well as reducing the hours worked, it would be possible to 'concentrate the labour power of the nation in the most active and vigorous years of life'.[38] For trade unions, reduction in the supply of labour was viewed chiefly as a means of increasing its price. (This mirrored employers' attitudes to the supply of goods.) In the 1920s they had relied upon state-subsidized unemployment to keep up the wages of those in work. By the 1930s they were more ready than they had been to see the dole converted into a permanent system of pensions and family allowances; and more convinced that their programme of raising wages and shortening working hours for those in employment required the abolition of the interest and rent due to the capitalist class.

The world depression and the political experience of 1929–31 gave Keynesianism its first firm foothold in the Labour Party. It also gave the socialist case a new urgency, and furnished additional arguments for it. How far would the Labour Party in power have been prepared to *act* on its new, or revised, insights, whether Keynesian or socialist? There are two dimensions to this problem, the external and the domestic. As I have

---

* See also Cole's further statement that rationalization 'might succeed in lowering substantially the cost of producing each unit of the national output: but it would only find itself unable to make use of the great new productive power of which it had become the master. For the problem of production cannot be solved unless the problem of distribution is solved with it; and the lowering of the unit cost of production, unaccompanied by a pouring of fresh purchasing power into the pockets of the consumers, will only mean a more determined policy of restricting output and a widening circle of unemployment.' Both passages are from Cole's *The Next Ten Years* (pp. 109, 116), quoted in T. E. Gregory, 'Rationalization and Technological Unemployment', *Economic Journal* (December 1930).

argued, the fact of British dependence on world markets, and still more importantly, the internationalist ideology growing out of it, had made it virtually impossible for British statesmen to conceive of a national solution to the unemployment problem, i.e., one that did not in some sense imply either an adjustment of the British economy to prevailing world conditions, or an attempt to modify world conditions to suit the demands of the British economy. In the 1920s, the British attempted a bit of both, without much success. Would a Labour Government in the 1930s have been prepared to pursue a policy of national capitalism – or national socialism? The question may be put more concretely: if foreign bankers had objected to a policy of deficit finance, would the Government have jettisoned the policy, or gone ahead regardless? This was not a purely hypothetical dilemma in the 1930s. Roosevelt had to confront it immediately on taking office. His answer was to torpedo the World Economic Conference of 1933 by devaluing the dollar. When Keynes wrote that 'Mr Roosevelt is magnificently right' he was defending not so much the specific policy as an attitude of mind which said: look after the domestic economy and the world economy will look after itself.

Was such a cavalier attitude possible for Britain in the 1930s? In its reply to the Mosley Memorandum, the Treasury had written: 'It is quite absurd to compare the conditions prevailing in the United States – a self-supporting country, with vast internal resources and a high protective tariff – with the competitive conditions under which the population of these islands must live and work if the standard of living to which we are accustomed is not to be radically altered.'[39] But as Sir Leo Chiozza Money pointed out to the Labour Party Conference of 1932, the task of building socialism in one country was not so difficult as imagined, since only one worker in seven now produced for export.* In his contributions to the *New Statesman* of 8 and 15 July 1933, entitled 'National Self-Sufficiency', Keynes attacked the theoretical basis of interdependence, arguing that every reasonably-sized country could produce for itself most of the things it needed; the small additional cost was not enough to outweigh 'the other advantages of gradually bringing the producer and consumer within the ambit of the same national,

---

* The British trend towards self-sufficiency was the inevitable result of the failure of exports. By 1938, with the home market expanding far faster than the export market, exports accounted for 11 per cent of the national income, and imports for 18 per cent, compared with 28 per cent and 31 per cent respectively in 1913. (See D. H. Aldcroft, *The Interwar Economy: Britain 1919–1939* (1970), p. 256.)

economic and financial organization'. (He went so far as to claim that 'economic entanglement between nations' was more likely to produce war than peace.) As Sir Roy Harrod says, Keynes had come to regard a 'change in mental atmosphere' as a necessary condition for the 'bold experiment in achieving full employment by the methods that he advocated'.[41]

In the Labour Party, Arthur Henderson and George Lansbury represented the traditional approach. In a major policy-statement of 25 September 1931, Henderson summed up Labour's international proposals in the phrase 'more buying and more lending'. Great efforts should be made to 'restore the normal flow of credits from the lending to the borrowing powers, to reestablish the normal volume of international purchases of goods . . .' (Henderson is still working with the nineteenth-century concept of normalcy.) Britain should 'give a lead' in tariff reductions. Only a decisive lead by Britain, 'the greatest power in the world . . . the centre of the financial system . . . pre-eminent in every quality that makes a nation strong' could avert the 'breakdown of civilization'.[42] In 1932, George Lansbury restated the traditional socialist view: 'We cannot get forward with Socialism without everybody else coming with us.'[43] With the failure of the World Economic Conference of 1933, this traditional perspective gave way to a more selective one. The failure of the Conference had proved conclusively that 'full and permanent co-operation is impossible within a system of International Capitalism'. The Labour Party therefore pledged itself 'from the outset to co-operate as closely as possible with Russia and other Socialist Governments in order to form a nucleus for International Socialist co-operation'.[44] However, the basic premise of interdependence was not challenged:

> In modern times, the world has become a single economic unit . . . The capitalist system is now cosmopolitan; its activities transcend political frontiers. In these circumstances, there can be no return to self-centred economic nationalism. The time is ripe for a great Socialist advance in the economic reorganisation of the world. Just as National Planning is a vital need to-day for every State, so on a larger scale, International Planning is necessary for the world . . . The Labour Party in its developing policy for the restoration of world trade, and the inauguration of a new era of prosperity, will work unceasingly for the

establishment of effective international economic machinery, etc, etc . . .[45]

How far any of this displayed a 'new mental atmosphere' is for the reader to judge.

Would a Labour Government have been prepared to confront boldly the domestic obstacles to a radical policy – to overcome refractory interests, and various forms of obstruction and delay; to deal with a 'crisis of confidence'? Did it, in other words, still accept the traditions of normal peacetime government, based on marginal interventions and incremental changes, or had it come to accept the idea of the executive State? There is some evidence that Keynes believed that his policies would never be tried out under normal peacetime conditions. In 1936 he wrote a notably warm preface to the German edition of the *General Theory*; and by 1939 he was doubting whether it was politically possible 'for a capitalistic democracy to organise expenditure necessary to make the grand experiment to prove my case except in war conditions'.[46]

Within the Labour Party, the orthodox parliamentarians confronted the left-wing radicals led by Sir Stafford Cripps. At the 1932 Conference, Cripps introduced an amendment to the NEC Report, *Socialism and the Condition of the People*, demanding (i) the immediate abolition of the House of Lords, (ii) the passing of an Emergency Powers Bill giving the government power to act by Orders in Council and (iii) the revision of parliamentary procedure to ensure the rapid passage of other legislation. The NEC agreed with Cripps that parliamentary procedures were 'devised to suit the purposes of the negative State in the nineteenth century, and are definitely unsuited to the needs of the positive State in the twentieth'. However, its actual proposals, accepted by Conference, were limited to dealing with the House of Lords only if it proved obstructive, using emergency powers only in emergency situations, and making greater use of the guillotine to speed up debate. Cripps claimed the victory, but it is clear he had been defeated on his major proposals.[47] A Labour Government would follow traditional procedures; abnormal methods would be used only in abnormal circumstances. The view that a situation of continuing mass unemployment was itself abnormal, requiring a 'revolution in administrative procedure' analogous to wartime (compare Roosevelt's Inaugural: 'In the event that Congress shall fail ... I shall ask Congress for the one remaining instrument to meet the crisis – broad executive power to wage war against the enemy, as great as the power that would be given to me if we were in fact invaded by a foreign foe') had evidently made little progress. A major obstacle to acceptance of Cripps's strategy was the widespread Labour hostility to 'dictatorship from either Right or Left'. Cripps's argument that his proposals were designed to forestall fascism failed to convince the trade union leaders. In fact, the power to legislate by Orders in Council was eventually granted by Parliament to the Government in 1939, not to fight the war against unemployment, but the war against Germany.

We can now attempt a brief answer to two questions. How far had Keynesian priorities replaced socialist ones in the 1930s? Would a Labour Government in fact have been willing to act in face of powerful foreign and domestic opposition? On the first point, although Keynesian thinking had made some headway, socialist priorities had been rendered more insistent by the capitalist collapse. In the 1930s, socialists of all persuasions were united on one point: that socialism was the only cure for unemployment. The nagging suspicion that Keynesianism might be quite an effective rival cure only strengthened the resolve not to let it cut across the political struggle for socialism.[48] At best it could play a supplementary role. Keynes, for his part, regarded schemes for nationalizing the joint-stock banks and major industries as crashingly irrelevant to the actual needs of the hour. On the second point, I have found little evidence that the Labour Party was psychologically or morally ready to become an effective engine of peacetime government, for the achievement either of Keynesianism or socialism. My own view is that had it come to power in the 1930s, there would have been a little Keynesianism and a little socialism, which would both have had a little effect on the unemployment figures; but that the bulk of unemployment would have been mopped up, as it eventually was in any case, by rearmament and war.

VII

My argument has been that the resistance to Keynesian ideas was rooted in the British political culture. This has been considered (i) as a set of traditional beliefs and values, (ii) as a particular vision of social progress based on those values and (iii) as a system for transmitting and perpetuating beliefs and values. The Labour Party was part of the British political culture. It shared its pride in the British achievement, most of its operating assumptions, and with the decline of the Liberal Party came to embody many of its hopes for a better future. Its distinctive and separate commitment was to the eventual elimination of the capitalist class. Up to 1931 it resisted what Keynes called the 'new notions of what is economically sound' chiefly in the name of the traditional and social reforming values it shared with the other parties. After 1931, although Keynesian ideas made progress in the Labour as in the other parties, it subordinated them to a socialist strategy based on a non-Keynesian analysis of unemployment. A certain break with gradualism in the realm of ideas, however, was not accompanied by a comparable break in the traditional political strategy, leading to the conclusion that had Labour come to power in the 1930s there is unlikely to have been a New Deal of the Roosevelt, or even the Swedish, type.

The decisive revelation for the Labour Party of the possibility of a new economic order based on a Keynesian consensus came not in 1931, but between 1939 and 1945. The war, as Keynes had foreseen, provided a fertile laboratory for new economic experiments which it would have been difficult to organize in peace. The Labour Party was able to accept the Second World War as it had not been able to accept the First World War; and consequently accept wartime achievement as the basis of peacetime construction rather than as an aberration from the 'norm'. Full partnership in government under extraordinary circumstances did more than anything else to turn the Labour Party into a 'party of government'. Finally, full employment was the irresistible political demand arising from the war, to which all else had to be subordinated. The mental and administrative leap from gold standard to full employment standard having been accomplished in war, and through war, the Labour Party was free to take up again the unfinished matter left over from the nineteenth century: how to moralize success? Now the Keynesian consensus in turn is breaking down and we have to see how the Labour Party will confront the reappearance of its old dilemma: the lack of any success left to moralize.

NOTES

1   J. M. Keynes, 'The Dilemma of Modern Socialism', *Political Quarterly*, April 1932.
2   A. L. Rowse, 'Mr Keynes on Socialism: A Reply', ibid., July 1932.
3   *Hansard*, vol. 256, cols. 72–82.

4   Quoted in Edmund Whittaker, *A History of Economic Ideas*, (1963) p. 154.

5   R. B. McCallum, *The Liberal Party from Earl Grey to Asquith*, (1963) p. 50.

6   G. B. Shaw, 'In Praise of Guy Fawkes' (1933), *Bernard Shaw, Platform and Pulpit*, ed. Dan H. Laurence, (1962), p. 240.

7   Susan Strange, *Sterling and British Policy*, (1971), p. 14.

8   P. J. Grigg, *Prejudice and Judgment*, (1948), p. 7.

9   PRO: T. 175/26.

10   N. G. Annan, 'The Intellectual Aristocracy', *Studies in Social History*, ed. J. H. Plumb, (1955), p. 285.

11   Donald Schon, *Beyond the Stable State*, (1971), p. 124.

12   Introduction to John Gorman's *Banner Bright*, (1973), p. 8.

13   J. M. Keynes, *Essays in Persuasion*, (1931), p. 325.

14   L. T. Hobhouse, *Liberalism*, (1964), p. 114.

15   Arthur Marwick, 'The Impact of the First World War on British Society', *Journal of Contemporary History*, January 1968.

16   J. R. MacDonald, *Socialism and Society*, (1905), pp. 23, 37. 'History is a progression of social stages . . . today we are in the economic stage. Yesterday we were in the political stage. Tomorrow we shall be in the moral stage.'

17   This point is well made by P. F. Clarke, 'The Progressive Movement in England', *Tr. Royal Hist. Soc.*, 5th ser., vol. 24, pp. 163–4.

18   Ibid., p. 164.

19   G. B. Shaw, 'The Transition to Social Democracy', *Essays in the Economics of Socialism and Capitalism*, ed. R. L. Smyth, pp. 44, 48.

20   H. Sidgwick, 'Economic Socialism', ibid., p. 35.

21   Donald Winch, *Economics and Policy*, p. 45 and ch. 2 generally.

22   W. H. B. Court, *British Economic History 1870–1914, Commentary and Documents*, p. 316.

23   Clarke, 'The Progressive Movement in England', p. 162.

24   Sidgwick, 'Economic Socialism', p. 26.

25   Winch, *Economics and Policy*, p. 32.

26   Sidgwick, 'Economic Socialism', p. 27.

27   Ibid., p. 30.

28   Elie Halévy, *Era of Tyrannies*, p. 258.

29   *Memoranda on Certain Proposals Relating to Unemployment* (1929), p. 23.

30   PRO: CAB 24/209.

31   Thomas Jones, *Whitehall Diary*, vol. 2, ed. K. Middlemas, (1969), pp. 258–9.

32   P. Snowden, *Autobiography*, vol. 2, p. 541.

33   *Labour's Immediate Programme* (1937). The Labour Party's *Pamphlets and Leaflets* are to be found in bound annual volumes in the Party's library, Transport House.

34   J. M. Keynes, *The Means to Prosperity* (March 1933), esp. pp. 15–16, 35–6.

35   My reference for this is the pamphlet *Socialism and 'Social Credit'* (1935)

by E. F. N. Durbin, Hugh Gaitskell and W. R. Hiskett. Discussing the various ways in which a Government might increase spending, the authors argue that it could 'unbalance the Budget on current account by reducing taxation and filling the gap with borrowings from the banks'. They continue: 'This method, however, in so far as it involves an unbalanced Budget, is not in accord with the Labour Party's official policy' (p. 31).

36 *Liberal Magazine*, April 1929.
37 Arthur Greenwood, *Unemployment and the Distressed Areas* (1935). Greenwood was a champion of this view, but far from being the only one. In *Planning or Chaos* (1938) Fred Henderson argued 'there is no choice for us concerning the leisure itself in one form or the other'.
38 *Socialism and the Condition of the People* (1933).
39 PRO: T.175/26.
40 Labour Party Annual Report, 1932, p. 201.
41 Sir Roy Harrod, *Life of John Maynard Keynes*, p. 446.
42 A. H. Henderson, *Labour and the Crisis*, reprint of speech at Burnley, 25 September 1931.
43 Labour Party Annual Report, 1932, p. 199.
44 Ibid., 1933, p. 166.
45 *Socialism and the Condition of the People* (1933), p. 7.
46 Winch, *Economics and Policy*, p. 266.
47 See *For Socialism and Peace* (1934), p. 27; Labour Party Annual Report, 1933, p. 159; also the Appendix to *Socialism and the Condition of the People* reproduced in Labour Party Annual Report, 1934, pp. 261–3. In this the Labour Party committed itself also to a greater use of delegated legislation.
48 The following from the 1939 Conference is characteristic: 'but we, in the Labour Movement, know that so long as there is capitalism so long will there be unemployment . . . we must not deceive the unemployed of this country by telling them there is any permanent solution for unemployment under capitalism' (Labour Party Annual Report, 1939, pp. 268–9).

CHAPTER NINETEEN

'*Our Age*'

Noel Annan, *Our Age: Portrait of a Generation*
[Weidenfeld & Nicolson, 1990]

LORD ANNAN has written a warm-hearted, but cool-headed, portrait of the generation which got its come-uppance from Mrs Thatcher – 'Our Age' he calls it. Whom is he writing about? Not all those as old as

Annan, but the 'intellectual aristocracy' – a term he first invented to describe a network of nineteenth-century families who moulded the high culture of Victorian England. In the twentieth-century version the family connections are looser, but other things remain familiar. Our Age went to university between 1919 and 1950, usually to Oxford, Cambridge or the LSE: many of them stayed there. Nearly all of them were men, mostly from the top public schools. They formed the *mentalités* of their time, and remained arbiters of fashion in thought, politics and the arts, until challenged in their turn by a new generation.

How useful is generational history? People at all times, Annan writes, are fascinated by 'the sense of belonging to a particular peer group who share common assumptions about their own society, and who are convinced they are different from their fathers'. Coming up to King's College, Cambridge, in 1935, Annan is located at mid-point in Our Age. His portrait of it is wide-ranging, erudite, stylish, somewhat discursive. He is too addicted to sporting metaphors, and there is the slight suggestion of the prurient schoolmaster, perhaps a legacy of his days at Stowe under Roxburgh. Yet he too has problems with the categories. He cannot dispense with a whole lot of Victorian and Edwardian foster-parents, who were not of his generation, but who taught it how, and often what, to think and feel: Russell, Moore, Wittgenstein, Strachey, Roger Fry, Virginia Woolf, Eliot, Pound, Lawrence, Joyce; Shaw, Keynes, Wells, Tawney, the Webbs; Diaghilev, Stravinsky and others. As he remarks, 'we played variations on our predecessors' themes'. And with 'deviants' from Our Age as formidable as Waugh, Leavis, and Oakeshott – he should surely have added Orwell – one senses a certain shrinkage of explanatory power.

There is also the problem of cohorts. Each decade had a different character. The 1920s were gay, the 1930s political, the 1940s austere. Do assumptions stay common through such shifts in mood? And if they do, isn't this less a matter of generations than of epochs? Finally, there is the Two Cultures problem raised by C. P. Snow. Of course scientists do help mould the *mentalité* of an age: the splitting of the atom in the Cavendish Laboratory in the 1920s is the classic example. This happened at the time Annan is writing about, but surely not *because* of the time. Generational history is more useful explaining changes in attitudes to art, literature, morals, manners, and perhaps politics than changes in scientific theory, even though scientists may have generational attitudes outside their scientific work. And it is not equally useful at all times. It seems that there has to be a subversive avant-garde in place from the previous generation. And there have to be events capable of generalizing the significance of its ideas.

The First World War shattered Our Age's faith in the public school ideal of the gentleman: too decent, manly, loyal, unimaginative and brainless to avoid the slaughter of the First World War, prepare for the Second, or govern properly in between. Modernism, collectivism and pacifism were the new gods of the alienated public schoolboy. I wish Annan had explored the connections between the first two. 'The modernists believed art should portray society as disintegrating and decomposing. If society is dehumanised, why depict people as recognizable human beings? They should squint out of paintings like the deformities they had become ...' Does not the totalitarian temptation spring from such a dehumanized view of individuals? And is it surprising that totalitarian regimes ruthlessly suppress modernism and replace it by an equally dehumanized view of the worker as a piece of heroic machinery?

To his trinity, Annan adds 'the cult of homosexuality', exemplified by the Oxford Wits in the 1920s and the Cambridge Spies in the 1930s. (Maurice Bowra, one of the Wits, dubbed them respectively the Immoral Front and the Homintern.) It is in this area of morals and manners that one seems to be both at the heart of Our Age, and of Annan's book. Whether or not they were gay – in the wide or narrow sense – the Edwardians were above all else hard-working. They still had a puritan sense of Duty – to themselves and to the world. The achievements of Bloomsbury, patchy though they were, came from a marriage of Victorian habits and post-Victorian sensibility. Our Age – at least in the 1920s – discarded the habits. They wanted above all to be amused and be amusing; to have a good time. This frivolity was the real enemy of promise. It helps explain why so many of the brilliant trend-setters of the 1920s achieved so little by comparison with the Edwardians. Annan's devastating verdict on Cyril Connolly – 'he lived on unearned pleasure' – will do for many of them. Evelyn Waugh, the one indisputable literary genius produced by the 1920s, needed St Augustine to keep him sane – and sober.

After visiting Soviet Russia in 1925, Keynes wrote: 'It is hard for an educated, decent, intelligent son of western Europe to find his ideals here, unless he has first suffered some strange and horrid process of conversion which has changed all his values.' The horrid process started with the young scientists at Cambridge in the late 1920s: their totalitarian fantasies still have the power to make one shudder. The cohort of the 1930s rushed towards Marxism and Communism, the two terms then being almost interchangeable: Brian Simon claimed that at the time of the Spanish Civil War, one thousand out of eight thousand Cambridge students were Party members. Political commitment went hand in hand with a revived puritanism. Communism, Annan rightly says, did not capture Our Age; but many of it were bound to the Communists by personal friendship and common causes, and for years after formed a protective belt which enabled the Soviet agents among them to go undetected.

Annan, who was not himself bitten by the bug, dutifully rakes over the old historical embers, without probing deeply into the causes of this mass conversion. Yet in his seminal essay on 'The Intellectual Aristocracy' he had provided a framework for understanding it. The Victorian world of religion and learning was both socially detached from business, and morally hostile to it. It could not square its conceptions of the good life with absorption in money-making. This hostility to the *spirit* of capitalism was central to the credo of the Edwardian avant-garde. The simultaneous breakdown of religious belief and the machinery of wealth-creation between the wars destroyed the delicate equipoise between the two. For a brief period, communism could combine the appeal of a religion, an explanation of breakdown, and a 'scientific' technique of social progress – a heady mixture for intellectuals without faith, hope – or power.

In the 1940s faith in communism rapidly waned, but not faith in social science. The Second World War, and the Labour Government which it produced, brought the technicians to power, integrating the last cohort of Our Age, and many of their aberrant predecessors, into the mainstream. Moderately collectivist, moderately hedonistic, moderately permissive; drawing their inspiration from Keynes, Beveridge and Tawney rather than Marx, they were the academics, politicians, civil servants, planners, and architects who helped build the social democratic Britain which started to be dismantled in the 1980s. What went wrong? Annan has an answer. Our Age had no sticking point. It could not hold any line. It could not fight against the distorted images of itself presented by the middle-class radicals of the 1960s, or against the sectional greed of the trade unions. It ended in a spirit of defeat, and puzzlement.

There is surely more to be said. Annan's generation saw itself as a clerisy; it ended up more like a *nomenclatura*. Once gurus become experts they lose their magic for the young, especially when the magic fails to deliver the goods. That's why I think the children of the 1980s probably do mark the start of a new generation in Annan's sense. Modernism and collectivism, the improbable bequests of Victorian high culture, have run their course. On balance, Our Age had a pretty good innings; and in Annan it has found a worthy chronicler.

CHAPTER TWENTY

Oxford in the 1920s

Christopher Hollis, *Oxford in the Twenties*
[Heinemann, 1976]

CHRISTOPHER HOLLIS is an interesting man. He started off conventionally enough: clerical family, Eton, Balliol, President of the Oxford Union. Then his life took an unusual turn. In 1923 he became a Roman Catholic. Catholicism took him beyond the shallow liberalism of his Oxford friends. He wrote a couple of unorthodox, Chestertonian, books on money, one of which earned him the friendship of Ezra Pound. *Death of a Gentleman* was an unusual evocation of rural England between the wars. He was a Conservative MP for ten years after the war, and has written extensively on Catholic subjects. One would like to know him better, but his writing tends to be impersonal and unvivid.

This is not a particularly good recommendation for a book about people. Mr Hollis offers us sketches of five of his Oxford friends of the 1920s: Maurice Bowra, Leslie Hore-Belisha, 'Crusoe' Robinson-Glasgow, Evelyn Waugh and Harold Acton. We do not get a distinct impression of any of them. His style is often leaden – for example: 'It cannot be denied that witty epigram was sometimes preferred to deeper truth or that to raise a laugh even those who were at heart kindly and genial at times did not forbear to say wounding things about their fellows.' On the other hand, Mr Hollis tells many pleasing anecdotes. I like George Moore's remark: 'Of all sexual actions copulation is the least deleterious.' Some of the stories have been doing the rounds a long time. 'Buggers can't be choosers', here ascribed to Bowra, I first heard as the comment allegedly made by Winston Churchill on the occasion of

139

Tom Driberg's marriage. Mr Hollis is much more successful in evoking a certain upper-class ambience; and it is for this that the book should be read. Remarkable about all the clever and self-assured young men who flit through these pages (I can't recall a single woman) is what they took for granted. Britain was still the centre of the world. The Empire was alive and well. All the persons worth knowing came from a few public schools and went to Oxford and Cambridge. Examinations were peripheral: a private income or at worst a sinecure teaching or literary job obtained by connections would leave plenty of time for the really important things like writing, painting, playing cricket. The idea that they might have to start producing wealth in a post-imperial age never occurred to them.

What then distinguished Christopher Hollis's Oxford from the pre-1914 version? Certainly not political radicalism: for undergraduates, the 1920s was a very unpolitical decade. Maurice Bowra was 'vaguely Left' but no one pretended that he 'ever very much consorted with the workers at any period of his life'. His political creed was liberal élitism: perfect freedom for himself and his friends to carry on more or less as they liked. Most would have agreed with Balliol's snobbish Dean 'Sligger' Urquhart that opportunities should be created for 'Birmingham, etc.' (Balliol even had a few token black men), but few did anything about it, or imagined that such egalitarianism might be at their expense. There was little interest in curricular or university reform. As for unemployment, their knowledge and interest would have been on a par with that of the famous cricketer, C. B. Fry, who, standing as Liberal candidate for Oxford and asked why England had more unemployed than France, made the memorable reply 'I have no idea – no idea whatsoever, bowled me middle stump – neck and crop'. Hore-Belisha was an exception to the lack of political involvement, but he was an adventurer.

No: what distinguished post-war from pre-war Oxford was a different attitude to duty. The post-war generation was much more private than the pre-war. Their favoured situation, the general discredit of traditional ideals of honour and duty in the war (Alec Waugh's *Loom of Youth* was very influential), plus the conviction that another war was unthinkable, led them to seek a life that was 'good in itself' rather than one dominated by service. They rejected not the public school ideal, but the Roman side of it, emphasizing the Greek side instead. Leadership, the prefect system, were devalued in favour of personal relationships, beauty, self-expression. Games were not rejected, but they were shorn of their moral claims.

This post-war Oxford privatism came out in a number of ways – in Maurice Bowra's incurable clever-silly irreverence, in the flamboyant aestheticism of the Anglo-Florentine Harold Acton, in the passion for cricket which reached a new intensity in the 1920s (Baldwin was writing a preface to a cricket book on the eve of the General Strike). But two special features may be noted. Most of those Mr Hollis writes about were homosexual or bisexual; and homosexuality had become more overt as private happiness took precedence over convention or public service. The second feature was the apparently almost continuous state of drunkenness. Here Evelyn Waugh set the pace. Clever jokes, aesthetic credos, cricket, homosexuality, boozing – these appear to be the main ingredients of Mr Hollis's Oxford.

No one except Evelyn Waugh fulfilled the promise he was thought to have in him. Bowra wrote almost unreadable books on romantic poetry and classical literature; Hore-Belisha never became the second Disraeli; Robertson-Glasgow failed to play cricket for England; Harold Acton's poems are now quite forgotten; Christopher Hollis himself remained on the fringes of interesting subjects and events. Perhaps none of them was as brilliant as he seemed at the time; or perhaps they were too spoilt to do anything much with their lives.

CHAPTER TWENTY-ONE

Vera Brittain

John Caitlin, Family Quartet: Vera Brittain and her Family
[Hamish Hamilton, 1987]

VERA BRITTAIN and her husband George Catlin were minor luminaries of the inter-war years. She was an ardent feminist and pacifist. She wrote forgettable novels and one autobiographical masterpiece, *Testament of Youth*, a chronicle of war-damaged high-mindedness. He was a more shadowy presence, even in her life. A gentleman academic on the fringe of politics, his books on political science are even more forgotten than his wife's novels; he also had to share her affections with Winifred Holtby, a fighter for women's rights and black liberation, who wrote one good novel, *South Riding.*

Why should we want to read about such people? Because, their son John Catlin explains, they represent 'a way of life between the turn of the century and the end of the Second World War'. The justification is reasonable. All three adults in his story were freelance members of the middle-class army of progress as it regrouped after the First World War. On the one hand, the war had broken down Victorian 'appearances', allowing 'modern' relationships to be lived more or less openly. On the other hand, it had destroyed not only loved ones, but the idea of 'automatic' progress; creating in its wake, and for both reasons, professional World Improvers: people who spent their lives preaching peace and brotherhood and often, with equal fervour, birth control, Esperanto, vegetarianism and other worthy causes. Vera Brittain and Winifred Holtby represented the inspirational side of the movement. Their idea of a refreshing holiday was to attend League of Nations debates at Geneva; they poured forth uplift on the platform and in the press. George Catlin tried to give the uplift a proper grounding in social science. Servicing the army of progress were two survivals from the Victorian age still considered indispensable: servants and unearned incomes. However, a child's perspective offers only a limited insight into what drove these people, and how they lived their lives. Nor has John Catlin really tried to supplement his own memories and reflections with wider reading and research. His parents must have left masses of personal papers: little or no use has been made of them.

They certainly left millions of published words. John Catlin did not read them when they appeared and did little to remedy this later. More damagingly, he is not a writer. *Family Quartet,* though brief, is awkward, repetitive and clogged up with wearisome details of forebears and unilluminating tittle-tattle about Laski, Wells, etc. Also, I think it exhibits an ungenerous, carping spirit. Clearly John Catlin grew to resent his parents and his famous sister, Shirley Williams. He tells twice the story of how Shirley, as a girl, used to pretend she was poor by going in and out of her parents' grand house in Cheyne Walk by the servants' door at the back. A typical remark is: 'I do not think Shirley has much imagination, any more than my mother had . . . Like most English people [she] is basically a philistine.' Well, perhaps . . . but what is his standard of comparison? The only really affectionate portrait is that of Winifred

Holtby, who gave him the love he felt he never got from his do-gooding, globe-trotting parents.

Vera Brittain was clearly a tiresome lady. She bulldozed her way through life, sacrificing family and friends to her causes. She was completely without humour. On the other hand she could be a great charmer; unlike many feminists, she also believed in looking nice. Beatrice Webb, usually censorious about such things, noticed approvingly: 'Her lips and nails delicate crimson, cheeks slightly and skilfully rouged ... attractive little body.' Her loss of brother and lover in the war and her subsequent battles to improve the world make her a figure at once tragic and heroic. George Catlin, on the other hand, despite his marked resemblance to Leslie Howard, became embittered by an accumulating weight of failures: failure to get an Oxford Fellowship, failure to become an MP, failure to get a peerage. For these things he largely blamed his wife. But in fact he was a superficial thinker, a prize bore, and an insufferable snob. As his son makes clear, he needed no help from Vera in mismanaging his career. What might have been a sympathetic effort of understanding turns out to be a rather sad essay in childhood resentment, made sadder by the death of the author just after he had finished his book. John Catlin is, of course, right. His parents *are* period pieces. The task remains to set them properly in their period; and also to show how their concerns, if not their achievements, transcend it.

CHAPTER TWENTY-TWO

Stanley Baldwin

WHAT causes fashions in statesmen to change? Stanley Baldwin, three times Prime Minister of England, is suddenly back in favour after almost thirty years in the shadows. Here was a man accused by his biographer G. M. Young of having failed to prepare England for war; a man who manifestly failed to address the problem of unemployment; a man whose name became a byword for lethargy and incapacity. Yet now his latest biographers, Barnes and Middlemas, compare him to Disraeli. With the aid of some dubious sociological theory, they have built him up into a model statesman for our times, a 'new style of leader'.

143

What has caused this transformation? Partly it is a technical matter. A whole mass of Cabinet Papers of the period has recently become available to scholars. These naturally emphasize Baldwin's active side – presiding over committees, pushing through measures, giving support to his colleagues; and it is a great temptation to judge people on what the documents show them to be doing rather than on what they should have been doing – which is something the documents leave out. But there is a more fundamental reason for Baldwin's reinstatement. His stock has risen in proportion as we have come to expect less and less of our politicians. The fact that he failed to solve problems counts less heavily against him because we no longer expect our modern politicians to solve problems. The fact that he was a second-rate man seems less reprehensible because we have got used to being governed by second-rate men. Keeping up standards in politicians seems to me just as important as keeping them up in everything else, which is why I want to take a more critical look at Baldwin. I want to show exactly why, for all his qualities, he should not be taken as a model statesman for our times.

The most striking thing about his first fifty years of life is that they were completely undistinguished. Harrow, Cambridge, his father's steel firm, local government – he passed through them all without leaving a mark. At the age of forty-one he was returned unopposed for his father's seat at Bewdley in the Conservative interest. The same pattern repeated itself. For almost ten years he was a respected, but hardly sparkling, backbencher. He dreaded making speeches and was an indifferent performer. Indeed, in 1916 he almost retired, but his wife Lucy persuaded him to stay on. Reward finally came a year later when, following the creation of the Lloyd George Coalition, he became Parliamentary Private Secretary to Bonar Law, the Tory leader. He was then exactly fifty. Six years later he was Prime Minister. It was an astonishing ascent. What had happened was that all the people in his way had suddenly been removed. Most of the ablest Conservatives remained loyal to Lloyd George. That put them out of the running. Bonar Law unexpectedly had to resign from cancer of the throat. Lord Curzon, the one remaining top-line Conservative, was a peer, before peers could renounce their titles. That left Baldwin the best of a pretty undistinguished bunch. He himself reflected on the irony of the situation. Here were these clever men, immeasurably above him. Now they had all collapsed like a pack of cards, leaving him on top. He was to stay there till 1937.

Nor did he change much in that time. Of course, high office gave scope to some qualities and developed others. The premiership provided him with the opportunity and confidence to display an undoubted gift for words, a capacity for expressing simple, even banal ideas in suitably uplifting language. Once on top, he took considerable pains to stay there, becoming, in Churchill's words, 'the most formidable politician I have ever known'. His gift for personal relations and his generous – over-generous – treatment of incompetent colleagues certainly helped him: without doubt he was the most liked politician of his time. Nevertheless, when all this is said, he remained unmistakably the mediocre man his first fifty years suggested, merely translated to a higher sphere. How, then, do we account for the phenomenon of Baldwinism – not just the contemporary acceptance of mediocrity in high places, but its veneration?

In part, it was a very natural recoil from the colossal effort of the First World War. Nations, like individuals, can put forward their best efforts only in short bursts, before relapsing again into the humdrum and the routine. The war was an exceptional experience, which most people wanted to forget about as soon as possible. So the cry was 'back to normalcy', and what could be more normal than Baldwin, with his pipe and his massive common sense? But Baldwinism signified more than the rejection of exceptional effort: it involved the rejection of intelligence as well. As a nation we have always tended to exalt character above brains, practical experience above theory. We have produced some of the finest brains in the world, but intellectuality as such has never been greatly prized. Moreover, in the inter-war period, and even earlier, it was discredited in the eyes of the practical man by its association with a new phenomenon – the socialist intelligentsia: 'a very ugly word for a very ugly thing', as Baldwin dubbed it.

There was another, more immediate, reason for the revolt against intelligence. The Lloyd George Coalition of 1918–22 was dominated by the clever men – the 'first-class brains', as they were known. Lloyd George, Churchill and Lord Birkenhead were a restless, inventive, brilliant trio. They represented the wartime tradition of energy and improvisation, when what the political classes wanted was less energy and more routine. Moreover, there was a strong odour of corruption in high places. Lloyd George himself despised party connection and the House of Commons; his Garden Suburb clique threatened the independence of the Civil Service and encroached on Ministerial responsibility.

He sold peerages quite shamelessly; his private life was scandalous; his diplomatic initiatives in the Middle East threatened to involve Europe in a new war. You never knew where you were with the Goat, as he was called. He seemed to epitomize brilliant opportunism and shady practice. Baldwin certainly regarded him as the chief corrupter of public life, and it was he who led the backbench Tory revolt which brought Lloyd George down. This was where your first-class brains got you! Far better to return to tested principles and men of unimpeachable character. 'We are sick of Welshmen and lawyers,' said Lord Winterton, 'of the best brains and supermen. We want the old type of English statesman, who is fair-minded, judicious and responsible, rather than the man who is so clever that he thinks ahead of everyone else.' Baldwin played on this longing with superlative skill. 'A dynamic force is a very terrible thing,' he told his audience at the famous Carlton Club meeting of October 1922. He himself was quite free from the charge of excessive dynamism, and no one who knew his record could suspect him of being a wizard or a superman.

The path to salvation, he declared in 1923, lay through faith, hope, love and work. Conspicuously absent was brains. The war had shattered the basis of England's old industrial system, leading to mass unemployment. On the Continent it was to throw up new movements and men who came to threaten England's security. To understand, to cope, to innovate, required, above all else, brains and ideas. Yet in the aftermath of the Goat, theory was disdained; clever men were at a discount. Keynes was never used; Churchill flung aside. In talking about the mood of the time, one is in danger of generalizing the opinions of the articulate people – those who write letters to *The Times*. It was they who sought to return to the pre-war world. Yet the mass of returning soldiers and their families were less interested in Back to Normality than in a New Deal. They had voted for a Land Fit for Heroes in 1918. Baldwin's political problem was somehow to reconcile this demand of the people to get something done with the desire of his party to do as little as possible. His principal solution to this problem was words.

In a famous speech in 1925 he called for 'Peace in our time, O Lord.' His words made a deep impression, the more so because they were so obviously sincere. As his biographers point out, the war had given him a sense of mission and he never forgot that he 'held power by sufferance of the dead'. In an act of rare and quixotic generosity he gave a third of his fortune – £150,000 – anonymously to the Exchequer: his own contribution to class peace. He despised the hard-headed business-men who looked as though they had done well out of the war, and attempted instead to display to the electorate the human face of Conservatism – its acceptance of social responsibility, its concern for the underdog. In this respect, recent Conservative writers see him as the rediscoverer of the Disraelian ideal of One Nation. Whatever the truth of this, he was certainly the discoverer and first consistent practitioner of what has since come to be known as consensus politics, which may be briefly defined as government from the moderate centre. If the Conservative, like the Labour, Party remained motivated by class interest, Baldwin contrived to veil the fact with decent reticence; and his successors have followed his example ever since.

But words do not build houses or provide work. Millions of people were doomed to a sad, hopeless life on the dole, on the edge of starvation. Action was required; and action required thought. In this situation Baldwin had nothing to offer. As a Treasury official of the time remarked, Baldwin 'took his economics from his nose'. He believed that the government's role was limited strictly to exhortation. Visiting a Glasgow slum, he almost cried at the horror of it, yet noted afterwards: 'They can't know how impotent one is to help.' It was a characteristic refrain. True to his beliefs, he refused to intervene in the General Strike, with the result that the coal-owners starved the miners into submission. This whole episode in some ways shows Baldwin at his most character-istic. He sympathized deeply with the miners and made it clear that he did so. After the strike was over he restrained his party's desire for vengeance to the best of his ability. But he never came up with a constructive solution. No wonder it was said of him that he usually hit the nail on the head, but it never went in.

In the early 1930s, even the human face of Conservatism disap-peared with the Means Test, the revival of the Poor Law, the cuts in education and social welfare, and the Sedition Act. It was in Baldwin's last period of power that the Hunger Marches took place and the town of Jarrow died. But by this time he had given up all hope of solving problems. There would always be mass unemployment in England, he declared, at precisely the moment when Keynes was completing his *General Theory*.

Had he succeeded in his one attempt at positive leadership, he might have been emboldened to try again. In 1923, in his first year as Prime Minister, he went to the country on a programme of Protection.

He had convinced himself that, with Europe in disarray, the only chance of getting rid of unemployment was by expanding Imperial trade. This required Imperial Preference and a tax on foreign food: a major departure from Britain's free trade traditions and one which had hitherto always been electorally unpopular. This was the policy Baldwin put to the voters in 1923. For the first and only time in his life he gave his people a lead. The result was a fiasco, ending in the installation of the first Labour government. From this Baldwin drew the conclusion that active leadership was doomed to failure. Yet the conclusion was wrong. The truth was that the 1923 campaign was sadly mismanaged: the timing was dictated by fears of a Lloyd George come-back; the circumstances were inopportune. Baldwin had not prepared his party or the country. He had not even worked out the policy. No one could understand his speeches. No wonder he failed.

In the 1930s the failure of the men in power to rise to the level of events becomes even more tragically apparent. A senile MacDonald and a rapidly ageing Baldwin left Britain unprepared to face the dictators. The latest evidence makes it clear that behind the scenes Baldwin was not as inactive as people have thought. Broadly speaking, he did as much as he could to expedite rearmament by stealth. But he never put the need for massive rearmament unequivocally to the people. Remembering 1923, he was afraid of the result. At the time, there seemed to be good reasons for his hesitation. Pacifism seemed to be sweeping the country. In those circumstances a rearmament election seemed likely to bring Labour back into power. 'Better insufficient rearmament from me than none from the Socialists' was Baldwin's view. But the facts were rather different. Labour's recovery owed less to pacifism than to the reversal of the abnormal situation created by the National Government victory of 1931. And even if this was not appreciated at the time, Baldwin was in an immensely strong position. His majority was 500. He could lose a packet and still return victorious. A bold leader would have dramatized the need for rearmament in the 1935 election and would almost certainly have won. Of course there were risks, but the risks to the country of inaction were even greater. The real charge against Baldwin is that he did not even try. The failure to try was ultimately the failure of self-confidence of an inadequate man.

Lesser things he could do well. He handled the Abdication crisis tactfully. He deserves praise also for his consistent support for the cause of Indian self-government. Yet a leader must be judged by his actions on the main issues confronting him. Baldwin failed to tackle the unemployment problem, and he left England inadequately rearmed to face the challenge of the dictators. This is an indictment which no amount of special pleading is likely to alter. And this is why we should be discriminating in our praise. 'Safety first', Baldwin's famous slogan, is not the spirit in which to face a new world.

CHAPTER TWENTY-THREE

The Taming of Labour

Maurice Cowling, *The Impact of Labour 1920–1924*
[Cambridge University Press, 1971]
Peregrine Worsthorne, *The Socialist Myth*
[Cassell, 1971]

ONE of the great themes of twentieth-century British politics has been the taming of the Labour Party. Its arrival on the scene had the ruling classes quaking in their beds and locking up their silver. Today they face the prospect of a Labour Government, if not with equanimity at least with the knowledge that not only will it not distress them too much, but that its muddles and failures will lead to a fairly speedy return to 'normal' Conservative rule. The twin themes of the evolution of a successful style of resistance to Labour by the Conservative Party and the inability of Labour to establish itself as a governing party are explored in two important books by Conservative writers.

Mr Maurice Cowling deals with the attempts to evolve a successful resistance to Labour between 1920 and 1924 – the key, in his view, to a proper understanding of the confused politics of that period. Birkenhead and Austen Chamberlain wanted to fuse the Liberal and Conservative wings of the Lloyd George Coalition into a constitutional, anti-socialist party. Lord Robert Cecil wanted to construct a party of high-minded aristocrats under Lord Grey. Lloyd George oscillated between hopes of fusion and dreams of leading a reunited Liberal Party which could undercut Labour's radical appeal. In the end the triumph of Baldwin established the 'politics of resistance' in 'viable party form', inaugurating a pattern of practical accommodation, 'decency', and soothing rhetoric

149

which kept Labour moderate and the Conservatives mostly in power. This is an important and illuminating theme, a detailed case-study of yet another successful adaptation by the British ruling class to pressures from below. It is not the only way to make sense of what was happening at this time: attempts to re-establish the historic Conservative and Liberal parties were just as important as efforts to construct a successful opposition to socialism, and by no means always, or even usually, coincided with the latter. Nevertheless, Mr Cowling's approach provides a new insight into many important issues.

For example, Baldwin's sudden leap into Protection in 1923 has always puzzled historians. It is sometimes thought that he was simply out to dish Lloyd George. Mr Cowling sets it in the context of a continuing attempt to evolve a successful Conservative riposte to Labour's ideological challenge. He provides entertaining sketches of those mostly forgotten peddlers of anti-socialist nostrums who abounded at the time: Horatio Bottomley with his 'John Bull' and his big business nationalism; General Page Croft with his patriotic National Party; Lord Salisbury and his Anti-Waste obsessions; the anti-Jewish, anti-Bolshevik groups round the Duke of Northumberland. In the break-up of the party system exotic blooms flowered briefly. But in spite of its many virtues, *The Impact of Labour* is an irritating and exhausting book. Mr Cowling has little sense of shaping a narrative or argument. He is never content with one illustration if ten will do. Big lists of names frequently appear in the middle of the page. The use of footnotes is often bizarre and pedantic. There is a sly undercurrent of sexual innuendo. Clearly Mr Cowling has a somewhat brutish view of human nature; larger purposes are always at the mercy of 'antipathy, self-interest, and mutual contempt'. This may be true; there is no need to relish it quite so much.

If Mr Cowling's theme is over-burdened with detail, Mr Worsthorne's is developed with a magnificent disregard of it. He starts with a concrete problem – why did Harold Wilson's Government end in failure and defeat? – and goes on to elaborate a completely theoretical explanation. A planned society, according to Mr Worsthorne, requires a communal spirit much more than does a capitalist society which relies on self-interest. This communal spirit can arise either from the masses, fired with revolutionary or patriotic zeal, or from a public-spirited governing class able to command the deference of the masses, as the old aristocracy used to. Unfortunately, the Labour Party can achieve neither. It cannot fire the revolutionary zeal of the workers because it is not revolutionary enough; at the same time it cannot appeal to their patriotism – beat the national drum – because patriotic themes are a monopoly of the Right.

Equally, its egalitarian ethic prevents it from creating a new governing class or using the existing one. Meritocratic élites based on the intellect are no good as governors because intellectuals are basically critical and have no contact with the people. At the same time, socialist taxation policies prevent the irresponsible plutocrats becoming responsible aristocrats as in the nineteenth century; prevent, in other words, the Clores from becoming the Alec Douglas-Homes. The result is a fatal contradiction in democratic socialism. 'Its collectivist economic policies require a markedly hierarchic system of status and rank, while its egalitarian social policies are aimed at producing the opposite.' Paradoxically, Tory paternalism is far more applicable to the needs of the socialist economy than is Labour egalitarianism. The party of the Right alone has the instincts and the prejudices needed to manage the economic society demanded by the party of the Left.

There is a great deal to criticize in all this; something to ponder as well. Democratic political theory, as Mr Worsthorne points out, has largely ignored the problem of leadership. In practice leadership was provided by the old governing classes, and in any case classic democratic theory never envisaged the problem of managing a modern industrial State. The fact is that modern politicians are faced with far greater challenges than their predecessors; mistakes are likely to be far more costly. Yet hardly any thought is given to the question of how to make men fit for the kind of power they are now called upon to exercise. The revival of an hereditary ruling class is not the answer, for the skills it implants are essentially those of the public-spirited amateur; one has only to cite Sir Alec to reveal the inadequacy of this preparation for modern conditions. Mr Worsthorne, stepson of Montagu Norman, comes from this background. For all his penetration and charm he remains, in the last analysis, an elegant amateur in a world inhabited by tough professionals like Mr Cowling. I sympathize with his predicament.

CHAPTER TWENTY-FOUR

Baldwin Revisited

Roy Jenkins, *Baldwin*
[Collins, 1987]

ROY JENKINS has cornered the market in the biographical essay. It's a role which suits him at this stage of his career. He writes elegantly; does no original research; doesn't aim at being exhaustive. One reads him therefore not to find out about Baldwin (for that one goes to the indigestible Middlemas and Barnes) but to find out what he thinks about Baldwin. He is one of the very few biographers (or historians) whose opinion (as opposed to scholarship) is worth having. Not that his subject has inspired him to great heights – any more than he did his 'authorized' biographer, G. M. Young. Mr Jenkins wrote the essay in the early 1970s as part of a larger project on Presidents and Prime Ministers which he never finished. He has altered and lengthened it for publication and added an introduction which reads as though it was written over an agreeable weekend. His publishers have added nasty black blobs on the page which refer to the potted biograpies at the end. It is a distinctly low-key performance.

This is understandable. The most interesting thing about Stanley Baldwin is that he was completely uninteresting. Consider the facts. For the first fifty years of his life he did nothing of note. One could call him a very late developer. By 1922, aged fifty-five, he had managed to become President of the Board of Trade. He then made a speech to Tory MPs at the Carlton Club which brought down the Lloyd George Coalition. Its key phrase was 'a dynamic force is a very terrible thing'. Less than a year later he was Prime Minister and leader of the Conservative Party. He clung to the top like a limpet for the next fifteen years – The Age of Baldwin they have been called. He then disappeared as though he had never been.

The only way, I think, to make sense of this story is to ask questions about the mood and circumstances in which inaction could be seen as the supreme political virtue. One does not have to be a Marxist to appreciate the force of John Strachey's remark in 1932 that Baldwin was 'a perfect statesman for an empire in decline: he realises instinctively that almost anything anyone *does* will only make matters worse'. But to set Baldwin's masterly inactivity in social and imperial contexts would have required historical ideas, of which Mr Jenkins has never had a large stock. What he offers instead is a well-focused narrative with strong asides. In eight years as Prime Minister and four more as *de facto* Prime Minister under the decrepit MacDonald, Baldwin acted decisively twice. In 1923 he asked for a mandate for Protection. The electorate turned him down. No one knows why he did it. Mr Jenkins at least asks the right question: 'Was it the pattern of politics or the future of Britain's trading arrangements which he wished primarily to influence?' The second occasion was his handling of the Abdication crisis in 1936. This probably saved the Monarchy. In between there were some notable speeches and much inattention. He made a memorable remark in 1931 when he accused the Press Lords Beaverbrook and Rothermere of aspiring to 'power without responsibility – the prerogative of the harlot throughout the ages'. His inattention to rearmament proved rather serious.

If none of this is the stuff of drama it offers considerable comic potential which Mr Jenkins, alone of Baldwin's biographers, has exploited. 'What can you do', a colleague of Baldwin's once complained, 'with a leader who sits in the smoking room reading the *Strand Magazine*?' Mr Jenkins comments: 'Baldwin ... was most likely not even reading the *Strand* but sniffing it and with it the atmosphere around him. He was also probably ruminating, feeling his way, nudging towards a variety of decisions ... This was a technique which made it peculiarly difficult to say when he was working and when he was not.' One of Baldwin's favourite ruminating spots was Aix-les-Bains, where he spent lengthy annual holidays. Holiday time was the time he liked best.

Baldwin has one major achievement to his credit. He established a pattern of Conservative cohabitation with Labour which lasted fifty years. He and MacDonald between them broke Lloyd George, the Liberal Party, and all those clever Centre Party ideas by which Lloyd George and others had hoped to keep Labour out of power. Baldwin actively welcomed Labour to office; and he was a master of emollient mood-creation which took the heat out of the class war. When he asked in the House of Commons for 'Peace in our time, O Lord', Labour Members were in tears. Writing in the early 1970s Mr Jenkins approves mightily of all this. He criticizes Baldwin for breaking his own pattern by forming the National Government with MacDonald in 1931. I wonder whether the inter-war years look quite the same from the SDP angle.

In the end, it's the political asides which one most relishes: the professional's judgment on the game. Mr Jenkins remarks shrewdly of Baldwin's failure to lead effectively in Opposition: 'His *forte* as Prime Minister was taking the heat out of debates . . . a technique which by its very nature was unsuited for use from the opposition front bench.' When Baldwin wrapped up his abandonment of Protection in circumlocutory language Mr Jenkins sagely remarks, 'It is never wise for a politician to use ringing words to announce a retreat.' And it is surely Labour's reforming ex-Home Secretary who comments on Baldwin's appointment of Joynson Hicks as Home Secretary in 1924 that it launched the Home Office 'upon a course of dour obscurantism from which it took three or four decades to recover'.

CHAPTER TWENTY-FIVE

Ramsay MacDonald

David Marquand, *Ramsay MacDonald*
[Jonathan Cape, 1971]

BIOGRAPHY is in a bad way. It no longer provides a generally acceptable method of investigating the basic biographical questions: why does a person hold the opinions he does, behave in the way he does, achieve what he does, become the person he is? All existing explanations are suspect. We no longer believe, with Bacon, that 'glory and honour serve as goads and spurs' to achievement. We don't accept the rationalist view that men can be reduced to bundles of principles, interests, qualities. At the same time, we rightly suspect the 'mental health' approach of the Romantics and psychoanalysts. Did Gramsci really become a Communist because he was a hunchback? Is greatness inevitably grounded in neurosis? That old stand-by, racial characteristics, is out as well. The result is biographical eclecticism: all possibly relevant 'factors' are listed, connections vaguely hinted at, and the reader left more or less in the dark as the biographer hurries on to describe what his subject actually did.

154

David Marquand's massive and formidable new biography of Ramsay MacDonald illustrates these problems. Born in 1866, the illegitimate son of a Scottish farm labourer and servant girl, MacDonald was the chief architect of the Labour Party – first as Secretary, then Leader, finally as Prime Minister of two Labour Governments. In 1931 he broke with his party to form a National Government largely manned by his lifelong opponents, dying discredited six years later. His was a remarkable and complicated career, influenced, to a quite exceptional degree, by unhealed psychological wounds and unappeased personal tensions. The challenge to the biographer is to explain the source of these and to relate them to what MacDonald did. Marquand tries hard to do so. In MacDonald's Diary, here used for the first time, he has a remarkably self-revealing document to help him. What he lacks are adequate techniques for exploring character and motive. Instead he brings to bear on the MacDonald problem the best virtues of traditional historical scholarship. His research, based on the MacDonald Archive, is thorough and scrupulous. He is equally at home with socialist theory, social history and economic policy. As a Labour politician himself, he has a firm grasp of the political situation. His writing is fluent and often elegant. He is sympathetic to MacDonald, but balanced. In short, he is a complete professional at everything except explaining his subject.

Admittedly, that is appallingly difficult. MacDonald's personality had two sides. He was both a mystic and a tactician. To explain this split, Marquand falls back on a familiar cliché: MacDonald sprang from a union of Highland and Lowland stock. But this is a substitute for an explanation. What is interesting about MacDonald's two tendencies is their extreme and unrelated character. On the one side was MacDonald's remarkably imprecise use of language. From the beginning, he treated certain subjects, personal and political, in a completely idealized way, enveloping them in mist and haze. On the other hand, MacDonald was an outstanding committee man, negotiator, party organizer. He brought many talents to this: the outstanding one was the capacity for obsessively hard work. From quite early on, fatigue was a problem, helped on by insomnia. Exhaustion haunts his diary; neurasthenia dogs his life. But he goes on driving himself till mind and body are completely worn out. By sixty-six he is a wreck.

This baroque language, this obsessive work schedule, points unmistakably to a sense of inner emptiness, unworthiness. Marquand quotes a most revealing entry in MacDonald's diary dated 15 July 1924: 'It is an

odd thing to have a dead man as Premier to look after a living world.'
The biographer attributes this and many similar remarks to Mac-
Donald's bereavement at the early death of his wife Margaret. But in
fact the thing which struck all MacDonald's most perceptive contemporaries was his hollowness. He was a man of substitutes, a truth captured
by Beatrice Webb in a famous phrase (not quoted here). It is not so hard
to guess what was being substituted for: religious faith on the one hand
(partly sublimated into Utopian socialism), and sexual fulfilment on the
other. MacDonald's public life was a flight from his own nature.

Biographical convention, which includes the pressure of relatives
as well as the personal embarrassment of the biographer, often prevents
the raising of such central questions. Like many passionate men in that
repressed era, MacDonald had enormous guilt feelings about sex. There
are too many references in his Diary to his solitariness and to his
imminent physical decay to disguise the nature and source of his anxiety.
He found relief in spiritual, idealized, relationships with a number of
women, in which, however, the underlying note of repressed sexuality is
quite evident. No doubt his marriage to Margaret Gladstone helped him,
but there is something curiously unreal about it. I find it quite remarkable, for instance, that when they became engaged, after a courtship
lasting several months, she should be asking MacDonald's mother 'by
what name I am to call your son? I only know him as Mr MacDonald
and really don't know what Christian name he uses.' MacDonald spoke
beautifully of her after she was dead, but what were their relations like
when she was alive? Marquand describes MacDonald's relations with
some other women. He wrote Lady Londonderry 'rather plaintive poems
full of Celtic twilight'. He held Cecily Gordon-Cumming's hand under
the rug in his official car. He flirted wistfully with Martha Bibesco.

Sir Oswald Mosley once told me about another flirtation. He and
his wife Cynthia had taken MacDonald on a Continental holiday in
1928. In Vienna, MacDonald introduced them to an agreeable older
woman. The pair used to go out together to look at museums. At a
country house party in Cornwall just before the 1929 election Mosley
again met MacDonald with the Viennese lady. MacDonald used to read
poetry to her. A few months later, Mosley, now a Minister, was
summoned to her flat in Horseferry Road. The Labour Prime Minister,
she told him, had refused her pleas for financial assistance, and she now
proposed to sell his letters, full of pornographic poetry, to the French
press. Mosley said he bluffed her out of it; but evidently she renewed her

attempts. Eventually, the letters were recovered by Sir Charles Mendl of the British Embassy in Paris for £20,000 sent over by Vansittart. Mendl read the letters before destroying them, confirming to Mosley their pornographic content. So what, one may ask? The point is that sexual guilt and repression in someone of passionate temperament help explain (I would put it no higher than that) some of MacDonald's chief political characteristics: the idealized quality of his socialism, his obsessive work habits and inability to delegate, his histrionics, prickliness, insecurity, inaccessibility. And these in turn had serious political consequences. He was never able to bring his Socialism into contact with real life, because it was a substitute for something real in himself. Tiredness led to serious political mistakes – over the Campbell prosecution, and Zinoviev letter for certain, but also in 1931 and the Stresa Conference probably. The crises of MacDonald's political career were confronted by a vulnerable, anxious, and exhausted man.

Marquand fails to develop another interesting interpretation of MacDonald suggested by Francis Williams. Williams saw MacDonald as the outsider desperately trying to get in on the inside, an urge made more desperate by his illegitimacy. MacDonald was a 'lad o' pairts', denied opportunities by the rigid class system. When his revolt drove him to radical politics, he was shut out of the Liberal Party. The Labour Movement gave him and other talented working-class leaders the chance to play a part in great affairs. Once MacDonald became successful his radicalism subsided. His success in politics, helped by his 'classless' Scottishness, gave him an entry into society. Yet even here the fruit was bitter. Inside the Labour Party, MacDonald was a hero. Outside, he was always a bit of a joke. He bored the pants off the Garsington sophisticates with his long anecdotes which never came to the point. Even friends like Harold Nicolson mocked his artistic, literary and intellectual pretensions. His tragedy was that he was prepared to trade his place in the Labour movement for an acceptance he could never win from fashionable society. No doubt King George V and Lady Londonderry liked him. But nevertheless he was used by the possessing classes and knew it.

Marquand explains better, and with more detail, than anyone else has done MacDonald's role in the Labour movement of his day. He was not just a right-wing leader who bamboozled the Left with fine words. There was a side of him which responded to the ethical temper of the early ILP much more than it did to the machine politics of Arthur

Henderson and the trade union and party bosses. MacDonald was never the candidate of the machine – and the conflict between him and Arthur Henderson which ran right through their careers and surfaced with new bitterness over foreign policy between 1929 and 1931 is crucial in explaining their break in the latter year. The secret of MacDonald's party position was that he embodied both Labour's moral aspirations and its instinct for power. Beyond that, the Gladstonian mixture of moral language and moderate politics helped make Labour appealing but safe to a large electorate. Yet though he was no more able than Gladstone to bring his morals and politics together, there was less excuse for him than for Gladstone. Society was not stable in MacDonald's day. To perfect a creed of evolutionary socialism on the eve of the First World War was, at the very least, to ignore major aspects of contemporary reality. Entirely lacking from MacDonald's thought was Burkhardt's perception that Europe had entered an 'era of wars', or Joseph Chamberlain's instinct that nineteenth-century internationalism was doomed, or any appreciation that Britain's industrial position was undermined, with its concomitant of mass unemployment. The future that MacDonald projected had no contact with the reality with which he, as a politician, would be faced.

And yet politically this was not a disadvantage – quite the reverse. His hold on Labour and British politics was assured by the step that seemed certain to destroy him – his resignation from the Labour Party leadership in 1914 to oppose the First World War. This established moral credentials which he never lost. Principles apart, the anti-war crusade filled an emotional void. Part of his nature responded to its moral exaltation. He was leading the Saints of the ILP against the Sinners represented by Lloyd George and the warmongers. This courageous stand dislodged his career from its former groove. Before 1914 he and his leading parliamentary colleagues seemed headed for places in a Liberal Cabinet. This would inevitably have produced in reaction a strong independent, and possibly revolutionary, party of the far Left. Instead MacDonald provided the Left with a cause and a leader within the Labour Party. By so doing, he ensured that the post-war Communist Party would remain insignificant. He also enlarged the Labour Party's appeal to the anti-war Liberals. These were his signal services to social democracy.

The book's climax is a strong defence of MacDonald's role in the financial crisis of 1931. His forming of the National Government,

Marquand argues, followed logically and inexorably from the decision to defend the gold parity which had been taken by the whole Labour Cabinet. He was prepared to accept the financial and political corollary of that decision; the Labour Cabinet was not. Central to Marquand's defence is that a £76 million cut in the budget, including a large cut in unemployment benefits, was essential to get the loan from New York to prop up sterling. The bankers insisted on it. If the government was to get the loan it had to produce economies of £76 million. But the Labour Government which wanted the loan wouldn't go beyond £56 million.

This sounds convincing, but is seriously misleading. The New York bankers who were being asked for the money never demanded a cut of £76 million, or any other figure. What they did ask for, in the words of Harrison, Governor of the Federal Reserve Bank of New York, was an economy programme which would be supported by 'all three parties'; in other words, a *national* commitment to economy. It was the Conservative and Liberal leaders, especially Neville Chamberlain, who insisted on the higher figure. And the reason they insisted on a cut higher than the Labour Government was prepared to contemplate was not because they thought the higher figure was necessary to secure the loan (it was their support for the programme that was vital for that), but because they saw a chance to break up the Labour Party. To the eternal discredit of MacDonald he allowed himself to be used for that manoeuvre. MacDonald, after all, was in a very strong position. All he had to do was to point out that a £76 million economy programme carried out by a Conservative–Liberal Government against a united Labour Party would do far less to restore confidence than a £56 million programme carried out with the support of all three parties. The electoral prospects for such a coalition in those circumstances would also hardly be inviting. But MacDonald never used these arguments to bargain for Opposition support for the Labour Government's programme of cuts. He threw away his hand. By so doing, he involved his party in the biggest catastrophe it has ever suffered.

Once Chamberlain, Baldwin and Samuel had got MacDonald's assent to the higher figure, it was a relatively simple matter to get him to do what they wanted. They knew that a combination of ignorance, vanity and disgust with his own party would probably make MacDonald available for the role of splitter. They also knew how strong was MacDonald's more admirable urge to prove that men of working-class origin were not inferior in patriotism to the traditional rulers. The irony was that the Labour leadership actually minded far more about 'saving the pound' than did the Opposition leaders who must have had an inkling that the gold standard was doomed, but who were not prepared to give up the political opportunities which presented themselves in its death throes. The final irony is that a politician as clever as Marquand should have presented such an 'academic' interpretation of the 1931 political crisis. Poor Labour Party, will it never learn?

CHAPTER TWENTY-SIX

Lloyd George

Peter Rowland, *Lloyd George*
[Barrie and Jenkins, 1976]

NO ONE has yet written a good biography of Lloyd George. For this there are many reasons. Lord Beaverbrook, who might have done it, commissioned instead a sub-standard life by Frank Owen which appeared in 1954. A. J. P. Taylor, who might have done it, instead wrote a life of Lord Beaverbrook. Latterly, the huge expansion of archives has posed a daunting challenge to any would-be biographer, though John Grigg has valiantly embarked on the journey. Also it seems that Americans are not interested in Lloyd George, which makes a biography an unattractive publishing proposition. But these explanations do not go to the root of the matter. The trouble is that Lloyd George's career has simply become too difficult to get into focus. He is too great to be ignored, too elusive to be understood. He foreshadows the future, but doesn't really fit either into what went before him, or what came after him. He is the puzzling product of a puzzling epoch – the age of war, revolution, and empire which opened in the 1880s and closed, perhaps, in 1950. Peter Rowland, who works with the Greater London Council, has scarcely met the challenge posed by this 'life and times'. What he has written is perfectly respectable and fair as far as it goes. His main strength is a firm grasp of political detail. His main weaknesses are a lack of interest in personality and context, and a truly monumental inability to see the wood for the trees. He is not helped by a wretched production, though it would doubtless have been less wretched had the book been less than 872 pages and 450,000 words. In short, the book lacks class, which is a pity as its subject has so much.

Of Welsh parents, David Lloyd George was born in Manchester in 1863, but grew up in Caernarvon. Brought up by his adoring and indulgent Uncle Lloyd, he soon developed a sense of destiny, a high belief in his own capacities, a determination to succeed in law and politics, and some standard Welsh grievances against Toryism, represented by English landlords, English brewers, and the Established Church. Although these may have had personal experience behind them, the motivating force in Lloyd George's life seems to have been the very natural desire of an outstanding young man to reach the commanding position to which he felt his talents entitled him, an ambition given a radical tinge by small artisan, rural resentments against squire and parson (rents and tithes) and a nationalist, anti-English, tinge by the fact that these feudal remnants symbolized English occupation. In the Liberal Party his hero was Joseph Chamberlain, not Gladstone: the 'unauthorized programme' plus federalism (which fitted Wales) was much more appetizing than Home Rule plus nothing. It is hard to tell from Rowland's account whether it was Chamberlain's betrayal of liberalism or his own emotional identification with small nations, which led Lloyd George, as MP for Caernarvon Boroughs, to take up such a bitter, populist, muck-raking, anti-Boer War line in 1899. At any rate, the parallels with Chamberlain's career are so striking that it is tempting to see both of them, for all their differences – Chamberlain's greater vision, Lloyd George's greater charm – as politicians of the same type: politicians of situation, rather than principle or class.

No assessment of Lloyd George's political personality can proceed far without confronting the deeply ambiguous concept of opportunism. To call a politician an opportunist is to suggest someone who sacrifices principles for the sake of political gain. But to call a footballer or tennis player an opportunist is to suggest rather someone with a flair for creative responses to chances and challenges. The converse of this kind of opportunism is not principle but rigidity. To confine the meaning of opportunism to the first case alone makes little sense in our century of accelerating change and enlarging government, which have forced on politicians prodigies of adaptation and manipulation which would have shocked their mid-nineteenth-century predecessors.

Lloyd George was an opportunist in the second sense, one whose fluidity of principle made him a creative politician for a period of great unrest and danger. He was a manager, not an ideologist or class warrior: a manager of genius. 'The difference between ordinary and extraordinary men,' he told Lord Riddell, 'is that when the extraordinary man is faced by a novel and difficult situation, he extricates himself by adopting a plan which is at once daring and unexpected.' And the point of the man of action is to get things done when there is danger but no consensus. At no stage in his career was Lloyd George ever at a loss for a plan, a solution, a way out, however intractable the problem appeared. His method of action was instinctive, but a certain preferred pattern emerges: the summoning of the best brains to provide policies; the appointment of executive types, mainly from business, to carry them out; and the exercise of political leadership to mobilize the necessary consent. With this approach Lloyd George could never be a good party man. If the party situation proved no obstacle to doing what the situation needed, all well and good. But like Joseph Chamberlain, he was prepared to break up parties, if necessary, to secure the required flexibility of response. Lloyd George's creative opportunism is best seen in the situation which most required it: the First World War. The standard 'selfish hypothesis' has him scheming non-stop to replace Asquith as Prime Minister. However, in three dense chapters, Rowland shows that Lloyd George's underlying commitment in all his jobs, including that of Prime Minister, was to create a machine capable of mobilizing the nation's resources for war and of imposing the civilian will on the military. The elimination of Asquith was never part of this plan. It was Asquith's unwillingness to accept the reality of his decline and hence a more modest conception of his premiership, that brought Lloyd George in December 1916 to a position he had not coveted.

To his managerial view of politics Lloyd George brought outstanding skills. He had an uncanny feel for what the situation required. He was highly receptive to new ideas possibly because, unlike Ramsay MacDonald, he actually listened to what people said. As a persuader he was supreme – sensitive to atmosphere, charming in private, magnificent on a platform. To get things done, too, Lloyd George was prepared to set aside standard procedure. No leading British politician has had a greater disdain for the established conventions of public life, sexual as well as political. Of the Irish settlement of 1922 Rowland writes: 'He had achieved it by typical Lloyd George methods – patient, conciliatory discussions, sudden storms of rage, truculence one moment and sweet reasonableness the next, pleadings, wooings, threats, frankness, generosity and guile.' But the Coalition elected in 1918 also illustrates the seamy counterpart of flexible response: the growth of a purely manipulative style of politics. Like Nixon, Lloyd George came to believe that everything could and should be fixed, managed or bought. His court developed many of the same paranoias and vices, illustrating what a thin line divides creativity from corruption. By 1922, as Rowland writes, 'everyone was on to Lloyd George. His slapdash methods, his blatant opportunism, his attempt to manipulate the Press, his network of spies and personal contacts . . . and lastly . . . the stench of the Honours Scandal, had given rise to widespread and very real repugnance.'

Yet the collapse of Lloyd George's career in 1922 is linked to a more fundamental problem: the failure of managerialism to generate either large objectives or a solid social base. For all his temperamental radicalism, Lloyd George was a fixer and patcher. But while he was laying the foundation of the Welfare State in 1911, even while he was winning the war, the politics of ideology and class were creeping up, leaving him stranded. Essentially what both Chamberlain and Lloyd George tried to do was to preserve flexibility of response by breaking up the two party system. Lloyd George's plan in 1920 was for a Centre Party under his leadership, isolating the Left from the Right on either side. Instead after a period of further confusion, the political battle lines formed up on the basis of Conservative versus Labour, with the Liberals squeezed out. In retrospect it is hard to see how it could have been otherwise, or how Lloyd George could have altered the outcome. By the 1920s, despite his brand new economic policy which hardly anyone understood, he already appeared, as Rowland says, a 'fascinating survivor from a vanished age'.

CHAPTER TWENTY-SEVEN

Life with Sylvester

A. J. Sylvester, *Life with Lloyd George*, ed. Colin Cross
[Macmillan, 1975]

ON 19 October 1922, David Lloyd George resigned as Prime Minister. He was fifty-nine years old. Although he lived for another twenty-three years, he never held ministerial office again. After 1931, his parliamentary following shrunk to his daughter Megan, his son Gwilym, and Goronwy Owens, a relation by marriage. These are the years covered by the shorthand diary kept by his private secretary, A. J. Sylvester, now most skilfully edited by Colin Cross.

There were many reasons for Lloyd George's fall. He was attached to a declining party – the Liberals. He remained a radical in a society which sought the security of doctrine and convention. 'It is time there was a row in England,' Lloyd George used to say. But the last thing the smooth men wanted was a row. Since Lloyd George's cynicism in small things offended the goody-goodies, and his audacity in big things appalled the political mediocrities at Westminster, his exclusion from power or influence became inevitable. Perhaps it was expecting too much of England to allow itself to be saved twice by the same Welshman.

This is a record not just of political, but of personal, decline. Lloyd George was all right till he was seventy-five. Then he slowly subsided. 'He would deal with one question very well,' said Lord Dawson of Penn, the King's Physician, in 1939, 'but when he attempted too much, the other questions would not have the same quality of mind applied to them' – which is a nicely long-winded way of saying he was still fine for three hours a day.

What kind of person emerges from this book? Lloyd George was, in many ways, a child of nature. His sense of humour was basic. Someone produced a bag of air which made rude noises when sat on. 'L. G. laughed himself almost to death.' He was credulous. He firmly believed in phrenology, and would judge people's character by the shape of their craniums. He loved singing hymns and telling funny stories about Welsh preachers. Everything had to revolve round himself. He gobbled his food and had his guests' plates cleared away as soon as he

164

had finished his so that he would not have to wait before starting on his next course. Given his dependence on the nonconformist vote, he took immense risks with his sex life. At this time of his life there was not perhaps much of it, but the complications of his triangular ménage with his wife Dame Margaret and his mistress Frances Stevenson increasingly engrossed his old age, and continued beyond the grave.

He made up for his unashamed self-centredness with great charm, and an entire absence of humbug. At 'whiskey time', which, Sylvester somewhat disapprovingly indicates, came increasingly often, he would comment on men and events in forthright fashion. The League of Nations was a 'factory for manufacturing flapdoodle'. Lord Grey was 'absolutely worthless'. Told about the King's objections to certain passages in his war memoirs, Lloyd George flared up: 'I owe him nothing; he owes his throne to me.' He was none too keen on some of his so-called great contemporaries. Neville Chamberlain failed the phrenological test. 'The worst thing Neville ever did was to let Hitler see him,' said Lloyd George in 1939. Baldwin 'had a happy knack of saying commonplace things in an emphatic way'. Ramsay MacDonald had 'sufficient conscience to bother him, not enough to keep him straight'. Yet Lloyd George was incapable of hating, and seems to have genuinely liked Baldwin, though the feeling was not mutual. Of Philip Kerr (Lord Lothian), Lloyd George remarked: 'His rudder is not equal to his horsepower.' Winston Churchill alone Lloyd George recognized as an equal (almost) but 'he has no convictions and no loyalties to a cause . . . He fights for himself.'

The last three observations are specially interesting, because the question which always arises with Lloyd George is whether he himself had any rudder. 'One catches in his company that flavour of final purposelesness, inner irresponsibility . . .' Keynes wrote in a famous passage which ends, 'Lloyd George is rooted in nothing; he is void and without content; he lives and feeds on his immediate surroundings.' This is unfair. Lloyd George was as much rooted in Wales as Keynes was in Cambridge. 'My one weakness', he remarked, 'is small nationalities . . . If Germany had not invaded Belgium, I would have been against the war.' Perhaps. What is undeniable is that he settled the Irish question – almost for good. He was also rooted in the radicalism of the Joe Chamberlain era, with its hatred of the landlord, and its vision of a prosperous peasantry and a decently housed and treated urban population. Like many great, and not so great, men he moved from the divisive

Left to the reconciling Centre, though rightly refusing to have anything to do with the sham National Government of 1931. Yet he was probably happiest fighting on the Left for the traditional radical causes. Late in life he said how much he would like to lead the opposition in Heaven.

To what extent did he succeed in bringing his radicalism up to date? In 1935 he launched his last public campaign to get the government to 'conquer unemployment'. His speech at Bangor on 17 January 1935, his seventy-second birthday, was a *tour de force*. But the language is not that of modern economics, less so than in 1929 when Keynes was advising him. What divided Lloyd George from Baldwin was not theory or even beliefs, but temperament. Baldwin himself pinpointed this when he remarked with horror in 1922: 'A dynamic force is a very dangerous thing.' At Bangor, Lloyd George said: 'I am not concerned about "isms" of any kind ... These things matter little in comparison with getting things done.' The determination to get things done was the key to his character. It is in the light of this frustrated activism that one should judge Lloyd George's praise of Hitler, following a visit to Germany, and two meetings with the Führer, in September 1936. 'He is a very great man', he remarked of Hitler after his first conversation. What Hitler represented to Lloyd George was precisely that ability and willingness to get things done so lamentably lacking at home. For Germany, Hitler was the 'resurrection and the life'. It is hard now to understand that for many in the 1930s the major interest of Germany was its 'rebirth', not its treatment of its Jews. Realization of the full price being paid for Hitler's social revolution came later.

Despite his admiration for Hitler, Lloyd George was against appeasement. But when war finally came, to the consternation of his friends and the subsequent embarrassment of historians, he turned defeatist and urged a negotiated peace. His assessment of the situation was characteristically forthright. 'It is clear that that damn fool Neville never gave a thought to that question – whether we should win – when he declared war. I am not against war, but I'm against war when we have no chance of winning.' No doubt Lloyd George underestimated the British capacity for snatching victory out of the jaws of defeat. It is also said that he misread the mood of his countrymen. I wonder whether this is so. 'The post which L. G. is receiving as a result of his speech in the House [advocating a negotiated peace] is the greatest I have ever known,' wrote Sylvester in October 1939. 'He has received thousands ... They all cry out for peace.' Lloyd George did not live to see a British victory.

Ennobled as Earl Lloyd-George of Dwyfor in January 1945, he died in Wales two months later. Frances Stevenson, now his wife, held his left hand and his daughter Megan held his right. Sylvester was there too, grumbling, but loyal, to the end.

CHAPTER TWENTY-EIGHT

Life with Pussy

*My Darling Pussy: The Letters of Lloyd George
and Frances Stevenson 1913–1941*, ed. A. J. P. Taylor
[Weidenfeld & Nicolson, 1979]

LLOYD GEORGE did not waste much time on love. Nor did he waste much time on his love letters to Frances Stevenson. Neither does Mr Taylor on editing them. Nor should the general public on reading them. They have no claims as literature; and Mr Taylor is reduced to the following peculiar advertisement for their historical value: '1917 was a year of crisis. The U-boat attack on British shipping across the Atlantic reached its climax . . . There was a revolution in Russia . . . The French army was in a state of mutiny . . . In October the Italians were routed at Caporetto. None of this is reflected in Lloyd George's correspondence with Frances.' Instead we read, 'I have loved you more passionately – more tenderly – more affectionately than ever. D.'

Frances Stevenson became Lloyd George's secretary and mistress in 1913; he married her in 1943, two years after the death of Dame Margaret, his first wife. The letters cover most of this period. They are mainly from him to her. 'I am so happy to think that my girl is getting nearer and nearer to the arms that are throbbing with a desire to enfold and crush her against my bosom,' the old boy scribbled lecherously; she in turn pined to 'feel your thrilling kisses on my lips'. So they amused themselves. 'Pop' (as Lloyd George sometimes signed himself) claimed he loved his 'Pussy' with 'a ferocity which is unchilled by the snows of age or the glaciers of domesticity'. But he displayed considerable ferocity on the side; and the glaciers of domesticity guaranteed the Nonconformist vote. Frances, too, loved elsewhere, notably Colonel Frederick Tweed, Lloyd George's political adviser; though Taylor argues

167

convincingly that it was Lloyd George, not Tweed, who fathered Frances's daughter Jennifer.

In all these acres of passion it is hard to find much politics. What there is of interest is provided not by Frances Stevenson's reports (printed at excessive length) but by some characteristic Lloyd George jibes at the expense of the plentiful supply of mediocrities who surrounded him. Of his Liberal No. 2, the sanctimonious Sir Herbert Samuel, he remarked acidly in 1929, 'If his courage and capacity were equal to his conceit I should resign in his favour.' On 4 February 1931 he wrote about the Labour Cabinet: 'I am full of trying to bring this cowardly government up to the mark – a hopeless task. Sisyphus is not in it with me. I am trying to roll a melting sloshing snowball up the hill.' And of its Prime Minister, Ramsay MacDonald: 'This ranting hero of the Socialist halls squealed with terror when he was invited to face the wrath of the financial weasels of the City. What leaders for the Revolution.'

Mr Taylor takes a limited view of his editorial functions. Pertinax was not a 'leading French journalist' but the *nom de plume* of André Géraud of *L'Echo de Paris*, who was. Lloyd George did not launch his Council of Action at the beginning of 1935, but in July 1935. And it is surely far-fetched to suggest that, but for his prostate operation, he would have headed the National Government in 1931. Mr Taylor's knowledge is encyclopaedic, but even he should not write history off the top of his head.

CHAPTER TWENTY-NINE

Rhodes James's Churchill

Robert Rhodes James, *Churchill – A Study in Failure 1900–1939*
[Weidenfeld & Nicolson, 1970]

CHURCHILL the hero was born in 1940. Two years earlier he had been written off as a failure. 'Thank God we are preserved from Winston Churchill,' wrote a senior officer in 1936 when Churchill was refused the new Ministry for the Co-ordination of Defence. It was a general sentiment. How had he come to count for so little after a lifetime of striving? Lloyd George blamed 'the distrust and trepidation with which mediocrity views genius at close quarters'. Robert Rhodes James disagrees. Churchill's wounds, he argues in his new book *Churchill: A Study in Failure 1900–1939*, were self-inflicted. Despite his brilliant gifts of mind and character, there was some 'tragic flaw in the metal' which denied him the trust accorded to lesser men. The theme is not new, but it is developed with all the eloquence and erudition which Mr Robert Rhodes James's admirers have come to expect. He builds up a formidable indictment against a man convicted repeatedly of erratic judgment and inconsistency of purpose.

The very qualities which made Churchill such a memorable talker were apt to make him a disastrous executive. His enthusiasm for half-baked ideas was notorious. Antwerp, the Dardanelles, intervention in Russia, his budgets as Chancellor of the Exchequer, India, rearmament – his career was littered with audacious and imaginative schemes which were either flawed in conception, or, while soundly conceived, had not been fully thought through. He was a prophet for a cause – but the cause seemed to vary from moment to moment. As President of the Board of Trade he championed social reform; as Home Secretary he sternly repressed sedition. As First Lord of the Admiralty he enthused over naval expansion; as Chancellor of the Exchequer he cut down naval estimates. The Little Englander who broke with the Conservatives over Joseph Chamberlain's Imperial visions of 1903 becomes the undeviating upholder of Empire in the 1930s; the Air Minister of whom it was written 'he leaves the body of British flying well nigh at its last gasp' emerges as spokesman for air rearmament in 1934. The fanatical anti-Bolshevist embraces the Soviet alliance in 1938.

Of course the charge of inconsistency can be overdone. The man who over a long life claims never to have changed his opinions is either a fool or a liar. Nevertheless the bewildering variety and contradictions of Churchill's enthusiasms (not to mention his switches of party allegiance) prompt the question: what did he stand for? What was Churchill's dream except Winston Churchill? These pages provide little evidence of serious political purpose. Rather we are transported into a world of romance, peopled with heroes and villains, echoing with drama and thunder-claps and last stands. Each situation is invested with the properties of fantasy and heroic achievement, always with Churchill in the role of the romantic lead. The great captain, the tribune of the people, the Iron Chancellor, the defender of the King, the champion of Liberty – these were the roles Churchill conjured up for himself, with events, circumstances, people to be moulded into the shape required by his inner drama.

Churchill's commitment to parliamentary democracy was always at the mercy of his flirtations with the heroic. Lloyd George likened him to 'a chauffeur who apparently is perfectly sane and drives with great skill for months, then suddenly takes you over a precipice'. A rail strike of 1911 finds him mobilizing 50,000 troops; fifteen years later as editor of the *British Gazette* during the General Strike he compares himself to the captain of a great battleship. With Churchill, as A. C. Gardiner has pointed out, 'it is always the hour of fate and the crack of doom'. The rhetoric was inevitably subject to the law of diminishing returns. All these mistakes, according to Mr Rhodes James, deprived Churchill of the influence he should have had in the 1930s. Yet the reason for his failure then is not that he had been 'wrong' so many times that when he was finally 'right' no one was prepared to listen; rather that he continued to be 'wrong' in the same way. His advocacy of bigger rearmament was ruined by obsolescent military views, and by his devotion to the crackpot schemes of his confidant, Lindemann. Potential support on the right was antagonized by his failure to link rearmament with political settlement; on the left by his failure to widen his simple anti-Germanism into anti-Fascism – he welcomed both Mussolini and Franco as bulwarks against the 'bestial appetites' of Bolshevism. His policy seemed to be truculence for its own sake; an old-fashioned Great Power romanticism, with half-fearful, half-joyful anticipations of Armageddon; or for those who had never trusted his motives, simply another ploy to bring an ageing politician back into the office his restless talents and ambition craved.

In the end we are hardly closer to unravelling the Churchill enigma. That he was fascinating, magnanimous, courageous, gifted, is beyond dispute; but over his seriousness of purpose a question mark remains.

CHAPTER THIRTY

Martin Gilbert's Churchill

Martin Gilbert, *Winston S. Churchill: Vol. 5, 1922–1939*
[Heinemann, 1976]

I HAVE never found Winston Churchill the most interesting of modern political leaders. He had many marvellous qualities, among which were courage, generosity, and the ability to express his thoughts in eloquent and inspiring language. But it is the thoughts themselves which leave me dissatisfied. Churchill was never interested in the economic and social forces shaping the twentieth century; he was 'unable', as Leopold Amery put it, 'ever to get the modern point of view'. He thus occupies a curiously isolated position in the politics of his time. Alone of all the great twentieth-century leaders he made no impact, in either thought or action, on the economic problem. Even when he and 'history' came together, as they did so triumphantly in 1940, this was more a matter of luck than judgment. I do not know why Churchill was so insensitive to his age. Perhaps it has to do with his own self-absorption. Whatever the case, and whatever Churchill's specific value in 1940, he must seem irrelevant to much of what was happening over a very long political life.

Martin Gilbert has plainly decided not to let such considerations prevent him from treating Churchill's life on the grandest scale. I have a most vivid, and agreeable, memory of visiting Gilbert, a few years ago, at his home near Oxford. The whole of the first floor, an immense room, was 'purpose built' to house the Churchill Archive. As we talked about Churchill, appeasement, and kindred subjects, he would rush to his files and extract document after document, each of which would be fingered lovingly before being passed to me for inspection and approval. It was the kind of love affair which the greatest historians have always had with their material. But the dangers of self-indulgence are very great. Documents can too easily become a substitute for judgment – and thought. It cannot be said that Mr Gilbert has entirely avoided these pitfalls.

The book is far too long. No historian should succumb as completely as Mr Gilbert has to the fascination of the documents themselves. Of course, much of the new material, from the Churchill and other collections, is genuinely absorbing. But there is too much. Was it really necessary to reproduce the letters of appreciation which Churchill received after every speech, major or minor? By putting so much in, Mr Gilbert allows the detail to overwhelm the theme. This fault is connected with another, and greater: the entire absence of independent historical judgment. Mr Gilbert's immersion in the Archive has deprived him of a detached perspective. He never asks: was Churchill right or wrong on this question, in the light of what we know and feel today? In fact 'what we know today' is almost entirely ignored. There is no attempt to incorporate the results of the latest historical research, whether it be on the return to the gold standard, or on the scale of Germany's air rearmament in the 1930s. There is no attempt to take into account such criticisms as those mounted by Robert Rhodes James in his *Churchill: A Study in Failure*. Now, if a man has been universally denigrated, there is something to be said for writing more favourably about him than one may perhaps feel in order to redress the balance. But Churchill is such a hero, such a myth, to so many people, that there is really no excuse for a serious historian to perpetuate the most uncritical aspects of the legend. But this is what Mr Gilbert does by deliberately refraining from comment. Mr Gilbert would no doubt reply that the documents speak for themselves. But if this were so, we would not need a biography, merely a collection of papers. The historian's task is not to reproduce original sources in a fair-minded way and link them together in tolerable prose, but to use those sources to interpret motive and behaviour. History, in short, should be argument. This is particularly necessary with Churchill, whose stands were so consistently controversial. Mr Gilbert's self-denying ordinance time and again fails to uncover the basic issues in the events in which Churchill was involved.

Consider the return to the gold standard in 1925. Mr Gilbert quotes from memoranda Churchill wrote, as Chancellor of the Exchequer, questioning the wisdom of the policy. Now, I think, and I think Mr Gilbert thinks, that Churchill's doubts were genuine, that he would have been happier with an alternative policy but lacked the knowledge and confidence to fight his advisers. But Mr Moggridge, who has written the authoritative book on the return to the gold standard, interprets the material differently. Mr Gilbert never refers to the book. It all hinges on what one thinks Churchill's motives were in writing the memoranda he did – the most basic question which can confront a historian. Mr Gilbert ignores it. He also never discusses the quality of advice Churchill was given as Chancellor. I think Churchill comes out much more creditably than is usually allowed. But no one would gather from the way Mr Gilbert discusses the matter that Churchill's association with the gold standard, and the ensuing deflation and unemployment, was to weaken his political position in the 1930s. By not discussing the enormity of the return to gold, and emphasizing instead Churchill's pension and de-rating schemes, Mr Gilbert gets his Chancellorship completely out of perspective. He was not a great reforming Chancellor, and was not regarded as such at the time, for all the brilliance and ingenuity of his budget speeches.

Mr Gilbert minimizes the provocation of Churchill's articles in the *British Gazette* during the General Strike of 1926, but rightly emphasizes his conciliatory gestures to the miners afterwards. A Churchillian attitude is revealed here which is of great relevance to his later stands on India and Germany, but which Mr Gilbert's 'no comment' approach to history prevents him from bringing out. This is Churchill's refusal to give way to pressure, allied with his generosity in victory. This is the patrician attitude; it is one of the main clues to both his greatness and his inadequacy. Declining empires are always subject to pressure, and offer few clear-cut victories for the display of magnanimity. A refusal to surrender to pressure thus becomes a recipe for endless confrontation, unless generosity comes in advance of pressure. But because Churchill never recognized the extent to which Britain's power had declined, he was unable to anticipate adverse circumstances. The two options he offered were thus to fight or to be humiliated. This was the basic motif which runs through his career, overshadowing everything else. When the Nationalists threatened British lives and property in Shanghai in 1927, Churchill demanded that the government 'send out plenty of tanks . . . to keep order'. The foreign exchange and budgetary costs to a Chancellor who had just put Britain back on the gold standard, and was trying to economize on military spending to finance old age pensions, never entered his head.

It is significant that Mr Gilbert can write over eleven hundred pages on Churchill between the wars without having to put the word Unemployment into his index. At the height of the Great Depression, Churchill's consuming political passion was to block any moves, however modest, towards Indian self-government at the national level. Mr Gilbert produces much new material on Churchill's campaign, particularly in connection with the Committee of Privilege. But he refuses to pass any judgment on the issue between Churchill and his opponents, on the interesting (if in my view fallacious) connection Churchill made between resisting Gandhi and resisting Hitler, and on the extent to which Churchill's association with the Diehards damaged his standing with the political classes. Clearly, and Mr Gilbert does well to bring this out, Churchill was not as remote from the corridors of power in the 1930s as people have often assumed. Although the BBC – with its usual robust concern for freedom of expression – twice prevented him from broadcasting, he was given access by MacDonald, via Sir Desmond Morton and others, to a great deal of classified information on the state of British and German armaments, which he was able to use in attacking government policy. Even as the Indian controversy dragged on, Churchill was playing a semi-official role in the tardy move towards British rearmament: that of an officially-sponsored critic prodding the government to further efforts.

But Mr Gilbert's historical methods let the reader down most badly when it comes to the clash between Churchill and the so-called Appeasers. It is quite unacceptable for a historian not to make some attempt to measure his protagonist's words and forecasts against the reality which the historian can see in retrospect. Churchill was magnificently right in demanding quicker and more massive rearmament; but almost entirely wrong in the specific arguments he used both for the need for rearmament and for the type of rearmament needed. He stated that Germany's industry was 'adapted on an unexampled scale for war'. This is not true. Although the issue is extremely complicated, all modern accounts I have read agree that Churchill's estimates of German aircraft production were greatly exaggerated. His assertion that the German air force was intended to murder 'our women and children' was untrue. Mr Gilbert also fails to bring out the central issue between Tizard and Churchill's friend, Lindemann, on the Air Defence Research sub-committee – whether it should concentrate on developing radar or dissipate its energies in investigating Lindemann's crackpot schemes.

The larger issue in all this concerns, of course, British policy towards Germany. Mr Gilbert ignores the whole revisionist school and simply assumes that Churchill was right all the way through. On the face of it, it seems plausible enough. As soon as the Nazis came to power in Germany Churchill declared that they meant to go to war. In 1939 war broke out. He seemed completely vindicated. Yet, judging from the evidence of this book, Churchill never provided convincing arguments to show why he thought Nazism meant war, why he thought German aims were limitless, or why he thought they were directed against Britain. My complaint throughout this book is not that Mr Gilbert takes up positions with which I might disagree, but that he never attempts to argue anything out.

CHAPTER THIRTY-ONE

Oswald Mosley

[1969]

IN A sense the life of Sir Oswald Mosley[1] can be seen simply as a personal tragedy. A man of brilliant gifts was ruined by fatal flaws of character. There is little to be said except pay a tribute to his qualities, describe his failings, indulge in a little psychologizing and speculating on what might have been, and pass on to more serious matters. Yet the uncomfortable feeling remains that this is not the whole story – though it is undoubtedly a considerable part of it. Why, after all, was the political system *not* prepared to adopt his unemployment policy in 1930–31? Why, in particular, did the radical party shrink from the only measures that would have enabled it to fulfil its pledges to those who voted for it? The question becomes even more puzzling when we recall that not just Mosley but *anyone* with ideas, courage, and energy, was excluded from power or influence in the inter-war years. The roll-call of the neglected and the discarded includes the three most distinguished names in twentieth-century British public life – Lloyd George, Churchill and Keynes. It is true that they all made mistakes: Lloyd George cheated over peerages, Churchill went wild over the General Strike and India, Keynes stood convicted of intellectual arrogance. Yet the fact remains that each had a unique contribution to make, not only to the saving of millions of lives in this country from the wastage of unemployment, but also to the saving of Europe from the much greater horror of another war. They were denied the opportunity, and even today well over half the people alive in England must be the poorer in health, wealth, experience and memory because of it – not to mention those who are dead.

Were these men excluded for their faults or for their virtues? The answer, surely, is that the two are inseparable. Great men usually have great faults: this is what makes them dangerous. But that is no reason for not using them, provided they can be subject to control, for they can achieve things beyond the power of lesser mortals. The real question posed by Mosley's life, particularly in his Fascist phase, is whether it is possible to liberate the dynamic forces in individuals or groups and at the same time preserve a civilized framework of public life. Energy is fundamentally amoral. It is no counter of heads, or respecter of rights; it despises weakness and passivity. It can certainly be attached to moral objectives, but need not be. In any case, it need not be associated with moral behaviour. The civilized regime deliberately seeks to dampen the fires of public energy for fear of the damage they might do to the social fabric. Yet the civilized regime, too, has a serious flaw. In Raymond Aron's words 'such regimes are capable, not of committing monstrous actions, but of passively suffering the consequences of monstrous phenomena'[2] – for example, the world economic depression of 1929–33. This is because they are by nature conservative, slow-moving, and small-thinking. Because they fear men eager to master great challenges, they are run by the mediocre and the timid – men incapable of doing great harm, but incapable of doing great good either. Moreover, such mandates as they might obtain from the electorate are largely undermined by the excessive influence they allow to what David Riesman has called the 'veto-groups' – strategically placed lobbies or pressure groups without effective power to initiate action, but in an excellent position to stop anything being done inimical to their interests.[3] Such regimes suffer from a paralysis of executive power which can become dangerous in any situation where big choices are called for.

The problem of injecting a new vitality into the British system Mosley saw essentially as a cultural one. British politics was a closed cultural system, dominated by habits of mind, spirit and conduct, which in his view no longer had much relation to the 'harsh necessities of this age' – an age dominated by an unprecedented rate of technical and cultural change. It attracted and produced a type of man 'to whom action has become impossible.' Mosley was not part of that culture. Nor, for that matter, were Lloyd George and Churchill. This may help to explain why all three saw certain things more clearly

176

than their political contemporaries – and why they were hated for doing so.

In his memoirs, Mosley writes of 'three very diverse experiences which wove me into the warp and woof of English life'. The first was his family background. He sprang from a family of landed gentry who traced their ancestry back to King John. Of his grandfather who dominated his early years he writes, 'His type and being were rooted in English soil.' Life had changed little at Rolleson, the Mosley Staffordshire seat, over the centuries. It was 'remote from the world, a remarkable, feudal, survival'. The economy was 'practically self-contained'. In true feudal fashion 'the warmest and most intimate friendships' developed between landlord and estate worker. 'This was really a classless society.' In his political life Mosley took the 'One Nation' ideal completely seriously. For the 'bourgeois Tory mind with its crude class divisions of the cities' he had little time. To the charge levelled against him by the Tories of being a class traitor 'my reply was simple: it is you, not I who betray our very English heritage, when you take the part of reaction against the people!' The Whig aristocrats had pioneered the major reforms of the nineteenth century. In the Labour Party, too, the aristocrats 'were a great disappointment to MacDonald . . . they at once joined the Left.' The great enemy was the bourgeoisie. MacDonald had fallen victim not to the aristocratic, but to the middle-class, embrace.

Another legacy of his early upbringing is what Mosley describes as the 'Cavalier attitude to life'. In the seventeenth century the Mosleys were prominently identified with the Royalist cause and in the eighteenth century were intriguing for the Young Pretender – 'a romantic tradition of opposition and insurgence' which, as Mosley writes, was transformed into the Whig gravity of the nineteenth century. But that was about as far as the Mosleys got to modern England. Nor was the transition complete. The reckless, Cavalier strain remained, especially in personal life. Of his mother's family he writes, 'They were by nature much more respectable than the Mosleys, who always rather shocked them . . . they had not the complete freedom from inhibitions which was a characteristic of many Mosleys.' Indeed, if the puritan approach to life can be summed up (in Reich's phrase) as a 'holding back', Mosley's was the exact antithesis. The young men of his class and generation 'rushed towards life with arms outstretched to embrace the sunshine, and even the darkness, the light and shade which is the essence of existence, every varied enchantment of a glittering, wonderful world; a life rush, to be consummated.' The strong flavour which emerges from these passages on his childhood of an aristocracy and a working class united, not only by feudal relationships, but, as Lord Randolph Churchill only half-flippantly observed, 'in the indissoluble bonds of a common immorality', has little connection with Victorian England, in which a rhetoric of high seriousness concealed the reality of an industrial exploitation inexorably compelling the masses to organize in their self-defence.

If Mosley took his healing vision from the aristocracy, he took from the Army a method of organization and a 'certain attitude to manhood'. From Winchester, Mosley had gone to Sandhurst; he fought bravely in the First World War, both as a volunteer in the infant Flying Corps, and later in the trenches, before being invalided out in 1916. Mosley was greatly attracted by the 'collective character of regiments', by the combination of discipline and trust which made possible their great achievements; a combination which might yet be adapted to peaceful purposes when the 'noble inspirations' used for war might be released for 'creative achievement'. Mosley brought to politics a definite military attitude. His most memorable remark – on Labour's perform-ance in 1931 – is a military one: 'What would we think of a Salvation Army that took to its heels on the Day of Judgment?' He set out to create an Army that would not run away, that would inculcate 'that sense of belonging to an *élite* of service and achievement' which he had found in the Army – an ideal which naturally attracted very much the same sort of recruit. 'Around me,' he recalls of his political army, 'were men wearing every medal for gallantry the army has to offer . . . They seemed to appear from nowhere, from the limbo into which Britain all too often casts those who have served it well.' For Mosley, the BUF was really a regiment – under his command. It provided 'the most complete companionship I have ever known'. He 'reverted to type and lived in the spirit of the professional army where I began'. Of the decision to put his men into uniform, he writes, 'The old soldier in me got the better of the politician.' It is not a bad summary of his political career.

His morality, too, is very much the morality of an army officer. A political commentator in 1931 described him as a 'Mussolini tempered by the decencies of Sandhurst'. Honour, chivalry, respect for a brave foe, fighting with the 'good clean English fist' are ideas that frequently crop

178

up in this book. Hitler's genocide programme ran contrary to 'the instinct of brave men ... that you cannot kill helpless prisoners'; the same reaction prompted his early political campaigns against the Black and Tans and General Dyer's Amritsar massacre in 1919. Mosley cannot be called an amoralist: but his morality has little to do with the Christian ethic or any belief in the brotherhood of man. It may be described as an intense loyalty and compassion to members of his own group, community, or 'culture'; coupled with a relative indifference to the fate of outsiders. As to his commitment always to 'fight clean', one can only say that to many observers it seemed to be more evident in the breach than in the observance.

If Mosley took his ideal from the aristocracy and his disciplined method from the army, it was to the working class that he looked to provide the energy for its realization. 'It was', he writes, 'the dynamism of the Labour Party at that time which really attracted me, and this came mostly from the rank and file.' For Mosley the working class was a regenerative force because it was uncontaminated by the political and personal inhibitions of the bourgeoisie. The two main centres of energy he found on the Clydeside and among the miners. He worked closely with the Clydeside leaders, who showed a 'real impulse of vital feeling'. Of John Wheatley he writes, 'he was the only man of Lenin quality the English Left ever produced.' He admired the 'blaring bands and flaunting banners' of the Durham miners' galas, symbols 'then anathema to the shy middle class with its ... inhibitions'; the 'gay panache' of the East Londoners. A. J. Cook, the demagogic miners' leader, he regards as 'a real product of England if ever there was one'. Mosley's identification with the working class was an active one. 'Every night', he recalls of his Labour Party speaking tours, 'was passed in the house of a different member, nearly all manual workers ... The wife cooked and looked after us, gave the very best they had, and I have never been better cared for and made to feel more warmly welcome and accepted.' In return, Mosley flung himself wholeheartedly on to the workers' side in the General Strike (which he nevertheless considered was a mistake), and was rewarded with considerable rank-and-file support. Indeed, he was the only major leader of the Labour Left who had had a strong union base – among the miners – though the bourgeois union leaders mistrusted him as an unsound intellectual.

179

The working class may well be uncontaminated by the political inhibitions of the bourgeois mind; large sections of it are singularly free likewise from bourgeois standards of public morality and respect for the rights of others that go with them. Mosley gradually added to his championing of working-class rights, a championing of working-class prejudices as well – against the Jews in the East End in the 1930s, against the coloured immigrants in the 1950s. These stands cannot be fully explained by considerations of *realpolitik*. Essentially they arose from the same feeling of sympathy for the *English* underdog that led him into the Labour Party in 1924, the feeling that the 'goody-goodies', as Churchill called them, were prepared to put every interest above that of their fellow-countrymen; though the psychological pressure on the orator to say things that he knows will stir his audiences cannot be ignored. Today, with the elimination of overt economic oppression, it would appear that racial questions are the only ones capable of radical-izing the working class. The long-term implications of this are not at all comforting. It would indeed be ironic and tragic if the British ruling class should have finally succeeded in creating what they have always tried to avoid – a 'know-nothing' proletarian party, chauvinist and racialist in outlook; and proving Mosley to be a precursor in this sphere, as in so many others.

Absent from Mosley's account of the 'warp and woof' of English life is any mention of the public schools, universities (he did not go to one), civil service, trade union or local government organizations, the legal profession, industry and finance: the great seminaries of the English governing *élites*, bastions of civic middle-class culture. This omission justifies the frequent view of Mosley as an alien politician – 'alien', that is, to the dominant political culture of his time, no longer nourished from the soil from which Mosley sprang. A hundred years ago, Bagehot discerned the underlying truth, then still obscured behind an aristo-cratic façade, that it was the middle classes who wielded 'the despotic power in England'; that what passed for public opinion was the opinion of the 'heavily sensible class – the last people in the world to whom, if they were drawn up in a row, an immense nation would ever give an exclusive preference.'[4] It was this class that gave to the 'fickle and protean' England of Tudor times[5] its recognizably modern shape and flavour – serious, sound, and sanctimonious. Its virtues were

180

worthy and mediocre rather than exciting, but it gave to English public life its 'rules of the game' – a civilized framework of public life which shielded it from the excesses of the Continent. Mosley was not part of this England. He spurned it, and it rejected him. Like so many activists, he looked to the losers rather than to the winners of the nineteenth-century social struggle to restore a lost heritage of dynamism and greatness.

I do not wish to imply that Mosley can be explained – or explained away – by his class background. A county background still produces choleric Tory squires, whose 'One Nation' thinking scarcely goes beyond the boundaries of their rural retreats. Able Sandhurst products become generals, not politicians. Certain personal qualities and one decisive circumstance carried Mosley to a leading position in English politics. The qualities were a powerful mind, a gift of eloquence, and an enormous energy. The decisive circumstance was the First World War. It was the war that turned his attention to politics. The war-time state had given him some inkling of the possibilities of social organization. It was easy for gallant officers to pick up parliamentary seats. The party battle was temporarily suspended. Above all, the catastrophic slaughter of the war gave him a strong sense of mission: to ensure that war never happened again, to build 'a land fit for heroes'.

It was this mixture of social idealism and raw intellectual energy, grafted on to a squirearchical-military stem, that produced the explosive phenomenon of Mosley the politician. The difficulties of classifying him emerge in some of the encomiums reproduced in this book: 'could well have been either Conservative or Labour Prime Minister', etc. In the space of ten years Mosley moved from Unionist to Independent to Labour and finally to Fascist, virtually taking in the Liberal Party on the way. His policies combined causes dear to the heart of progress with causes dear to the heart of reaction. 'The most irrational antithesis of our time', he writes, 'always seemed to me to be the conflict between the progress of the Left and the stability of the Right . . . My programme cut right across it . . . Progress was impossible without stability, and stability was impossible without progress.' Nor do alternative classifications along a 'tough-minded–tender-minded' axis help very much. Many of Mosley's political attitudes, Left or Right, were certainly 'tough-minded': on the other hand, he has been a pacifist in international relations and a libertarian over personal questions. He was neither an honest Tory with old-fashioned prejudices, nor an honest Liberal with new-fashioned ones. Nor is it easier to fit his methods into a recognizable syndrome. He combined the most gentlemanly behaviour in private with very ungentlemanly conduct in public; the methods of reasoned argument with those of demagoguery – 'the high road' and the 'low road' as one commentator remarked of his 1959 North Kensington election campaign. History yields many examples of similar ideological and temperamental syndromes. The fact nevertheless remains that Mosley is not a contemporary English political type. It is as if a character from the sixteenth or seventeenth century had suddenly been transported into the modern English world, with a mission to make his mark upon it. 'The great secret', Mosley writes, 'is to be in the rhythm of your age.' As far as the English political classes were concerned, Mosley certainly was not. He disturbed their rhythm, with its muted oscillations. He was both too old-fashioned and too advanced at the same time.

Nevertheless, this ideological and temperamental remoteness from the modern world did have certain definite advantages. The essence of creativity is the ability to see familiar phenomena in new combinations and juxtapositions, to approach the raw material of life with an imagination unencumbered by stale images or conventional categories. It is no coincidence that the universities have not produced a single creative politician in the last hundred years: Joseph Chamberlain, Lloyd George, Winston Churchill, Mosley – none of them were university men. What they all had in common was an intuition that the world was not quite as their contemporaries saw it. They were sensitive to certain important currents of their time which escaped those trained to think in a certain way. Chamberlain saw that the free trade world of nineteenth-century liberalism was dying. Lloyd George saw that the social question had destroyed the rationale of *laissez-faire* at home. Churchill saw with a terrible prescience the coming struggle between England and Germany. The sources of these profound intuitions vary. Churchill's was derived from history; Joseph Chamberlain and Lloyd George knew no history: they were hyper-sensitive to the vibrations of the external world. Mosley, too, heard the distant hoofbeat of history. Again, it is difficult to say from where. He was not a historical generalizer like Churchill; he knows history, but his vision is not derived from it; it is brought in to support conclusions reached quite independently of it. Nor was his attitude to life formed by ideas: he admired Shaw, Nietzsche, Goethe, Keynes; he studied the great men of action; but all they did was to provide words or illustrations for what he already felt to be true. Mosley learnt whatever he knew 'from life', not from books. He absorbed from it what was necessary to the fulfilment of his own nature. His mind was uncluttered by intellectual luggage. This was a great strength – and weakness. It enabled him to focus on many of the right questions: it also made him blind to many others which should have been weighed in the balance.

The most notable aspect of Mosley's thinking is the entire absence of any 'isms'. This is not to say that he didn't have strong attitudes to life, that there were not certain things he passionately wanted to do. But he did not view the world through the intellectual constructs which dominated the minds of his political contemporaries. Of the free trade/ Protection debate he writes: 'My approach to it was purely pragmatic. Whether you had one system or not was a question of circumstance. If it was raining you needed an umbrella, if the sun was shining, you did not.' It was as if a fourth-century church leader had proclaimed his indifference to the Athanasian–Arian controversy! Similarly, he was untouched by the other great contemporary debate, between socialism and *laissez-faire* capitalism. He regarded these questions as questions of means rather than ends. The same attitude marked his approach to parties: were they or were they not effective instruments for doing what had to be done? In the *Sunday Chronicle* (23 July 1933) he wrote, revealingly, 'We were right to give Socialism a chance. We were also right, when the Labour Party failed, to abandon the old party system . . .' Nothing could be more indicative of his approach than this view of the instrumentality of ideas and movements. How different from Keynes who in the *General Theory* describes his long struggle to 'escape from habitual modes of thought and expression'. Mosley's habitual modes of thought and expression were non-political, for he was not a child of the political culture. That is why he did not have to divest himself of them before he could begin to think creatively about politics.

His capacity to discern important shifts in reality ahead of his contemporaries is indeed impressive. In the 1920s Mosley sensed that the economic debate between *laissez-faire* capitalism and bureaucratic socialism was irrelevant. He discerned that demand rather than distribution was the overriding problem of Western society at that time. Hence he was able to focus his energy on the unemployment problem, and emerge, well ahead of his time, as the prophet of a 'managed capitalism'. This is not all. A visit to America convinced him that modern techniques of mass production had destroyed the basis of small-scale, national economies. It followed that Britain had to enter into a larger economic system. In the 1930s that system was the Empire; by 1947 he was urging that Britain take the lead in creating a united Europe. In the 1930s he saw that any major European war must result in the division of Europe into American and Russian spheres of influence, thus destroying the possibility of its independent development. He was probably wrong in thinking that a war could have been averted on any terms consistent with England's safety and independence; but he was right in foreseeing its consequences, and right – it seems to me – in the conclusion which he drew from it that the old world must unite to redress the balance of the new. He saw again that the existing English system of government and politics seriously inhibited the adaptations England needed to make to new circumstances – a view which is once more on the verge of serious discussions – though he was certainly wrong in seeing Fascism as the 'modern' answer to the problem.

These perceptions were extremely unwelcome to the Establishment. Mosley's success in thinking up good policies was matched by his inability to get them adopted. English political life over the last fifty years has not lacked in ideas. The English have continued to produce good ideas, like good inventions. The trouble is that more often than not they are adopted abroad rather than at home. Keynes's economic policies were tried in other countries before England got round to using them; Liddell Hart's chief disciple was the German General Guderian. It is not enough to explain the failure to use good ideas simply by the inertia of institutions. Some institutions are more inert or unreceptive than others. Why is it that the forces of 'conventional wisdom' in this country have become so strongly entrenched? Or put another way, why is it that the energizing vital forces have become so attenuated? Mosley's explanation is rather uneven. He recognizes the largely unacknowledged hold of certain powerful ideas – particularly the idea of internationalism which, as he remarks, makes British socialism a *de facto* ally of finance capitalism – but does not really pursue this line much further. He is alive to certain defects in the machinery of government and has, at different times, proposed changes – smaller Cabinets, reorganization of the departments, speeding up parliamentary procedure – which have also been canvassed by many others. Of the civil service he has a surprisingly high opinion, blaming most of its alleged failings on the incompetence of its political chiefs.

It is indeed on what he considers to be the psychological failure of the political class that he directs his main attack. Here he plunges somewhat rashly into Freudian explanations – though denying them any validity for an understanding of his own character. The attitude of political 'negation' which Keynes criticized in 1930 he identifies with the 'catastrophe of Puritanism'. He traces a link between personal inhibition, derived from a puritan upbringing, and public inhibition characterized by a negative response to big challenges. Thus he identifies public failures with failures of puritan, middle-class culture. He contrasts this with the amoral energy of a Lloyd George, an energy which the civilized political groups viewed as threatening and disruptive, just as society feels threatened by breaches of its sexual and moral codes. Yet it was Lloyd George, he writes, who 'in tragic paradox' might have realized the 'fine ideals' of the class that feared him. 'His faults were obvious . . . what did they matter in comparison with his extraordinary capacity to get things done, if he were under the right influence, aimed in the right direction? They should have forgiven Lloyd George's minor faults, and embraced his genius to use it for fine ends.' No doubt he had himself very much in mind when he wrote this passage.

This account, especially in its implication that somehow political energy is associated with sexual freedom, is unsatisfactory as it stands. The 'inner-directed' puritan is usually considered capable of great achievement precisely *because* his energy has been diverted from instinctual gratification to the 'tasks of life'. Repression is the spur to achievement, not a hindrance to it, by permitting the concentration of energy on one object, rather than allowing it to be dispersed over many. Mosley would be on much firmer ground, in my view, if he made a distinction between the puritan culture at its zenith, which equipped its leaders with a superb self-confidence, and the puritan culture in its decline, which riddles them with self-doubts. It is this decline which is probably the chief explanation of the humbug which he finds such a characteristic feature of the current political scene: something which arises when real commitment has become a cliché, no longer believed in, but somehow too painful to abandon. In this sense, no doubt, MacDonald, Baldwin, Hoare, Simon and all the 'old gangs' of the 1920s and 1930s were 'whited sepulchres' as Mosley claims; not because they were sexually repressed, but because they lacked inner conviction.

Mosley could have done with some good old-fashioned puritan self-discipline in his own life. I very much doubt whether he would ever have been a very successful party leader, though he might, under suitable circumstances, have been an extraordinary Prime Minister. What he had to do above all else was to avoid discrediting himself beyond repair. A 'reputable' Mosley might have been able to swing British opinion behind Europe in the 1950s, to play Joe Chamberlain to Macmillan's Balfour. Yet discredited he did become through a series of misjudgments that deprived him of any chance of serving his country. It was largely a matter of temperament. Although Mosley likes to picture himself as a model of 'cool determination' and 'icy realism' he was in fact a hot-head who time and again ruined his chances by rash action. One commentator has noted perceptively: 'His defects are those of a cavalry officer under a temperamental compulsion to charge.' In this he resembles his Cavalier ancestors. He was a Prince Rupert rather than an Oliver Cromwell.

This, I am convinced, is the right way to view Mosley's actions in the 1930s and afterwards. He was by instinct a fighter, not a Machiavellian, for no Machiavellian would ever have been so unsuccessful. Moreover, he was a fighter who had only one response: *Charge!* 'We shall win; or we shall return upon our shields,' he cried in 1931 – not just to encourage his troops, but because he felt that way. He describes a number of disputes with fellow cadets at Sandhurst, generally ending with Mosley challenging his opponent to a fight. He says he was 'already becoming too adult for that sort of thing'. This judgment is not borne out by his political career which, from its earliest days, was marked by an extreme pugnacity, by a wounding invective, by an over-reaction to slights and insults (real and imagined) and in general, by a method of controversy that polarized opinion. Whereas many of Mosley's ideas, though revolutionary in terms of the British political culture, were ideas of the centre, capable of winning wide and distinguished 'moderate' support, his methods were those of the extreme, gradually alienating those who would gladly have worked with him, but who were not prepared to stomach the 'Biff Boy' elements which he increasingly considered necessary to his crusade. One can overdraw this picture, for on occasion – as in his resignation of 1930 – Mosley was capable of behaving with tact and decorum. Throughout 1930 in fact we see him at his very best, with his concern for the unemployed conveyed in speeches and arguments remorseless in their logic, dignified in their expression, and passionate in their feeling. But he was incapable of holding this, admittedly difficult, balance for any length of time. The demonic urge for action *at all costs* gripped him. The politics of self-discipline gave way to the politics of self-expression, with results fatal to his career and the causes for which he stood.

And yet a lingering doubt remains. Given the English political system, could that balance between creative thought and civilized political behaviour ever have been maintained for long by someone who actually wanted to get things done, rather than wait for history's verdict? Is civilized political behaviour always the supreme virtue? Was it not worth dislocating the civilized routines of British politics to cure mass unemployment? Most people would rightly accept a certain level of economic suffering in preference to a Fascist or Communist dictatorship. But what about a temporary parliamentary dictatorship of the kind Lloyd George and Churchill exercised in war – and headed by similar people? Would that not in fact have been the answer? Was this not the only method which would have enabled radical solutions to be applied in a political framework that remained recognizably civilized and humane?

For Mosley's Fascist career is an illustration of what happens when a common-sense solution is denied by a political system. The creative thinking is separated from the civilized political framework in which it can find no expression. That framework comes to be seen not as a necessary defence against excess, but as an impediment to action of any kind. Not only are the particular policies of the 'old gangs' repudiated, but also the whole political environment in which they operate. If the distress is great enough, whole sections of the population are shifted from their stable and relatively 'safe' political moorings and become mobilized into radical movements. In this way radical ideas which in themselves offer no threat to civilized political behaviour become attached to social forces and methods which do. A perfectly reputable case against international finance degenerates into an anti-Semitic one; a nationalist case into a racialist one, and so on. The radicalization of one section produces a parallel radicalization of the other, and the politics of violence and villains comes to replace the politics of reason. This is what happened on the fringes of English politics in the 1930s and it might easily have spread had war, and the preparation for war, not supervened.

By all means, then, let us blame Mosley and give full weight to all the temperamental traits that led him to his dismal present. But this no more disposes of the problem posed by his life than does the 'betrayal' of Ramsay MacDonald dispose of the problem of Labour's failure in 1929–31. In both cases we have to deal not just with the faults of men but with the faults of the systems they tried, and failed, to work. Only with that extra dimension does the story of Mosley become fully comprehensible.

NOTES

1   Sir Oswald Mosley, *My Life* (1969).
2   Raymond Aron, *Democracy and Totalitarianism* (1968), p. 103.
3   David Riesman, *The Lonely Crowd* (1961), pp. 213f.
4   Walter Bagehot, *The English Constitution* (1963 ed.), pp. 247–8.
5   The phrase is Max Nicholson's in *The System* (1967), p. 34.

CHAPTER THIRTY-TWO

British Fascism

[1981]

BRITISH fascism is associated above all with the name and personality of Sir Oswald Mosley. There had been a few fascist groups in the 1920s. The British Fascists, founded in 1923 by Miss Rotha Lintorn-Orman, was an extreme right-wing body, disproportionately staffed by generals and admirals, and dedicated to unrelenting struggle against bolshevism. The Imperial Fascist League had been started in 1929 by Arnold Spencer Leese, a retired veterinary surgeon and specialist in camel diseases. An anti-semitic publishing company, the Britons, founded by Henry Hamilton Beamish, dated from 1919. These groups had virtually expired by the early 1930s, though the IFL, reduced to a few dozen members, maintained a raucous, anti-semitic presence throughout the decade. In 1937, William Joyce and John Beckett formed the National Socialist League, a breakaway from Mosley's movement. It attracted about one hundred members. We are left with the British Union of Fascists, founded on 1 October 1932. It campaigned for almost eight years, before being dissolved on 23 May 1940. Although it never came near to power, and in fact never won a single parliamentary seat, it was, for most of that period, a definite

188

factor in British domestic politics and may, at its peak, have had a membership of between 30,000 and 40,000. Its importance was almost entirely due to the outstanding qualities of its leader and founder, Sir Oswald Mosley. The first part of this essay will deal with Mosley's career and personality. Then I shall give an account of the BUF itself, before turning to the wider question of Fascism and the British political culture.

Mosley's career and personality

The salient facts of Mosley's career up to the time he formed the BUF are as follows. Born in 1896, the eldest son of a wealthy and prominent Staffordshire county family – his grandfather was the original of John Bull – he was educated at Winchester and Sandhurst. One of the earliest volunteers to the Royal Flying Corps, he was invalided out of the war in 1916, after a spell in the trenches. Elected MP for Harrow in 1918 on the Coalition Unionist ticket, he crossed the floor in 1920 in protest against the Black and Tans; in 1924 he joined the Labour Party. When Ramsay MacDonald formed his second Labour government in 1929, Mosley, then thirty-three, was appointed Chancellor of the Duchy of Lancaster with special responsibilities for unemployment. In May 1930 he resigned from the government, after the rejection of his Memorandum on unemployment policy. In February 1931 he quit the Labour Party and formed the New Party with a handful of his parliamentary colleagues. This was wiped out at the general election of October 1931 which returned a massive 'National' majority. In the following year, after a visit to Italy, Mosley launched the British Union of Fascists.

Certain features of this story help to explain Mosley's characteristic attitudes to the problems of his day. Politics was far from being his natural vocation. He was born into the squirearchy, or minor aristocracy. This class had traditionally provided local, not national, leadership: in its three hundred years as a leading country family, the Mosleys had sent only two back-bench MPs to Westminster. Mosley himself grew up in a feudal world, unconnected with industrial England. His education was completed at Sandhurst, not Oxbridge. He thus entered parliament without the benefit of a modern political apprenticeship – an émigré from a dying enclave of old England, with something of the attitude of a professional soldier.

Probably he would not have come into politics at all but for the

189

First World War. The war ended the Mosley connection with rural Staffordshire. Even more important was the experience of war. His experience in the air and in the trenches worked on a powerful imagination, giving him a vision of an England reborn, and instilling a hatred of the 'old gangs' who had blundered his country, and Europe, into an appalling blood-bath. Martial values, and wartime organization, might be applied to build a 'land fit for heroes'. The chivalry of air combat might create a more durable basis for European conciliation than the calculations of old-fashioned diplomacy. Mosley desperately wanted to become an air ace. Instead he crashed his aeroplane at Shoreham, before his adored and adoring mother. This probably saved his life, since he was soon afterwards invalided out of the war. But one feels that thereafter he always needed to prove to himself that he was a hero.

For the twenty-two-year-old Mosley, the parliament of 'hard-faced men' was a disillusioning and also misleading experience. The disillusion lay in the failure to build a new world, and the all too depressing prevalence of old political habits and ideas. Idealistic hopes for a reconciling peace, and an effective League of Nations, foundered on the machinations of politicians and diplomats. European statesmen were exploiting, so it seemed to Mosley, the sacrifices of the soldiers in order to pursue the projects of nineteenth-century imperialism – in Russia, the Middle East, and the Ruhr. The Amritsar massacre, and Lloyd George's use of the Black and Tans in Ireland – the issue on which Mosley broke with the coalition – seemed to display the same unregenerate attitudes. Finally, the economic collapse of 1920–21 put paid to immediate hopes of a 'land fit for heroes', ushering in instead a decade of mass unemployment.

Mosley's experience of coalition politics misled him as much as it depressed him. The war had disrupted the two-party system. Politics between 1918 and 1922 were dominated by the attempt to construct a new 'centre' party from the bits and pieces of historical Liberalism, allied to 'patriotic' Labour and 'moral' Conservatism. Mosley was involved in a couple of such attempts, the lead being taken by his patron, Lord Robert Cecil. The dream of a non-ideological, non-class party of the centre never left him. The Conservatives, he told Lord Robert, had sold out to the 'bourgeois profiteer'. Socialists, on the other hand, were too concerned with 'ultimate issues'. Although the leftward evolution of his own ideas, plus the failure to establish a viable centre party, was to carry Mosley into the Labour Party in 1924, he was basically out of sympathy with this redivision of politics into Labour and Conservative. He failed to appreciate its deep sociological roots. He continued to believe that beyond Westminster there was the potential movement of the war generation awaiting the kiss of life. His experience in holding Harrow twice as an Independent strengthened this conviction. And his success at Westminster itself in elegantly hopping from one group to another fed the illusion that party commitments were as fragile as his own.

But Mosley was not just a politician of war-nostalgia. He was determined to give his 'middle way' some intellectual content. Mass unemployment of 10 per cent of the insured labour force in the 1920s gave him his chance. The result was his pamphlet *Revolution by Reason*, written in 1925 with his Labour Party friend, John Strachey. It was a striking attempt to break new ground, intellectually and politically. Orthodox and socialist thought on unemployment alike took its stand on the old political economy inherited from the nineteenth century, the central contention of which was that there could never be a general glut – that is a general insufficiency of demand. The problem, therefore, must lie in some disturbance in proportion. Business spokesmen, and most orthodox economists, argued that as a result of better trade union organization wages had become too high for full employment. Socialists tended to argue the reverse: that wages were too low under capitalism for the purchase of a full-employment output. Both sides therefore tended to explain the mass unemployment of the 1920s in terms of a maldistribution of rewards to the factors of production. The situation was to be remedied either by lowering real wages or – in the socialist version – by redistributing income from the rich to the poor, which was held to require in the end the public ownership of the means of production. The solution, in either case, involved class struggle – which the moderate leaders of both main parties shrank from, particularly after the experience of the General Strike of 1926. Mosley's break with this line of reasoning comes out in the following key statement in *Revolution by Reason*:

At present Socialist thought appears to concentrate almost exclusively upon the transfer of present purchasing power by

191

taxation, and neglects the necessity for creating additional demand to evoke our unused capacity which is at present not commanded either by the rich or by the poor.[1]

The influence of Keynes on this formulation is obvious, though Mosley went further than anything Keynes was actually proposing at the time. What he advocated was that, under the cover of a floating exchange rate, the budget should be unbalanced to the extent necessary to raise actual production to the level of full-employment production. The struggle over the distribution of the existing product would be replaced by a joint sharing of an expanded product.

Revolution by Reason had little resonance in the 1920s, even on the left. Both its intellectual daring and its conservative implications were lost on Mosley's contemporaries. It was for a later generation to discover in Keynesian 'demand management' the intellectual basis for 'consensus' politics. Yet Mosley's later political evolution cannot be fully grasped unless one realizes that he believed he had discovered the way out from the 'dogfight between Capital and Labour' – a basis for a positive consensus to replace the Baldwin–MacDonald politics of 'decency' which, by refusing to push intellectual premises to logical conclusions, bought political peace by betraying the hopes of the war generation.

At the time it was not Mosley's programme but his political style which attracted (mainly unfavourable) notice. Mosley broke ranks not with his search for mass consent, but with his methods of communicating with the mass mind. This first came out during the rowdy by-election in which he was returned to Parliament as Labour MP for Smethwick in December 1926. The conservative press found something deplorable in the spectacle of an aristocrat, the son-in-law of Lord Curzon, who spent his amply provided private life in beautiful houses and a 'jet set' of fashionable artists and writers, inflaming the passions of the mob. The contrast between Mosley's 'reason' and his 'populism' was thus established quite early in his career. Mosley excelled on the public platform. At his best, he had an almost unique ability – perhaps only Joseph Chamberlain is comparable – to bring technical economic arguments to life for a mass audience. Only by investing reason with passion could popular support for progress be mobilized in an era of mass democracy. Much more could be said about Mosley's 'high road' and 'low road'. Here it is sufficient to note that Mosley's power of platform appeal, his ability to generate excitement and devotion, blinded him to the extent to which modern political support is institutional, not personal. He came to believe that the basis of political power lay in the response of large audiences to stirring speeches, rather than in the habitual loyalty to parties. He came to prefer the theatre of politics to its substance; which is, perhaps, another way of saying that deep down he wanted to be a legend rather than an achiever.

As Chancellor of the Duchy of Lancaster in MacDonald's second Labour government, Mosley set to work with a high sense of destiny: 'Before we leave this mortal scene, we shall do something to lift the burdens of those who suffer . . . We of the war generation are marching on.'[2] In practice, Sir Oswald marched straight into the impenetrable wall of Philip Snowden's orthodoxy at the Treasury. There was simply no money, declared the Iron Chancellor, to lift the burden of suffering from the increasingly large number of unemployed. As the world depression deepened, Mosley bombarded the ministries with lucid, but unavailing, memoranda. Finally, he decided to amalgamate them into one big Memorandum, and send it to the Prime Minister. The nation, he told MacDonald, must be mobilized for a supreme effort. He proposed a small 'war cabinet' serviced by a 'think-tank' headed by Keynes; a protected home market, with government money for modernizing the older, and developing the newer, industries; a £200 million programme of centrally organized public works; and a great increase in the public debt to provide the money. It was a nationalist programme to fight the depression. When it was rejected, Mosley resigned office. 'I perhaps misunderstood you when I came into the Labour Party,' he told MacDonald.[3] Eight days later, on 28 May 1930, Mosley defended his alternative before a packed House of Commons, in one of the most remarkable speeches ever delivered to that assembly. He ended:

What I fear more than a sudden crisis is a long slow crumbling through the years . . . a gradual paralysis, beneath which the vigour and energy of this country will succumb . . . What a fantastic assumption it is that a nation which within the lifetime of everyone has put forth efforts of energy and vigour une-qualled in the history of the world, should succumb before an economic situation such as the present. If the situation is to be overcome, if the great powers of this country are to be rallied and mobilised for a great national effort, then the Government and Parliament must give a lead. I beg the Government tonight to give the vital forces of this country the chance they await. I beg Parliament to give that lead.[4]

In the next few months Mosley's oratory reached new heights as his fortunes waned. A speech to the Labour Party conference at Llandudno in October 1930 was rapturously acclaimed; but the party managers were able to stave off the challenge with some ease. Meanwhile, Mosley was convinced that history was at last living up to his sense of drama. The party system which thrived in normal times would surely break up under the impact of the impending collapse of the world economic system. The moment had come to revive the 'centre party' ideas of 1919–22. Mosley's programme for fighting the depression was designed to reunite the scattered and frustrated survivors of the 'war generation'. Surely the Tory and Liberal ex-officer politicians of his own age, like Harold Macmillan, Oliver Stanley, Walter Elliott, Henry Mond and Archibald Sinclair, could be brought together with his Labour supporters, John Strachey, Aneurin Bevan and W. J. Brown, into a new Mosley Party?

It was, in fact, a non-politician from the pre-war generation who gave Mosley the decisive push. Mosley's conversations with the young Tories had led nowhere; his attempt to form a 'Manifesto Group' in the Labour Party had petered out. But then, early in 1931, the car manufacturer, Sir William Morris, handed him a cheque for £50,000, about £1,000,000 in today's values. On 28 February 1931 Mosley launched the New Party. Six MPs – five Labour, one Conservative – resigned their Whips at the same time.

The New Party reflected the diverse strands of Mosley's personality and experience: the search for a political framework adequate for his ideas, the instability of the party system, his conception of himself as a man of crisis, his penchant for the dramatic gesture. The most interesting statement of its early political purpose is contained in an article by C. F. Melville, which appeared in the journal *Fortnightly Review* in May 1931. The central assumption of the New Party was:

> The trouble is not that we have a class war so much as we have a class deadlock. The deadlock must be unlocked. We shall try to do something towards unlocking it.

Melville found strong similarities in the policy, though not in the methods, of the 'German and English movement':

> Both movements are in effect National-Socialist parties which, while appealing to the working masses, attract to themselves the support of the industrialists; thereby becoming the protagonists ... of industry versus banking finance.

Thus, Melville thought, 'Sir Oswald Mosley and his associates propose to help both industrial capital and the industrial worker to their mutual benefit', a policy which suggested to him the Mond–Turner conversations of the later 1920s. His prognosis of the New Party's future was not pessimistic:

> It is obvious that the New Party hopes – and it seems to me to have a good chance of eventually realising this hope, provided it can succeed in reconciling the many aims and as many interests which it represents – to become the principal magnet for a new 'Centrum' in British party politics ... In this sense it cuts right across the old arguments about *Left* and *Right*.

Although the New Party started out, in Strachey's words, as 'an entirely Utopian appeal for social compromise', social forces, as well as Mosley's conceptions and temperament, had already started to push it towards Fascism before Mosley formally adopted the label. The fundamental sociological fact was that Mosley started his 'centrist' career with the organized forces of Labour ranged against him. This estrangement was completed by the New Party's intervention at the Ashton-under-Lyme by-election on 30 April 1931 which was generally considered (wrongly) to have handed the Labour seat to the Conservatives. At meeting after meeting, New Party speakers faced organized disruption from Labour and Communist militants. Mosley's response was to organize a 'private army' of stewards, initially un-uniformed, and trained by the Whitechapel boxer Ted Kid Lewis. At the same time, Mosley observed to Harold Nicolson, his most prestigious non-parliamentary supporter, that 'The main response we are getting ... comes from the younger Conservative group.' Thus the hostility of organized Labour, Mosley's pugnacious response to it, and the nature of the New Party's grass roots support, all pushed the party towards the right.

195

However, the crucial point is that Mosley did not want to be there. To John Strachey's question – whether to come down on the side of working-class revolt or ruling-class reaction – Mosley replied 'On neither side'. He would not become a Communist, or return to the party of 'predatory plutocracy'. The movement towards Fascism arose essentially from Mosley's refusal to choose between left and right in a situation of mounting social crisis. Rather, it seemed to him that Fascism was the natural legatee of the centre party idea. It was based on the notion of having a government strong enough to control both Communism *and* predatory plutocracy, while using the power of the state to build the higher civilization which would put both out of business. Such was the direction of Mosley's thoughts in the final months of his parliamentary life.

Whether he would ever have carried these ideas to their logical conclusion had the New Party retained a parliamentary base is open to question. As it was, the parliamentary side of the New Party (already diminished by the desertion of W. J. Brown, Oliver Baldwin and John Strachey) was obliterated in the general election of October 1931. From the point of view of building up a parliamentary following, Mosley's timing had been disastrous. He assumed that the economic crisis would force the Labour and Conservative Parties into an unholy alliance to defend the pound, leaving the field free for a true 'national' alternative. MacDonald and Baldwin did their bit by joining up to form a National Government on 24 August 1931 – the consensus of 'decency'; but MacDonald failed to carry the Labour Party with him. Thus the two-party system was not broken. Opposition to the National Government still had its natural focus in the Labour Party. The New Party, along with other splinters, became a political irrelevance. But its very collapse in the general election of October 1931 convinced Mosley that parliamentary centrism had to give way to a grass-roots variety. On 1 October 1932 he launched the British Union of Fascists from the remnants of the New Party and deserters from existing Fascist organizations, campaigning for a 'Greater Britain'.

The British Union of Fascists

Mosley's policy for winning power, expounded in his book *The Greater Britain* (1932), was a recapitulation and development of the proposals and arguments of his Labour and New Party days. It consisted of three parts: an economic argument designed to show why Britain must extricate itself and its empire from the crumbling international system in order to realize the post-war dream of a high-wage, full-employment economy; an argument for an 'executive' system of government capable of decisive action and free from detailed parliamentary control; and the proposition that the new system of political economy could be brought about only by a new political movement, Fascism. The economic argument is an adaptation of Mosley's original ideas of 1925 to the world economic collapse of 1929–32; the argument for 'executive' government and a new 'type' of politician, first formulated in the Memorandum and New Party proposals for a small 'war cabinet' to organize the fight against the depression, reflects Mosley's experience of government in the minority MacDonald administration; the argument for a 'new movement' develops Mosley's old dream of a 'centre party' of the war generation. The distinctively new element was the linking of the economic argument for greater national and imperial self-sufficiency with the prospects for world peace. 'The measure of national reconstruction already described', Mosley wrote, 'involves automatically a change in our foreign policy. We would be less prone to anxious interference in everybody else's affairs, and more concentrated on the resources of our own country and Empire.'[5] Essentially this remained the programme for the rest of the decade, though its presentation became increasingly populist. The 'international economy' was progressively personalized in terms of 'alien' or 'Jewish' financiers; parliamentary democracy became the domain of the corrupt 'old gangs'; Jewish interests, too, were preventing peace by making bad blood between Britain and Germany. The idea of dictatorship also became more explicit, with electoral choice reduced to an 'occupational franchise' for an advisory parliament, and national referenda in which voters could reject the ruling set of Fascist ministers, leaving the monarch the task of choosing a new Fascist Prime Minister. There were also proposals for a 'corporate' reorganization of industry, with the government settling any dispute: strikes and lock-outs were to be abolished. 'In such a system,' Mosley wrote, 'there is no place for parties and for politicians. We shall ask the people for a mandate to bring to an end the Party system and the Parties. We invite them to enter a new civilisation.'[6]

The BUF was an expression of sociological optimism, not a response to sociological pressures. The main hope was that in time of crisis, comparable to war, sectarian loyalties, rooted in class, would give way to a rallying of 'patriotic' Britons behind a non-class, non-sectarian movement. The initial situation of economic collapse seemed favourable. Further, before starting the BUF, Mosley had assured himself of the support of Lord Rothermere, the press proprietor; a promise fulfilled in January 1934, when the *Daily Mail* and its sister papers came out for the 'blackshirts'. The publicity boost created a minor bandwagon in the BUF's favour in the first six months of 1934, its membership peaking at between 30,000 and 40,000. There was no special concentration by the BUF at this stage on target areas or target groups. Members were joining from all round the country at a satisfactory rate. Nevertheless, it seems clear that in the 'Rothermere' phase, the membership was heavily middle-class, Mosley attracting what Baldwin called 'ultra-montane' Conservatives, offended by the consensus of decency and stagnation. Noticeable also was the attraction of the movement to young people, which was to remain a permanent feature.

Nor, in this period, was the BUF seriously organized for electoral politics. The official myth was that it would come to power in a violent situation – probably resisting a Communist attempt at take-over. The organization was to be based on a number of big headquarters in the main urban areas (the main one was 'Black House' in Chelsea), organized as military barracks, in which squads of uniformed blackshirts would live and train for the great day. Their other function was to provide support for the platform, as Mosley and the BUF speakers put the Fascist appeal to audiences which often contained fiercely hostile sections. This phase of British Fascism ended in the disorders of the Olympia meeting of 7 June 1934, after which Lord Rothermere backed out. Also, by 1934, the first real impact of economic recovery was starting to be felt. The BUF shrank as rapidly as it had grown.

The second phase – from the summer of 1934 to March 1937 – marks the beginning of a more orthodox attempt to win power, based on a national party headquarters staffed by 140 full-time officials, the rudiments of a constituency organization, and a series of campaigns directed at particular areas, groups and themes. This phase was marked by a much higher degree of centralization. The military model was retained, though military aims were abandoned. Local Fascist bigwigs, who had tried to organize independent satrapies, were removed, and their groups brought under the control of Neil Francis-Hawkins, Director-General of Organization, and a system of National Inspectors. Ward

and action units were established as the basis of constituency organization. By 1938, the BUF was ostensibly organized to fight about eighty
seats. The whole system, intended to provide an unbroken chain of
command from the Leader at the top to the humblest active member,
was in practice riddled with personal jealousies and divided jurisdictions.
Supreme policy was made in a Policy Directorate, but little is known of
its working. It seems that the usual friction prevailed between the
bureaucrats who valued the organization as an end in itself, and the
political propagandists, William Joyce, John Beckett and Arthur Chesterton, who wanted a more daring, risk-taking, propaganda appeal, based
on anti-semitism. On the whole, Mosley sided with the administrators.
Curiously, the conservative elements in the BUF, represented by the ex-
military men, proved as bad for its image as the anti-semitic radicals: for
it was their love of uniforms and elaborate organization for violence
which helped turn the parliamentary politicians against the BUF in 1936.

In the summer and autumn of 1934 the first systematic attempt
was started to concentrate propaganda on certain regions and groups. In
the autumn of 1934, Bill Risdon, an ex-ILPer, was sent to 'open up'
Lancashire, home of the ailing cotton industry. The ex-miner and boxer
'Tommy' Moran went to the South Wales coalfields. John Beckett
concentrated on the Tyneside. Rural areas (the BUF had intervened in
the East Anglian 'tithe war' of 1933) were assiduously wooed. From late
1934, too, dates the growth of support in East London, where the BUF
started to champion Gentile grievances against Jewish immigrants.
Although the BUF tried to win support in the depressed textile and coal-
mining industries, its main *class* appeal was directed towards the petty
bourgeoisie and the unorganized sections of the working class. On the
one hand, it directed its propaganda at the 'small man with his
independent firm [who] is caught between the upper millstone of
trustification and the lower millstone of socialisation'.[7] On the other
hand, it exploited the grievances of shop assistants, cinema usherettes,
barmaids, servants, etc., particularly where these could be shown to be
exploited by big Jewish employers. Finally, throughout the 1930s, the
BUF tried to pick up support through single-issue campaigns – the 'Mind
Britain's Business' campaign of 1935, connected with the Abyssinia
crisis, the 'Stand by the King' campaign of 1936, and the Peace campaign
of 1939.

By the mid-1930s, the BUF's presence on the political stage was
giving rise to severe problems of public order. From the moment he

broke with the Labour Party, Mosley had had to face militant opposition, to which he reacted by organizing his 'private army' of uniformed stewards who travelled round with him to meetings, and whose presence in turn offered a provocation to his opponents. In forming the BUF, Mosley adopted a creed and livery hateful and offensive enough to a section of left-wing opinion to ensure the further development of active hostility. The opposition was generally mobilized, co-ordinated and directed by the Communist Party, which saw in Fascism a threat, a competitor, and a chance for its own growth. The announcement of a BUF parade and meeting in a large urban centre would be the signal for a 'counter-demonstration' at or near the vicinity, which often led to violence, with the police in the position of defending the Fascists against their enemies. Indoor meetings were protected by Fascist stewards, but these meetings, too, were penetrated by opponents determined to prevent the speech from being made. Few large BUF occasions in the main urban and industrial centres escaped some violence in the 1930s, though elsewhere the Fascists were relatively unmolested. The most famous disturbance took place at the Olympia stadium on 7 June 1934, when the bulk of an audience of 12,000 watched, disgusted or admiring as the case may be, the efficiency or brutality with which the stewards ejected several hundred demonstrators.

Politicians and the police tended to attribute the violence to the provocation of the Fascist uniform – initially a black shirt tucked into grey trousers: later a more elaborate affair with jacket, boots, breeches, belt, cap, etc., worn as a privilege of rank or service. This was a superficial analysis: what Fascism stood for was provocative enough; and violence did not die with the end of the uniform. It was also widely argued that provocation was deliberately used by the BUF as a tactic to gain publicity, or to impress opinion with Fascist ruthlessness in dealing with the 'Reds'. There is something in this, but it is exaggerated. Marches were intended primarily to advertise meetings and as an activity for members. Insults directed by Fascist speakers at hostile elements in their audiences generally arose out of the context of the meetings themselves. To try to assign responsibility for the violence is probably a pointless exercise: Mosley claimed the right to propagate a creed which was sufficiently offensive to ensure militant opposition. Violence flowed from this basic dynamic. Nevertheless, some Fascists and Communists no doubt enjoyed violence for its own sake; and passionate politics released instincts which in more tranquil times are confined to football matches.

At the heart of the BUF's confrontation with its opponents in the streets and halls of urban Britain lay its clash with the Jewish community, particularly in East London. This requires some consideration.

Mosley himself had no known personal history of political or cultural anti-semitism. At the start of the BUF he declared that 'anti-semitism forms no part of the policy of this Organization, and anti-semitic propaganda is forbidden.' It is easy to conclude that his later espousal of political anti-semitism was purely oportunistic – an attempt, from late 1934 onwards, to re-establish a declining movement by exploiting a base prejudice. The fact that the only place where the BUF succeeded in winning a mass following was in East London with its large Jewish community of first and second generation immigrants lends support to this interpretation. But the story is more complicated than this. East London Fascism was a fairly spontaneous growth. Its leader, 'Mick' Clarke, was not a BUF officer sent to 'open up' a new area, but a native East Ender who saw in the BUF an effective instrument for ventilating deeply rooted local Gentile grievances against East London Jews, ignored by the established political parties in the area. Gentile East London with its combination of tiny businesses, sweated workers, lack of trade-union organization, appalling slums, and a strong local Jewish capitalism, found in the BUF a 'natural' political vehicle; and the BUF's growing involvement in East London in turn coloured its whole political stance. The conventional interpretation also ignores or minimizes the role of Jewish anti-Fascist militancy, stimulated by Hitler's victory in Germany, but also dating back to the post-Russian Revolutionary connection between East London Jews and Communism, in making the BUF as a whole 'Jew-conscious'.

Having said this, there remains a substantial element in the BUF's anti-semitism which cannot be explained either by reference to the anti-Fascist opposition offered by Jews themselves, or by the existence of local anti-Jewish grievances in East London. Anti-semitism was the nearest thing Fascism ever had to an all-embracing ideology, capable of rivalling those of liberalism and Marxism. It provided a comprehensive explanation of social ills, in terms of a malign Jewish dynamic, which in the modern world has had the appeal of religious faith to a small minority of intellectuals and fanatics. In other words, it has provided the devotional core which any mass party needs to stay afloat in lean times; and was, in fact, the only ideology available for a movement like Fascism. Mosley himself, it is clear, never accepted the anti-semitic ideology; but he increasingly picked on Jews as the main targets of his denunciations. There are a number of reasons for this, which are listed in no definite order of importance – we cannot, after all, be sure what went on in Mosley's mind. Firstly, he needed some anti-semitism to retain the 'devotional core' – his militants and tireless propagandists. Secondly, he clearly saw the propaganda utility of concentrating all his fire on a single opponent. The masses required both something to love and something to hate, he is alleged to have remarked. They could not be taught to hate capitalism, since Mosley only wanted to control it, and anyway hoped for business donations. Nor could simple, straightforward anti-communism deliver the support of the non-socialist radicals. Anti-semitism was a way of being radical without being Communist. It was an ideology of radical nationalism; and Jews were just prominent enough in the activities Fascism denounced (international finance and Communism) to give the imputation that they dominated in these spheres a superficial plausibility. Thirdly, but linked to the second point, Mosley deliberately used anti-semitism as the chief weapon in his peace campaign. The avoidance of another European war was a genuine political commitment dating back to his first days in Parliament; reinforced, but not caused, by his later sympathy with the Fascist powers. How far he actually believed that Jews constituted a powerful, or dominant, war lobby is impossible to say; but he increasingly categorized them as such. Finally, although Mosley, and probably most of his followers, had no previous history of anti-semitism, this is not to say that they were not liable to react to Jews anti-semitically under certain conditions. The potential for anti-semitism is deeply rooted in European history and culture, based on the predominantly unfavourable stereotype of Jews which is the inheritance of the Jewish diaspora in Christian Europe. It only needed the active opposition by 'foreign' Jews to his political projects – he once referred to hecklers as the 'sweepings of the ghetto' – to activate Mosley's dormant anti-semitic prejudices.

So how can we sum up the BUF's turn to anti-semitism in the mid-1930s? It had a definite sociological basis in East London. Beyond this, it seems to have been a calculated attempt by Mosley to achieve a propaganda coherence or edge, made possible by an inability to think of Jews in the mass as either fully British or indeed fully human, once Jews had started to impinge on his politics.

The second phase of British Fascism ended in the East London 'battle of Cable Street' on 4 October 1936, the passing of the Public Order Act two months later, and the mixed local election results which the BUF chalked up in three East London boroughs in March 1937. These events marked the climax of the BUF's rowdy penetration of East London and the government's reaction to it: the Public Order Act banned political uniforms and gave chief police officers the power to ban marches in their areas for up to three months at a time. This political blow to the movement's *élan*, coupled with its failure to win local power in East London, produced, or perhaps merely brought to a head, an internal crisis, financial, ideological and political. In one afternoon, Mosley sacked over a hundred full-time officials of his inflated head-quarters staff. The emphasis thereafter was on decentralization and local initiative. Despite this, financial solvency was not restored. Except for the money provided by Sir William Morris, Lord Rothermere and Mussolini, Mosley had never received large donations. Now the supply of funds virtually dried up, and he had to spend £100,000 of his own money to keep the movement going in its last two years. Significant for the BUF's ideological complexion was Mosley's dismissal of Joyce and Beckett, who, together with A. K. Chesterton who left about a year later, formed the radical anti-semitic group in the leadership. By this move, Mosley repudiated the strategy of full-blooded anti-semitism; and in fact anti-semitism thereafter tended to become less important. To the political crisis there was no immediate solution, and it became more acute in the months ahead, with falling membership, and the closure of propaganda outlets, as the Metropolitan Commissioner used his new powers to ban Fascist marches in East London, and as municipal and private owners withheld permission for the BUF to use their halls for meetings.

The last phase of BUF activity was dominated by the 'peace campaign' of 1938–40 which brought the movement fresh support, a new vigour, and, perhaps, a new integrity. For the first time since he launched British Fascism Mosley was able to identify with a cause which had deep roots in English radical politics, though under peculiarly unrewarding conditions. The BUF – which had advocated rearmament for the sole defence of the British Empire, but otherwise wanted non-interference in European affairs – now made strange contacts with the pacifist fringe; and for a time it seemed as if Mosley might emerge as leader of a 'peace front'. In July 1939, the BUF staged its last great rally at the Earls Court Stadium, Mosley declaring that 'a million Britons shall not die in your Jews' quarrel'. But events were now moving too swiftly and Mosley was reacting too slowly to the new possibilities. The BUF was too much identified with Nazism for it to be able to mobilize the powerful peace sentiment under its own banner; and Mosley was not prepared to abandon Fascism for the cause which now claimed his allegiance. After the outbreak of war on 3 September 1939 Mosley was still capable of getting an enthusiastic response in East London to his call for a negotiated peace; but BUF candidates fared miserably in a number of by-elections. With the opening up of the war in the west and the fall of Chamberlain's government, British Fascism was doomed. On 23 May 1940, it was disbanded under Regulation 18B. Mosley and 700 of his supporters were interned as security risks. It was ten years, almost to the day, since his resignation from the second Labour government.

The BUF and the domestic political context

Between 1932 and 1940, the BUF failed to establish itself as a serious contender for power. Nor did it have much prospect of improving its position without the support of a German victory, though had war been avoided, Fascism would no doubt have remained a larger factor in British and European politics than proved to be the case after 1945. For most of the 1930s, the BUF was about the same size as the Communist Party, larger in the early 1930s, perhaps a little smaller at the end, when it may have had about 20–25,000 members. Clearly Fascism had only a limited scope for growth in Britain. Why was this so? The reasons for the BUF's failure can be grouped under four main heads: firstly, its own tactical mistakes; secondly, the nature of the British political system; thirdly, the character of the British social structure; and fourthly, the economic and international context in which it operated.

The BUF's chief tactical failure was its inability to prevent itself being saddled with responsibility for violence and public disorder. This led not only to the passage of legislation specifically designed to cripple it; but also to the progressive closure, through informal, local or police pressure, of its main propaganda outlets. In short, Mosley failed to solve the tactical problem posed by unrelenting left-wing opposition. His boast that his strong-arm methods had 'secured free speech' was in fact the reverse of the truth: because by the late 1930s all the big halls were closed to him, and he was not allowed on the radio or to write in the press. (The BUF only got the Earls Court Stadium in 1939 through a last-minute cancellation.) The blackshirts won the 'battle of Olympia' itself, but lost the propaganda war which followed, as well as Lord Rothermere's support. The 'battle of Cable Street', contrary to legend, led to an *increase* of Fascist strength in East London; but it also led directly to the passing of the Public Order Act and the ending of Fascist processions in East London. How Mosley should have handled his tactical problem is difficult to say. He seemed to face an unenviable choice of being ineffective or brutal. He would have done better had he learned earlier the lesson he tried to impart to his followers after the war, that 'You win not by the punches you give but by the punches you duck.'

The BUF's mishandling of the problem posed by its opposition undoubtedly limited such scope for growth as it possessed in Britain. But this does not lie at the heart of Mosley's political failure. What decisively constrained Fascism's advance was not its lack of ability to exploit favourable opportunities, but the lack of favourable opportunities to exploit. The British political system was a crucial barrier. There are three aspects worth noting here. Firstly, there was an absence of political ideas favourable to Fascism such as existed on the European continent. There was no *nationalist* ideology of the kind developed by Corradini in Italy. There was no anti-semitic ideology of any importance. Overt racialism was frowned upon. Social imperialism was dead. 'Chesterbelloc' provided only a tiny trickle of Roman Catholic social thought. In short, liberalism remained the hegemonic public philosophy, with socialism as a somewhat deviant branch; there was no resonant set of anti-democratic, or anti-liberal ideas, waiting to be taken up by a Fascist movement, as was the case elsewhere. This situation was reflected in the paucity of intellectual support which Fascism received. In so far as the younger intellectuals rejected liberalism, they turned to Marxism. Fascism, by contrast, had few intellectual fellow-travellers, and they tended to be isolated, eccentric figures: Ezra Pound, Wyndham Lewis (for a time), Bernard Shaw (in certain moods), the novelist Henry Williamson. There was no Fascist equivalent of Trinity College, Cambridge.

Secondly, the British parliamentary system was politically very efficient. Dangerous situations did not produce a crisis for political institutions as they tended to do on the continent. Even when the world financial crisis shook the two-party system in 1931, it did so in a way which did not help Mosley. Those who would normally respond to a straightforward 'patriotic' appeal to save the nation had the National government; those who wanted reform and reconstruction could still pin their hopes on a Labour Party purged of its collaborationist leadership. The instinctive cleverness of the political arrangements which got England through a dangerous decade is astounding. Certainly, the sheer *political* competence of the English parliamentary system in this period is remarkable.

Thirdly, Mosley assumed that the failure of the British political system to cope with the economic problem would bring it down. He forgot the other half of the equation. The stability of a political system depends not only on its efficiency in solving problems, but on its *legitimacy*, the respect in which the system is held. People who love and respect their institutions are less likely to change them in haste. German democracy collapsed in 1933, not just because the economic crisis was too severe, but because the Weimar Republic had too few supporters. Eventually even legitimacy will succumb to inefficiency, but it takes a long time.

Other political explanations of Mosley's failure are less convincing. The British, it is said, hated anti-semitism. At the level of the élites, this may have been so; and, in so far as anti-semitism led to the closure of propaganda outlets, it was counter-productive. But at the mass level it is doubtful if Mosley was harmed by his attacks on Jewish financiers, though outside East London they did not win him a mass following. There has always been a certain tension between élite and popular levels of British politics which Mosley tried to exploit in the 1930s, as he did in his populist Labour Party days. But a combination of a party system seen to be effectively competitive on economic issues, a National Government which satisfied the patriotic feelings, and a governing class capable of co-opting able dissidents with all the skill of the old Roman senatorial order, served to keep the political system legitimate for the mass of voters. The social basis of British democracy was also much more secure than in many European countries. This, too, put a decisive limit on the growth of British Fascism.

The crucial point is that there was no important social group which was not adequately represented in the existing political system. British democracy arose out of social competition. The competition in feudal times between the monarchy, the great nobles and the towns established the original balance of the British constitution. In the eighteenth and nineteenth centuries there was the competition between the aristocracy and the middle classes which in turn let the working class into the political system through successive extensions of the franchise, as each side sought to establish a mass following. As a result of this long development, every important social group acquired a stake in the system and a share in running it. Because access was relatively satisfactory, individuals retained strong attachments and loyalties to the institutions which represented them at the centre: their political parties, trade unions, pressure groups, etc. In the language of political science, they were not available for 'mobilization' by new movements. Robert Benewick writes, 'Fascism's ultimate dilemma was the presence of a sense of community which at one and the same time contained and was nurtured by competing interests and loyalties.'[8] This was the social basis of the successful MacDonald–Baldwin politics of accommodation and decency.

Mosley tried to overcome this dilemma by building a coalition of gentry, small men providing services (traditionally to the wealthy) and 'deferential' and 'patriotic' workers, urban and rural: a coalition based very much on the social structure of the Staffordshire estate in which he grew up; a traditional coalition put together from the 'losers' of modernization, whose numbers he hoped would be swelled by progressive economic failure. And he did recruit from all three groups, but not enough. Mosley did not win significant support from the gentry class which remained attached to conservatism. There was quite a strong ex-officer element in the BUF; but, on the whole, the military section of the population – those who had served in the regular forces – found their outlets either in their own organizations, like the British Legion, or in Conservative patriotic organizations, like the Primrose League. More importantly, the British army was stationed abroad, and had adequate outlets for its Fascist values in ruling the empire. Fascism did recruit among small shopkeepers, furniture makers, tailors, etc. These were the people who gave Fascism social space to grow all over Europe. But in Britain, the world's most advanced (or senile) industrial economy, these intermediate groups were less heavily populated than elsewhere, and had been more effectively absorbed by the main parties. Mosley's biggest failure was to win substantial support from the working class. The loyalty of working-class people to the Labour Party and their trade unions proved unshakeable. Sections of the working class gave him support while he was in the Labour Party, but their support was not transferable. Fascism's pickings were meagre: some Conservative Lancashire working men and women, a few servants and shop assistants.

Nor did the strategy of trying to win support through minority politics offer better prospects. There were too few deprived, isolated, ethnic or religious minorities, unrepresented, or under-represented, in the British political system: East London, where the BUF was able to exploit communal tensions, was an obvious exception. There was clearly some potential for this kind of politics, as the post-1945 successes of Scottish and Welsh Nationalists show, as do the Protestant and Catholic politics of Northern Ireland. But at the time these national and religious issues were dormant. British Fascism was anyway not equipped to exploit them, and anti-semitism only had a strong appeal in East London, especially in north-east Bethnal Green, site of an earlier Huguenot immigration. One minority somewhat susceptible to Fascist propaganda was the Irish Catholics. British Fascism did disproportionately well in this group. But it was small beer.

Finally, we must look at the economic context. Even though Mosley was wrong in thinking that his chances of success hinged on the severity of the depression, he was right to suppose he would gain from profound economic distress. His greatest miscalculation was to suppose that economic collapse was inevitable. In doing so, he seriously underestimated the underlying strength of the British economy. The Marxist analysis was that capitalism's need to 'withdraw' concessions from the working class in order to restore profitability would shift working-class allegiance from Labour to Communism. Mosley's hope was that the same crisis would shift a section of the bourgeoisie and working class towards an anti-Communist movement which stood for a system of national and imperial economy promising full employment, high profits and high wages. In fact what occurred was a gradual movement of opinion towards the concept of the Keynesian-Welfare state which would make both Communism and Fascism unnecessary. But this took place in an economic environment unsufficiently stimulating to produce success for violent remedies. And the lack of Communist growth in turn weakened the rationale for the Fascist alternative.

What is striking in retrospect is the shallowness of the British depression and the speed of recovery from it in the absence of any deliberate fiscal stimulus. British unemployment, 2.9 million at its peak in late 1932, was half Germany's and a sixth of America's at the same date. From 1933 onwards there was a steady recovery (briefly interrupted in the winter of 1937–8) so that John Stevenson and Chris Cook in their recent study, *The Slump*, could conclude that 'most people were better off by 1939 than they had been ten years earlier.'[9] Between 1933 and 1937 inclusive, the British economy grew at 4 per cent a year, unemployment fell from 22.8 per cent to 9.5 per cent, output and real wages rose above their 1929 level.

The relative mildness of the British depression was caused by a number of factors. There was a substantial, though unintended, fiscal stimulus in the worst years, arising from the fact that government spending did not fall as fast as government revenue. (In the depth of the depression, the real value of social services and unemployment benefits was going up owing to the failure of government economies to match the fall in the cost of living.) Secondly, Britain's external position held up relatively better in the depression years than that of either Germany or Japan. In the period of collapsing world economy, the legacy from the past, in the form of captive empire markets and income from foreign investments, helped keep up demand. The imperial connection, which made Britain a 'satisfied' power, also undercut the kind of appeal to unsatisfied foreign ambitions which Fascism was able to exploit in Germany and Italy. Specific policies of the National Government, notably protection and cheap money, helped produce a 'home market' recovery. Finally, the remaining slack was taken up by the rearmament programme after 1937.

The resilience of the British economy damned Mosley's much more strenuous plan for securing British prosperity as it had Joseph Chamberlain's campaign for tariff reform and by the same token gave British Fascism an unfavourable domestic context, unlike in Germany where the national socialists could integrate the problem of mass unemployment with their nationalist, anti-Versailles, anti-reparations propaganda in an explosive mixture.

Summary

Oswald Mosley saw his mission in politics as to create a policy and political framework capable of expressing the ideals of the war generation. He was much more successful in the former than in the latter. His Keynesian approach to economic problems in the 1920s could have made Keynesianism a more powerful political force sooner had he stayed in conventional politics. Instead, he saw the economic and political crisis of the early 1930s as a chance to realize his dream of a new party of the centre. The failure to achieve this at Westminster threw him back on the grass-roots alternative which, given his own background and temperament, the nature of his recruitment and opposition, and the emergence of Fascism as a European-wide phenomenon, was bound to take the form of an attempt to establish a British Fascist movement. The logic of the Fascist struggle itself – its need for an ideology capable of holding together the militant core and unifying the disparate elements of its appeal, the nature of the opposition it aroused, and its sociological possibilities and limitations – drove Mosley into the politics of violence and anti-semitism. But although this discredited him, it was not the cause of his political failure. In reality, the whole project of trying to establish a new centre party, capable of drawing off substantial support from the existing parties of the right and left, was misconceived in the British context of the time. It underestimated the inventiveness and resilience of the political system in the face of crisis, and the congruence between existing arrangements and the values and aspirations of the main social groups. It also banked on a far greater degree of economic collapse than in fact occurred, or was plausible to expect. As a result, British Fascism failed to establish a mass base, except in East London; and never became a serious contender for power, though, partly because of its nuisance value, partly because of the fear it inspired, and partly because of Mosley's own charisma, it remained an element in everyone's political calculations. The final impression left is of a tragedy of wasted talents, rather than of a real danger to British democracy.

NOTES

1   Oswald Mosley, *Revolution by Reason*, a pamphlet read to the ILP summer school at Easton Lodge, August 1925, pp. 16–17.
2   Quoted in *Labour Magazine*, 1 May 1929.
3   Quoted in Thomas Jones, *Whitehall Diary*, ed. K. Middlemas, vol. 2, (1969), p. 259.
4   Parliamentary Debates (1930), Hansard, vol. 239, col. 1372.
5   Oswald Mosley, *The Greater Britain* (1932), p. 140.
6   Oswald Mosley, *Fascism* (1936).
7   Quoted in *Action*, 21 May 1936.
8   Robert Benewick, *Political Violence and Public Order*, (1969), p. 305.
9   John Stevenson and Chris Cook, *The Slump*, (1977), p. 5.

CHAPTER THIRTY-THREE

Nicholas Mosley on his Father

[1] Nicholas Mosley, *Rules of the Game: Sir Oswald
and Lady Cynthia Mosley 1896–1933*
[Secker and Warburg, 1982]

OSWALD MOSLEY was the stuff of which tragic heroes are made.
Robert Boothby wrote of him in 1925 that he had the 'Divine Spark'.
His flaw was *hubris* – the feeling that everything was possible, that he
could get away with anything. In 1921, soon after the start of his
Parliamentary career, his wife Cynthia wrote to him: 'My sweet . . . if
you can't be good be careful.' It was the kind of advice Oswald habitually
ignored, until it was too late. In business life he might have made and
lost several fortunes – and kept the last one. In political life, which
allows brilliance, but not brilliant achievements, his gamble on Fascism
in 1932 was one gamble too many. He was compulsorily retired into
another game: the game of might-have-been, or the myth-making game.
He and his opponents between them conspired to make him taboo – the
embodiment of forces too dangerous to be useful in public life. I wrote a
book about him in 1975 in which I tried to reduce him to the more
mundane proportions of history. But he still lives in that part of life
made up of myths and legends; and will no doubt continue to do so.

To his eldest son, Nicholas, born in 1923, Oswald Mosley also
appeared as a somewhat magical figure. In Nicholas's world parents and
children had very little routine contact – separated by nannies and
governesses and the spaces of large country houses. Adults appeared to
him as performers, constantly play-acting. Oswald would clamber down
the chimney dressed as Father Christmas, or intone nonsense rhymes
with a far-away look in his eye. Nicholas's parents and their friends,
devotees of the fun-life, as it was known, would get up to absurd pranks,
fall around, dress up in odd clothes, make weird noises. Every so often
they would all rush off to the South of France. Nicholas concluded that
the grown-up world was completely mad, but that the madness might
have some meaning at a level beyond his understanding.

As he grew older the childish image of his father confronted the
political legend, and the two got confused in his mind. Oswald Mosley

211

now presented himself to Nicholas in the guise of Superman, the supremely rational being, baffled by the forces of inertia and wickedness in his attempts to save the world from another war, and build a land fit for heroes. In the Second World War Nicholas fought with the Rifle Brigade in Italy and spent his leaves visiting his father at Holloway prison. They discussed Goethe and Nietzsche and the Greek tragedians. 'Darling Nick,' Oswald wrote to him in 1943, 'I can never tell you what a joy it was to know you as an adult and to find what a perfect community of mind and spirit we had in searching together through all the higher and lovelier things of life.' But something seemed to Nicholas to be not quite right. What had these 'higher and lovelier things' to do with marching around in black shirts, saluting, street-brawls, and attacking Jews in the East End of London? He started asking questions. Oswald explained patiently. He was in the revolutionary business: one could not make an omelette without breaking eggs. He had a complete answer to every objection. Time and again Nicholas retired baffled, but with the growing conviction that his father was the master of one thing only – the manipulation of words and arguments to shed the best possible light on himself. His father's language, he felt, had lost all contact with moral or practical reality. From the age of seven Nicholas had started stammering. He now developed a theory about it: that stammering on some level 'is simply a protest against a too easy flow of words; against one's own and other people's terrible tendency to bury living things under a verbal lava-flow'.

Defeated in verbal exchanges with his father, Nicholas equipped himself to win the last argument. He studied psychology and philosophy. He took to writing novels and biographies about the games people play in their private and public lives, about their use of words to obscure the truth. But the game he wanted to understand above all was the game his father played – the marriage game he had played with his wife Cynthia, Lord Curzon's daughter, who had died when Nicholas was nine, and the political game. Oswald Mosley died on 3 December, 1980. Ten days before that, when Nicholas told him he hoped to write a book about him, Oswald said he could have his papers. 'It was as if', Nicholas writes, 'he knew as part of him had always known that if anything was to survive of what he had cared about it would be to do with efforts at truth.'

Less than two years later Nicholas Mosley's 'efforts at truth' have yielded a merciless exposure of his father's verbal pretensions. The first

212

of two volumes takes the story up to 1932–3, by which time Oswald, who was still only thirty-six, had run through his first marriage and most of the eligible society women of London, and through all the political parties. It is a story above all about the corrupting effect of a way with words. His father is presented as someone who manipulated words to transfer the contradictions and paradoxes of his married and political life from a sphere where they should influence and restrain action to a sphere where they need not – where they can be reconciled by proclaiming that they have been. It is the story of how a marriage and a political career were ruined by an inexhaustible capacity for rationalization. It is about the use of the arts of seduction to enslave women and audiences. What Nicholas Mosley does is to provide a running commentary on his father's prose – his intimate words to his wife, his political speeches and writings – which has the effect of a needle pricking a balloon. For example, in his autobiography Oswald explained his participation in London's social life as necessary for 'Ganzheit' or wholeness. Nicholas comments, 'What these *salons* were useful for, of course, was the business of men picking up women.' This is typical of the illusion-stripping exercise. Nicholas writes about his relationship with Oswald: 'From my side at least there was loyalty and some hostility, anger and bewilderment, nearly always love.' But the memory of the verbal humiliations which Oswald inflicted on him is too great, one suspects, for much loyalty and love to come through; or any undue consideration for the feelings of his father's widow, Diana.

Whatever Nicholas Mosley's motives in writing the book, it is the results which concern us. And there is no doubt that he has achieved something dazzling – a book which is immensely clever and interesting on many different levels. There is a brilliant chapter called 'The Riddle of the Sphinx' in which he tries to sum up his view of his father – which is basically that of a hero ruined by lack of self-knowledge; able to pierce through other people's deceptions but blind to his own. Also interesting is Nicolas Mosley's controlling theme that individuals must work out their destinies within the 'rules of the game' if they are to save themselves and others from destruction. His book also works very well in human terms. The pace is fast, the characters are vivid, his mother's death suitably moving. Much of this effect is created by his skill as a novelist; but Oswald and Cynthia Mosley live up to the demands of art.

The doubts about his efforts at truth arise at a different, and more banal, level – the level of facts. Nicholas Mosley tries to confront his father's fantasies with reality. But his own notion of reality is itself a highly abstract one. He seeks to illuminate truth by myth and metaphor. The trouble is one can play precisely the same game with his own ideas about reality as he plays with his father's – that is to say that they do not represent the facts of life in their obvious, common-sense, meaning. Mr Mosley finds it very difficult to get out of the legendary game which his father set up for talking about his career. Like Oswald he is full of very interesting hot air. But one sometimes asks: what relation has it to what actually happened?'

Take, for example, his account of his father's marriage to his mother. He presents Oswald (or Tom as he was known) as a kind of sexual monster, who enslaved Cimmie with baby talk, while he went off and had affairs. He sees the marriage as exemplifying Oswald's destructive use of words – in this case, they destroyed his mother. She could not win her arguments with him, she could not resist his naughty boy letters to his 'darling soft nosed wog-tail' protesting his undying love for her, she could not stop adoring him – yet she felt a falseness: if he really loved her, he would not carry on in the way he did. In the end, Nicholas Mosley writes, 'she felt death as a condition in which human beings might at last be all-of-a-piece'. And her own death, from peritonitis, at the age of thirty-four, seems to give artistic and moral point to the story. Yet this is not the point. The destructiveness lay in the situation, not in Oswald's manipulation of it to keep the marriage going. They were two incompatible people held together by love, and for whom separation would have been more painful than the pain they caused each other. Mr Mosley feels that had his father tried to deal with his mother as an adult she might have grown up to understand and accept the complexities of their situation – the 'rules of the game' as the upper classes played it, which allowed affairs on both sides. But I doubt if this is true. Cimmie does not seem to have been that kind of person. The destructiveness of Oswald's marriage to Cimmie was followed by forty-four years of happiness with his second wife, Diana. Whatever the moral of the tale it does not seem to be the moral which Nicholas Mosley wishes to draw.

Another major misunderstanding arises about the relationship of his father's economic ideas to the political game. As Nicholas Mosley sees it, politicians trade ideals for office, because they recognize that to be fully serious about realizing ideals would require dictatorship. That is why they talk a lot about making the world a better place, but do not do much about it. This seems to me fair. But he then uses this framework to explain the politicians' rejection of his father's plans to cure unemployment, which seems to me to be simply wrong. He writes:

> Of course unemployment could be solved: a leader could say –
> You will be employed in this way or that way or you will be
> shot. Most people did not think of this solution because it did
> not seem relevant: it might work, but they assumed it would be
> worse than the curse. But they did not quite say this, because it
> would seem that they were not interested in solving unemploy-
> ment which they were. And so they said nothing. And they were
> devoured. And the city starved. The riddle was not solved not
> because it was too difficult but because it was too undesirably
> easy. But what was also unpalatable was the fact that in that
> case perhaps the only solution was that there was no solution –
> one had to learn to live with the curse.

This is interesting and well put, but what on earth has it got to do with his father's unemployment policies, the main points of which, partly derived from Keynes, have since become routine in systems which undoubtedly remain liberal and democratic? (Only in recent years have they started to be challenged.) Nicholas Mosley sees his father's plan in 1925 for an Economic Council to 'estimate the difference between the actual and the potential production of the country' as a call to dictatorship. This task has long since been performed, on the Treasury computer. The truth is – and we are dealing with efforts at truth – that there was nothing in Oswald Mosley's economic plans which were incompatible with the rules of the game as they were then understood. It just needed time for the new ideas to sink in. Nicholas Mosley says the rules of the political game were needed as defences against the 'dark forces' in his father's character, and this is true. But they were not needed in defence against his father's policies. The confusion arises, I think, partly because Mr Mosley is not really at home with the economic argument, and partly because he tends to see his father's policies as rationalizations of his drives and obsessions. In this he does him an injustice. This is a shame, for an appreciation of his father's desire and capacity for constructive statemanship, as well as an exploration of its sources, would have balanced Mr Mosley's picture of a mainly self-justifying rhetorician. In the many excellent photographs of Oswald Mosley in this book, the only one in which he does not seem to be performing is when he is shown with John Strachey and Fenner Brockway at an Independent Labour Party Summer School, obviously talking about something which interested him. This side of him is rarely allowed to emerge.

Oswald Mosley's break with the political game in 1931–2 had less to do with the disappointment of the rational man who sees his plans rejected at some level he cannot understand than with the recklessness of a rich young politician who senses that his world – and the game – are collapsing and decides to 'have a go' and see what he can rescue from the wreck. The torrents of rationalization which Nicholas got from his father came later – after the gamble had failed, and the legend-building had begun. For the years covered in this book, one is left with the odd feeling that Mr Mosley has constructed a fascinating apparatus of thought to understand things which were not happening.

[2] Nicholas Mosley, *Beyond the Pale: Sir Oswald Mosley 1933–1980*
[Secker & Warburg, 1983]

SHORTLY before my biography of Oswald Mosley was published in 1975, its subject appeared on a television programme called *Today*. He was then seventy-eight, and was allowed on the box from time to time, as though he were some monstrous exhibit to be gawped at like the Elephant Man. Sir Oswald, still a magnetic performer, used such occasions, when allowed to by his interlocutors, to 'peddle his ideas' – then chiefly to do with the need for a united Europe and continued dialogue with the Soviet Union to avert a nuclear catastrophe.

I wrote him a letter, which I now regret, telling him that his demeanour showed signs of megalomania. I have no record of a reply. But I met him some time later. He must have been going on about how he could have saved, or might still save, the world from a terrible fate, for suddenly he stopped short. 'Ah, megalomania again,' he said, and laughed conspiratorially. One of the disarming things about Oswald Mosley was this ability to laugh at himself as a great man. But it made me wonder what his act really was. I had been protectively anxious that he should make a 'reasonable' impression, for had I not written about him as someone who might have been a great peacetime leader? But of course it was silly to feel this way. Oswald Mosley was 'beyond the pale'. So why should he not be megalomaniac if that gave him pleasure?

The interesting issue raised by Nicholas Mosley's two books about his father is to what extent, if at all, Oswald Mosley ever was in that 'other' game – a real seeker after power to do good, as he said he was, or even a real seeker after power. Mr Mosley sees his father as someone who gambled for power on his own terms, and lost. But he also sees, and I think rightly, that Oswald Mosley was not prepared to put everything into the gamble; which is why, although he lost, he survived. Mr Mosley feels he has found a way of writing about his father's life in such a way as to turn its failure into some kind of success.

His first volume took the story of his father up to 1933. Sir Oswald was presented as a man of lavish gifts and energies, political, intellectual, and sexual who had a 'crazy belief that he could get away with almost anything' – a belief which left him, at the age of thirty-six, with a sadly depleted estate; his first wife, Cynthia, and his political career, expiring at almost the same time. There is the same juggling with love and politics in volume two. Mosley married Diana Guinness (née Mitford) in Berlin in 1936, though the wedding was kept secret till 1939; but for much of the 1930s he divided his time between Diana and Lady Alexandra Metcalfe, Cimmie's younger sister; an older sister, Irene Ravensdale, looked after the children at Savehay Farm, the family home. On holidays in France and Italy, Alexandra (Baba) would leave as Diana arrived; once Diana arrived early, a situation which 'provided a social and personal challenge worthy of the mettle of someone like my father – on his tightrope, as it were, juggling with his plates above Niagara'. In politics Mosley ran a movement – the British Union of Fascists – which tried to be all things: political and anti-political, law-abiding and revolutionary, rational and prejudiced, pacific and aggressive, honest and dishonest.

Nevertheless, there was a change of pattern. Oswald and Cynthia Mosley had been a political team; Diana simply wanted to adore her husband, amuse him, make him happy. She emerges as the heroine of volume two, not on account of her political opinions, which could be even more chilling than her husband's, but because she provided him with a home, which Cynthia had not, and thus saved him from self-destruction: his wartime letters to her, when he was in Brixton and she in Holloway, are loving, tender, and adult. He did not need to use the 'baby-talk' which covered up the emptiness of his marriage with Cimmie. She, of course, would not accept Mr Mosley's accolade on these terms.

Mr Mosley's tone towards his father becomes kinder as his political

217

failure becomes more palpable. But his is not the pity for a father who disgraced himself, but rather a celebration of survival. Of course as a son (and for many years a favourite son) he saw the best sides of his father: his genuine passion for ideas, his sense of fun, his geniality and, ultimately, his serenity. But above all, he came to feel that his father's politics might not be the most important thing about him. Mosley, unlike Hitler, was not sucked into 'the black hole of willed self-destruction'. He came through, without doing too much damage to himself or to others. One part of him could to some extent look at what the other parts were doing, and draw back – though he never found an appropriate language to talk about this. This is not an interpretation likely to appeal to those who felt themselves to be the victims of Sir Oswald's verbal onslaughts, or the attentions of his political movement. They might well feel that their fears were too high a price to pay for his survival; or alternatively, that it was little thanks to him that their apprehensions proved groundless. Nevertheless, Mr Mosley's account has the ring of truth. There is the same fault, as in volume one, of not taking his father's political passions seriously – either in their effects on him or on others. Despite this, one feels one is in the hands of a master craftsman, who has fashioned a language adequate to the ideas he wishes to convey; and that those ideas are important – having to do with what life is like, the games people play, and how one talks about these games. And there is the interest in the chief player, despite (or because of?) his failure.

How well does Nicholas Mosley's biography succeed on the level of history? That austere biographer, Bernard Crick, says: 'damn the ring of truth, give me the footnotes'. There are no footnotes here; but the history is well done, and there is new information to interest students of British Fascism. Mr Mosley reproduces memoranda and letters from Fascist officers and sympathizers, including Major-General Fuller, which throw light on the reorganization of the BUF in the summer of 1934, following the fiasco at Olympia and the withdrawal of Lord Rothermere's support. What Mosley did was to inaugurate a review of strategy. The advice he got shows that some Fascist minds were still working politically. He was warned against attempting to 'defend the Hitler regime'; told that the scurrilous propaganda emanating from William Joyce would put off decent people; urged to get rid of undesirables. Fuller advised him to make the Blackshirt Defence Force as 'inconspicuous as possible'; to delegate authority; to make better use of talent. At the same time Mosley was receiving other kinds of suggestion from radicals like Joyce and A. K. Chesterton to the effect that the Jews were Fascism's main enemy, and that he should nail the movement's propaganda to the mast of anti-semitism. (Even 'sensible' Fascists like Fuller were apt to go dotty on the subject of the Jews: while advising Mosley not to allow his followers to 'knock little Jews on the head', Fuller wrote about them in *The Fascist Quarterly* as the 'cancer of Europe'.) Mosley went on juggling. He accepted most of Fuller's organizational reforms (which did not, however, end the atmosphere of intrigue and jealousy which riddled the movement); at the same time he defined the Jews as Fascism's leading immediate opponent in his Albert Hall speech of 28 October 1934, thus opening the sluice-gates to what Mr Mosley calls 'an intrinsic anti-semitism in the BUF'.

Mr Mosley writes skilfully and sensitively about this subject and period: 'Members of the BUF were feeling both persecuted and belligerent: they were comrades-in-arms in a tough struggle: if they were to survive, they needed solidarity and courage. It must have seemed that now was not the time to think of casting out – of too severely reprimanding even – party stalwarts like Joyce of whom there could be no doubts about their almost reckless courage.' Oswald Mosley was trapped in complicity with the 'dark forces' – including those in himself.

Mr Mosley establishes beyond reasonable doubt that his father was subsidized by Mussolini between 1933 and 1935, probably to the tune of £100,000. The important new source he uses consists of letters to and from Count Grandi, the Italian Ambassador in London, which were known to exist, but which have only recently come to light through the efforts of the historian, David Irving. These letters show that Mosley was receiving £5000 a month from Italy, and that on one occasion, following a personal interview with Mussolini on 9 January 1934, he was personally handed £20,000. (January 1934 was a good month for the BUF: Rothermere's 'Hurrah for the Blackshirts' appeared in the *Daily Mail* the day before Mosley saw Mussolini. The Italian dictator, being a journalist himself, had the usual difficulty in distinguishing between newspaper events and what was actually happening.) There are a couple of nice twists to this story, suggestive of the constant interplay between private and public lives which we know goes on, but which historical biography can rarely footnote. It transpires that Grandi and Mosley were rivals in love – a fact not unconnected with Grandi's advice to Mussolini to suspend payments in 1935. The most bizarre twist, though, was that W. E. D. Allen, an ex-Conservative MP and Belfast businessman, who received the Italian payments on Mosley's behalf, apparently worked for British Military Intelligence. Mosley later claimed that he had always known that Bill Allen, a close friend who had married one of his former girlfriends, Paula Casa Maury, was a secret agent.

Bill Allen's role becomes significant in relation to Mosley's internment on 23 May 1940 under Regulation 18 B (1A) – which gave the Home Secretary power to detain any members of an organization 'subject to foreign influence or control', or whose leaders 'have or have had associations with leaders of enemy governments' or 'sympathise with the system of government of enemy powers'. Mosley appealed against his detention; on 3 and 15 July 1940 he was cross-examined for a total of sixteen hours by an Advisory Committee headed by Norman Birkett KC, as a result of which his detention was confirmed. The transcript of this hearing has never been made public; nor the advice which this Committee gave the government; even less is known about the Defence Security Executive, headed by Lord Swinton, which in Mr Mosley's words was 'the effective power behind the legalistic façade of Birkett's Advisory Committee'. (What on earth was Alfred Wall, described by Mr Mosley as 'a communist activist in South London', doing on this Executive?)

Recently Diana Mosley and Stanley Newens, former Labour MP for Harlow, have been campaigning for the release of government papers relating to Mosley's internment. Lady Mosley hopes they will prove her husband's detention to have been 'unjust and unfair'. The Labour side expects the papers to reveal a conspiracy, linking Mosley with members of 'the Establishment' to do a deal with Hitler to end the war in 1939–40. On Friday 21 October of this year, it was announced that the Home Secretary, Leon Brittan, was lifting the hundred-year ban on some papers relating to the British Union of Fascists, but not apparently those to do with Mosley's internment.

The conspiracy theorists are almost certainly barking up the wrong tree, as conspiracy theorists generally do. The important people contemplating a negotiated peace in 1939–40 had nothing to do with Mosley: what could he offer them? But Lady Mosley's hope that the release of the internment papers will somehow 'vindicate' her husband seems equally misplaced. Quite apart from the fact that Regulation 18 B (1A) was framed in such a way as to leave him little effective defence on publicly known facts, there were two embarrassing episodes which were known only to the security services. The first was the Mussolini subsidy; the second, and more important, had to do with Mosley's plan, just before the war, to set up a network of commercial radio stations outside Britain, on the model of Radio Luxembourg, to beam entertainment to Britain. The most important of these stations was to be located in Germany. Since the Führer controlled the wavelengths, his permission was needed. Diana Mosley, who was a friend of Hitler's, acted as go-between. As Mr Mosley tells it: 'During 1938 she saw Hitler several times in Berlin; she succeeded in re-awakening his interest in the plans.' Hitler's attention was diverted by minor diplomatic projects such as the annexation of Austria and the dismemberment of Czechoslovakia, but by 1939 arrangements for setting up a radio station in Heligoland were almost complete: profits were to be split 45/55 between Air Time Limited (Mosley's front organization) and a German company.

There was nothing necessarily sinister in all this. But it was hardly the kind of activity likely to convince the Advisory Committee that the Mosleys were not security risks. For of course everything was known to the security services, including Diana's visits (under the name of Mrs Guinness) to the insomniac Führer's Chancellery late at night. To quote Mr Mosley: 'How were they [the Defence Security Executive] to know that what was talked about was no more than charming gossip about the state of the world? or rather – what more evidence might such men as those who worked for the Executive require, when it was probably in their minds to imprison my father anyway?'

But what game exactly were Oswald and Diana playing? No doubt Mosley needed money to continue his movement: as he put it, 'I would have achieved my ambition to be the first revolutionary in history to conduct a revolution and at the same time to make the fortune which assured its success ... with good clean weapons of relatively decent commerce, which at least provided the people with an entertaining alternative to the dreary schoolmasters of the BBC.' But for a leader of a British Fascist party to have pursued a commercial plan depending on Hitler's patronage in 1938–9 when war with Germany had become probable was to show either astonishing naivety, or a reckless disregard for consequences, both to himself and to those who depended on him. His son inclines to the second interpretation: 'My father's insouciance was in keeping with his image of himself as a gambler going for very

221

high stakes: he took risks about money for the sake of what he believed about the fate of Britain and Europe.' What I think is at issue is not whether Mosley was gambling on a German victory as a prelude to his own success, but the extent to which his commercial hopes, which depended on Hitler, influenced the tone of his peace campaign, with its absolute refusal to criticize any German actions. I now feel I understand something which has always puzzled me: which is why Mosley made no attempt to organize a broader-based peace movement in the two years before the war. His hands, it seems, were tied by his own negotiations with Berlin. He was still juggling; still sacrificing public causes for private considerations.

How then does Mr Mosley make sense of all this? In order to understand how he handles the riddles of his father's life, one must remember that he is not just his son, but a novelist with a definite project: to develop a language for talking about life's riddles – an idea which may have come to him because he was his father's son: what could be more 'impossible' than winning a Military Cross, as Mr Mosley did, fighting, in a war he did not believe in, while his father was locked up in jail as a security risk? In his novel, *Imago Bird*, Bert, like Mr Mosley, stammers. He says, 'Stammering, it seems to me, is often caused by a person's wanting to say two or more things at once; which, it also seems, is often the only way in which things can be made to sound true. But ordinary language is not suited to this: or at least, not without struggle.' The structure of language is logical; but life is self-contradictory. What is needed is a new kind of language able to contain, and convey, its contradictions; a stylized stammer, so to speak. It is a language of people talking about people talking about things: what Mr Mosley calls a 'knowing' language. Nicholas Mosley's novels are filled with people who confront impossible predicaments and have to find a way of dealing with them. When Bert, the stammerer, is psychoanalysed, he thinks: 'One of the patterns that seemed to be emerging from my sessions with Dr Anders was the way in which she claimed to have spotted in me a liking for turning things into mysteries; while I claimed that it was life itself that consisted of mysteries; which I tried to observe truly but which other people always seemed to be trying to turn into simple dramas that were false.' Mr Mosley's 'efforts at truth' involve the avoidance of 'simple dramas' in which characters and events are coherent, all of a piece: good or bad, rational or irrational, winning or losing. His 'knowing' language is witty, ironic, paradoxical, allusive; expressive

222

of an attitude of mind which makes it possible to live with impossibilities, rather than simplify them out of existence. His is a post-Christian answer to other post-Christian attempts to discover purposes and patterns, attempts which, being partial, end in death and destruction. His stylized stammer is his answer to his father's way with words.

Oswald Mosley, too, was aware of incoherence: of people's desires being contradictory, of good and evil being intertwined, of private wants constantly cutting across public purposes. What he consciously tried to do was to get beyond these contradictions by a language of rational political synthesis: Nietzschean self-will must be pressed into the service of the Christian will to help humanity; these reconciled tendencies must be aligned with the findings of modern science, etc. But Mr Mosley tells us life is not like that, nor was his father's. He survived, as a human being, because he allowed his nature to take its contradictory courses, doing on the whole what he was good at and enjoyed (he was, writes Mr Mosley, like a dynamo who turned on lights in people), not sacrificing the whole to the parts, the left hand more or less cancelling out the right hand. A. J. P. Taylor has something of the same idea when he writes: 'Mosley had other, more human weaknesses. Strangely enough, despite his resolute appearance he was not a sticker. Time and again after launching some crusade, he lost interest and went off to Venice for a holiday. Often at a moment of crisis the self-appointed saviour of his country was not to be found: he was at a fencing match or playing practical jokes in high society. The true dictators, Hitler and Mussolini, thought of politics and nothing else. Mosley often gave the impression that politics were for him an exciting hobby, pursued with an intense concentration and then superseded by some equally absorbing activity. Again, though he spoke repeatedly of action, this worked out in the sense of putting on a performance rather than of practical work. As possibly the greatest orator of his day he lived by words . . .'

What Taylor regards as his 'weaknesses', Mr Mosley regards as his saving graces. At the 'battle of Cable Street' on 4 October 1936, his father was ordered by the Metropolitan Commissioner, Sir Philip Game, to call off his projected march through East London, after police had failed to disperse the militant opposition. Mosley told his followers to turn round and march back home 'to cries of disappointment'. Before he dismissed them he orated 'The Government surrenders to Red violence and Jewish corruption. We never surrender.' Mr Mosley points out the absurdity of 'a revolutionary movement prepared for a crisis who in a

crisis did exactly what they were told by the authorities. People wondered – what on earth was Mosley doing in his jackboots?' What they
did not know was that he was due in Berlin the next day to be married
to Diana Guinness. There is something not unengaging, after all, about
a person who calls off a revolution to get married.

PART THREE

The Era of Wars

CHAPTER THIRTY-FOUR

War and Change

Gerd Hardach, *The First World War 1914–1918*;
Derek H. Aldcroft, *From Versailles to Wall Street 1919–1929*;
Alan S. Milward, *War, Economy and Society 1939–1945*
[Allen Lane, 1977]

ACCORDING to the historian Geoffrey Barraclough, the contemporary era started in the 1880s. The forces which have shaped today's world first became apparent then. These three books, following on Kindleberger's *World in Depression 1929–1939* in the same series, are a great help in understanding what those forces were. The problems created by an unstable system of political economy have dominated our era; and much of modern history, including the two World Wars, has consisted of attempts by different countries and different political systems to solve, mitigate or evade them. So economic history, if broadly conceived, can offer great understanding of contemporary political and social dynamics. A first and final volume in this series will undoubtedly enlarge that understanding yet further; but certain themes stand out from the four already published.

The first question concerns the place of the two World Wars in contemporary history. Did they change its course? Did they strengthen existing trends? Were they outside shocks from which the system soon recovered? Like most interesting questions, these are impossible to answer firmly. But two broad approaches can be noticed. The Marxist approach tries to integrate war into the dynamics of capitalist imperialism. War has been a tool of national monopoly capitalisms in their fight for relative advantage. It is not accidental or exogenous, but a way of redividing the world to reflect a shift in productive power which has already occurred. Thus wars register and accentuate existing trends, but are not prime movers. This is Hardach's view.

By contrast, Alan Milward stresses the innovative and creative effects of war. War sets special organizational problems which bring about a shift of productive and other forces, domestically and internationally, which might otherwise not have occurred. There is nothing inevitable about war: it is, says Milward, 'a policy and investment

227

decision by the state'. But certain consequences follow from it. Organizational problems common to all belligerents in 'total war' produce economic, political, administrative and social solutions, which in turn influence life in the ensuing peace. Neither view does justice to the peaces which in fact emerged in 1919 and 1945. The 1920s saw a very determined attempt, known as the 'return to normalcy', to pretend that the war had never happened. Its organizational expedients were on the whole dropped. The dominant war power, the United States, did not try to play a comparable peacetime role. Nor was the Marxist thesis vindicated. The war for the supposed 'redivision' of the world in favour of the dynamic powers left the two undynamic powers – Britain and France – with larger empires than before. The Second World War gives much more support to both theses: the problem of choosing between them is not thereby made any easier.

The question of how important war is in bringing about change is very relevant to a second theme of modern political economy: the rise of the United States to world leadership and the decline of Europe. Did America pursue a world policy, including war, in order to win economic hegemony, as the revisionists Kolko and William Appleman Williams argue? Or was greatness thrust upon it unwillingly by the actions of the Europeans? The evidence from all three books makes it clear that the two wars themselves were critical in the rise of the United States, by simultaneously strengthening America and weakening Europe. Crucial to the former was the position of America in both wars as the 'arsenal of democracy'. This gave a tremendous boost to American productive capacity, exports and finance. In both wars, the western powers needed American goods to fight the war, but could not pay for them. Thus, through war, America was able to build up a dominating creditor and exporting possition in the world markets, destroying in the process earlier imperial connections forged by the European belligerents. The wars also weakened Europe absolutely, and relatively to Asia, Latin America and Africa. For example, the estimated European population deficit from the First World War (deaths and those who would have been born to the dead or disabled) came to 22 million, excluding Russia. The war caused 'a serious depletion and deterioration in the quality of Europe's population' (Aldcroft). Losses in the Second World War were heavier. The demographic basis of European supremacy in Asia and Africa was thus undermined. The terms of trade shifted heavily against

Europe after both World Wars; the periphery countries were given their chance to industrialize and revolt; and Europe's manufacturing performance remained sluggish right through the 1920s.

The most important single aspect of this process, not completed till 1945, was the replacement of Britain by the United States as the underwriter of the capitalist world economy. It was the completion of this shift which produced a stable and prosperous 'free world' after 1945; it was the absence of such an underwriter which made the interwar economy so unstable. Aldcroft, like Kindleberger in his volume, attributes the depth and duration of the Great Depression of 1929 to the incompleted American hegemony. As he sees it, structural imbalances between the manufacturing and primary producing countries were adjusted, in the nineteenth century, by Britain's willingness and capacity to lend abroad, long and short, and keep on open market for imports. As the result of the First World War, structural imbalances had worsened and multiplied, but the United States was not ready, and Britain not able, to 'manage' the economy; hence the collapse of 1929 and the growth of autarky in the 1930s. (The importance of the two wars and depression for the rise of economic nationalism and Fascism is one of the many themes which cannot be explored here.)

Aldcroft's account of the slump of 1929 stresses 'real' not 'monetary' factors, especially in the American downturn, which in turn brought down the world. Yet an equally plausible turning-point was the collapse of American foreign lending in 1928, in order to fuel the Wall Street boom. It was this which actually destroyed the world financial system; which gives point to the French charge that it was excess credit creation made possible by the gold exchange standard which made the system so unstable. Absent from Aldcroft's rather conventional interpretation is any account of the French assault on the gold exchange system in the late 1920s which foreshadowed in a remarkable way De Gaulle's challenge to the dollar in the 1960s.

Another major theme of the period is the growing involvement of the state in economic life. Here again we can choose between a number of explanations. For Marxists, the state's growth resulted from the difficulties of monopoly capitalism which therefore became 'state monopoly capitalism'. In this system, big business simply uses the state to further its ends – both in making war to secure monopoly profits and running the war in such a way as to achieve the same result. Hardach's account of business/state relations in the First World War, particularly in Germany, rests heavily on this argument – 'the government machine, both as regards personnel and ideology, was dependent on industry.'

Milward's account is more complex. The state's growth is largely a response to the 'needs of war'. The political consequence of eliminating the price mechanism is the concentration of economic decision-making in a few hands, immune from legislative interference. This happened in all belligerent countries. The Lord President's Council in Britain, the War Production Board in the United States, Speer's Ministry of War Production in Germany all had the same job: that of allocating resources in line with national priorities. The staffing of both decision-making and implementing bodies by businessmen signifies not the subservience of governments to business interests, but their reliance on business expertise and co-operation to meet their targets. This government/industry partnership changed the structure of the peacetime political economy. There was less reliance on market mechanisms to achieve desirable results, more on state action in a corporate setting. As Milward puts it: '. . . the two worlds of business and government administration were never again seen as the separate worlds they had still been in the thirties.'

War, of course, has not been the only cause of the growth of state intervention: the depression was another. The great weakness of Aldcroft's book, which is also a weakness of conventional economic history, is the lack of a political economy dimension. In the 1930s, even in the 1920s, new forms of state intervention were being legitimized, new relationships being forged between the government and the interest groups. What was Rathenau's 'organised capitalism'? What was the significance of the Mond–Turner conversations? On all this, the traditional economic historian – tied, like the economic theorist, to the 'market' model of how an economy works – remains silent.

A final development of great importance has been the rise of the working-class movement. It is generally agreed that both World Wars greatly strengthened the power of organized labour. But did they alienate the workers from the state or integrate them into it? Hardach concludes that, despite the regrettable tendency of German labour leaders to betray the cause of 'international proletarian solidarity', the war brought the German proletariat's class consciousness 'more nearly into accord with their objective class condition than had previously been the case'. But the evidence is conflicting.

War in the twentieth century has, of course, been a great revolutionary force. Leninist Russia and Maoist China were creations of world war. Both wars strengthened the revolutionary left in Europe and Asia, partly by discrediting and weakening the old ruling classes who had either mismanaged the war or embraced Fascism. On the other hand, world war has also served to make the labour movement into a pillar of bourgeois society, by giving it for the first time an effective political role, and by greatly strengthening the movement for social reform. On all these matters the historical debate continues.

CHAPTER THIRTY-FIVE

Fascism and Expansion: An Essay in Interpretation
[April 1977]

I

Between the wars the expansionist states were the Fascist states. That there was a connection between Fascism and expansion is generally agreed. The precise nature of the connection is less clear. There are three ways of looking at the problem. First, one can see Fascism as having an in-built tendency to expansion. Expansion arises from the ideology, psychology or structure of the Fascist regimes, and the domestic problems they create. Secondly, one can view Fascist expansionism in the context of the 'crisis of capitalism'. This is the classical Marxist position. Both Fascism and the drive for empire result from the internal crises of certain great capitalist states – characteristically 'latecomers' in the world capitalist system. Fascism is the political agent of capitalism in such states. There is a modern neo-Marxist position which has a more complicated view of the internal crisis which produces the drive to expansion. Finally, Fascist expansionism can be analysed in the context of the international system of that time. The relevant (and perhaps connected) developments are the breakdown of its economic harmonizing and policing mechanisms. Expansionism results both from dissatisfaction with the benefits flowing from membership of the international system *and* the existence of opportunities forcibly to reshape that system

231

to the benefit of the dissatisfied powers. Fascist government is both the result of the dissatisfaction, and the instrument for the reshaping. I shall develop all three approaches in more detail, but with particular emphasis on the third, because this is the least familiar in the literature on Fascism, though not in the literature of international relations. Particular attention will be paid to the Great Depression as a possible cause of Fascist expansionism.

Two preliminary comments may be made. First, it is possible and necessary to use all three explanations, while emphasizing one or the other. Each can illuminate certain aspects of the expansionist dynamic. As between the first and the other two it is sometimes a question of the appropriate level of analysis. Secondly, the discussion of the connection between Fascism and expansionism is at the same time a discussion of the question of why Fascism succeeded in some countries and not in others. Historians have had less to say about this than about the common roots of Fascism in all modern or modernizing societies. (Barrington-Moore is an exception.) Yet, among the Great Powers, Fascist support was much weaker in Britain, America and France than in Germany, Italy and Japan; among the smaller powers, it was much weaker in Western than Eastern Europe. This disparity needs to be explained. In my view, it was only in those nations radically dissatisfied with their international standing, or in national groups dissatisfied with their position in existing states, that Fascism could mobilize enough popular support to pose a serious challenge to prevailing liberal values and patterns of rule.

II

There are many variations on the theme 'Fascism causes war'. Expansion is said to stem from the 'warlike philosophy' of Fascism, from its 'eminently military characteristics', from its militarist psychology.[1] Mussolini is often quoted in support: 'Fascism does not, generally speaking, believe in the possibility or utility of perpetual peace . . . War alone keys up all the human energies to their maximum tension and sets the seal of nobility on those peoples who have the courage to face it.'[2] Such attitudes involve the rejection of the doctrines of progress and natural harmony, clearing the way for applying crude social Darwinism to international relations.[3] Fascist expansionism can also be seen as ideological, designed to spread Fascism, much as Communist expansionism

232

today is sometimes attributed to Marxist ideology. Thus Carocci sees the subversion of the existing liberal world order as inherent in Fascism.[4] An anti-Bolshevik crusade was perhaps also inherent. The British Fascist leader Oswald Mosley, while insisting on the need for European peace, kept open the possibility of a European war against the Soviet Union.[5]

Other scholars have seen war and expansion as implicit in Fascism's rejection of 'transcendence' and modernity. This is Ernst Nolte's position. Fascist regimes sought, through conquest, to acquire the space and autonomy to realize their alternative plans of life, based on colonization and rural values. Conquest and colonization as a way back to social health were espoused by Hitler, Mussolini, and the Japanese Kwantung army in Manchuria. Others see in Fascist culture a passion for destruction, rather than the quest for alternative constructions. J. P. Stern has portrayed Nazism as the political manifestation of the Romantic striving for authenticity. When the actual tendencies of life are seen as inauthentic, such a quest inevitably leads to nihilism, to Rauschning's 'revolution of destruction'. Hitler's 'existential project' could not but fail to be 'catastrophic', involving Germany, the Jews, and himself in ruin. Stern thus locates both the source of war, and the failure to conduct the war rationally, in Fascism's Romanticism.[6]

This kind of analysis is extremely useful in showing the particular temper and direction Fascist ideas gave to the expansionist impulse. Hitler's plans for eastward expansion were not the same as the Kaiser's; nor were his methods. However, such analysis on its own ignores the functional aspect of ideas. A warlike rhetoric may heighten warlike feelings; it does not explain why martial values were able to strike a responsive chord in some places, not others. Certainly in Britain and France martial rhetoric had become completely *passé* after the First World War. Regenerationist, anti-industrial rhetoric is likely to be more popular in some places, at some times, than in other places at other times.

Fascist expansionism can also be seen as diversionary. Its object is neither to realize some 'socio-ethical purpose'[7] nor to solve the economic problem, rather to solve the political problems of the Fascist regime, particularly its lack of legitimacy. In the classic manner of dictatorships, the regime tries for a *coup de théâtre* to take people's minds off troubles at home. The ostensible objects of expansion – *Lebensraum*, markets, sources of raw materials, social renewal – are all more or less fraudulent, myths for popular consumption. Imperial expansion plays much the same role in Fascism as anti-semitism. It provides a spurious goal, a spurious enemy, in place of 'real' programmes of reform. Since Fascism was not willing to create a better society at home, its only way of keeping up support was by mobilizing the country against a foreign enemy.

This is the standard analysis of Mussolini's assault on Abyssinia, which also fits the current view of Italian Fascism as the least serious of the Fascist systems. The function of Mussolini's imperialism, writes Denis Mack Smith in a recent book, was to 'divert attention from pressing problems at home'. He quotes with approval Lord Perth's comment that Mussolini created foreign enemies to prevent public opinion from becoming 'dangerously introspective and critical of the internal doings of the regime'. The fraudulence of the claims for African empire can be shown by the results: there were hardly any settlers, the colonies were a great economic burden to Italy, there was little or no attempt to exploit their resources.[8] These arguments are not conclusive. Not only was there very little time to develop the empire before it collapsed; but in so far as the Fascist colonial enterprise was a flop, this may be due to the inefficiency and corruption of the regime, rather than the fraudulence of the policy. After all, a sizeable number of white settlers had previously established itself in Northern Africa, including over 100,000 Italians in Tunisia. Had the Axis won the war, a serious colonization programme might well have been attempted in Libya and Abyssinia.

In his work on Nazi Germany, T. W. Mason has attempted to relate expansion to the crisis of Hitler's economic policy. Mason argues that lavish Nazi spending on public works had produced an acute shortage of labour and raw materials by 1936, forcing up prices. The Nazis needed either to curtail rearmament, or reduce domestic consumption by means of wage controls and the direction of resources to strategic industries. Both were politically impossible. Rearmament was needed for a strong foreign policy, and wage controls were impossible for a regime which needed, yet feared, the working class. 'A war for the plunder of manpower and materials lay square in the dreadful logic of German economic development under National Socialist rule. The sequence of international events was not thereby predetermined, but the range of possibilities was severely circumscribed.' The argument is not wholly persuasive. The problems of Germany's overheated economy in the 1930s too closely resemble those of Western democracies of the 1960s and 1970s to inspire confidence in Mason's conclusion that a war of plunder was the most plausible way out for the Nazi economic system.[9] What he seems to be doing is using Germany as a historical illustration of today's 'crisis of capitalism'.

The main weakness of the theory that Fascism causes expansion – for whatever of the reasons discussed above – is that strong expansionary tendencies had existed in Germany, Italy, and Japan before Fascism appeared. Mason's argument involves isolating Nazi expansionism from that of Imperial Germany. In reply, A. J. P. Taylor has pointed out that 'The foreign policy of National Socialism merely restated the German problem'.[10] Historical investigation shows a remarkable continuity in the foreign aspirations of the three powers from the late nineteenth century through to the 1940s. It was these aspirations which gave Fascism its chance under specific historical circumstances – a chance which it did not have elsewhere.

III

In the Marxist interpretation, imperialism and Fascism are linked to each other through the continuing crisis of capitalism. The argument can develop endless complications, and modern Marxists are much more sophisticated about it than were the Marxists of forty or fifty years ago, when the crude formulations of the Comintern held sway. But common to all versions – the minimum doctrine – is the notion of the 'internal crisis' of capitalism which seeks an external resolution, of which Fascism is the eventual instrument.

The 'crisis of capitalism' as portrayed by Marxist writers during the Depression years ran from over-production caused by exploitation and the subsequent limitation of the internal market, through the export of capital and the opening up of new continents for exploitation, to the inevitability of imperialist wars for the redivision of the world. The detailed argument ran as follows. There were two possible solutions to the crisis of over-production: increasing mass consumption or creating 'external' markets. Big business would not allow the first, since this would reduce profits. It was therefore forced to the second solution. External markets were of two kinds. One of them could be provided by government purchases, especially of arms. By providing a market for heavy industry government could maintain profits and employment for a time, but at the cost of an arms race and inflation. The traditional external solution was to open up new countries to provide outlets for surplus capital. This had been the classical nineteenth-century pattern. But in the era of rival national 'monopoly' capitalisms, the exploitation of new countries could take place only by establishing political control of these areas. Here rearmament took its place, not only as a means of employment, but as a means of conquest. However, these 'solutions' were radically unstable, involving both increased global exploitation and world wars.[11]

This account of the inter-war 'crisis of capitalism' was much less sophisticated than later versions. Because their political hopes pointed in that direction, Marxist writers of the 1930s assumed a *general* crisis of capitalism, leading to the possiblity of both Fascism or socialism in *all* advanced industrial countries. The universal character of the Depression reinforced this. Although they were perfectly familiar with Lenin's concept of *uneven* capitalist development, they made little use of it to explain the differential impact of the crisis on, say, Britain and Germany, and hence the different ways of internal adaptation to it.

According to Lenin, it was uneven capitalist development which made the international system so unstable. Young monopolies needed to expand just as much as the older ones had before. They too needed to secure access to markets and raw materials; also to secure the 'super-profits' of imperialism to bribe their own working classes. But with the world already carved out among a few great empires, such expansion could take place only at the expense of older monopolies. 'When the relation of forces is changed, what other solution of the contradictions can be found under capitalism than that of force?' Lenin asks. A situation has arisen in which capitalist states in relative decline have great colonial possessions and the more dynamic ones have small and inadequate colonial possessions. Then begins an era 'of particularly intense struggle for the division and redivision of the world'. Written in 1915, Lenin's words have undoubted explanatory power.[12]

The English Marxists Palme-Dutt and John Strachey were both aware of the significance of uneven development for international relations. According to Palme-Dutt in 1934, Anglo-American imperialism was 'sated', while German–Japanese imperialism was 'hungry' and therefore expansionist.[13] Similarly, Strachey argued that 'Fascist economic policy is . . . wholly dependent upon the waging of a successful war' because it involves expansion which can be achieved only by conquest. 'A new German (or Italian) empire can arise only from the defeat and partition of the British, French, or some other Empire – or from the defeat and partition of the USSR.'[14] But neither of them at first saw the different domestic structures of, say, Britain and Germany as the result of their different world situations. Both writers needed Britain's domestic crisis to be as severe as Germany's to sustain their revolutionary optimism.

The notion of Fascism as the internal system particularly suited to the weaker imperialist powers has recently been made familiar by Poulantzas, among others. 'The uneven development of the imperialist chain,' he writes, 'has an effect within each national formation. The *concrete form* . . . of politics within each national formation depend(s) on its "historical" position as a link in the chain'. It was thus not surprising that the first, Communist revolution should occur in Russia, the weakest member of the pre-1914 imperialist club. It was equally understandable that 'Fascism arose in the next two links, i.e., those which were relatively speaking, the weakest in Europe at the time', the 'late-comers . . . to capitalism'.[15] Thus Fascism is seen as a form of adaptation by the 'weaker' imperialist nations to the crisis of capitalism; and by extension, the instrument of their expansion to overcome it. This is a powerful insight, taking us out of the world of 'diversions' into one of real problems.

At the same time, the Marxist concept of the 'internal crisis' has become more complex. In Lenin's model, forcible expansion was a simple function of 'lateness'. This is indistinguishable from the argument Fascist apologists like Corradini themselves used for expansion, when they divided the world into 'proletarian' and 'plutocratic' nations. (Of course, Lenin never thought that any country's 'crisis of capitalism' could be *permanently* solved by successful war: but this qualification was hardly likely to deter a would-be conqueror.) Hence Poulantzas's insistence that the international weakness of Germany and Italy must not be seen simply as a result of their late 'arrival', but also as a function of 'an accumulation of economic, political, and ideological contradictions' within their societies.[16] A complex relationship is posited between domestic and external factors, as well as between the various elements of the internal crisis.

The modern Marxist notion of the 'internal crisis' is thus considerably more eclectic than earlier ones, involving largely unacknowledged borrowings from 'bourgeois' writers like Schumpeter and Veblen. Poulantzas's formula of the 'exceptional capitalist state', whose social crisis is resolved in Fascism and war, is one that assimilates much non-Marxist historiography.

The main structural characteristic of this kind of state (Germany, Italy and Japan are the main examples) is now seen as the absorption of the most advanced technology by a largely traditional society in an unprecedentedly short time. Modernization was imposed from above by a bureaucratic, and in Germany and Japan, dynastic, state, rather than by a 'hegemonic' bourgeoisie. This meant retention of political and ideological control by the pre-industrial ruling class: the great agrarians in Prussia, the great feudal lords in Japan, metamorphosed into industrialists by the commutation of their feudal dues. In Italy, a weak bourgeoisie manned the state, but on condition of allowing the 'big landowners to maintain their economic and politico-ideological hold over the Southern peasantry, and at the same time to thwart the strategy of the Northern bourgeoisie'.[17] In these three states there thus emerged a fundamental contradiction between the 'rational' needs of capitalist modernization and the entrenched position of the pre-capitalist social order.

The first consequence was an 'irrational' economic development based on a high tariff alliance between government-sponsored heavy industry and traditional agriculture. (In Japan, a landlord–industrialist coalition also controlled politics, but without a tariff deal as in Germany and Italy.) This reduced the internal market, forcing industry and agriculture to seek external outlets; but at the same time reduced the international market still further by provoking retaliation. Thus an irrational economic policy created internal and international difficulties which a policy of territorial expansion was then designed to overcome. A second consequence of retaining the traditional social order was imperfect democratization and only superficial unity – in Italy, as Adrian Lyttleton puts it, 'a limited and artificial democracy' was set in the midst of an unmobilized electorate.[18] The result was that the masses, workers and peasants, remained outside, and antagonistic to, the state. The problem of integration could be tackled only through foreign policy. Imperialism offered this basis: the democracy of conscription rather than the ballot-box.

This kind of analysis can obviously be carried forward to the era of Fascism. In both Germany and Italy the war radicalized the masses, weakened the traditional order, destroyed the old techniques of government, and created massive new problems without, however, producing a real transfer of power. The result was *stasis*. As Schoenbaum has put it, 'Fascism appears to have been a product of industrially underdeveloped, but not undeveloped, countries, where parliamentary-democratic pegs failed to fit in vacant feudal or absolutist holes.'[19] Because Fascism inherited, without resolving, the contradictions of the 'exceptional capitalist state', it, too, was forced into wars of expansion.

However the 'internal crisis' is perceived, the essential point remains that expansion and Fascism both result from it. Fritz Fischer is quite explicit on this point. Germany was a dissatisfied member of the international community, but its dissatisfaction was the result of domestic strains.[20] Similarly, Hans Ulrich Wehler writes that the Wilhelmite policy of *realpolitik* had its origins 'in the social and political tensions between on the one hand the authoritarian state, the landed nobility and the feudalized bourgeoisie, and on the other hand, the advancing forces of parliamentarisation and democratisation and, most important, the social democratic movement towards emancipation'.[21] To explain Fascist expansionism in terms of social structure is undoubtedly illuminating; many manifestations of foreign policy are the outcome of social strains. However, as Barrington-Moore has reminded us, social structure is only one variable in explaining political development, others being 'time and external circumstances'.[22] Moreover, the views just outlined suffer from two specific weaknesses.

First, the view that the expansionist impulse after 1880 was economically 'irrational' implicitly assumes the rationality of the dominant liberal, free-trade commercial system. This may be a reasonable assumption before 1914, but what about the inter-war years? What internal reforms would have made expansion unnecessary, or at least unattractive, for weakly-placed great powers in the 1930s? Wehler and Barrington-Moore talk of enlarging the home market.[23] But quite apart from the fact that it took the Keynesian revolution to establish a democratic method of doing this, it is unlikely that domestic measures themselves could have compensated for the disorder which had by then developed in the international system. It took the Keynesian revolution *plus* American hegemony to restore the 'natural' harmony of interests of the free world after 1945; and central planning *plus* the Soviet army to enforce harmony in the Soviet empire.

Secondly, certain elements of imperialism cannot be reduced to class analysis. Nationalism is the chief example. The argument that a social revolution would have destroyed nationalism is very dubious. As

Ludwig Dehio has pointed out, though nationalism was present throughout society, it was much stronger in the middle and lower classes than among the traditional property owners.[24] On the other hand, in so far as expansionism was a 'rational' survival strategy for certain great powers in a given set of external circumstances, it does not *require* a class explanation. The fact that certain groups benefited, or hoped to benefit, from war and expansion does not mean that war and expansion were undertaken at their behest. As Karl Polanyi well puts it: 'The fate of classes is much more often determined by the needs of society than is the fate of society determined by the needs of classes.'[25]

IV

The view that the explosive situation of the inter-war years arose out of the unsatisfactory location of certain Great Powers in the international system was brilliantly expounded by E. H. Carr. His book, *The Twenty Years Crisis*, published in 1939, has two ideas relevant to our enquiry. The first is that international relations between the wars were dominated by the division between status quo and revisionist states. The second is that a country's internal system is largely determined by its position in the international system. Thus the division of the world between status quo and revisionist powers corresponded to that between 'welfare' and 'power' states.[26]

Carr offers a powerful insight into the political evolution of Germany, Italy and Japan in the fifty years or so before 1945. For this was an exceptionally fluid period in international relations when, unlike today, large and decisive shifts in power were possible. The rapid spread of industrialization at the end of the nineteenth century had fragmented significant power among half a dozen nations, bringing to a close the long era of the *Pax Britannica*. After 1945, the hegemonic void was filled by the US–Soviet condominium. But for half a century the situation was open for smaller great powers to try for their 'place in the sun' before it was too late. Carr leaves open the question of whether such ambitions were rational. Like Taylor he believed them to be inevitable in a world system of sovereign states. Great powers will always strive to increase their power unless checked.[27] As it stands this statement is incomplete. To understand the power bids of Germany, Italy, and Japan in the period 1880–1945 we must examine the peculiar nature of the vulnerabilities perceived by these powers in the international system of the time.

The feeling of *cultural* vulnerability was common to all three. The German intelligentsia felt threatened by Anglo-Saxon cultural dominance and also invented a mission to save Europe from the Slav: the theory of the so-called 'third domain' between America and Russia. In Japan, cultural and racial resentments came together in the notion of a Japanese mission to control and organize North China and exclude the Occident from East Asia. The idea of Italy's civilizing mission had been inherent in the Risorgimento. It was given fresh intensity by the failure of the Risorgimento to achieve its prerequisite: national unity. Mazzini foreshadowed the main theme of Italian nationalism when he wrote: 'Yes; unity was and is the destiny of Italy. The civil primacy twice exercised by Italy – through the arms of the Caesars and the voice of the Popes – is destined to be held a third time by the people of Italy – the nation'.[28]

Strategic vulnerability offered a second motive for revisionism. Germany was perpetually faced with 'encirclement'. Italy was trapped in the Mediterranean. Japan's defensive position was good, but like Germany and Italy, it lacked raw materials. Industrialization was making all three increasingly dependent on external sources of supply and, therefore, vulnerable to British blockade. This suggested a policy either of friendship with Britain or challenge to it. (In Japan's case, America, after 1918, was the power with the potential stranglehold.) Of course, strategic vulnerability only offered a rational motive for expansion on two assumptions: (a) that the dominant seapower could be successfully challenged, and (b) that the international economy worked systematically against the welfare of the strategically vulnerable countries.

Here then was the third motive. *Economic* vulnerability became much more of a real problem for these countries after the First World War, as we shall see later. But even before 1914 world integration on a competitive basis was producing severe internal strains through the transmission of economic fluctuations from one economy to another. Were national interests being harmonized or torn apart by trade and finance? If the former were true, it was rational to maximize the international division of labour. If the latter were the case, it might be more rational to lessen one's dependence on the world market. This debate was particularly acute in Germany. But already before 1914, protectionist and even autarkic ideas were very much in the air. In the case of the smaller great powers these ideas implied expansionism.

Even before 1914 these dissatisfactions produced a distinctive intellectual and political temper that differentiated the revisionist from the status quo powers, though this cleavage was not nearly as great as after the war.* Doctrines of Nationalism, Realism and Romanticism received their most incisive formulation in Italy and Germany. Economic policy was frankly mercantilist. Heavy industry was deliberately promoted in Germany, Italy and Japan to enhance these countries' military capacity. Agriculture was protected for the same reason. (In Britain, where the expectation was that the New World would be a reliable granary in a peaceful world policed by the British Navy, agriculture was allowed to decline.) Both Italy and Japan witness the beginnings of the movement to staunch the permanent loss of population through emigration. This implied acquiring areas for colonization: Libya for Italy, Manchuria for Japan, both objects of military penetration in the years leading up to 1914. The special position of the Army in the politics of Germany and Japan was not just an unfortunate 'atavism' in the Schumpeterian sense, but testified to the widespread acceptance of foreign policy aims which called for military force.

Germany, Italy, and Japan all entered the First World War to acquire empires.[29] Although all three powers were incorporated into the Versailles and Washington treaty systems of the 1920s, the outcome of the First World War was a defeat for their imperial ambitions, even while the war itself seemed to demonstrate their relevance to contemporary life: the British Empire reached its territorial zenith after 1918. While Britain, the United States and France became pacific, Germany, Italy and Japan remained strongly dissatisfied and revisionist. The main hope of containing these dissatisfactions lay in establishing an improved system of international economy, such as was achieved after 1945. But neither the abilities and knowledge of statesmen, nor the balance of economic power, was up to the task, and a fragile prosperity collapsed into the Great Depression of 1929–33 – an event which made Fascism a world-historical force.

What the Depression seemed to do was to settle the debate between

---

* Nationalism and revisionism were also powerful forces in France following the loss of Alsace-Lorraine in 1871 – a situation in which a Dreyfus affair and *Action Française* could develop. However, they died away after the First World War.

world integration and national or imperial self-sufficiency, initiated by the 'new imperialism' of the 1880s, in favour of the latter. The reason is that after 1918 there was no single power able to 'underwrite' the world economy as the British had done in the nineteenth century. This is the major theme of Kindleberger's important study of Depression. The result was that the world economy broke up in the 1930s into a number of economic blocs, loosely connected.

Kindleberger's argument is that a stable international economy needs an underwriter. In the inter-war years, the British could not and the Americans would not provide the necessary leadership; the French preferred the role of the spoiler. Thus the countries responsible for the international political order of the 1920s failed to ensure its economic underpinning. From 1924 to 1928, American (and to a lesser extent British) foreign lending, starting with the Dawes loan of 1924, kept the world economy afloat. But American foreign lending dried up after June 1928 as savings were diverted to the stock exchange boom. This destroyed the financing of agricultural stocks, leading to a huge collapse in the prices of foodstuffs and raw materials. Instead of keeping an open market for distress goods – one of the functions of Kindleberger's underwriter – the United States put on the gigantic Hawley-Smoot tariff of 1930 'which made it clear that in the world economy there was no one in charge'.[30] The Bank of England's $7 million one week credit to Austria on 5 June 1931 marked 'the end of Britain as lender of the last resort'.[31] Britain left the gold standard on 21 September 1931 and abandoned free trade with the Import Duties Act of April 1932: both measures transferred deflationary pressure to others, particularly Germany. By setting up the Exchange Equalisation Fund Account in 1933, the British monetary authority finally gave up responsibility for the international economy.[32] The United States did so even more dramatically that year when Roosevelt devalued the dollar and refused to consider exchange stabilization, declaring that 'the sound internal situation of a nation is a greater factor in its stability than the price of its currency'. France throughout 'sought power in its national interest, without adequately taking into account the repercussions of its position on world economic or political stability'.[33] In short, the leaders of the world economy broke it up in order to protect themselves.

In this situation, the favoured countries were those with a high degree of self-sufficiency or with markets and supplies over which they had some control. Among the great powers the former included the

United States, the Soviet Union and France (which also had a large African empire). The main example of the latter was Great Britain, which was able to raise its exports to the empire and sterling bloc countries from 45 to 62 per cent of the total between 1929 and 1938 and imports from 42 to 55 per cent. Least favourably situated were those great powers whose economy depended on markets, supplies, and finance over which they had little political control. In this category were Germany, Italy and Japan.

Germany was in a very weak position. The Versailles treaty deprived it of 30 per cent of its coal and iron capacity and 7 million of its population. After the disastrous inflationary collapse of 1921–3, the German economy was refloated by American loans which, however, left its industry dangerously dependent on short-term foreign funds. It had no 'sheltered' foreign markets or supplies. The termination of foreign loans after 1928 wrecked the financing of private industry and the municipalities. It was these external features of the German situation, as well as the foolish deflationary policies of Bruning, which made the Depression so severe and, because of that, gave Hitler his chance.

Italy 'was one of the countries hardest hit, because of the weakness and imbalance of its economy and because the world crisis was superimposed on the still-active crisis provoked by the revaluation of the lira'.[34] American, British and French restrictions on Italian imports left it virtually defenceless. Japan was also very badly balanced. In 1929, 42.5 per cent (by value) of its exports, mainly raw silk, went to the United States. By 1933 this had fallen to 26 per cent. In all three cases, the severity of the Depression can be related to attempts to play the 'rules of the game' from weak international positions. This was not entirely voluntary. The more dependent a country was on external factors, particularly external finance, the more it felt constrained to behave in 'orthodox' ways, and the more resentful it would become at the 'dictatorship' of foreign bankers. The dependence of all three countries on foreign capital, and the extent to which the severity of the Depression could be blamed on this dependence, played an important part in the political developments of the 1930s.

Japan was the most successful of the three revisionist powers in overcoming the Depression. In 1932, the Finance Minister Korekiyo Takahashi launched a ' "full employment" policy ... four years before Keynes's *General Theory* provided him with a theoretical justification'.[35] By 1934 public spending accounted for 38 per cent of the net domestic product.[36] Almost half of this was on military spending, greatly stimulating production in the heavy industries. Externally Japan managed to achieve a most remarkable shift of trade from the United States and Europe to the 'yen bloc' of Korea, Formosa, Manchuria and Kwantung – that is, to the Japanese empire. Trade between Japan and these area rose from 24 per cent to 55 per cent of Japan's total trade between 1929 and 1938. Manchuria became a major outlet for capital investment.

The adaptations of Germany and Italy were less successful. Hitler too was able to cure unemployment, before Keynes had finished explaining why it occurred, by a mixture of industrial subsidies and public works. But Germany was much less successful in securing its foreign position, its trade with Eastern Europe, competitive with that of both France and Britain, rising only from 5 to 13 per cent of its total trade between 1929 and 1938. In that sense Mason is right in saying that Germany had not solved its economic problem in the 1930s. But this was as much due to external as internal factors. Italy attempted to relieve the Depression through land reclamation (the 'battle for wheat') and by setting up state holding and credit organizations (IRI and IMI) to bale out the defence-related heavy industries. But the bulk of its foreign trade, like Germany's, remained scattered and beyond its control.

The relationship between Fascism, the Depression, and expansion is complex. Academics in the three 'have not' great powers often argued the expansionist case on economic grounds. Thus an Italian pamphlet of 1938 claimed that the breakdown of the welfare guarantee through the international division of labour forced states to become self-sufficient. But for Italy such self-sufficiency had to be on an imperial basis in order to obtain secure access to raw materials and extra living space for Italy's 'prolific and industrious masses'. Professor Predöhl of Kiel University argued, like the Italians, that the breakdown of the international system meant autarky. But his argument for a *Grossraum* was based on the insufficiency of relatively small national markets for modern mass production industry. This suggested strongly integrated regional economies. The historian Masamichi Royama wanted East Asia to become a vast self-sustaining region where Japan would acquire economic security and immunity from such trade boycotts as she had experienced at the hands of the Western powers.[37] The line of all these arguments leads from welfare to empire.

Fascism's claim to rule was based on its promise to change for the better the international situation of the unfavourably placed powers. Its ideology and internal structure were defended as functional to that end. Specifically, it set out to create (a) a mass base for an ideology hostile to liberalism, pacifism and humanitarianism, (b) a social system which would abolish class conflict, (c) a political system which would give unity of direction and clear purposes, and (d) an economic system which would give adequate support to the regime's foreign policy aims.

That Fascism tried to organize its societies for wars of conquest seems indisputable. But it is much too simple to see the expansionism of these powers purely in terms of world economic breakdown. The connection between the Depression and expansion is clearest in the case of Japan's seizure of Manchuria in 1931. But even here the causation is indirect. The Depression did not so much stimulate a positive programme of economic imperialism as destroy the most telling argument against it: that it would sacrifice economic prosperity. It thus strengthened the political position of those who wanted to change the existing inter-national system *for other reasons*. The Japanese Army's argument that expansion was needed to create an autonomous war-making power gained its new force from the destruction of the liberal argument that growing economic prosperity was making war an anachronism.

The link between the Depression and expansion is even less direct in the case of Italy and Abyssinia and Germany and East Europe. The dominant note being struck is not that the breakdown of the liberal system *requires* the establishment of an alternative welfare basis. It is rather, that the breakdown gives the opportunity for those societies willing to grasp it to reshape their lives on healthier lines. For example, Predöhl rejected the international division of labour not just because it had broken down, requiring second-best strategies, but because it was bad in itself. 'The benefits accruing from such a division of labour and the purchase of commodities in the cheapest market are obtained at the cost of injury to agriculture, population growth, cultural and social objectives, and at a great cost to national security. What may be sensible from a purely economic point of view may be absurd from a political standpoint.'[38] What the Great Depression did was to bring back into practical politics more traditional concepts of the 'healthy society'.

A good example of this is Mussolini's population policy. Italy's 'prolific' population is given as the reason for empire. Yet Mussolini's policy was to increase the population (the 'battle for births') with special rewards for spectacular feats of fertility, in order to make possible the founding of empire. As early as 1927 he had said: 'If a nation diminishes, gentlemen, that nation does not found an Empire. It becomes a colony.'[39] In other words, war and empire were values quite independent of the Depression. What the Depression did was to provide opportunity. Japanese and Italian demographic arguments for expansion (to provide space for colonization) did have some basis in the collapse of emigration outlets, especially in America. But the rural bias of Fascist social policy was dictated by other motives – to restore social health, to maximize military power, or simply to keep down the numbers of the industrial proletariat.

Also it is going much too far to say that Germany's international situation in the 1930s required a war of conquest. There is little doubt that the 'Schachtian' system of regulated trade could have been developed and intensified to give Germany effective control over the economic life of central and Eastern Europe without war. Arguments like those of Predöhl might have led a regime less obsessed with national glory and racial cleansing towards the project of a European 'common market' as a *rational* response to world economic breakdown.

Finally, the Depression not only gave domestic opportunity to put certain political principles into practice, it also created a more fluid international situation – one more favourable to revisionism. To give one very important example: the economic leverage that creditor nations could exert through finance was removed when capital markets became moribund. The contrast is between 1931, when France had been able to block Customs Union between Germany and Austria by taking its funds out of both countries, and 1938 when it stood passively by while Germany annexed Austria. The removal of non-military deterrents from international relations, shown also in the weakness of the sanctions policy against Italy in 1935, gave the initiative to those powers willing to risk war to get their way.

To sum up: the Depression provided mass support for revisionism in Germany, Italy and Japan by linking it directly to 'bread and butter' questions. Fascism exploited this situation. In Japan a ruined peasantry provided the mass base for the Army's socio-ethical and strategic programme in North China. In Germany, the Depression gave National Socialism mass support for the first time: revisionism and economic prosperity no longer seemed to be in conflict. In Italy, Fascism had, of course, come to power before the Depression. But the Depression brought out its radical potential. What the Depression did in all three cases was to seem to make politically relevant criticisms of actual tendencies which had proliferated in those great powers unfavourably situated in the international system.

V

The survey of the relationship between Fascism and expansion gives no conclusive answer to the old debate about the primacy of domestic or external politics. The fact that, after a number of stunning successes, the Fascist regimes went down to defeat and ruin in the Second World War should guard us against any undue tendency to think of Fascism as a rational adaptation of domestic politics to fit the 'objective' needs of unfavourably-situated great powers: a view which unites the cruder versions of Marxist historiography with Fascism's own apologists. Although the Depression gave the Fascist powers the opportunity, incentive, and support to try to change the international balance of power, the nature of Fascism's external project was highly influenced by Fascist ideology, the structural characteristics of the Fascist regimes, and internal social strains which had little or nothing to do with international politics or economics. However, in trying to explain the link between Fascism and expansion historians need to pay more attention than they have done to the pressure for expansion generated by the state of international relations at the time. This essay is a modest attempt to do just that.

NOTES

1   Otto-Ernst Schuddekopf, *Revolutions of Our Time: Fascism* (1973), pp. 151–6.
2   Benito Mussolini, *Fascism, Doctrine and Institutions* (1935), p. 19.
3   Eugen Weber, *Varieties of Fascism* (1964), p. 33.
4   Giampiero Carocci, *Italian Fascism* (1975), p. 71.
5   Oswald Mosley, 'The World Alternative', *Fascist Quarterly* July 1936, p. 392.
6   See Ernst Nolte, *Three Faces of Fascism* (1965); J. P. Stern, *Hitler, The Führer and the People* (1975).
7   H. A. Turner, 'Fascism and Modernization', *World Politics* June 1972.
8   Denis Mack Smith, *Mussolini's Roman Empire* (1976), pp. 32, 65, 81, 85, 122.
9   T. W. Mason, 'The Primacy of Politics – Politics and Economics in National Socialist Germany' in S. J. Woolf (ed.), *The Nature of Fascism* (1968); 'Some

Origins of the Second World War' in E. M. Robertson (ed.), *The Origins of the Second World War* (1971), p. 125.

10 A. J. P. Taylor in Robertson, p. 139.

11 See R. Palme-Dutt, *Fascism and Social Revolution* (1934), pp. 15–22, 215; John Strachey, *The Menace of Fascism* (1933), pp. 67f.

12 V. I. Lenin, *Imperialism: The Highest Stage of Capitalism* (Foreign Language Publishing House, Moscow, n.d; first pub. 1917), pp. 139–40, 16–17, 165, 214.

13 Palme-Dutt, *Fascism and Social Revolution*, p. 215.

14 Strachey, *The Menace of Fascism*, p. 71.

15 Nicos Poulantzas, *Fascism and Dictatorship* (1974), pp. 22–5.

16 Ibid., pp. 23, 34.

17 Ibid., p. 34.

18 Adrian Lyttleton, *The Seizure of Power: Fascism in Italy 1919–29* (1973), p. 8.

19 D. Schoenbaum, *Hitler's Social Revolution* (1967), p. xiv.

20 Fritz Fischer, *War of Illusions* (1975), pp. viii–ix.

21 Hans Ulrich Wehler, 'Bismarck's Imperialism 1862–90', *Past and Present*, 48, (1970), p. 151.

22 H. Barrington-Moore Jr, *Social Origins of Dictatorship and Democracy* (1969), p. 252.

23 Ibid., p. 290–91. 'It is legitimate to ask why business and the agrarians (in Japan) could agree only on a programme of domestic repression and foreign expansion. Perhaps there was something else they could have done. There was, I believe, though it ran the risk of political suicide. To raise the standard of living of the peasants and workers and to create an internal market . . . would have threatened the exploitative paternalism upon which their authority rested . . .'

24 Ludwig Dehio, *Germany and World Politics in the Twentieth Century* (1959).

25 Karl Polanyi, *The Great Transformation* (1944), p. 152.

26 E. H. Carr, *The Twenty Years Crisis 1919–39* (1939), p. 120.

27 A. J. P. Taylor, *The Origins of the Second World War* (1971), p. 9. 'In a world of sovereign states, each does the best it can for its own interests; and can be criticised at most for mistakes, not for crimes.'

28 Giuseppe Mazzini, *Selected Writings*, ed. N. Gungalee, p. 67.

29 For Germany, see Fritz Fischer's two books, *Germany's Aims in the First World War* (1967) and *War of Illusions* (1975). For Italy, C. J. Lowe and F. Marzari, *Italian Foreign Policy 1870–1940*, pp. 148f; M. H. A. Macartney and Paul Cremona, *Italy's Foreign and Colonial Policy* (1938), p. 55. For Japan, Ian Nish, *Japanese Foreign Policy 1869–1942* (1977), pp. 60–61.

30 Charles P. Kindleberger, *The World in Depression 1929–1939* (1972), p. 134.

31 Ibid., p. 151.

32 Ibid., p. 180.

33 Ibid., p. 303.

34 Carocci, *Italian Fascism*, p. 80.

35 G. C. Allen, *A Short Economic History of Japan* (1966), p. 136.

36 Kindleberger, *The World in Depression*, pp. 165–6.

37 'Autarchy' (Instituto per gli Studi di Politica Internazionale, Milan, 1938); H. Predöhl, 'Summary Prepared by State Department' (1942); Masamichi Royama, *Foreign Policy of Japan 1914–1939* (Tokyo, 1941), pp. 11–12.

38 Predöhl, 'Summary'.

39 Mussolini's Ascension Day speech, 26 April 1927, quoted in *The Demographic Policy of the Fascist Government* (Rome, 1939), p. 15. Mussolini was obsessed by the declining fertility of the white races relative to the rest; which gives point to Barraclough's penetrating view of Fascism and National Socialism as 'a characteristic by-product of the old world in decline' in *An Introduction to Contemporary History* (1969), p. 32.

CHAPTER THIRTY-SIX

The Diplomatic Diaries of Oliver Harvey

John Harvey (ed.), *The Diplomatic Diaries of Oliver Harvey 1937–1940*
[Collins, 1970]

I REMEMBER talking to a senior and distinguished civil servant soon after devaluation in November 1967. He was saying how much easier our situation would have been had we taken the plunge much earlier, in July 1966 for example. I asked him why, holding the view he did, he had not tried to persuade a leading Minister known to be in favour of expansion (e.g. George Brown) to resign and lead the fight for an alternative policy. His reply was 'If you want to be an impresario, you must first of all have a star.' Sir Oliver Harvey, the author of these *Diaries*, fancied himself as just such an impresario in 1938. There was no nonsense in his mind about a civil servant keeping out of politics. His star was Anthony Eden, his Foreign Office chief. A career diplomat and a fervent anti-appeaser, Harvey sought to 'promote' Eden into a national alternative to the Prime Minister, Neville Chamberlain.

We have become so accustomed to thinking of Eden as a strawman that it is hard to understand how he came to be cast in the role of hero in the mid-1930s – and for many years afterwards. It probably had less to do with his own qualities than with the absence of any plausible alternative. The incomparable Winston Churchill was out on a limb; the Labour party had no one; the Conservatives were still ruled by the old gangs left over from 1914. *Faute de mieux* the youthful, seedily good-looking Eden became the repository of the hopes of the young, the idealistic, the forward-looking.

Harvey was convinced that if Eden resigned the Government would fall and Anthony would return as PM. Eden duly resigned on 20 February 1938 (after much prodding from his Private Secretary), Halifax taking over his job. He made speeches up and down the country. From his own reports to Harvey, they were enthusiastically received (this is hard to believe as his oratory was notoriously uninspiring). Far from toppling, the Government never trembled. If only A. E.'s impeccable sentiments could be expressed somewhat more *crisply*, his impresario sighed. 'I feel A. E. must develop a programme,' Harvey was writing on 13 November 1938 – something he might have thought about before encouraging Eden to embark on his populist career. Soon he was agreeing with Halifax that Eden paid too much attention to his 'image' and not enough to his homework. Eden for his part 'wants to be back dreadfully' in the Government – almost on any terms. But the telephone call from No. 10 never came.

Harvey had clearly misjudged the man and the mood of the country, still far more drowsily non-interventionist than he allowed. But perhaps a more important failing of the alternative national leader was the lack of an alternative policy. Chamberlain wanted a political settlement with Hitler. Churchill wanted to ring him round with Britain, France and Russia and anyone else who would come in. Eden's policy, apparently, was to keep him guessing, so that 'Germany could never be sure that HMG would not intervene in Central Europe and the French could never be sure that we *would* – hereby [for some obscure reason] discouraging both from forward policies'. Anything more calculated to cause war by miscalculation could scarcely be imagined – especially with gamblers like Hitler and Mussolini around. Eden was popular with Harvey because he was a Foreign Office man – and the 'guessing policy' was just another name for the traditional Foreign Office dislike of any fast commitments – thus encouraging one's enemies and discouraging one's friends.

Indeed the 'guessing policy' was so obviously stupid, given even the most elementary insight into the psychology of the dictators, that one wonders whether something more than mere Foreign Office traditionalism was involved in it. After all, both Churchill's and Chamberlain's policies were peace policies – the former's aimed at deterring the aggressor, the latter's at removing the causes of conflict. The Foreign Office policy was designed to accomplish neither of these two aims. It was almost as if men like Harvey had come to believe that war was the least of all the possible evils. His diaries are full of references to the fundamental incompatibility between the Hitlerian and the democratic system – strangely enough he was far less worried about Russia. He had become convinced, he writes, that no peace was possible till the Hitler regime had been overthrown. It is a very short step from this to actually becoming a supporter of making war. Of course he could not say, or even think, this openly, in a democracy, but if this was his policy – half-admitted only to himself – then no more admirable instrument for the purpose than the 'guessing policy' could be devised for tempting the dictators into making war through miscalculation.

There's another point, which links up with the 'promotion' of Eden as an alternative to Chamberlain. Harvey was convinced that England needed a 'new deal' *à la* Roosevelt. He is constantly urging Eden to come out with a big social programme to heal class divisions. Increasingly he came to feel that this spirit of national solidarity could only be evoked by war. He constantly accuses Mussolini of seeking foreign adventures in order to solidify his own regime. Yet there is little doubt that by 1939 war offered some kind of solution to the problems of the democratic regime as well. This is not true just in the limited sense that rearmament 'cured' the unemployment problem. But in the absence of any real intellectual, moral, or political thrust for a genuine Keynesian New Deal, war offered the best, perhaps the only chance of uniting the nation and sweeping away the old men enthroned by an ailing democracy.

If I am right in my assumption that a semi-conscious war party existed in the Foreign Office, then this throws an important light on the whole question of the operation of the so-called appeasement policy. Appeasement, it must never be forgotten, was Chamberlain's personal policy for ensuring 'peace in our time'. It was not the policy of the British government of which he was Prime Minister. In fact it was carried out largely by stealth behind the backs of the Foreign Office officials – who protested repeatedly against Chamberlain's 'amateur' diplomacy. Whenever he attempted to bring it out into the open – as on the issue of giving Germany back its colonies or in his relations with Mussolini – Chamberlain was checkmated by the Foreign Office. It's interesting how contemptuous Harvey and his group are of Vansittart, who was violently anti-German but agreed with Chamberlain on the need to try to detach Italy from the Axis. Again this was a perfectly reasonable strategy given that one's aim was to avoid war. It made no sense to those with a vested interest in war.

There is much that still remains to be explained. There is, for example, the curious episode of Tilea, the Rumanian Minister in London who comes to the Foreign Office on 17 March supposedly with the story that the Germans have just presented Rumania with an 'ultimatum'. This starts the whole British avalanche of guarantees to Eastern Europe. Yet the Rumanian government denied the story the next day and Tilea subsequently denies ever having said anything of the sort. What is one to make of that? Then there is the obscure episode of the Anglo-German economic negotiations of January–March 1939, briefly touched on in these *Diaries* ('that mountebank Montagu Norman is off to Berlin'). It is not so much the facts we lack, as a new interpretation of all these events. When that book is written, Sir Oliver Harvey's *Diaries* will be an indispensable source.

CHAPTER THIRTY-SEVEN

The Impact of Hitler

Maurice Cowling, *The Impact of Hitler: British Politics and British Policy 1933–1940*
[Cambridge University Press, 1975]

MR MAURICE COWLING is high priest of a school of political history which concentrates on what it calls High Politics. According to this school, issues of public policy can best be understood as instruments in political conflict. *The Impact of Hitler* is about Hitler's impact on British politics, not on British security or the Empire. Foreign policy 'became the form that party conflict took'. It might have been unemployment or Protection. Indeed Mr Cowling implies that one reason party conflict was about Hitler and not about unemployment was that no one had anything very convincing to say about unemployment. The context of British High Politics, familiar from Mr Cowling's previous books, is the survival problem of the Conservative Party. This arises from the fact that the Conservatives are a natural minority in a society dominated by class conflict. The perennial problem of Conservatism is thus to convert this 'natural' minority into an 'unnatural' majority. Claims to Conservative leadership have to be staked in terms of themes capable of breaking up the anti-Tory majority. This was the circuit into which foreign policy was plugged in the 1930s. Once foreign policy became central, or could be made central, the problem was which foreign policy – appeasement or resistance – could best sustain the dominating position – 'governing centrality' Mr Cowling calls it – which the Conservatives had so surprisingly won in 1931.

The book opens with Baldwin's search for a 'theme' to repair the 'electoral dilapidation' suffered by the National Government in the by-elections of 1934. Abyssinia and the Peace Ballot provided it. Hoare's strong speech at Geneva on 17 September 1935, 'struck oil in liberal areas where the Conservative Party felt vulnerable and where its managers wished to generate support'. Baldwin's successful 1935 electoral theme was to link up the Peace Movement with Collective Security. The process of tailoring foreign policy to the requirements of the Conservative Party had begun. But in Baldwin's theme there was a dangerous snag. Suppose Collective Security meant not Peace but War? With his 'mid-summer of madness' speech of 10 June 1936, Neville Chamberlain identified himself with Peace against Collective Security, leaving the alternative position in the hands of the political Outs, including those in the Tory party. The central political conflict in the later 1930s is thus between Chamberlain's attempt to fuse Imperial Isolation with the Peace Movement and the Churchill/Eden attempt to construct an alternative coalition of moderate Labour, Liberal and liberal Tory round Collective Security and resistance to the dictators. Chamberlain achieved a dominating position at Munich. Thereafter, Hitler undermined his credibility. This convinced Halifax, for whom Conservatism was a 'porous container' which had to be filled with liberal decency, that Chamberlain's policy would destroy the Conservative Party. To save himself, Chamberlain adopted the war policy of his critics in the expectation that war would never have to be fought, even if it had to be declared. It was the destruction of this assumption in Scandinavia early in 1940 which eliminated Chamberlain, and enabled the Tory Party, rather than the Labour Party, to superintend the great historic shift to the Left which occurred in the war years.

This is a highly stimulating, original, and intelligent approach to the problems of the 1930s. Historians are not very good at discussing issues in terms of politics, partly because the documents they rely on are adept at concealing 'political' motivations, partly because, not themselves being actively involved in managing power, they tend to minimize its importance for making policy. Mr Cowling's approach is doubly illuminating when applied to the 1930s since it takes us one stage further still from uncritical acceptance of the Churchill line, which until quite recently provided a substitute for serious historical analysis. I like, too, his view of Conservative strategy as preserving the social structure 'by talking about something else'. In general, it is refreshing to have a cool and cynical eye cast on democratic myth making; and to be reminded that it is not only dictatorships that are liable to get involved in foreign conflicts to divert people's attention from domestic difficulties. Having said this, there remain serious criticisms.

First, and most obviously, Mr Cowling's view of issues as instrumental works much better for some groups than others. It is probably better for the Conservative Party than the Labour Party; it is certainly better for the Outs than for the Ins. To treat all political history as High Politics is, therefore, at best a partial view, a corrective to taking what politicans say at face value, but far too limited even in its view of politicians' motivation to offer a generally valid model. It is by no means clear how well it works even for the 1930s' leading political actor, Neville Chamberlain. Although Mr Cowling does the best he can with Chamberlain's political skill in capturing the 'peace position', he does not seriously dispute the revisionist view that Chamberlain's foreign policy was dictated by 'objective' factors. But his method makes it impossible for him to deal with those factors.

Chamberlain's foreign policy was a desperate atempt to balance the accumulating weaknesses of a declining power – strategic, military, economic and moral weaknesses – against the traditional conception of Britain as upholder of the European balance and its associated freedoms. The attempt to do this produced a necessary illusion: that Hitler could be satisfied without altering the balance of power. The occupation of Prague destroyed Chamberlain's policy not because it showed that Hitler wanted world domination, but because it contradicted what

Chamberlain had said Hitler wanted. Mr Cowling's methods do little to unravel the Chamberlain enigma. He is clearly by far the ablest and most interesting of the senior governmental figures of the 1930s. Pehaps his chief offence was not that he failed to pursue a readily available alternative foreign policy (there was none), but that he pursued with such confidence and self-righteousness a policy which was almost bound to end in disaster.

A second question concerns evidence. One can perhaps talk about groups of nations in terms of logic of situations. But when one is talking about individual motives one needs evidence. Eden's 'synthetic jacobinism' (an excellent phrase) is, I think, amply documented here, as it was by Oliver Harvey. But where is the evidence for the view that Churchill took up the anti-dictator crusade to get back to the 'centre of the scene'? Isn't it just as plausible to say that he genuinely believed in the balance of power; and that he played politics in order to win policies rather than the other way round? Again, where is the evidence for saying that Halifax turned to obstructing Hitler 'because Labour could not otherwise be resisted'? I have not found it in the book. Mr Cowling writes that this view came to 'embody Conservative wisdom'. Yet he actually says very little about Conservative sentiment and nothing to explain how Chamberlain commanded such passionate support right to the end. Mr Cowling prefers to concentrate on exotics and oddballs. More 'low politics' would have helped.

His problems of establishing motive is compounded by the way he uses evidence. He has been through a splendid collection of private papers (the secondary material is much less impressive), but rarely stays long enough with a subject or a document either to establish the point he is making or to bring out the evidence supporting it. The book is in fact extremely wearying to read, both on account of its literary brutalities, and its lack of intellectual shape. It can also be amazingly inaccurate, as though Mr Cowling knows the politics of the period much better than its history. Perhaps the publishers are prudent to ask £15.00 for it. One dreads to think of the cost of his next promised work, *The Impact of Inflation.*

CHAPTER THIRTY-EIGHT

Going to War with Germany

Between Revisionism and Orthodoxy

[1972]

NORMALLY, historians are expected to say something new. The origins of the Second World War is the one subject on which they are expected to say something old. The parameters of the discussion are by now well-worn. On the one side there was Hitler who unleashed his wicked war of world conquest. On the other side there were the timorous democracies who after vainly trying to appease him by shameful surrenders, finally screwed up their courage to the sticking-place and ventured forth to battle with the forces of evil. Deviations from orthodoxy have so far been largely confined, as Mr John Vincent put it, to consenting historians in private. Mr Taylor, it is true, has had his say.[1] His attempt to reduce Hitler's foreign policy to less than satanic proportions, and to place the German problem of the 1930s in its historical, rather than in its moral, or ideological, context, led to a reply in this journal.[2] In a nation where brilliance is admired, but originality profoundly suspect, Mr Taylor's fate was inevitable: he became a licensed eccentric, a man who delighted in perverse judgments, an *enfant terrible*. The exorcism was humane, and indeed highly profitable, but unmistakable.

It is perhaps on the appeasement side of the picture that the most notable attempts to revise the orthodox views have been made. If the task of 'rehabilitating Hitler' has been considered too unrewarding, the task of rehabilitating Chamberlain and the Men of Munich has aroused somewhat greater enthusiasm. The portrait of the man who myopically pursued his 'mission' has gradually been softened into a picture of a realistic statesman, weighed down by the knowledge of Britain's weakness and the strength of her potential enemies, who courageously bought time for rearmament and the creation of Imperial and national unity. Appeasement is now increasingly seen as an atempt to buy time rather than buy off Germany. The difference between appeasers and anti-appeasers is seen as one of tactics rather than strategy. The consensus is being projected backwards into the 1930s. The implications of this view,

257

suggested by two recent books,[3] are striking, to say the least. For what, then, is left of appeasement as a policy for the peaceful redress of German grievances? The evolution of Mr Chamberlain into an exponent of *realpolitik* already foreshadowed by Donald Watt in 1965[4] would appear to diminish somewhat the unique wickedness of 'Herr Hitler'.

Before looking at the evidence for this reinterpretation, two further questions may be asked. Why has the orthodox view proved so resilient? And why has revisionism flowed into this particular channel? The vulgar answer to both questions is simply that 'the facts' point in those directions. But the truth is that history has very little to do with raw facts, and everything to do with their selection and arrangement, which always reflect shifting needs and changing outlooks. As Goethe said, 'The history of the world must be rewritten from time to time not because many events of the past are being rediscovered, but because new vistas are opening up, new ways of looking at things, which show the past in a different light . . .' This has always been the motive of real revisionism. A changing society always rewrites its history; a static society confirms its historical orthodoxies. The Second World War was Britain's last heroic moment; it also established the contemporary British consensus. There has been no major new political or social thinking in Britain since the Second World War: merely a filling-in of the detail. To challenge the existing interpretations is therefore to challenge in a sense everything that came out of the War – as well as to deprive ourselves of our last true moment of glory.

There has been a somewhat different, though related, transatlantic motive for buttressing the conventional wisdom. As a result of the Second World War, the United States inherited Britain's world position. American Empire replaced the British Empire, and with it a commitment to preserve the status quo against a new challenger, Russia. To question the wisdom of United States involvement in the Second World War was to question the whole edifice of American foreign policy which arose from its victory in the war. In particular, 'Munich' became synonymous with 'appeasing Communism'. Here the situation was fundamentally different from that which followed the First World War. The First World War had destroyed the challenge to the British-controlled world order. The Second World War immediately raised a new challenger to the American-controlled world order. The opprobrium attached to appeasing the dead dictator in Berlin was attached to appeasing the living dictator in Moscow; to affirm Munich was to deny NATO. In this way the lessons of the 1930s were drawn in the context of the Cold War; and it was essential to these lessons to portray Hitler as bent on world conquest, and appeasement as a fatal mistake which had almost enabled him to achieve it.[5] With this perspective in mind, it is possible to interpret the 'rehabilitation' of Chamberlain as part of an attempt by conservative British historians to include Chamberlain – and, further back, Stanley Baldwin and Ramsay MacDonald – in the Second World War consensus: to bring the traditional *Guilty Men* of inter-war Conservatism out of the cold into the cosy warmth of the 'central' British tradition as established by the Second World War. This kind of revisionism is thus basically a conservative undertaking; its motives have little to do with an attempt to elucidate the mysteries of the origins of the war itself. It is significant that the revisionist touch of Mr Keith Middlemas[6] had earlier been applied to Stanley Baldwin.[7]

This general intellectual enterprise has been greatly facilitated by the release of Cabinet Documents. A historian who carps at the mass of new primary sources which have recently flooded on to the academic market may be regarded as simply churlish. Yet he cannot escape the conclusion that the release of official papers has led to the writing of some very official history. It is almost as if twentieth-century historians have been co-opted into the Establishment *via* the Public Record Office. From a Machiavellian perspective one could regard the release of these papers at this time as a marvellous Establishment plot to buy off historical discontent! In fact the tendency of official papers to produce conservative history has a simpler explanation. On any but the most resolute historian, all those memoranda have the same effect they had on the Ministers for whom they were first produced: to show that nothing different could possibly have been done. A historian who comes 'naked' to the corridors of power is almost as likely to *write* conservative history as is the politician who arrives in the same condition to *make* conservative history.

This is not to say that the new history of appeasement written from the 'inside' is worthless. Far from it: Mr Middlemas, in particular, has produced an excellent book on Chamberlain's diplomacy of 1937–8, especially strong on the machinery of government, its firm grasp of the central issues of debate, and its wide coverage of Cabinet Papers.[8] It is a pity that he breaks off after Munich, which is traditionally seen as both the culmination of appeasement and the beginning of its decay. There was much more continuity between 1938 and 1939, and of a different kind, than either orthodox or revisionist historians have allowed: only on this assumption do the extraordinary British actions of March 1939 become comprehensible. But this is a subject for another book. What light meanwhile do the recent books throw on the nature of appeasement?

A striking preliminary insight into the character of appeasement is afforded by Chamberlain's first two foreign policy initiatives as Prime Minister. He decided to offer Germany some African territory, mainly at the expense of Belgium and Portugal; he also pressed for *de jure* recognition of Mussolini's conquest of Ethiopia. Far from promoting peaceful revisionism in Europe, these moves were clearly designed to reinforce the European status quo. Concessions in Africa were designed to forestall claims in Europe; 'appeasement' of Mussolini was designed to get him to oppose German Anschluss with Austria. As Middlemas rightly notes, 'The central principle of British policy was to avoid any disruption of the existing order.' F. S. Northedge writes of a 'basic Conservatism in regard to the prevailing international order'. This perspective was shared alike by appeasers and anti-appeasers and of course severely limited the possibility of 'peaceful revisionism'.

In what sense, then, were the appeasers doing something different than the traditionalists in the Foreign Office or the group round Churchill? The fundamental difference between Chamberlain and his critics was in their attitude to war. From the first, Chamberlain repudiated a policy that carried the risk of war or tried to employ the threat of war as a weapon of diplomacy. This reflected a genuine horror of war; it also reflected his consciousness of Britain's military weakness. The two reinforced each other. In combination they dictated a policy of trying to achieve some kind of agreement with Germany. But this was not to be an agreement which involved any major redistribution of power in Germany's favour. The aim was 'coexistence with Germany on Britain's terms' (as Middlemas describes it). The illusion of the appeasers was that coexistence was possible on Britain's terms.

This illusion was a necessary consequence of Chamberlain's abandonment of deterrence – at least of British deterrence. For if one wanted to maintain the status quo without deterrence, then one had to believe that Germany's demands were 'reasonable' i.e., such that Britain could accept them without impairment of her European interests. 'I formed the impression', Chamberlain told his colleagues on his return from Berchtesgaden, 'that Herr Hitler's objectives are strictly limited.' This was the necessary premise of appeasement as Chamberlain pursued it. In its name he exposed himself and Britain to the humiliation of Munich. Once its unreality had been exposed by the events of March 1939, the way was left open to adopt the alternative assumption – that Hitler was bent on world conquest. This was just as unreal a guide to diplomacy as the previous one, and directly involved Britain in the Second World War. But psychologically it was an inescapable consequence of the first illusion. The elderly Chamberlain reacted like a lover spurned; and the British nation, which he had involved in his maladroit wooing, and whose pride, like his own, had been humbled by its scornful rejection, reacted in the same way.

It is only from this perspective that we can make sense of Britain's persistent involvement in the affairs of Central and Eastern Europe. The usual view is that Britain only committed itself to the status quo in Eastern Europe *after* Hitler had shown, by his dismemberment of Czechoslovakia, that his plans were Napoleonic. It is true that military guarantees to Poland, Rumania and Greece, as well as military conversations with Russia, followed only after the occupation of Prague, and in this sense mark a change in strategy. But the aim of preventing changes in the territorial or even economic status quo was present even in the heyday of appeasement.

It is, of course, true that Britain faced the constant danger of being dragged into war on the coat-tails of France, with its entangling alliances in Eastern Europe. This was the nightmare of the Chiefs of Staff; and was a powerful motive for Chamberlain's rejection of the Foreign Office's 'guessing game' in favour of a more active policy of *détente*. If he was going to avoid risk of war then he had to rush in to try to 'solve' the Czech question before the Germans tried to do the same thing, whether by force or not, and thus involve France in the defence of Czech integrity. As Taylor rightly commented, 'The Czechoslovak problem was not of British making; the Czech crisis of 1938 was.' The same comment might be made of the lesser Austrian crisis of March 1938. This crisis arose essentially from Schuschnigg's refusal to accept client status, buoyed up with hopes of playing off Britain, France and Italy against Germany. Had Britain told Austria clearly that it would not act and that Schuschnigg must reach the best possible arrangement with Hitler, he might have carried out his part of the agreement of 12 February 1938.

As it was, the Anglo-Italian conversations of 20 February led Schuschnigg to hope that he would not be deserted and precipitated his fatal proposal for a plebiscite which led to German occupation.

The French system of alliances was, to be sure, a serious obstacle to Britain washing its hands of Central Europe; but it was not the decisive one. Had the British really been determined to give Germany a 'free hand' in the East, as many politicians and Foreign Office officials discussed in private, then Britain could have brought strong pressure on the French to break their guarantees – and also the Franco-Soviet Pact – in exchange for a much firmer British military guarantee of the defence of France itself. The reason this alternative was never seriously pursued was that Britain had no intention of washing its hands of Central and Eastern Europe. This is clearly revealed in the case of Austria. But it emerges most strikingly in British attempts in 1938, described by Middlemas, to build up an anti-German economic bloc in Eastern and South-Eastern Europe. How many times in the diaries of Cadogan and Oliver Harvey, as well as in the Cabinet Papers, do we find apparent acceptance of the idea of Germany's natural 'sphere of influence' in Eastern Europe. Yet in the heyday of appeasement Britain was trying to checkmate Germany there through a policy of political loans, involving acceptance of imports that no one in Britain wanted – a policy described by Halifax as adding 'an extra man to the small countries' team'. Encirclement at 6 per cent might be a more accurate description.

It is this sort of evidence of Britain's continuing involvement in the status quo of Eastern Europe that prevents acceptance of the explanation that it was Hitler's methods that finally undermined appeasement and brought about war. Certainly these methods were alarming; and thus played their part in turning public opinion against appeasement. Yet even so it is legitimate to ask how much revisionism Hitler would have got had he not been prepared to use military blackmail. Halifax had talked vaguely to Hitler of 'possible alterations' in the European order, involving 'Danzig, Austria, Czechoslovakia'. From Hitler's point of view the British were simply trying to string him along with fair promises while they built up their military strength and system of alliances. If any revisionism was going to be achieved he had to do it quickly and brutally. This feeling was widely shared in Germany even by anti-Nazis like Adam von Trott who came to 'have within himself an elemental feeling derived from historical experience that in the end, the only way left open to us was the use of force'.[9]

Of course, there were a number of groups in Britain who rejected this conception of appeasement; who advocated the bargain that Hitler must always have hoped for – 'a German deal with the British Empire at the expense of the Soviet Union'.[10] But such cynicism (or realism) was foreign to the British Establishment. It could not have been done in Chamberlain's non-Fascist Britain. Here we have another dimension to the notion of the status quo. This was not simply a power notion: it was an ideological commitment. The British Establishment may have been more pro-Fascist than pro-Communist. The point is that they disliked both. 'How far apart we are from these people,' Ciano noted in his diary as Chamberlain, rolled umbrella at the ready, walked down a passage to Mussolini's study lined with youths with drawn daggers. The defence of Britain's power in Eastern Europe involved the defence of parliamentary democracy, of the rule of law, of world finance and trade, of bourgeois respectability; in short, of the whole Anglo-Saxon world-order fashioned in the nineteenth century. The fact that its defence was in the hands of men riddled with self-doubt – in the hands of a Chamberlain rather than a Gladstone – is what gave Hitler his chance. But the lines of conflict were perfectly clear.

They were clear to that *doyen* of appeasement *The Times*. *The Times* was never prepared to concede Germany a 'free hand' in Eastern Europe. It wanted 'reasonable change', 'revision by agreement'. The trouble was that what *The Times* thought reasonable differed widely from what even the conservative anti-Nazi opposition thought reasonable. Even Dr Karl Goerdeler insisted on the incorporation of the Sudetenland, the 'liquidation' of the Polish corridor, a colonial settlement – demands which led the Foreign Office to believe that he was a 'stalking horse for German *military* expansion'.[11] Prussian socialism was not Nazism; but it, too, had little in common with British liberalism.

What was true of *The Times* was true of the other British newspapers. We know from Frank Gannon's book that no newspaper, except perhaps Lord Rothermere's *Daily Mail*, favoured 'any kind of continental arrangement with Nazism.' In fact the ideological conflict raged most strongly outside the editorial offices where judicial statements of what was 'reasonable' were composed; and this had important consequences for public opinion. Few people, after all, read – or remember – editorials. Public attitudes are formed by the selection and packaging of news, the day-to-day reporting of events. The major foreign correspondents of the time were 'radical and socialist . . . To them what was at issue was a civil war of European dimensions between democracy and totalitarianism.' Their Europe was centred on Moscow or Geneva. They were bitterly hostile to Fascism; and their reporting highlighted the most atrocious features of the German and Italian regimes.

Ideology was strengthened by sensationalism. Bad news sold more copies than good news. Crisis – even simulated – made good copy. Hitler's speeches and domestic manoeuvres were given crisis-treatment so that in the end even the jittery Government came to expect some dramatic new demand every time he opened his mouth; and in the overheated atmosphere of Central Europe, where no one knew exactly what was happening, every rumour was elevated into a journalistic scoop (with incalculable effects, especially in that month of rumours, March 1939). Much work still remains to be done on the influence of the Press on Anglo-German relations. Press activities sharpened the ideological divide and thus further curcumscribed the limits within which the appeasement could operate.

The reasons for appeasement's failure are, thus, reasonably clear. There was always an irreducible gap between anything the British were prepared to concede and what even the anti-Nazi Germans wanted. This was true of nearly all groups in Britain; the main exception was Sir Oswald Mosley's British Union of Fascists which was alone serious about giving Germany a 'free hand' in the East. Whether the 'public' would have been prepared to accept such a policy is difficult to say. According to a Gallup Poll quoted by Middlemas, 43 per cent were against going to the support of Czechoslovakia, with 33 per cent in favour, and the rest undecided. What is certainly true is that the actual way appeasement was conducted turned the mass of the people against it. The public saw no foreign policy except a series of surrenders – Nanny scuttling away from the Big Bad Wolf. And so they too became ashamed of their umbrella-waving representatives. Yet these humiliating confrontations were the inevitable consequence of a policy of endless interference without the force to back it up or the real willingness to strike a bargain.

Was the alternative then always a policy of status quo backed by deterrence? Churchill's 'Grand Alliance' backed by proper armaments? It all depends on whether one believes that such a policy would really have averted war. It is easy to read back the idea of deterrence into a pre-nuclear age. Few people at the time thought that such a 'Balance-of-Power policy' was a peace policy. How could they? It had always led to war in the past. The central fact which emerges from 400 years of European history is that there was no system of deterrence capable of stopping a hegemonic bid by a determined power. No Grand Alliances had ever been formed *in advance* of such a bid: they only crystallized after the bid had started.

The question of the rival merits of bargain and deterrence as peace policies is unanswerable. What can be said is that the implicit choice for war in March 1939 had little justification in terms of Hitler's 'plan of world conquest' which Chamberlain discovered on 17 March. The antithesis between status quo and world conquest was a pure illusion created by the actual evolution of Chamberlain's appeasement policy. There were whole areas intermediate to this which had barely been explored; could not be explored by very reason of the unrealistic assumptions of appeasement. How far would a redistribution of power in Europe – or the world – have had to go before Germany was 'appeased'? The general trend of the 1930s was towards autarchy – or a system of self-sufficient economic blocs. America in the early New Deal period and the Soviet Union were the chief examples of autarchic systems. Japan was trying to create a 'Co-Prosperity Sphere' in the Far East. England itself had made the first tentative moves towards an imperial system. Hitler's *Lebensraum* theory was not identical to autarchy as understood by economists in the 1930s but was a German variant of the same basic design.

For one thing it had a racial element; for another, it was in a deep sense anti-industrial. There was no way in which the Fascist or Nazi ideology could fulfil itself in a highly urbanized society. Full employment, housing, road-building: these were essentially engineering operations. The deepest longing of Fascism was for rejuvenation; and rejuvenation could only come from the soil. Its horizon was the 'frontier'; its 'ideal' social unit, the peasant–warrior commune. Hitler dreamt of 'a people which no longer needs to shut off its rising generations into the big cities as factory workers, but which instead can settle them as free peasants on their own soil.'[12]

Whether this quest for living space and longing to reunite all Germans would have taken him towards the Eastern plains of Europe to link up with the communities of 'lost' Germans is impossible to say. What can be said is that *Lebensraum* and autarchy, taken together, led not to world empire but to the creation of an empire in Eastern Europe, large enough to supply the bulk of its food and raw materials and with sufficient empty space for colonization. The idea sounds so romantic and 'unmodern' that A. J. P. Taylor cannot take it seriously; and he thus assumes that Hitler did not take it seriously either. For Taylor it was just idle dreams in odd moments; for the orthodox historians simply a stepping stone to 'world conquest'. Whatever the truth, much more research has still to be done into the connections between Nazi ideology, foreign policy, and the development of the Nazi economy before more precise statements can be made about Nazi Germany's possible evolution.[13]

In any event, the heaviness of Germany's eventual 'weight' in the world did not depend on Hitler alone. It obviously depended on the 'weight' of others, including such intangible factors as the moral and spiritual weight of contrary systems. Fear of Germany's world domination had no basis in detailed power calculations, using as measurements manpower, raw materials, territory, and industrial strength. The fear was essentially psychological; the response of debility to vigour, however barbaric. A vigorous Western system might have been able to limit German gains without war, for then the intangible factor of morale would have been differently distributed. But the pre-war decay of the West European political and social systems was such that reinvigoration could only come about through war itself.

This is the real reason why appeasement was damned by the best at the time and has remained accursed ever since. It is undyingly associated with the decadence of a ruling order which oscillated between illusory hopes and exaggerated fears. It is only at this level that we can explain the enormous sense of relief of all the active elements in conventional British politics when Chamberlain, suicidal even in his boldness, made his decisions for war in March and September 1939. They sensed that parliamentary democracy could only survive through war, however terrible the cost, because only war would give it the sinews and the will to rejuvenate itself and create a world that was worth living in.

NOTES

1   A. J. P. Taylor, *The Origins of the Second World War* (1961).
2   H. R. Trevor-Roper, 'A. J. P. Taylor, Hitler, and the War', *Encounter* July 1961.
3   Neville Thompson, *The Anti-Appeasers* (1971); Frank Gannon, *The British Press and Germany 1936–1939* (1972).
4   Donald Watt, 'Appeasement: The Rise of a Revisionist School?', *Political Quarterly*, 36 1965.
5   In America it is no coincidence that a Revisionist school has grown out of the decay of the Roosevelt–New Deal consensus created in the war and post-war period. In fact there have been two Revisionist schools, of Right and Left. The Right revisionists started earlier, with their allegations that the United States was inveigled into the Second World War by the unscrupulous British and by crypto-Communists round Roosevelt: see H. E. Barnes (ed.), *Perpetual War for Perpetual Peace* (1953); Charles Callan Tansill, *Back Door to War* (1953); David L. Hoggan, *Der Erzwungene Krieg* (1963). The Left, reading Viet Nam backwards into the 1930s, postulates an Imperialist motive for US involvement in both Japanese and European wars: see Noam Chomsky, *American Power and the New Mandarins* (1969) and Gabriel Kolko, *The Politics of War: The World and United States Foreign Policy, 1943–1945* (1968). The link between both schools is isolationism.
6   Keith Middlemas, *Diplomacy and Illusion* (1972).
7   Keith Middlemas and John Barnes, *Baldwin* (1969).
8   Two other books using the Cabinet Papers for this period should be mentioned: Ian Colvin, *The Chamberlain Cabinet* (1972) and Roger Parkinson, *Peace for Our Time: Munich to Dunkirk – the Inside Story* (1972). Both have their virtues. Colvin was the anti-appeasement Berlin correspondent of the *News Chronicle* in the late 1930s and played an important role in precipitating the guarantee to Poland; there is a whiff of *Guilty Men* about this book.
9   Christopher Sykes, *Troubled Loyalty* (1968).
10   Donald McLachlan, *In the Chair: Barrington-Ward of The Times, 1927–48* (1971).
11   David Dilks (ed.), *The Diaries of Sir Alexander Cadogan 1938–45* (1971).
12   Telford Taylor (ed.), *Hitler's Secret Book*, (1961), p. 210.
13   The chief English-language research into this fascinating and important field is being done by T. W. Mason. See his essay 'The Primacy of Politics' in S. J. Woolf (ed.), *The Nature of Fascism* (1968).

CHAPTER THIRTY-NINE

The Meaning of the Polish Guarantee

Simon Newman, *March 1939: The British Guarantee to Poland*
[Oxford University Press, 1977]

ANYONE who has thought seriously about Anglo-German relations this century must be aware of a considerable anomaly in the conventional view. According to this view, Britain on two occasions fought a war of self-defence against German aggression. The problem is that on neither occasion was Britain the object of German war aims. So the conventional thesis has to be supplemented by the argument that Britain had to go to war in both 1914 and 1939 because if Germany achieved its actual aims it would be in a better position to conquer Britain later. The larger goal of eventually limitless expansion is assumed to be self-evident from the nature of the German 'character' or its political and social structure. Ironically, the task of demolishing this mountain of special pleading has been left to British historians. German historians now appear to accept without question the 'war guilt' thesis. They spend their time excavating the social, economic and political roots of Germany's unique international wickedness, forgetting that other countries exhibited similar symptoms and attitudes, and forgetting above all that Germany was part of an international system of states the *sum* of whose ambitions and fears, and not just Germany's alone, produced two great wars. In particular, the recent attention lavished on Germany has prevented consideration of Britain's role in the generation of twentieth-century European conflicts. Only when British policy is subjected to the same critical scrutiny will it become fully apparent why Britain and Germany could not get together till both powers' capacity for destroying Europe had been eliminated.

Germany's twentieth-century foreign policy has been exhaustively and critically explored. It was dominated by the ideas of space and time. To be a great power in the sense of Britain, but more especially America and Russia, Germany felt it needed a great land empire. This was the commonly accepted geopolitical basis of world power.

Moreover, such an empire had to be won quickly, before the much greater potential of the United States and Russia would shift the balance of power irretrievably against Germany, dooming it forever to medium power status. Desperation to acquire extra territory before it was too late explains the enormous risk-taking characteristic of German foreign policy.

Such ideas were common to both Imperial and Hitlerian Germany. What had changed in the interval was the role assigned to Britain. Before 1914 there was much greater acceptance of the view that German expansion was contrary to Britain's interests and would therefore be bound to bring the two nations into conflict. Hitler's foreign policy, by contrast, was based on the assumption that a weakened Britain now had a mutual interest with Germany in weakening Russia and ultimately holding the balance against the United States, and that the traditional realism which to Hitler had always marked British foreign policy would force the British to come to terms with him. Hence Hitler persisted in wooing Britain right into the phoney war period. The felt need to strike quickly, however, came into conflict with the logic of waiting for the British, so that Nazi foreign policy was eventually ruined by exactly the same mistake as Hitler had warned against in *Mein Kampf*: making the bid for world power with the British as enemies, not friends.

Britain, on the other hand, was never prepared to accept voluntarily a redistribution of world power in Germany's favour. There were several reasons for this. One, which should not be underestimated, is that the two countries actually had very little concrete to quarrel about. Consequently they never acquired the experience of co-operation through negotiating their differences. Had there been more occasion for limited deals like the Anglo-German Naval Treaty of 1935, an alliance might have been built up incrementally. Secondly, before 1914 Britain never saw itself as sufficiently weakened to *need* an alliance on equal terms with another power. The Anglo-Japanese alliance of 1902 was made with a power of inferior rank. The *ententes* with France and Russia were not full alliances and arose out of the settlement of particular conflicts in Africa and Asia. Thirdly, to the extent that Britain did recognize its growing weakness, especially after 1918, Germany was not considered by the British as a fit partner to share global responsibilities. Intense economic rivalry before 1914, as well as profound cultural and political differences, contributed to this feeling. Britain was prepared to pass the torch to the United States, not to share it with Germany.

It is in this context that we must consider Simon Newman's new book on the British guarantee to Poland in March 1939 – the most important discussion on the origins of the 1939 war since A. J. P. Taylor's classic of 1961, and all the more remarkable as the first work of a young academic. It has many virtues. Mr Newman does not scintillate like Taylor (who does?), but he writes clearly. He is technically proficient in the use of documents and the language of diplomacy. His work has benefited greatly from a multidisciplinary background of PPE at Oxford and the study of international relations at the Johns Hopkins School of Advanced International Studies in Washington. This shows to particular advantage in his handling of economic issues which diplomatic history usually ignores. But the book's importance derives above all else from Mr Newman's honesty. He has looked at the Foreign Office and Cabinet Papers with a mind uncluttered by war propaganda and has come to two striking conclusions. The first is that Britain never pursued a serious policy of appeasing Germany. The second is that Britain's guarantee to Poland was intended to set up a preventive war with Germany. The March 1939 guarantee was thus not a reversal of policy, but an intensification of the policy of resisting German expansion. Let us examine Mr Newman's two conclusions in turn.

The conventional story has it that Britain appeased Germany, from whatever motives, before March 1939, and started resisting it after Hitler occupied Prague on 15 March. But according to Mr Newman, even before March 1939 Britain had never abandoned the pursuit of balance of power in Europe. The difference between the appeasers and their opponents was one of method, not principle. The appeasers were in office, and therefore much more constrained by military and economic weakness, and also public and imperial opinion. But this did not lead them to contemplate abandoning Eastern Europe to the Germans. Mr Newman defines British policy before March 1939 as one of 'opposing the spread of German influence within the limits of [Britain's] power', i.e., by all means short of war.

Chapter 3, 'Silver Bullets', deals with what Mr Newman calls the 'Anglo-German struggle for power and influence in central and south-eastern Europe'. As a result of Foreign Office pressure, an Inter-Departmental Committee was set up under Sir Frederick Leith-Ross ('Leithers') in June 1938 to counter German expansion in south-eastern

Europe, the idea being that 'this area of Europe shall look specifically for leadership to this country, and generally towards the Western Powers, rather than feel obliged in default of any other *point d'appui* to allow itself to be exploited by Berlin' (FO Memorandum, 24 May 1938). Mr Newman describes the resulting policy of loans as 'a limited policy of insurance against German monopoly in the area, which the Foreign Office sought to implement by economic means until such time as British resistance could be strengthened'. What is significant is British resistance to *peaceful* German penetration. Following Munich, Mr Newman argues, Chamberlain continued to work for a general agreement with Germany, but again on terms which did not involve a change in the balance of power. In return for colonial concessions, Hitler was to disarm and abandon autarky and the system of bilateral trade relations with Eastern Europe. At no time, then, before March 1939 was Britain prepared to abandon Eastern Europe to German control, however achieved. Mr Newman makes a firm distinction between the intentions and results of appeasement. The intention of British policy was to tie Germany to the European status quo by making concessions in Africa. Its result was to tilt the European balance in Germany's favour. But this was an unintended consequence. Munich marked the defeat of appease-ment, not its victory. It was the inevitable result of trying to run resistance on a shoe-string.

This argument is largely, but not wholly, convincing. The most plausible alternative interpretation is that the British Government would in fact have been prepared to abandon East Europe to Germany and was only brought back to resistance by the violence of Hitler's methods. Certainly from Munich to Prague Hitler's foreign policy was extraordi-narily ill-adapted to the purpose of winning Britain's acquiescence in Germany's eastward expansion. The anti-Jewish pogrom, the war of nerves, the insolence of the Prague occupation, all made further dealings with him politically impossible; a fact which Chamberlain was forced to recognize in his 17 March speech at Birmingham. No doubt Hitler continued to believe that the logic of events would force Britain to settle with Germany on his terms and therefore felt he could ignore British feelings in the short run. If so, he was mistaken in much the same way as was the Kaiser in the early 1900s. Manner is as important in international relations as matter. How far the British would have been prepared to concede had the Germans behaved better is a moot point.

But in his eagerness to establish continuity from 1938 to 1939, Mr Newman minimizes the impact of German actions on the *politics* of British foreign policy in this crucial period.

The core of the book deals with the evolution of the British guarantee to Poland. Skilfully using Cabinet and private papers, Mr Newman shows how the British response to Hitler's occupation of Prague developed between 17 and 31 March from an official proposal to consult with other powers if Germany threatened the independence of any European country into an unconditional, unilateral guarantee of Polish independence. Two questions arise. How did the British response come to focus on Eastern Europe? And what was the purpose of the Polish guarantee? The fact that the British were very angry with Hitler's occupation of Prague goes without saying. In fact, Mr Newman could well have set the diplomacy of the guarantee more firmly in the context of domestic British politics. The growth of Conservative opposition to further accommodation with Hitler was especially important in deter-mining Halifax's actions. Halifax was convinced that further 'appease-ment' would break up the Conservative Party. Some striking gesture was needed to restore the Government's prestige.

But intensity of feeling does not explain the direction into which it was channelled. There were many possible 'firm' British responses which did not involve guaranteeing Poland. Conscription might have been introduced, Churchill and Eden brought back into the Government, the Anglo-French alliance strengthened on its military side. Or to take another instance, a determined attempt might have been made to bring Russia into an anti-German front. It is not enough to explain the Polish guarantee by British anger. The spilling out of the anger in that way needs explaining.

Mr Newman does well to emphasize the role of rumour. At various times in this critical fortnight, the British Government apparently believed that Rumania and Poland were under imminent threat of German attack; and British actions can be causally related to these rumours. It was the claim by the Rumanian Minister in London, Virgil Tilea, on 17 March that Germany had presented his country with an ultimatum which first suggested the plan for a Four Power Declaration. The report turned out to be false, Mr Newman surmising that Tilea was acting on behalf of King Carol who wanted to weaken the pro-German party in his government. On 29 March, Ian Colvin, Berlin correspondent of the *News Chronicle*, reported that Germany was about to attack

Poland. Halifax flew Colvin to London to persuade Chamberlain of the need for an immediate British guarantee to Poland. Again the report was false. Of course, these and other rumours were made credible only by the style of Hitler's foreign policy. More importantly, they were significant only in the context of a prior British interest in keeping these countries out of German hands. It is here that Mr Newman's emphasis on the continuity of British foreign policy helps explain Chamberlain's 'diplomatic revolution'.

Why was Britain not prepared to let Poland and Rumania fall into the German sphere of influence, even peacefully? Clearly the dominant consideration was the balance of power. German control in Eastern Europe would shift the balance in Germany's favour in two ways: by providing Germany with strategic materials (especially Rumanian oil) to beat the blockade, and by foreclosing the possibility of an immediate second front. It is clear from the documents that the Foreign Office were not prepared even for a peacefully established German hegemony over the area. This very possibility had, of course, been opened up by Hitler's destruction of Czechoslovakia. With Czechoslovakia gone, loans were no longer sufficient to keep the East European countries available for British and French purposes. Military guarantees alone would do the trick. The Foreign Office was particularly terrified in March 1939 of a 'corrupt bargain' between Germany and Poland whereby Poland would pledge neutrality in return for Germany accepting less than 100 per cent of its claims in Danzig and the Polish Corridor. Britain in effect had to force protection on Poland and Rumania in order to stop them making the accommodations with Germany which would tilt the European balance in Germany's favour.

So much for the motives. What purpose was the Polish guarantee meant to serve? As we have seen, British policy was governed by the balance of power. But there was a crucial ambiguity in the concept. Was an alliance designed to *deter* an aggressor or *defeat* an attempt at aggression? Although the distinction was coming to be understood it was still too novel to produce precise thinking about the purpose of military alliances. Chamberlain, for example, said the object of the Eastern guarantee was to 'check and defeat' Germany's attempt at world domination, which suggests both deterrence and military victory, two logically opposed ideas. Halifax invoked the deterrence argument in presenting the guarantee proposal to the Cabinet on 30 March 1939. But earlier he had repeatedly accepted that the guarantee meant war.

273

Indeed, the main thrust of the documents is not about deterrence, but about the need to put Britain in a better position to fight the coming war. This is reinforced by two further considerations. Had deterrence been the unequivocal objective, Russian rather than Polish requirements would have been met, because Russia alone could have held up the German army long enough to make credible the threat of a two-front war. Secondly, if deterrence was indeed the aim, it turned out to be wildly misplaced. Six months later Britain and Germany were at war. In fact, it was the British guarantee to Poland that directly precipitated Hitler's decision to find a military, rather than a negotiated, solution to the Danzig problem.

This raises an important question posed by Mr Newman's book. Did the British in guaranteeing Polish independence intend exactly that result? Were they setting up a preventive war against Germany by under-writing the status quo in the most volatile and unstable area of Europe – Danzig and the Polish Corridor? Mr Newman believes they were. He cites in evidence Colonel Mason-MacFarlane, the British military attaché in Berlin, whose two memoranda in March 1939 demonstrably influenced both Halifax and Cadogan. MacFarlane's argument was that the longer Britain waited before fighting Germany the more the balance of power would shift in Germany's favour through East Europe falling peacefully into the German sphere. Kirkpatrick noted of MacFarlane's memor-andum on 30 March that Britain obviously could not force war on Germany. But there was a very general recognition that guaranteeing Danzig was the nearest thing to doing so. Mr Newman's argument is that if British policy-makers foresaw the consequences of their guarantee they must be held to have intended these consequences. The inclusion of Danzig in the guarantee (or rather the failure to exclude it) must have been designed to precipitate war between Germany and Poland.

There were probably some in the Foreign Office who were con-sciously working for a preventive war. There was also the feeling that making an alliance with Poland and Rumania was a way of avoiding making an alliance with Russia. But the dominant view in March 1939 seems to have been that war with Germany was inevitable given the character of the Hitler regime, and therefore Britain should prepare for it as best it could. To that extent Mr Newman's attack is misdirected. The British Government were not plotting to provoke Hitler to war. Where they were culpable is in drawing the unwarranted conclusion that the German occupation of Prague showed that Hitler meant to conquer the world. This was a *non sequitur*.

It is a pity that the book stops in March 1939. An equally careful study of the next fifteen months is needed to show whether, or to what extent, the policy of March was adhered to. Whatever such research shows, Mr Newman has made a notable contribution to the discussion of the failure of Britain and Germany to reach the accommodation which might have spared Europe two great wars. It is the fashion to blame Germany for these catastrophes. Careful historical analysis now reinforces a view common sense has always suggested: that Britain must take its share of the blame. It was still a Great Power in 1939, wielding equally with Germany the supreme decision for peace or war. Mr Newman's conclusion is that Britain's unwillingness to accept the *peaceful* absorption of much of East Europe into the German sphere was a major cause of the 1939 war. It deserves to be carefully pondered. It may well change our way of thinking about these matters.

CHAPTER FORTY

Adam von Trott

Klemens von Klemperer (ed.), *A Noble Conflict: The Letters of Shiela Grant Duff and Adam von Trott zu Solz 1923–1939*
[Oxford, 1988]

OF ALL the 'good' Germans of the 1930s, the enigmatic Adam von Trott is the one who most caught the English imagination. A Hessian aristocrat, he came to Oxford on a Rhodes scholarship in 1931, where his charm, looks and cleverness won over such luminaries as A. L. Rowse, Maurice Bowra, Isaiah Berlin, David Astor and Goronwy Rees. He himself was captivated by a fellow student, Shiela Grant Duff, who had prominent Liberal connections on both sides of her family. A German patriot, who loathed Hitler, he rejected the alternatives of being 'a Nazi or an émigré'. He returned to Germany for the last time in 1938, after a year in the Far East, determined to pursue a double policy of promoting German interests while working for the overthrow of the

Hitler regime by the Army. He was executed in August, 1944 for his part in the July plot against Hitler's life. Shiela Grant Duff (now Mrs Sokolov Grant) still farms in Ireland.

Their correspondence, somewhat intrusively edited as *A Noble Conflict*, is an extraordinarily moving account of a friendship wrecked by politics. Neither is a first-class letter writer. Shiela writes passionately about politics, but is not good at description; Adam has an eye for vivid detail, but the expression of his ideas is tortuous. Part of the problem was his addiction to Hegel; partly it was the effect of the censor. It is the pathos of the situation which, in the end, makes their exchanges as painful for the reader as they clearly became for the writers, who broke off contact in 1939.

Their relationship was difficult enough without the politics. Adam found it impossible to love singly: there was Shiela, her friend Diana Hubback, and an old flame, Miriam Dyer-Bennet, an American divorcée with five children. He eventually proposed to Shiela in 1934; when she turned him down they agreed to form an alliance between 'two sovereign states . . . something which two independent lives can share and create from two different worlds.' For Adam this was the model of the friendship he sought between Britain and Germany. At Oxford it had been easy. He and Shiela could happily attribute the First World War to capitalism rather than to German wickedness; the British liberal could denounce the Versailles Treaty as fervently as the German nationalist. Hitler's arrival changed all that.

Shiela came to see an inherent conflict between Western and German values; Adam clung to the hope of a synthesis between British liberalism and German 'feudalism'. Hitlerism might, despite its barbarity, be seen as the primitive stirring of a new economic system, one which would overthrow the 'bourgeois greed and stinginess' which he and Shiela both hated. Shiela was more impressed by the barbarity. 'When you affirm your German character, you deny your European character,' she wrote to Adam in 1935. Adam attacked her 'scanty rationalism', he accused her of basing socialist ideals on British imperialism. Shiela was moved to vigorous defence of the British Empire. At least it was inspired by the notion of self-government, whereas 'you [Germans] believe in the unaltered and unalterable inferiority of all races to one you call Aryan which does not exist.'

In the 1930s Hobbes proved a better guide to international affairs than did Hegel. The European idealism with which both Shiela and

Adam started their dialogue – 'children of a yet unborn civilisation' Adam called them – gave way to increasingly strident affirmations of national differences. In 1936 Shiela went out to Prague as *Observer* correspondent and embraced the cause of Czech independence. She increasingly saw Germanism, not Hitlerism, as the problem. 'When a nice, unfanatical German boy says to me', she wrote to Adam in 1936 during a visit to Saxony, 'that England is finished, France is going under, Jews, Christianity and communism are the three united enemies of Europe . . . the German race must rule, I wonder if it is not time to count my soldiers.'

Adam accused her of taking 'vulgarian Saxons' too seriously, adding 'I'm afraid most journalists' habits of thinking and feeling end with counting one's soldiers and not only counting them.' His line was that all nations were equally to blame: the German problem must be recognized as a European problem. 'You haven't any right', he wrote to Shiela in 1937, 'to denounce the policies of a country which is rather blindly and – I certainly admit – viciously groping for some economic outlet from the assumed moral superiority of a country which has all she wants and has got it and maintains it with methods which are in many respects as blind and vicious.'

So the arguments and misunderstandings went on, Shiela's moral absolutism confronting Adam's equivocations, until the frame of a loving friendship could no longer contain them. Even without Hitler one wonders whether a 'feudalistic' Germany could have cohabited with a liberal Britain. By an appalling irony, it was Hitler's wholesale liquidation of 'good' Germans like Adam von Trott in 1944 which reconciled post-war Germany to liberal Europe. Liberal and National Socialist could at least agree on one thing: there was no place for the old German aristocracy in the new Europe.

CHAPTER FORTY-ONE

The Cambridge Communists

THERE were two widespread reactions to the recent 'Blunt Affair'. The first need not detain us. This was the revulsion against Anthony Blunt in the name of the traditional loyalties which he betrayed. It was a mixed reaction whose emotional roots lie in tribal values, a philistine distrust of aesthetic culture, and the populist hatred of privilege; but whose strength reflects the contemporary disenchantment with a left-inclining, tender-minded intelligentsia, whose alleged antipathy to patriotism, the domestic virtues, the work-ethic, and business profits is felt to have brought Britain to its present sorry pass. Analysis of this type of response can be left to the political sociologist of contemporary Britain. Here it is sufficient to say that the 'simple' loyalties and virtues in whose name Blunt has been attacked have always been problematic to the thinking person, and never more so than in the aftermath of the First World War, when it was rightly seen that traditional, stereotyped, responses to new situations had inflicted on Europe a disaster unparalleled since the Thirty Years War.

The second reaction, that of survivors of the Marxist or the Communist generation of the 1930s (the two terms were much more interchangeable than they are now), deserves closer attention from the historian. It is surprising that no one – except Philip Toynbee – actually defended what Blunt was prepared to do. For on certain assumptions, which were shared by the whole Marxist generation of that time, there could be no moral objection to spying for the Soviet Union. Moreover, it is clear from the published comment by some survivors of this generation on the Blunt Affair that many of their assumptions about that period are still vigorously held today. The facts which continue to define for Philip Toynbee the reality of the 1930s are 'a group of heartless politicians ... two million unemployed ... appeasing the rampant Fascist regimes in Germany and Italy', and 'rapidly expanding' Fascist sympathies in Britain (*Observer*, 25 November 1979).

Or take the letter to *The Times* of 23 November 1979 from Professor Eric Burhop (FRS; eminent scientist; Trinity College, Cambridge undergraduate; and Communist sympathizer of the 1930s). 'Huge unemployment, malnutrition, the dole, means test, hunger marchers –

these were the realities of the time.' Capitalism 'had failed'. Nazism 'appeared the most evil thing any of us had seen'. The British Government was 'hell-bent on appeasing Hitler'. 'The only force that stood staunchly against Nazism . . . was the Soviet Union and its Red Army.' Given these facts it was hardly surprising that 'the brightest spirits of our universities' turned to Marxist solutions. As James Hemming remembers it (*Guardian*, 23 November 1979):

> the establishments of all central Europe were sympathetic to Hitler and Co. as the only means of checking communism and controlling labour. In Spain, a democratically elected government had been overthrown by the Franco–Hitler axis with barely a cheep from the Western powers. Italy was securely fascist under Mussolini. France was rotten with quislings. In the East End, the police were supporting the Mosleyites against the Communists . . . Nor should we forget that the Soviet–German alliance was forced on Russia as a means of buying time after the pusillanimous collapse of the League of Nations.

What is remarkable to the historian is how resolutely this 'world view' of the 1930s has survived the assault of historical evidence. Its essential elements are: the horrors and despair of Depression and mass unemployment; the intellectual and moral bankruptcy of Capitalism; the menace and spread of Fascist barbarism; the pro-Fascist leanings of the Establishment and Government; the pusillanimous or sinister appeasement of Hitler; the progressive anti-Fascist, anti-capitalist, alternative being developed in the USSR; and Communism (including the Soviet Army) as the embodiment of the will to resist Fascism and preserve civilization. If all this were true, to spy for the Soviet Union, had the opportunity arisen, would have been the plainest duty. 'I would undoubtedly have accepted that proposition with pride', writes Toynbee, 'even with joy.' The crucial point which needs to be made is that the facts were very far from being as the Marxist generation saw them. The fundamental criticism of Blunt is not that, given his convictions, he spied for the Soviet Union, but that he and the rest of the Marxist generation were political simpletons. They took a very small selection of the available facts of their time, and imposed on them rigid and absurd interpretations.

*

It remains an article of faith to the Marxist generation that the 1930s were for Britain a decade of unrelieved economic misery and despair. This is simply not true. No one would deny that the Great Depression of 1929–33 was the greatest shock that the modern economic system has ever experienced; or that Britain was profoundly affected by it. During the depth of the Depression in 1932 unemployment in Britain reached 2.9 million, or 22.8 per cent of the insured labour force. However, from 1933 onwards there was a steady recovery (briefly interrupted in the winter of 1937–8) so that John Stevenson and Chris Cook in their recent study[1] could conclude that 'most people were better off by 1939 than they had been ten years earlier.' Between 1933 and 1937 inclusive the British economy grew at 4 per cent a year, unemployment fell from 22.8 per cent to 9.5 per cent, and output, real wages, and the real value of social services (including unemployment benefits) rose above their 1929 level. It was in these years that the transformation from a nineteenth-century economy based on cotton, coal, ship-building, and railway construction to an economy based on housebuilding, mass consumption, and service industries was largely accomplished. 'Distressed Areas' remained, and these were dreadful blots. From today's perspective, far too many people were ill-fed, ill-clothed, and ill-housed. But the relevant standards of comparison were with what had existed before; and from this perspective, the improvement is clear.

It may be argued that this improvement only became apparent with hindsight: that the 'realities of the times' *seemed* as Professor Burhop described them. But for most people they did *not* seem so. Extremist movements such as Fascism and Communism were numerically insignificant. The 'Hunger Marches' attracted only tiny numbers. Much more important was the political dominance of the Conservative Party throughout the decade. The huge 'National' majority of 1931 can perhaps be explained by a panicky 'flight to the Right'; not so the election result of 1935, which gave the Conservatives a majority of 200, and in which Labour's failure to recover lost support in the booming Midlands was particularly significant. 'In 1939', Paul Addison writes, 'Labour ... looked all set to lose another general election.'[2] These political reactions reflected the solid gains of the decade.

Raymond Aron has drawn attention to the flaw of democratic systems – incapable of monstrous action, but allowing monstrous phenomena. It should be noted that during the worst years of the Depression, when the

Soviet Union was widely praised for having 'abolished' unemployment, Russia was a monstrous society in both senses of the word. There was widespread famine, and Stalin liquidated the kulaks, both accounting for millions of lives. To allow millions of people to remain unemployed, though cushioned by the dole, is horrible; but to kill millions, or allow them to die, is surely far worse. Even at its nadir, the moment at which it compared least favourably with the Soviet Union, world capitalism was far less monstrous than Bolshevism as an *economic system* – quite apart from the latter's denial of basic human rights and civil liberties to which attention had been drawn by Keynes, Bertrand Russell, and so many others. And this was all before the insane purges of the mid-1930s which opened yet another window on the reality of life under Stalin.

A central belief of the Marxist generation was that capitalism was bankrupt, and that its sole remaining resource was Fascism. Wrong again! That there were grave faults in the functioning of an unregulated market economy was obvious to most thinking people. That a system based on individual greed was both morally unlovely and produced unjust results were propositions widely accepted: they were the inspiration of the whole movement of social reform. But the view that capitalist democracy had no self-correcting or self-improving potential could have been, and was, held only by the most arrogant, ignorant, and foolish persons. One of the historical facts, and puzzles, of the 1930s is that the out-of-date, and virtually incomprehensible, economic theorizing of a nineteenth-century German émigré had a greater pull over Trinity College, Cambridge, than the eminently sane, generous, exciting, and lucid commentaries emanating from King's College, Cambridge, a stone's throw away.

> The prevailing world depression, the enormous anomaly of unemployment in a world full of wants, the disastrous mistakes we have made, blind us to what is going on under the surface – to the true interpretation of the trend of things. For I predict that both of the two opposed errors of pessimism which now make so much noise in the world will be proved wrong in our own time – the pessimism of the revolutionaries who think that things are so bad that nothing can save us but violent change, and the pessimism of the reactionaries who consider the balance

of our economic and social life so precarious that we must risk no experiments.

So wrote J. M. Keynes in 1930.[3] The eventually successful search for a 'middle way' between the two 'errors' – by Keynes and others in England, by the New Dealers in the United States, by the *hauts fonctionnaires* in France, by the Social Democrats in Sweden, by Henri de Man in Belgium – testifies to the intellectual and moral vitality of capitalist democracy in its period of crisis, a vitality which has not yet been fully explored by historians, who have tended to concentrate on the sterile intellectualizing of the Marxist generation.

But, it will be said, Keynes's optimism of 1930 predates Hitler's accession to power in Germany which changed everything. From 1933, the duty of 'resisting Fascism' took priority over everything else. Marxism was the only ideology, Communism the only political movement, the Soviet Union the only military and industrial force, willing and able to mount such a resistance. Hence the most famous false antithesis of the 1930s, 'Communism or Fascism', by which the stand of the Marxist generation is ultimately justified.

The first step in demolishing this proposition is to point out the false chain of reasoning which supported it. The most important link in the chain was the assertion that capitalism could survive only on a Fascist (i.e., a terroristic or violent dictatorial) basis. Consequently, domestic and international relations would be simplified, and polarized, into a straightforward confrontation between Fascism and Communism. It was into this process of polarization that the Marxist generation fitted the Spanish Civil War, the appeasement of Hitler by the National Government, the international role of the Soviet Union. In fact, the analysis was little better than nonsense, and was seen to be so by most thoughtful people at the time.

From a purely theoretical point of view, the maintenance of capitalism did not require Fascism. To assert the contrary was to deny any creative role to intelligence and democracy. It was also wildly implausible as a statement about what was happening in the real world. In the 1930s Fascist movements made little headway in the United States or Western Europe: the phenomenon was largely confined to Central and Eastern Europe. Corporatist, planning, and authoritarian ideas certainly had some vogue on the Right (and also on the Left) of democratic politics; but such ideas could be equated with Hitlerism only by the most perverse stretch of the imagination. Nor did the Spanish Civil War have any real connection with the Marxist scenario. Franco's uprising had little to do either with the problems of 'Spanish capitalism', or with political issues outside Spain – the latter at least was proved by Spain's neutrality in the Second World War. Even the role of the Spanish Civil War as a testing ground for Axis weaponry and strategy has been greatly exaggerated.[4] That the Franco regime turned out to be a particularly unpleasant clerical–military dictatorship did not justify the star billing given to the Spanish Civil War at the time, any more than the fact that British Communists fought and died heroically in Spain absolves the historian from pointing out, as did Orwell, much censured at the time, that 'the cause' for which they died was not as they perceived it. One can perhaps be a hero without understanding what is happening.

The problem of 'resisting Fascism' boiled down to the problem of preventing Germany from establishing a hegemony over Europe – a project which would have endangered Britain's security. As A. J. P. Taylor pointed out long ago, the dominating international issue of the 1930s was 'the German problem', not the Fascist problem. German Fascism, or Nazism, was a hegemonial instrument for realizing expansionist aims. In Walter Lippmann's phrase, Nazism was 'the elaborate and intense militarisation of a people for a war of conquest'.[5] Nor was this project the outcome of any 'objective' crisis of German capitalism, either before or during Nazi rule; but rather of an interaction between the general economic difficulties of the time, 'pre-capitalist' values which had retained an exceptional hold on traditional German society, and the humiliation of the Treaty of Versailles, particularly its annulment of Germany's victory over Russia in 1918. As for Mussolini's original Fascist regime, the worst that can be said against it was that it was repressive and uncreative, and harboured imperialist ambitions much more modest than those pursued by Britain and France down to the end of the First World War. The crucial point is that there was little or no basis in contemporary reality for interpreting international events in terms of an ideological struggle between Communism and Fascism, or even between democracy and Fascism. There was a special German problem dating from the 1890s; a peculiar Japanese problem dating from the same period; and a minor Italian problem. The first two were sufficiently serious to bring about another World War; but they were basically susceptible to analysis and treatment in terms of classic balance-of-power theory; and it was neglect of these considerations which contributed mightily to the eventual catastrophe.

Indeed, from the point of view of containing Germany, adherence to Marxist theory and Communist practice was massively counterproductive. The project of 'resisting Fasicism' might at least have suggested the rearmament of democratic Britain. But it did no such thing – because from the Marxist perspective the National Government was a potential if not actual part of the Fascist International, and must therefore be deprived of arms. Thus, in practice 'resisting Fascism' meant *not* resisting Hitler, whose rise to power had actually been facilitated by the German *KPD* on impeccable dialectical grounds; but resisting the admittedly inadequate efforts of the National Government to rearm Britain against Hitler. Such were the consequences of Marxism's distorting spectacles.

One of the hardiest myths of the 1930s is that the National Government, and more generally 'the Establishment', was 'pro-Fascist'. This led to the 'appeasement' of Fascism, at home and abroad. Such views have little contact with reality. The chief determinants of the appeasement policy were the state of public opinion at home and in the Dominions, including the highly ambiguous attitude of the Left to rearmament; the need to balance the accumulating weaknesses of a declining power – strategic, military and economic – against imperial and global commitments inherited from the days of Britain's supremacy; and, finally, a failure of nerve at the time of Munich which allowed Hitler to outbluff Chamberlain. One might have thought, as Senator Harry Truman was later to argue, that *realpolitik* should seek to involve Germany in an exhausting war against Russia: diplomats have not usually regarded it as an error to divert one's enemies to other targets. But there is no evidence that this is what Chamberlain was trying to do.

Admittedly, neither the British nor the French were keen for an alliance with the Soviet Union, and this has often been held to be convincing proof that they were not serious about opposing Hitler. But the obstacles in the way of an Anglo-Soviet alliance had nothing to do with the British Government's alleged pro-Fascist proclivities. First of all, as historians have recorded, Russia itself in these years was 'the scene of the most nightmarish, Orwellian orgies of modern totalitarianism'

(George Kennan). Secondly, the governments of the countries most threatened by Hitler did not want to be protected against him by the Soviet Army, itself a force of dubious value in the aftermath of the 1936–8 purges. Thirdly, the price demanded by Stalin for an alliance was extremely high: handing over to Russia the Baltic states; and compelling Poland and Rumania to accept Soviet troops on their territory if, in the opinion of Stalin, the situation warranted it. One did not have to be pro-Fascist to have hesitations about going to war to 'defend the independence of small nations' on such terms, and in such company.

The fact is that Stalin was no more committed to the Versailles settlement in Eastern Europe than Hitler was. But only Hitler could give him part at least of what he wanted – on the basis of a division of the spoils. And Stalin was quite capable of the *realpolitik* strategy of which Western leaders were accused by Western Marxists but from which they in fact shrank: i.e. turning Germany the other way. It was these long-term considerations, rather than a purely tactical effort to 'buy time', which determined Stalin to reach agreement with Germany. He 'obviously thought that the pact had value, not only as an immediate manoeuvre, but over a long period.'[6] Like everyone else, he was taken by surprise by Hitler's rapid victory in the West.

To summarize: the Marxist generation was wrong about the condition of the economy, wrong about the intellectual resourcefulness of capitalist democracy, wrong about the Spanish Civil War, wrong about the nature of the menace facing the West, wrong about the motives of the British Government, wrong about the Soviet Union. Confronted by systematic error of this kind, one is naturally driven to seek the source, or sources, of such distortion. The circumstances of the time cannot of themselves explain the appeal of Communism to a section of Britain's intelligentsia. What needs to be explained is why the circumstances were perceived as they were.

The answer to such a question cannot be simple. But I think John Maynard Keynes put his finger on the essential point when he remarked to Roy Harrod on the 'recrudescence of the ancient strain of Puritanism in our blood'.[7] The one misleading word in this acute phrase is 'recrudescence'. From the standpoint of Bloomsbury, the dogmatic-theological mood of the Marxist generation might well appear to be a 'recrudescence' of vanished Victorian instincts. But from a wider perspective, Bloomsbury's own anti-puritan ethic, with its emphasis on 'the arts' and 'personal relations' (to which was added in the 1920s a doctrine of 'self-expression' derived from Freud), was by no means the most characteristic way out of Victorianism for the educated middle class. On the whole, the puritan instincts of this class were not abolished, but redirected towards politics, particularly left-wing politics. This seems to me to be the right context in which to consider the Marxist generation of the 1930s.

If we try to see the period 1880 to 1945 as a whole, we become aware of a remarkable coincidence between social and economic crisis and the loss of religious belief. This crisis of faith was particularly acute for those whose upbringing had been more than conventionally religious – for the sons and daughters of clergymen and Nonconformist families. It also hit those with a 'need to believe' which could no longer be satisfied by orthodox religion. From the 1880s onwards a massive transfer of moral and intellectual energy took place from the service of God to the service of Humanity. Underlying this transfer was a fusion of the sense of personal sin with a sense of social guilt. It was not, as Beatrice Webb said, that social questions had taken the place of religious questions – they had *become* religious questions. And with the collapse of the old faith came a search for a new 'Religion of Humanity', a gospel of Progress with secure doctrinal foundations. A great deal of the middle-class input into the late Victorian reform movement can be explained in these terms. The progression from loss of faith to dedication to social causes can be traced in the lives of almost every late Victorian, middle-class reformer; the intellectual 'systems' of men like L. T. Hobhouse and J. A. Hobson are essentially substitutions of evolutionary for Christian theology.

The Marxist commitment of the 1930s was, of course, an ideological response to the social, economic and international problems of that decade. But it was also a spiritual revolt against old faiths which no longer seemed adequate by a generation which had been brought up to believe in *something*. There was Christianity itself, which had enjoyed a powerful revival in the 1920s, in reaction to the amoral and destructive activism of the First World War. A number of Marxist millenarians of the 1930s came from church or religious backgrounds.[8] Others were children of late Victorian social reformers, who had lost their belief in the 'evolutionary' creeds which had been their parents' substitute for religious belief, and who needed to establish the 'gospel of progress' on securer foundations. Still others were in revolt against the aesthetic theories, and even more, the aesthetic credo, which had been Blooms-bury's substitute for religion.[9] To an educated middle-class generation near enough to the Victorian age to need a secular religion, Communism, in the circumstances of the 1930s, provided a faith, a cause, a theology, a morality, a church – and, in reborn revolutionary Russia, an example of a new heaven on earth.

Trying to 'explain' the Marxist commitment of the 1930s rather than accepting it as a reasonable interpretation of the events of the time will always seem objectionable to some who still fancy themselves as 'the best and the brightest' of the day. My only justification is that the systematic misinterpretation of these events – a misinterpretation which was confined to a small minority of young middle-class intellectuals – leaves someting to be explained. It also provokes a reflection about the kind of political attitudes most conducive to a tolerable state of society.

I used to believe millenarianism was a necessary ingredient in politics: for without it what large motive for hopeful reform would exist? I am less sure today. Could it not be that we have in democracy and market economy mechanisms whose *tendency* is to bring about improvement in social conditions? . . . provided always that public life continues to attract men and women of high skill and creative intelligence without which no society, or civilization, can master its problems? If this is so, it would certainly be wiser to seek non-political spheres of endeavour for the religious, theological, aesthetic, and putatively heroic sides of our nature. In this light the Marxist commitment of the 1930s cannot be seen as that generation's 'finest hour'. If to condemn some of them as traitors is simple-minded, no less so is the myth that they were betrayed by Stalin. It is not that they were wrong about Russia: they were wrong about their own civilization.

NOTES

1   John Stevenson and Chris Cook, *The Slump: Society and Politics During the Depression* (1978), p. 5.
2   Paul Addison, *The Road to 1945* (1975), p. 15.
3   J. M. Keynes, 'Economic Possibilities for our Grandchildren' in *Essays in Persuasion*, Collected Writings, vol. 9, p. 322.

4   A. J. P. Taylor, 'Spain and the Axis' in *Rumours of War* (1952). 'The third volume of documents from the archives of the German Foreign Ministry ... contains little evidence of a Fascist conspiracy and none at all of British or French connivance in it.'

5   Walter Lippmann, *The Good Society* (1934), p. 64.

6   A. J. P. Taylor, *The Origins of the Second World War* (1964 ed.), p. 319. See also George F. Kennan, *Russia and the West* (1961), pp. 312–13.

7   R. F. Harrod, *The Life of John Maynard Keynes* (1951), p. 451.

8   Donald Maclean was a lapsed Scottish Calvinist; Anthony Blunt, Cecil Day-Lewis, Louis MacNeice and others had clerical parents. Joseph Needham saw Communism as a secular expression of Christian ethics. See Neal Wood, *Communism and British Intellectuals* (1959), pp. 64–9, 80.

9   Julian Bell, the son of Vanessa and Clive Bell, is an example of this reaction. Bloomsbury's theories were inappropriate in an age of 'unemployment, economic crisis, nascent fascism and approaching war' (Peter Stansky and William Abrahams, *Journey to the Frontier*, 1966, pp. 94–5). Marxists like Bell and Auden, while theoretically committed to fighting against 'War', were fascinated by violence. They made politics a moral arena for the waging of the 'just war' – against Fascism.

CHAPTER FORTY-TWO

The Science of Treason

Andrew Sinclair, *The Red and the Blue: Intelligence,*
Treason and the Universities
[Weidenfeld & Nicolson, 1986]

ANDREW SINCLAIR – double-first in history at Cambridge, almost an Apostle – has written a profound and disturbing essay about the ways in which people at or from Cambridge passed information to the Soviet Union in the 1930s and 1940s, the motives for their actions, and the effects of those actions on our lives. The great merit of his book is that it shifts attention from the Cambridge spies to the Cambridge scientists – from the world of Bloomsbury and the Apostles, which nurtured the traitors Anthony Blunt, Guy Burgess, Donald Maclean et al., to that of the Cavendish Laboratory, international centre of experimental physics, where the atom was first split in 1933, and where the presence of the brilliant but enigmatic Peter Kapitsa from the Soviet Union ensured the Russians legal access to the first fruits of atomic research.

'The acts of the Apostles', Sinclair writes, 'were small change to the constructions of the Cavendish.' His account turns on the contrast between these two Cambridge traditions; partly defined in terms of C. P. Snow's 'two cultures', but more importantly in terms of the conspiratorial attitudes of Cambridge secret societies on the one hand and the ideal of an 'open exchange of knowledge' held by Rutherford and the Cavendish scientists on the other. The nineteenth-century roots of the Apostles lay in undergraduate rebellion against the Establishment, then chiefly represented by the Church of England. But to proclaim openly an attachment to rationalism, agnosticism, and the spirit of free enquiry was to damage one's chances of promotion and preferment. The peculiarly English solution to this dilemma was to create a private space for subversive thinking, protected from intrusion by secrecy and by homosexual attachments, while continuing to enjoy all the advantages which membership of the Establishment provided.

Sinclair directly traces the treachery of the 1930s generation of Communist Apostles to the habits of thought and loyalties engendered by this double existence. 'Clandestine association', he writes, 'was an intellectual aphrodisiac, inducing closet ways and a sense of innate superiority. To be an Apostle was not only to be among the best, but to be set apart in splendid stealthiness . . .' What the traitors got from The Society was above all the 'double language of the Jesuits, the words spoken to other Apostles seeking the truth, and the words spoken to the masses, who could not understand the truth'. Perhaps all this 'created the conditions for becoming an agent with dual loyalties' as Sinclair avers. But many other conditions also had to be present. The traitors were the dregs of a tradition, not its finest flowers. Mostly the double morality worked to protect conventional standards, by channelling subversion from the public to the private sphere; or, in the case of Keynes, giving public activities an aspect of improving conservatism. The spectacle of a Blunt publicly willing to serve the Queen as Surveyor of her Pictures while privately happy to pass on secrets to the Soviets was the perversion of an ideal, not its culmination.

But the 'best' at Cambridge between the wars also included the scientists, none of whom made it to the Apostles. The leading figures were John Rutherford and his protégé Kapitsa, and two left-wing physicists, John Crockford who actually 'split the atom' and Patrick Blackett whose work led to the discovery of the neutron. Kapitsa's role was crucial, as a galvanizer of experiments in Cambridge and in conveying their results to Moscow. A mixture of genius and inspired clown, Kapitsa 'was to become the father of nuclear research in the Soviet Union' and, after his detention in the Soviet Union in 1934, 'an adviser on the making of the Russian atom and hydrogen bombs'. With another Rutherford protégé Niels Bohr at Copenhagen and the French Communist scientist, Joliot-Curie, also feeding information to Moscow, Russia had acquired the theory to make the atom bomb by 1939 – most of it developed and supplied by Western scientists. As Sinclair makes clear this voluntary flow of knowledge was far more crucial to that achievement than the later treachery of the atomic spies, Klaus Fuchs, Bruno Pontecorvo and Alan Nunn May.

Thus the two Cambridge cultures both ended by producing a one-way flow of information to Moscow. This makes one wonder how apart they really were. In assessing the motives of the scientists, one cannot evade the question of political allegiance. Nor does Sinclair try to, though he fails to give it its due weight, for fear of undermining the dramatic contrast on which his book is built. The two Cambridge élites were equally impregnated with Communism. The scientists did not need to learn Jesuitical double-talk from the Apostles. Playing on the ambiguities of the word 'science' they persuaded themselves, and sought to persuade others, that the Soviet Union was the first scientific state – the first to apply the scientific method to social organization. The Cambridge biochemist Joseph Needham believed that Communism 'was a biological imperative, for advanced life was essentially organisation and order'. The Cambridge geneticist Desmond Bernal 'supported the state control of scientific research so that researchers could be directed to work only on what directly benefited the masses'. Both élites set their own personal and professional judgments above communal loyalty. They were both in the business of building a brave new world centred on the Soviet Union – and their own societies were part of the bad old one.

These considerations rob the contrast between the activities of the Apostles and the scientists of much of its value, and the 'open' transmission of knowledge to the Soviets of much of its virtue. (There was no comparable flow to Nazi Germany.) Treason, after all, is merely the illegal end of a continuum. The Cambridge scientists had no need to 'betray their country', for the knowledge they were passing on in the 1930s had not yet been classified – largely because the government was ignorant of its military implications. Is it really credible that the scientists were unaware of them? As Sinclair notes, Kapitsa himself was never in doubt: that is, presumably, why he was put in charge of atomic research in Russia after 1934. This raises an interesting question. Were certain Western scientists determined to get the theoretical knowledge to Moscow *before* it was classified as top secret by their own governments – in order to give Russia the means to defend the Revolution?

There is one final twist to the story. After the war, Patrick Blackett was a founder of what is known as deterrence theory – the theory of war prevention based on the threat of nuclear destruction. Most defenders of deterrence argue that it has been the *joint* possession of nuclear weapons by the United States and the Soviet Union which has prevented another World War. Less frequently noticed is the fact that joint possession is also the condition of protecting the Soviet system from the vastly greater material and spiritual resources of the West. Was this outcome accidental, ineluctable, or in some sense intended? Did Kapitsa come to the Cavendish voluntarily or was he planted there? Whatever the answers to these questions we can agree with Sinclair that the coming of Kapitsa to Cambridge at the dawn of the golden age of experimental physics was a decisive event in world history.

CHAPTER FORTY-THREE

War Correspondents

Philip Knightley, *The First Casualty: The War Correspondent as Hero, Propagandist, and Myth Maker from the Crimea to Vietnam*
[André Deutsch, 1975]

WAR POSES an agonizing problem for the media. A key function of the press is to expose official cant, corruption and incompetence. Never is this more needed than in war when millions of lives may be at stake. Yet war also makes a diametrically opposite demand: to write or show nothing which can help the enemy or weaken one's own side. Once convinced of the media's importance, war leaders saw it as part of the war effort. So one gets the dilemma. Truth is desperately needed, but cannot be allowed. In order to keep up morale, politicians and generals must apparently be given *carte blanche* to blunder away lives and destinies.

Here is the story of how the press has allowed itself to be suborned to their purposes. At each stage of the process a growing official awareness of the usefulness of the media has been met by a growing willingness of the media so to be used. If Philip Knightley's book disappoints, it is because he does not deal with this developing relationship systematically. He writes about the main modern wars as separate episodes. The same reporting problems keep coming up in each one, but there is no sense of a developing argument. In other words, he has used the wrong framework to deal with this subject. But the subject *is* important. Knightley has assembled a great deal of scattered information on war reporting. He gives a fascinating insight into the psychology of the war correspondent. Above all, he is scrupulously fair, thus providing in his own book a model of what he thinks good reporting should be.

War journalism proper starts with William Russell's famous dispatches to *The Times* from the Crimean War – which contributed to the appearance there of Florence Nightingale. This was a high peak of integrity scaled only rarely afterwards. Almost from the start, the war journalist identified completely with his 'side'. 'It is not within the province of your correspondent to criticise what has been done by the army or the navy . . .' wrote a Northern journalist in the American civil war. It was a typical attitude. At first, the army was far from identifying with the journalist. Military men regarded him as an infernal nuisance, to be kept as far away from the battlefield as possible. Soon they began to appreciate his possible utility. Good publicity could advance a general's career, a fact exploited by such supershowmen of our own day as MacArthur and Montgomery. Governments, too, realized the value of having successes written up or invented, war aims explained or fabricated, in an attractive style. Thus the initial bias to simply suppressing all bad news gave way to cautious acceptance of the press as junior partner in a common effort.

How did the media come to accept this role? One explanation has to do with its own development under competitive conditions. The popular press grew up in the late nineteenth century to cater to the needs of a newly literate public, including its apparently insatiable appetite for violence and slaughter. This encouraged a simple type of 'us–them' reporting, based on the heroic incident or dramatic visual image, which exactly suited the way governments and generals wanted wars to be reported and presented. What it discouraged was any analytic, reflective approach, any emphasis on context and justification. Covering wars in gory detail has been both a way of making money and of strengthening public identification with military exploits. Contrary to widespread belief, there is little evidence, according to Knightley, that saturation coverage of Vietnam on American television hurt the war effort; some evidence that it may have helped it.

A second factor is the tremendous pressure that government and military can put on the media at all levels. At the highest, they can promise proprietors and editors substantial personal rewards – ennoblement or other honours, a special relationship, even political office – if they play the game, and threaten official censorship if they don't. Churchill wanted *The Times* commandeered in the First World War in order to secure 'an authoritative means of guiding public opinion' – a singularly inept choice, as *The Times* has always furnished a classic example of voluntary identification with power. At a lower level, the media were entirely dependent on military patronage to get at the news and to get it onto people's breakfast tables or (later) television screens. This dependence has, if anything, increased over time.

The psychology of the war correspondent has also been very important. Knightley points out that most war reporters in the later nineteenth century were soldiers *manqués*, driven by a thirst for adventure to escape the dullness of bourgeois life. War, as one of them put it, was a 'big factor in the joy of living'. This pattern continued in the twentieth century. According to Philip Gibbs, war correspondents are 'all the men who get lost somewhere between one war and another'. A photographer, Tim Page, who had been badly wounded covering Vietnam, was asked by a publisher to write a book which 'once and for all' took the glamour out of war. Page's response was incredulous. 'Jesus! Take the glamour out of war. How the hell can you do that? You can't take the glamour out of a tank burning or a helicopter blowing up. It's like trying to take the glamour out of sex. War is *good* for you.' Even for the unromantic, the pressure on the war correspondent to get 'on side', the guilt at detachment, must be immense.

War in the nineteenth century could still be regarded as an adventure. Paradoxically, it was the growth of its horrors which cemented the relationship between the media, the military and the government. The more 'total' war became, the greater the need for government to mobilize the 'home front' and the more crucial the role of the press for that purpose. In the First World War, the media emerged for the first time as a fully fledged arm of the war machine. For the war to continue at all, says Robert Graves, it became necessary 'to make the English hate the Germans as they had never hated anyone before'. To this end the British developed a 'propaganda machine . . . that became the envy of the world' – as well as the model for Goebbels. Its main weapon was the atrocity story, made more vivid by the use of photography: the same pile of corpses could do service for any number of horror stories. It fed on German ineptness in handling 'human interest' cases like that of Nurse Edith Cavell. In fact, reports of German soldiers raping Belgian nuns, which combined pornography and propaganda in an unbeatable combination, were mostly invented by British Intelligence. When correspondents, further, presented their own troops to readers as 'greyhounds on the leash, impatient to leap out of the trenches and charge from shell-hole to shell-hole, from cheer to cheer' it became clear that the aim of concealing the truth from the enemy had degenerated into a conspiracy to conceal from populations the criminal ineptness of High Commands. The cost in human lives of this double process – inventing a uniquely wicked enemy and concealing one's own blunders – ran into tens of millions of lives; to Europe's future it is incalculable.

The final ingredient in what Knightley sees as an increasingly corrupt relationship was provided by ideology. With the rise of Communism and Fascism, ideology became a powerful instrument of political manipulation, demanding committed media. At the same time, it became a reality for many of those engaged in transmitting news, and thus affected the way they handled it. Ideological hatred for Communism led all but a handful of editors and correspondents – notably John Reed and Morgan Philips Price – grotesquely to overestimate White Russian strength in the Civil War. Almost all the correspondents covering the Spanish Civil War consciously invented or suppressed facts to help the side they supported. Finally, in the two post-1945 Asian wars fought by America – in Korea and Vietnam – racism has provided a powerful psychological support for free world rhetoric.

In all this, there are many fascinating questions which Knightley touches on but does not develop. One is posed by William Randolph Hearst's famous 1898 telegram to a bored photographer in Cuba: 'You furnish pictures, I will furnish war.' How important has the press been in creating the wars, and incidents in war, which were so good for selling copy? Another question concerns the merits of formal and voluntary censorship. Editorial self-censorship has been the characteristic Anglo-

Saxon adaptation to war conditions. Yet the evidence of this book suggests that the truth is sometimes more likely to come out when government controls the press than when editors censor themselves. Germany alone of the Second World War combatants was prepared to admit a major military defeat – when it declared four days' national mourning for the loss of its army at Stalingrad. The best reporting of the decisive Russian front came from Cuzio Malaparte, writing for *Corriere della Sera* in Mussolini's Italy. This is an aspect which would repay further study.

Perhaps the real significance of war for the media is that it exposes in the sharpest form an ongoing tension between the claims of criticism and the claims of morale. Without criticism society freezes; without morale it disintegrates. The media generate both criticism and morale. One's final reflection on this book is how difficult it is to do both simultaneously, no less in peace than war.

CHAPTER FORTY-FOUR

Churchill's War

R. W. Thompson, *Churchill and Morton: Correspondence between Major Sir Desmond Morton and R. W. Thompson*
[Hodder & Stoughton, 1976]

IT WAS in 1960 that the war correspondent Reginald Thompson began his attempt to assess Churchill 'as a person and a personality, and his impact on his times in that light'. He had become convinced that while Churchill's eloquence and courage had helped save Britain in 1940, the war leader had later sold Britain and Europe down the river, leaving them to be carved up between the United States and Russia. The nub of the matter, as he saw it, was Churchill's failure to preserve an independent foreign policy in the war years. Such a policy would have rejected unconditional surrender and tried for a compromise peace with a non-Nazi Germany. This would have preserved Germany's defensive capacity in Eastern Europe, and kept Europe as an independent force in world politics.

Churchill's failure to defend Britain's interests has to be understood,

Thompson insists, in personal terms. The clues are to be found in his mixed Marlborough/Yankee ancestry. The first led him to play the part of Supreme War Lord, with disastrous results which undermined Britain's position in the Middle and Far East. The second led him to subordinate Britain's interests too readily to those of the United States. (The triumph of the Yankee in him was helped by his tortured relationship with his American mother: adoring her, but denied her love, he offered her his father's kingdom.) Thus Churchill renounced Britain's European mission. 'Europe was Winston's continent. There lay his role. Without his American obsessions, which were in his blood, he might have been one of the greatest Europeans of all time.'

So writes Thompson to Sir Desmond Morton in this fascinating exchange of letters written between 1960 and 1962, and now published for the first time. They were a kind of intellectual preparation for Thompson's book *The Yankee Marlborough* (1963), with Sir Desmond Morton, formerly of military intelligence and an intimate of Churchill for thirty years, acting as a sounding board for Thompson's ideas and an initiator into the mysteries of the Churchill personality. *The Yankee Marlborough*, and Thompson's other books on the same subject, seem to have sunk with hardly a trace. One can see why. He doesn't carry the historical guns to compel attention. Moreover, his theme is controversial – 'blasphemies about the Father-figure' – but not fashionable. For most people the point about the war was the defeat of the Nazis. It matters little whether Britain emerged quite as strong as it might have. Besides, the type of anti-Churchill critique which Thompson requests has come mainly from the military lobby, and everyone knows that generals, and their defenders, always blame politicians for preventing victory, or robbing them of its fruits, particularly if the politicians in question fancy themselves as strategists, which both Hitler and Churchill did.

Yet, for the historian, it remains a tremendous subject which has never been properly tackled. Britain went to war in September 1939 to preserve itself as a Great Power. To say afterwards that the war was justified because Nazism was destroyed and British territorial integrity preserved is to invent quite different war aims from the one with which Britain started. That original one was clearly not achieved. Britain has struggled through the post-war years as an increasingly enfeebled satellite of the United States, because the war destroyed, or fatally undermined, all the props of its previous position. The Second World War, in short, is a central episode in Britain's astonishingly rapid decline. So the question arises: was there some serious misjudgment in the decision to go to war in 1939? Or did the flaw in British policy develop during the war itself?

Thompson, Liddell Hart, and other critics of unconditional surrender believe the second to be true; and what these letters mainly discuss is the way Churchill's personality may have contributed to that flaw. We meet an aristocratic warlord who wages war erratically and capriciously because of a certain personal insecurity in face of the officer and gentleman class; a marvellously fertile mind with but little capacity for 'basic toil' on uncongenial, but necessary, subjects; an incurable romantic enslaved by the phrases which made each situation so vivid to him; a total egocentric who expected life and people to fit the pattern of his own interests and enthusiasms; a soldier of fortune whose very lack of 'navigation' was liable to trap him in the first available drama. These traits are paraded to support a major conclusion: that Churchill was incapable of an 'objective' analysis of a situation; that the extent of his absorption in one task made him incapable of seeing that task in relation to others. Specifically, his obsession with destroying Germany, added to his American sympathies, blinded him to the part Germany ought to play in preserving Britain's, and Europe's, independence.

Much of this character study is genuinely absorbing. Morton's view of Churchill as a 'magnificent character', one who does great things, independently of whether they are good or bad, hits him off perfectly. But how relevant is Churchill's character to Britain's failure to preserve its freedom of action? To suggest that he could have forced on his allies the idea of a negotiated peace with a non-Nazi Germany is fantasy. The Americans were never interested in it (perhaps they should have been); the Russians had no possible interest in it once the war had started to go their way. Nor could Churchill have gone unilaterally against Unconditional Surrender: Morton points out rightly that 'Power, in the sense of money, men and arms was in the hands of the Americans. I do not think that Winston's hatred of the Nazis comes in there . . .'; nor, he might have added, his Yankee sympathies. Britain's fate as a Great Power was decided the moment it locked itself into wartime partnership with the United States. Could that have been averted? I doubt it. Britain could survive as a Great Power only if it kept both the Germans and the Americans out of Western Europe. Once the Germans had reached the channel, Britain was forced into dependence on the United States, and American policy, for its very survival. By a tragic irony, its finest hour marked the terminal point of its imperial greatness. It was the decisions between March 1939 and April 1940, rather than anything Churchill did thereafter, which paved the way for Yalta, Potsdam, and the division of Europe.

Of course, over a longer period, the charge of Yankeeism is justified, against Churchill as well as against a governing class that since the late nineteenth century has been steadily marrying into American money. It helps explain why Britain over this period has chosen growing dependence on the United States to an alliance of equals with Germany. It is obviously not the whole story. Germany's own ambitions, before both 1914 and 1939, posed vast problems. Perhaps even more important, though, Britain's rulers were never really prepared to accept the German claim to equality. They were the Romans, the Germans the barbarians. It was an attitude endorsed by the Yankee Marlborough.

CHAPTER FORTY-FIVE

The Resistance

M. R. D. Foot, *Resistance: European Resistance to Nazism 1940–45*
[Eyre Methuen, 1976];
Graham Lyons (ed.), *The Russian Version of the Second World War*
[Leo Cooper, 1976];
Arthur Marwick, *The Home Front: The British and the*
Second World War
[Thames and Hudson, 1976]

THE SPATE of books about the Second World War continues. But the historical results are not especially impressive, since few of them are actually written for historical reasons. A large number are written and mainly read by those who want to justify and relive, not understand, the past. War books and films offer simplified emotions to mass audiences; there is also the continued pornographic interest in the Nazis, of which the insignia of punk rock provide the latest example. This use of the past for nostalgia, profit, or sexual titillation, does not make for good history. The ratio of propaganda to truth is too high. Too many assumptions are unargued. Statements are made on the basis of poor, or non-existent, evidence, because they fit popular sterotypes. Take an example from M. R. D. Foot's *Resistance*. On page 50 Foot writes of the 'ghastly atrocity of Kharkov – about a hundred thousand people massacred in an afternoon'. The source is given at the bottom of the page as 'conversation with a survivor, 1953'. Now it may be that the Germans did massacre that many civilians at Kharkov in one afternoon, though I have not heard it. But Foot must know that his conversation provides no kind of evidence for that statement, because a mere survivor could not possibly have known how many died.

As a British Army officer who served with the French resistance in Brittany, Foot is a notable survivor himself. Much of his book is about resistance work in its various aspects – intelligence, deception, escape, sabotage, attack and politics. He describes the techniques used, and provides a fascinating compendium of resistance lore. He gives potted histories of resistance movements and intelligence operations in all the main theatres of war. In fact, the book is partially misnamed since, although intelligence gathering was the main function of the resistance from the allied staffs' point of view, it took place quite independently of it. The breaking of the German military cipher, the most important intelligence achievement of the war, had nothing to do with the resistance, and was based on information supplied before the war had even started.

Foot's assertion that resistance was based on character, not class, contains an important, but not sufficient, truth. As he himself admits, Communists played a leading role in the resistance almost everywhere. They were uniquely equipped for it by ideology (after the attack on Russia), organization, and long experience of subversive politics. They performed it with great heroism. By overemphasizing Conservative and Liberal involvement in the resistance, Foot minimizes the extent of collaboration, active and passive – particularly the extent to which Nazi propaganda succeeded in converting the German war of conquest into an ideological war against Communism. Geoffrey Barraclough was not the first to notice that 'resistance to Hitler from within Europe was incomparably weaker in 1939 than resistance to Germany had been in 1914'. In practice, most resistance movements gathered momentum only when a German defeat had become certain.

Again, the whole thrust of the book, though not the sober final conclusion, is to exaggerate the effect of the resistance on the outcome of the war. The breaking of the German code was, as we have seen, done independently of the resistance. With the exception of the Rjukan raid which destroyed the German supply of heavy water, and thus aborted their not very advanced attempt to develop an atom bomb, the results of sabotage were negligible. The resistance movements caused German garrisons in occupied territories to be larger than they would otherwise have been, but garrisons of some kind were in any case required for the Nazi policy of exploiting the occupied territories. The fact was that in the moment of their greatest territorial expansion, in the summer of 1942, the Germans had lost the war, and Hitler knew it. The reason is that the German war potential, even after Speer's belated attempt to mobilize it, was much less than that of the Allies. We don't need the resistance to explain either the fact or the timing of the German defeat.

People are reluctant to accept this. There is a very understandable feeling that heroism ought to get its reward; the idea that the sacrifices of the resistance were useless goes against the grain. And, of course, they were not useless; but their use lay elsewhere. It was, first of all, in restoring the self-esteem of nations beaten in battle. Secondly, it was in shaping the politics of post-war Europe: post-war 'consensus' dates from alliances formed in the resistance movements. Even the Communists found, through resistance, a place in their national communities which they had not had before the war. And it was in resistance to a Fascist dominated Europe that the democratic European movement was born. But somehow this larger significance of resistance gets lost in Foot's crabbed and over-technical account.

The Russian perspective on the war, clearly put together by Graham Lyons from Soviet school textbooks, is not more distorted than the standard Western offerings. The Russians believe, quite rightly, that it was they who bore the brunt of the fighting and the horror. They also claim, in my view rightly, that it was they who defeated the Germans, with rather minimal help from the Western Allies. We read of the Normandy landings that 'the Anglo-American forces met with practically no resistance from the Hitlerites, and advanced into the heart of France.' The Russians were painfully aware that German resistance was much stronger on the eastern than on the much-delayed western front; and this feeds the underlying theme of Soviet war historiography: that the deepest longing of the Western leaders was to get together with the Nazis in attacking the Soviet Union, a longing only frustrated by imperialist rivalry, arising out of the contradictions of capitalism. Given the basic historical model of class conflict, the case is reasonably argued and by no means absurd. The main fault in the text lies elsewhere: in not properly understanding the domestic context of other countries' foreign policy, and therefore assigning the wrong weights to people's reputations and remarks. But this is a fault of parochial history, not Soviet history as such.

The main problem facing the writers of Russian war textbooks is to explain the catastrophic defeats sustained by the Russian armies in the summer of 1941. The result is a classic diversionary tactic. 'Up to the moment of its attack on the Soviet Union,' we read, 'the economy of Fascist Germany had been fully directed towards war-production.' This explanation (which is anyway untrue) of initial German military superiority is intended to hide the appalling effect on the Russian military machine of Stalin's purges, his suspicions, and his initial mistakes.

Compared with the Russians, the British had a light war. Of Arthur Marwick's *The Home Front*, published by Thames and Hudson, the best that can be said is that the 167 illustrations are more enjoyable than the text, though not much more. Marwick has written so much better on this subject before that one can only suppose that his mind was on other things when he dashed it off. At one point he describes Mrs Churchill as a 'truly charming and gracious lady'. This just about registers the level of the book's historical and literary inspiration.

CHAPTER FORTY-SIX

The Road to 1945

Paul Addison, *The Road to 1945: British Politics and the Second World War*
[Jonathan Cape, 1975]

THE SECOND World War is the supreme irony of British history. In its 'finest hour' Britain lost the game. The huge nostalgia industry cannot disguise this fact: it lives on it. Nor is it enough to say that the defeat of Nazism was justification in itself. Nations are not like individuals. We may admire individuals who sacrifice all for the cause they believe in. Nations which do the same are merely foolish: at least in the eye of history. Britain had a very great international position in 1939. It went to war to preserve it. As a direct result of the war it lost it. For many years one could believe, even as Britain's power crumbled, that economic and social gains more than offset vanished imperial glory. Today it is difficult to believe this. By sacrificing the empire Britain sacrificed much of its inherited economic strength, without guaranteeing itself an alternative basis of successful existence. Even the war's social achievement proved superficial. Class has been in the ascendant for most of the post-war period; and what remains today of the war's promise of national renaissance?

It is the chief flaw in Paul Addison's very fine, elegantly written book that he does not see the politics of the Second World War in their full historical context. Up to the minute in its research, the book's perspective is yet dated. 'We were – *almost* all – Butskellites then,' writes Addison about his own formative years; and his perspective remains Butskellite. He looks back on the war as one might have done in the late 1950s or early 1960s when it still looked all eminently worthwhile. Yet this was the immediate prelude to a collapse in Britain's position and morale sufficiently spectacular to compel reappraisal of the war experience.

Addison is too good a historian to ignore this dimension altogether. He understands the meaning of appeasement. In the 1930s John Strachey had perceptively seen in Baldwin 'the perfect statesman for an empire in decline' since he realized that 'all action is prejudicial on the long view to British interests'. The point about appeasement, which Addison brings out well, is that it was a Byzantine strategy of preserving the empire by avoiding direct confrontations; the strategy of foxes, not fools. He agrees with Maurice Cowling that as late as April 1940, Neville Chamberlain was still hoping to avoid fighting the war he had been forced to declare, relying on stalemate on the western front. His strategy in peace and phoney war alike was destroyed by the interaction between Hitler's brutal thrusts and a domestic opposition which wanted Chamberlain out for many reasons of which foreign policy was only one.

Chamberlain's opponents numbered at least one lion, Winston Churchill, and others who learnt to roar for the occasion. (Attlee, however, continued to resemble the 'frog who sits motionless on a stone, occasionally snapping up an insect with its tongue'.) War was Churchill's last chance to 'win the Derby' as he sometimes put it. He believed that only by spending, not hoarding, Britain's power could that power be

302

preserved; conscious of national decline, he looked for confrontation with Germany to restore 'moral health and martial vigour'. The Labour Party, too, stood to gain from war. Since 1931 it had made no progress on domestic issues. Confrontation with Germany provided it with unprecedented opportunity to combine patriotism and ideological commitment. A real war, as every Labour leader knew from the previous one, would guarantee a working-class advance on all fronts – political, industrial, economic. It might be the only way of securing it. For others, prospect of war gave an outlet to fantasies which had to be repressed in peace. Robert Boothby wanted a Committee of Public Safety, martial law, curtailment of Parliament. None of these people consciously aimed for war, though psychologists might have a field day with their unconscious drives. They were not, however, prepared to take risks for peace. In this respect, they were no different from Hitler. More seriously, they did not see that Britain could not 'win' the war even if Germany lost it; because Germany could not be defeated except by powers which had almost as much interest in weakening Britain as in crushing Hitler.

What, then, about the other side of the coin – the internal transformation which was to provide an alternative basis for British existence? Addison sees Churchill's government as the 'greatest reforming Administration' since Asquith's. He makes the now conventional connection between war and social reform: 'Churchill's arrival marked the real beginning of popular mobilization for total war ... This experience bred the demand for a better society when the fighting was done ...' Yet he himself admits that the 'reforming consensus' implied 'only very modest changes in society itself' – far too modest to provide for national renewal.

One reason for the modesty of reform was the success of the war effort itself. No more than the 1914–18 war did the Second World War modernize the British economy, that is, adapt it for life without the empire. As Henry Pelling has remarked, victory in war convinced the British that 'somehow or other, things in their own country were arranged much better than elsewhere in the world ...' In this connection, the success of wartime finance left a dubious legacy. Keynesian budgetary management was first introduced in order to avoid the inflation which had characterized war finance between 1914 and 1918: consumer demand was to be damped down in order to release resources for war production. The success of this 'demand management' prompted the full employment commitment of 1944: demand was to be kept high enough to employ the whole working population. The long-standing Treasury view that the British unemployment problem was basically structural, to be 'cured' by making British exports more competitive or even Hubert Henderson's more pessimistic argument in favour of retaining the empire as an economic bloc, were simply brushed aside. As a result, the Coalition made very extensive, and very expensive, social commitments before a sound economic basis for post-war survival had been secured. Attlee demanded that policy be based on the 'conception of . . . abundance'. For Britain, this was a dangerous myth, based on the abundance of American credit. Here, as in other ways, war proved to be an inappropriate context for radical reform. It was an interlude of illusion, which bred facile solutions.

Equally doubtful is the view that war by itself changes social consciousness. It does have revolutionary possibilities, but the suspension of politics drastically limits them. This means that war reform tends to be 'whiggish' rather than 'radical'. Addison talks about the 'demand' for reform, but from whom did the demand come? The general mood was cheerfully egalitarian and populist; the title of Nicholas Davenport's book *Vested Interests or Common Pool?* gives a flavour of the rhetoric of the time. But the mood was virtually empty of political content; and there was no Lloyd George capable of turning a people's war into a people's peace. Churchill could not do it. He was a Whig patrician, not a demagogue. Sir Stafford Cripps and Beveridge tried; but they were easily brushed aside. The men of the system who ran the war remained as before: cautious, pragmatic, unimaginative.

The dynamic for reconstruction came from another source: the intellectuals. It was their mobilization for war purposes which created an 'effective demand' for social reform. The cleverest people, functional to the war machine as they had never been to the peace machine, defined the agenda of politics for the post-war period. Addison shows how the war brought the left-wing intellectual out of the cold into the cosy warmth of the BBC, there to fight the 'war of words' against Fascism. More important still for the content of reform, the war brought into politics the advanced ideas of professional groups, largely ignored in the 1930s. 'Professional bodies like the BMA and the Town and Country Planning Association, centre pressure-groups like Political and Economic Planning and the Next Five Years Group, advisory committees like those of Spens and Barlow, the school of Keynesian economists, the social investigators of poverty and malnutrition like Rowntree and Boyd Orr –

these were the architects of reconstruction and consensus.' What fired them? In a few suggestive sentences which surely might have been expanded, Addison talks of the existential crisis of the intellectual in a situation where the real heroes are those who risk their lives in battle or 'produce for victory'. 'Usually of comfortable background and liberal persuasions, he most likely felt a sense of guilt before the war at the conditions of the working classes. Now the underdog was a hero . . . How could he be rewarded? At this point the intellectual could cast himself as the manufacturer of the moral weapon against Hitler. By designing an idealistic programme of war aims, he could at once reward the working classes, and by inspiring them to even greater efforts take his own place in the front line as the man who built the moral Spitfire . . . Hitler suffered a million deaths by typewriter.' So did the war's radicalizing potential.

One begins to appreciate better why the war was such a limited and limiting experience. It shifted the consensus leftwards: it did not create a continuing vitality. Thus 'Attlee's consensus' which replaced Britain's imperial position provided no basis for tackling the 'British disease'. From today's perspective, few things are more tragic than the comments of the 'young Radical' in 1944:

> We've shown in this war that we British don't always muddle through; we've shown we can organise superbly – look at these invasions of the Continent which have gone like clockwork; look at the harbours we've built on the beaches . . . Using even half the vision and energy and invention and pulling together we've done in this war . . . what is there we cannot do?

PART FOUR

Commonwealth
and Europe

CHAPTER FORTY-SEVEN

The Commonwealth Experience

Nicholas Mansergh, *The Commonwealth Experience*
[Weidenfeld & Nicolson, 1969]

MOST EMPIRES have been lost on the battlefield. Our own period is no exception. The German, Italian and Japanese empires this century all collapsed in military defeat. The French empire foundered at Dien Bien Phu and was finally sunk in Algeria. These bloody endings have had at least one beneficial consequence. They have dramatized the fact of change in a manner which no civilized, orderly, gradual transition could possibly have achieved. They have created a kind of *tabula rasa*, offering the opportunity, indeed necessity, for a fundamental rethinking of past and future.

The British empire, as is well known, did not fit into this pattern. It evolved, first into the British Commonwealth of Nations, finally into the Commonwealth. Today it is just as much a fact of contemporary British life as was the old empire of a hundred years ago, probably more so. Then, as now, there were big debates about its future: what was the point in having it? Was it worth the cost? Did it fit the new economic facts? Did it unnecessarily cramp the future? These debates, as they have been ever since, were inconclusive. Already there was a feeling that in some deeper, elusive sense the empire was a fulfilment of Britain's destiny, part of its historical experience and image of itself. This feeling has grown, rather than diminished, with the years, as that empire was divested of its crumbling Great Power supports, and transmuted into a moral ideal of a multiracial fellowship. Even today, few find it emotionally easy to swap Commonwealth for Common Market.

It was the triumph of the commonwealth ideal which saved the British empire from the violent destruction which is the common lot of huge and artificial human constructs. Such a triumph needs to be explained, and Professor Mansergh has set out to do so in a profound and sensitive book. As he rightly notes, there is a sharp antithesis between the idea of empire, which means the government of men by a superior authority, and the idea of commonwealth, which means the government of peoples by themselves. He attributes the unique growth of the commonwealth experience to the fact that large areas of the British empire were in origin colonies of settlement rather than areas of conquest: Canada, Australia, New Zealand and, to a certain extent, South Africa, all provided in their European, and especially in their Anglo-Saxon stock, the 'necessary popular foundation for commonwealth' which the other great western empires lacked.

The existence of settler communities was a necessary, but not sufficient, condition for the growth of commonwealth. Other mid-Victorian tendencies promoted the same result, especially the victory of free trade and *laissez-faire* which destroyed the mercantile rationale for a centralized empire, and made the imperial government increasingly reluctant to shoulder the costs of a colonial administration. Professor Mansergh might have made more of the particularly English contribution to the commonwealth experience. The readiness of England to concede responsible government to its white colonies stemmed largely from the fact that England alone of the imperial countries had responsible government itself. It was a particularly English interpretation of political unrest – whether in the empire or at home – to attribute it to the lack of adequate representation of the 'interests' in the scheme of government. Continental powers were still in the grip of paternalist theories of government and protectionist theories of economics which would have been difficult to reconcile with the grant of responsible institutions to their colonies even had the requisite 'popular foundations' existed.

The main challenge to the commonwealth theory of imperial development came at the turn of the century from such centralizers as Joseph Chamberlain and Alfred Milner, who advocated an imperial federation. One reason for the popularity of this thinking, especially in the Conservative party, was the intractable domestic problem of Ireland which could not be assimilated to the pattern of commonwealth experience. But international considerations were not lacking. Security needs in what many thought to be a dawning age of global struggle seemed to require a centralized defence system, and especially a unified naval command. To the Colonial Secretary, Joseph Chamberlain, an imperial *Zollverein* seemed the only answer to the challenge of German and American industrial competition. In practice, none of these ideas, strongly held, not only on the right but also on the left of politics, came to very much. As Mansergh remarks, 'the colonies were instinctively averse to any development which might impose a limit on the growth of their autonomy.'

310

Professor Mansergh has little doubt that the opponents of centralization were right – and history seems to bear him out. The unanimous rallying of the self-governing dominions to the British cause in the two World Wars proved that the sentiment of autonomous British communities provided a better guarantee of support in moments of danger than any central organization could have; indeed, this feeling could only be operative in the absence of such organization. However, against this were certain disadvantages attaching to a mere relationship of sentiment which could have been profitably explored. The Commonwealth undoubtedly helped Britain in war: it is less obvious that it did so in peace. Economically, its existence produced a dangerous complacency about the problems which Britain needed to solve, without providing the protection which a proper imperial *Zollverein* on the Chamberlain model might have done: as Hobsbawm has recently argued, empire became a psychological substitute for readjustment to changed conditions. Again, though the Commonwealth rallied to Britain in 1939, its refusal to contemplate war until the whole gamut of appeasement had been run undoubtedly made it more difficult for the British government to stand up to Hitler. The desire not to get involved in Europe was understandable: but the existence of empire disguised the fact, not least from the British themselves, that Britain's fate was much more closely bound up with Europe than with the Commonwealth – that it was New Zealand and not Czechoslovakia which was the 'far-away' country of Neville Chamberlain's description.

However successful the British had been in evolving the white commonwealth out of the empire of settlement, it was by no means obvious that they would be equally successful in creating a coloured commonwealth out of the empire of conquest. Yet already in the nineteenth century we find the germ of an imperial policy towards native races that was to make possible the post-1945 multiracial commonwealth; and which was to lead to the alienation of such settler communities as South Africa and Rhodesia, determined to preserve white supremacy. The British government, in establishing representative institutions in the Cape Colony in 1854, insisted on a 'colour blind' franchise: all were entitled to vote on a common roll, subject to a financial qualification. The far-reaching implication of this measure, by no means fully thought out at the time, was that responsible government was the right of all races, and that there would be no attempt to keep the coloured empire in subjection against its will. This made possible a peaceful handover of power: it did not ensure continuing association in a commonwealth. This question came crucially to the fore in the 1949 debate on India's application for membership as a republic. The traditional basis of membership, enshrined in the 1931 Statute of Westminster, was a common allegiance to the crown. Refusal to accept a republican member would have, in effect, restricted the Common-wealth for ever to its original white settler area: it would have remained a white man's club. Acceptance opened the way to the multiracial Commonwealth of twenty-eight members that exists today. The second alternative was more imaginative; the first would probably have been more realistic.

For however restrictive the old basis was, it represented something real. It was because the settler dominions felt themselves to be British that they rallied to England's side in its two wars. The common allegiance to the crown symbolized this obligation of feeling; the adoption of republican institutions by the post-war Commonwealth members signified its absence. An association of sentiment was replaced by a 'concert of convenience'. As Mansergh notes of India's application, 'there were mutual and substantial interests in making a settlement, on the British side of trade, investment and security, and on the Indian of stability, aid and as a counterpoise to Pakistan.' But, with mutual convenience as the new criterion of association, it immediately became legitimate to ask whether Britain's own convenience would not be better served by membership of some other grouping.

Of course, there was more than just self-interest to it. There was the multiracial ideal; there were shared institutions. For Britain in particular commonwealth offered a psychological escape from the bleak prospect of abdication. Nevertheless, we are forced to wonder, with Mansergh, whether the Commonwealth of today has not stepped over the border from reality to nothingness.

CHAPTER FORTY-EIGHT

Suez *

[1970]

IS THERE anything new to be said about Suez? Judging from the mountain of books produced on the subject, the answer would clearly seem to be no. We now know almost all that there is to be known – at least from our side of the story. Egyptian and Russian policy-making still remain mysterious. Would the Russians have intervened had Britain and France not agreed to a cease-fire on 6 November? Was Nasser ever prepared seriously to compromise or negotiate? And if so, what tactics would have been most efficacious to secure that result? We cannot be sure. However, there is no reason to suppose that the present outlines of the story will be substantially changed in the future.

Why then return to the subject? The answer is, because the historical treatment has been curiously unsatisfactory. Historians have, on the whole, refused to pass judgment. They have fitted together all the pieces, often with consummate skill.[1] But a certain timidity, or perhaps ordinary prudence, has inhibited them from taking up the broader issues. They have preferred to remain above, or perhaps below, the battle of ideas. The partisan accounts tend to be faulty in another way. They assume agreement with (largely) unstated premises or prejudices, Left-wing or Right-wing, pro-Arab or pro-Israeli. They do not really pretend to present a reasoned case one way or the other. An exception is Professor Herman Finer's *Dulles over Suez*, a powerfully argued condemnation of American foreign policy in the crisis. Anthony Nutting's recent pro-Arab book on Suez is entitled *No End of a Lesson*, but I cannot for the life of me discover what the lesson is meant to be.

To make up for their lack of a truly critical approach to the arguments advanced in 1956, the historians have resorted to some fashionable psychologizing. The Anglo-French reaction to the nationalization of the Suez Canal has been described as an 'imperial reflex' – a reaction based on prejudices and attitudes inherited from the nineteenth century but quite inappropriate to the modern world. But historians have

* See chronology on p. 332

313

been loath to define what these attitudes were and to explain exactly why they were inappropriate. Hugh Thomas suggests that the graceful surrender of Empire and influence had built up vast resentments in Britain which demanded for their release a 'spot of adventure', 'a daring stroke', one last final fling, before the nation was prepared to settle down to sedate and unexciting middle age. Eden's actions have been subjected to similar psychological, even physiological, scrutiny. The Tory Press's demands for the 'smack of firm government' began to prey on his over-sensitive nature; he wanted to prove himself a Churchill; his political position needed restoring by a bold coup. Illness played its part: 'the poison from the damaged bile-duct', writes Anthony Nutting, 'was eating away at his whole system'. Thus he too was driven into deviation: for a mad, intoxicating moment, Talleyrand saw himself as Napoleon.

These explanations are not without value or interest, but they should not absolve the historian from the task of examining the actual reasons adduced and arguments deployed. Professor Popper has described as 'a widespread and dangerous fashion of our time ... the fashion of not taking arguments seriously, and at their face value ... but of seeing in them nothing but a way in which deeper irrational motives and tendencies express themselves'. The historians of Suez have by no means been immune from this fashion. This approach is particularly disappointing because Suez brought into sharp focus certain fundamental questions about the nature of our response to the modern world: questions about the morality and practicability of the use of force in the nuclear age; questions about the consequences of the new nationalisms for peace and international order; questions about the role of Britain in the world and the purpose and scope of the United Nations. In other words, the Suez episode has many lessons to offer which the historical literature has largely ignored, or dealt with only by implication.

It may be objected that history has no lessons to teach; that each historical situation, like every other kind of situation, is unique. Yet people's thoughts and actions are in fact modified by experience; and history is, after all, only a special kind of experience. In fact the main participants in the Suez drama were very free in their appeals to history. Much anti-Suez opinion argued that the price of attempting to solve disputes by force had become unacceptably high. Others thought that

314

what Eden was trying to do was, in a vague way, historically 'not on'. 'Suppose', E. H. Carr wrote in his book *What is History?*, 'that someone informed you that he proposed to devote himself to conducting a campaign for the reunion of [Britain and America] under the British crown; you would probably reply that he would be wasting his time. If you tried to explain why . . . you might even commit the cardinal sin of speaking of history with a capital H and tell him that History was against him.' Pro-Suez opinion, as is well known, set great store by the 'lessons of Munich'. It viewed Nasser with eyes haunted by the vision of Hitler, and argued that experience showed that the appeasement of force merely whetted dangerous appetites. Even Eisenhower searched round, somewhat desperately, for historical arguments to convince Eden of the need for patience. In the first draft of a letter, he wrote: 'It took your nation some eighteen years to put the original Napoleon in his place.' The sentence was cut out when Dulles pointed out that Napoleon had been overthrown by force.

There is another motive for returning to the subject of Suez at this moment. Every account so far has preceded the Arab–Israel war of 1967. Certain complacent observations uttered before that event now appear, to say the least, somewhat dated; for example, the comment in the BBC symposium *Suez Ten Years After*: 'The Canal today is, of course, in better condition than it was before the Suez crisis began'; or again Herbert Nicholas's remarks in the same book: 'What the world actually got out of Suez was . . . a peace-keeping force.'[2] The conclusions which follow from these statements need revision. Historians apart, informed opinion was nevertheless bound to draw certain conclusions from the Suez affair. And the failure of the Right's policy has seemed in retrospect to vindicate the view of the Left, viz., that the attempt to discipline smaller nations by Great Power force having failed, as it was bound to fail, the only secure hope of international peace and order lay in strengthening the United Nations. In my view the attitude of the Left has turned out to be as illusory as the policy of the Right was obsolete; and in the following pages I will try to indicate why.

If the initial British reaction to Nasser's nationalization decree of 26 July 1956 was an 'imperial reflex', then it was certainly one very largely

315

shared among all sections of opinion. The Press and Parliament were unanimous in condemning his action. But what is of interest is the terms of the condemnation. Imperial and Great Power affront were very much in the background; what we heard was the authentic voice of liberal internationalism raised up in protest against the actions and style of nationalistic dictatorship. This was as true of Conservative reaction as of Labour's. There is a tendency to regard the authentic voice of Conservatism as the voice of a primitive atavism; but as E. H. Carr has more justly remarked, 'a typical English Conservative . . . when scratched turns out to be 75 per cent a liberal'.

How does this reaction square with that of imperial affront? Are we to reject the 'imperial reflex' thesis? By no means; for the two terms, imperialism and internationalism, are, in British experience, very largely interchangeable. By imperialism we mean that process whereby the major white nations established a hegemony, physical, economic and cultural, over the rest of the world. Now it is perfectly true that Nasser's action threatened British hegemony in the Middle East, latterly based on the Baghdad Pact and the Hashemite dynasties in Iraq and Jordan; although Eden undoubtedly overestimated Nasser's power to enforce the rather romantic dreams of Arab power outlined in his book *Philosophy of Revolution*. His action also challenged Britain's economic interests: the uninterrupted flow of oil was vital to the British economy. As Eden put it, a man of Nasser's record could not be allowed to 'have his thumb on our windpipe'. Personal antipathies played their part: both Eden and Pineau, the French Foreign Minister, detested Nasser. 'I want him destroyed, can't you understand?', Eden bellowed over the telephone to Anthony Nutting. The French believed that Nasser's destruction was the key to victory in Algeria.

But that is by no means the whole story, or even perhaps the major part of it. For it does not exhaust the definition of imperialism to say that it is the domination of one power over others. It establishes common conceptions and systems of law and justice, rights and obligations; it promotes economic interdependence; it preserves peace, stability and order beyond the bounds of the nation-state; it encourages the inter-mingling of peoples and the interchange of ideas; all of which to the internationalist are undeniably good things, even if, in the case of empire, they stem from the original act of force or colonization. The British were the true internationalists among the nineteenth-century empire-builders.

Owing to its island position and its early reliance on trade, Britain had pioneered the idea of economic interdependence. The free movement of capital and goods, the prompt payment of debts, the sanctity of contract, freedom of navigation, international peace and stability – these were all national interests which evolved over time into an international code of mutual benefit. This code flourished in the confidence that every reasonable person would recognize it to be in his own best interest that it should; with the true cultural evangelism typical of the age, the nineteenth-century English liberal did not doubt that God had given to the British nation the duty of universalizing the principles of true felicity, and looked forward to the time when such residual Great Power supports as economic sanctions and the British Navy would no longer be necessary.

To the critic – whether in nineteenth-century Berlin or in mid-twentieth-century Cairo – it seemed only too obvious that the true felicity these principles ministered to was that of the English middle classes, and that the facts which sustained them had less to do with universal human nature than with British economic and naval strength. The English liberal gave little thought to the energies, frustrations, resentments and passions bottled up by the Pax Britannica. Balkanization ought to have given him a clue as to the likely outcome of a withdrawal of imperial power; but at the time he believed that there was nothing in that situation that could not be put right by a railway from Berlin to Baghdad and the development of democratic institutions. The First World War was a more profound shock, but that could just about be explained away as the last agonized writhings of the beast in man. Since then the shocks have come fast, furious and frightening: the world economic collapse of the 1930s, Hitlerism, Stalinism, Auschwitz, Hiroshima, the nuclear threat, racial struggle, surging nationalisms, the ever-shrinking area of liberal democracy. It was certainly a period of transition, but it was less easy to feel optimistic about the outcome. The favourite international institutions beloved of the liberal mind seemed at best marginal: instead of the concert of powers envisaged by the United Nations, there was the balance of terror.

Yet the English liberals clung to their faith in world order and British responsibility for it, even though the voices of men like Eden and Gaitskell seemed particularly ill-attuned to the increasingly raucous noises of Black Power and White Power, of Red Guards and Young

317

Turks. They spoke of 'theft' and 'law' when something more primitive stirred. They crossed Parliamentary swords with old-fashioned courtesy, while the sorcerer from Cairo 'conjured up from the bowels of the earth the legions of hate and fury'.

The deepest theme of Suez is, as Martin Wight well puts it, 'the quest for civilised behaviour in a world of dissolving standards'. Both Eden and Gaitskell, for all their inability to get on with each other – Eden wrote of Gaitskell: 'in all my years of political life I had not met anyone with his cast of mind and approach to problems'[3] – shared a civilized, middle-class disgust at the actions and style of an upstart and a parvenu. Both men had felt the same about Hitler, and would have felt the same about any Englishman who had challenged his opponents with the words 'May you choke to death on your fury'. As Morrison put it, 'it is not a civilised . . . way of conducting business'.

Both Eden and Gaitskell were, of course, conditioned by the experience of Hitler. Indeed Gaitskell was the first Parliamentary speaker to draw this analogy: 'it is all very familiar. It is exactly the same that we encountered from Mussolini and Hitler . . . before the war.' What impressed them was the similarity in style rather than the similarity in power; and if Britain's security was not directly at stake in the same way, Israel's certainly was. Like Hitler, Nasser was out for theatrical effects. 'He wanted', said Gaitskell, 'to make a big impression. Quiet negotiation, discussion round a table . . . would not produce this effect.' And this was why both Tory and Labour leaders felt that he could not be trusted. He was not a gentleman – unlike General Neguib, for whom Eden cherished fond memories. He had 'torn up' agreements concluded with the Company only a few weeks before. He had acted, according to Gaitskell, 'suddenly, without negotiation, without discussion, by force'. 'One can have no confidence – no confidence', Eden repeated the word for emphasis, 'in the behaviour of a man who does that.'

The consequences for the international order of the new nationalisms exemplified by Nasser's Egypt were thus well to the forefront of the early Parliamentary debates on Suez. Two statements illustrate the point. First, Herbert Morrison [Labour]:

> I say . . . that we can have a situation in which the foe of genuine internationalism can be the modern nationalist, hysterical state,

determined to act on its own irrespective of the interests of the rest of the world.[4]

Second, Sir Robert Boothby (Conservative):

I believe that the rabid nationalism which is now developing is reactionary and atavistic – a revolt against the demands of the modern world and of life itself . . . [Nasser's language] is the language of Hitler and the rule of the jungle; and if we were to allow him to get away with it, it would be a most damaging blow to the whole conception of international law . . .[5]

Few Labour, and no Conservative, MPs dissented from these remarks. An exception was Anthony Wedgwood Benn who, pointing out that the Company concession would in any case revert to Egypt in 1968, asked: 'Can it possibly be an act of aggression to anticipate something that would be lawful in twelve years time?' – which showed at any rate that Wedgwood Benn had a strange idea of law. On the whole, though, Epstein is perfectly right in his summary that 'there was no substantial dissent from the Prime Minister's statement . . . that Britain could not accept an arrangement leaving the canal in the unfettered control of a single power'.[6]

It could be argued that this arrangement had in fact been accepted by the British Government in 1954 when it agreed to withdraw its troops from the Canal base. At that time Antony Head, later the Minister in charge of the military preparations against Colonel Nasser, had said: 'I do not see the slightest reason why the Egyptian Government should close the Suez Canal, because it is as much of a life-line to them as to anyone else.'[7] Jo Grimond was more sceptical: 'Have the Government any proposals for putting the Canal under international control or putting in an international force to protect it, if we are not there ourselves?', he asked.[8] In Eden's defence it could be said that at that time Neguib, a moderate, was still in power; the regime, according to Eden, 'showed no signs as yet of those wider ambitions which Colonel Nasser was later to proclaim and pursue'.[9] Besides, the Company's presence seemed to offer practical guarantees of effective maintenance, service and development of the Canal; it was a buffer between Nasser and physical control of the Canal, which is why Eden was later to claim that it was an integral part of the 1888 system guaranteeing free navigation.

The common aim of the British Government and Opposition was thus to restore some kind of international control of the Canal; but differences soon emerged as to the means. It has sometimes been claimed that the Labour Party retreated from the strong stand taken in Gaitskell's speech of 2 August 1956. Technically this is not so. Such inconsistencies as were to emerge in the Labour position were already present in that speech. What Gaitskell said may be paraphrased as follows: Nasser's action was abhorrent to civilized people; it reminded him of the style and methods of Hitler and Mussolini; it was not only a challenge to the West's position in the Middle East which had to be taken up, but also vitally threatened the future of Israel, and of civilized international behaviour. But the British Government in its reaction to that challenge must not go beyond the measures laid down in the United Nations Charter. These limited the use of force to self-defence or to collective military measures approved by the United Nations. It followed that Britain would be justified in using force if the United Nations sanctioned it; but 'we must not . . . allow ourselves to get into a position where we might be denounced in the Security Council as aggressors, or where the majority of the Assembly were against us'. Earlier he had laid it down as a principle of British foreign policy to avoid 'any international action . . . contrary to the public opinion of the world'.[10] Eden agreed with Gaitskell's assessment of Nasser's action, but he argued that it followed from that assessment that Britain should as a last resort be prepared to use force to impose international control even if United Nations authorization was withheld.

These differences became clearer in the debate of 12–13 September. By this point the Government had committed a major tactical error. The sequence of events as originally evisaged by Eden seems quite clear and straightforward. First there was to be the 22-Power Conference; if that failed to find a satisfactory solution there was to be an appeal to the Security Council; if that failed, the military expedition was to sail. The recall of Parliament in September was to coincide with the second stage of this strategy, the appeal to the United Nations. This was the 'clean line' that would have made it difficult for the Labour Party to divide the House.

This strategy was sabotaged by Dulles. He saw that the Anglo-French proposals would be vetoed by Russia in the Security Council, giving the British and French Governments an excuse to use force. He was determined to keep the parties talking, come what may, till after the

320

United States presidential election. He therefore introduced the red herring of the Suez Canal Users' Association, 'the poisoned apple' as Finer puts it, or in Paul Johnson's words 'The Dulles Double-Cross'. Briefly, this plan envisaged a consortium of users who would sail their ships in convoy through the Canal, using their own pilots and paying dues to a central office and not to Nasser. If Nasser tried to stop the users' ships, Dulles argued persuasively to Eden, then that would be a breach of the 1888 convention justifying stronger measures. Eden, in an effort to keep the Americans on his side, acquiesced reluctantly in this extraordinary proposal. But the Dulles plan made sense only if it was backed by sanctions. As Dulles gradually made clear, he intended none: he could not force American ships to pay dues to the Association rather than to Nasser; and if Nasser stopped the ships, well, then they would have to sail round the Cape. To the British Labour Opposition the plan seemed both provocative and ineffective. They urged Eden to abandon it and go straight to the United Nations. When he refused, they voted against him.

Eden's capitulation to Dulles enabled the Opposition to claim that it was in favour of going to the United Nations while Eden was not. It obscured the real point at issue which was what would happen at and after such an appeal? What should be done if the Russian veto were applied, or if, as was very likely, Britain and France failed to secure the support of the General Assembly, or even if, having secured a favourable resolution, Nasser ignored it? These questions the Opposition resolutely refused to face.

Since the appeal to the United Nations remained a purely hypothetical proposition on 12 September 1956, the Labour Opposition was able to claim that Nasser was an honourable man; that he would, in the last resort, be prepared to respect the rule of law, provided only that sufficient 'moral' pressure was brought to bear on him. Indeed, they had to take this line, for they knew perfectly well that the UN would not sanction the use of force against him. The Labour Party was in a painful dilemma. For if Nasser were like Hitler, then only the threat of force would stop him; yet the Labour Party was renouncing the threat of force. This renunciation entailed a revision of Nasser's psychology. He was no longer a Hitler; his admitted refusal hitherto to negotiate had to be explained in other ways.

Thus the Opposition devoted the debate of 12–13 September to the task of rescuing Nasser from Gaitskell's unfortunate comparison of

2 August. His intransigence was now blamed on Allied provocation. Robens argued that he had refused to compromise because he felt 'insulted'; Eden's words were 'provocative'.[11] Kenneth Younger went further. 'The trouble was that [the 18-Power Plan's] chances of acceptance were largely ruined by its being put in the context of the Anglo-French threats.' He doubted whether even 'the Soviet Union would have opposed us if we had gone to the Security Council . . .'[12] Crossman declared that if only 'the Government had started negotiating straight away, a settlement could have been reached which would have been regarded as perfectly honourable and would not have looked like a triumph for Nasser'. Yet a moment later he declared that any settlement would have to end Egypt's right to blockade Israel. How easily, one wonders, would a settlement have been reached with that stipulation?[13]

Menzies formed a different estimate of Nasser's psychology, more in keeping with Gaitskell's original assessment. Eisenhower's renunciation of the use of force, Menzies wrote, fortified Nasser in his belief that all he had to do was to 'sit tight, reject the Dulles proposals, reject any watered-down proposals . . . and continue the process until he had "written his own ticket". Meanwhile his practical grasp of the Canal would be consolidated, and the *fait* would be completely *accompli*.' Menzies' conclusion was: 'I cannot regard it as an element in statesmanship to relieve one's opponent of anxiety.'[14]

One or two Labour speakers did, it is true, deal with the possibility of frustration at the UN, but in an inconclusive way. Robens argued that 'a breach of a United Nations resolution would be a challenge to world authority, and no Government could successfuly do that' – adding, it seems as an afterthought, perhaps remembering Israel, 'if the United Nations is to survive'.[15] Arthur Henderson, the son of Labour's 1929 Foreign Secretary, said that the correct procedure was to go to the Security Council, and if the Russians vetoed the Western proposals there, to activate the Uniting for Peace Resolution; this would give Britain the 'moral authority to enforce the recommendation'. Suppose the UN refused to recommend anything? 'That would be a clear indication', Henderson went on, 'that we cannot look to the Charter as the instrument for safeguarding the security of the various nations of the world.'[16] In that case, would Britain be justified in using force on its own? Henderson did not say. Instead the Labour Party as a whole contented itself with the restatement of the principle that no action must be taken contrary to the United Nations Charter. Force should only be used 'within the Charter'.[17] Given the composition of the UN, the Labour stand, in Epstein's words, amounted to 'the advocacy of inaction'.[18]

The United States position was equally ambivalent. In view of the fact that none of its own vital interests were involved, it could afford to take the high moral line; at the same time Dulles and Eisenhower did give Eden grounds for belief that in the event of an Anglo-French recourse to force, the United States would preserve a benevolent neutrality. In public, Eisenhower contented himself with statements whose moral flavour must have seemed as hypocritical as their meaning was obscure – for example, the following on 11 September:

> Now, if they are guaranteed the free use, then it – and it says – and then provides methods by which co-operation with Egypt may be achieved, I think that they are justified probably in taking steps and conferring with President Nasser looking forward to the free use of the Canal. But I don't – that doesn't mean that they are justified at that moment in using force. I don't think that – I think this: We established the United Nations to abolish aggression, and I am not going to be a party to aggression if it is humanly possible or likely to lead – to avoid or I can detect it before it occurs.[19]

The Anglo-French reaction to Nasser seemed to justify all Dulles's suspicions of colonialism and imperialism. Like all the actors in the Suez affair, he too was captive to a historical dream – that of America's mission to cleanse the world of the evils of colonialism, whether Soviet or British. In 1938 he had argued that the British and the French, with the typical arrogance of the 'haves', were trying to deprive such impoverished 'have-nots' as Germany and Italy of their rightful place in the sun. His arguments had not changed much since the 1930s. Nor for that matter had the Labour Party's. They too were repeating in the new situation lines learned long ago. They wanted to stop Nasser, like Hitler, through collective security; they were even prepared to suggest force, so long as the actual question of using force never arose. And yet in the 1930s there was more excuse for trusting in collective security than in 1956. For then the League of Nations was dominated by big powers who at least had an interest in stopping Hitler; in 1956 it was dominated by the smaller powers willing to condone or support Nasser.

Of course, there was a new factor in the situation: the threat of a nuclear holocaust. 'The advent of the hydrogen bomb', declared Aneurin Bevan, 'has stalemated power among the great Powers. The use of the threat of war . . . is no longer available to statesmen . . . without running the risk of universal destruction.'[20] This is a perfectly tenable view, but it was not the reason given by the Labour Party for its opposition to unilateral action. For in theory it was perfectly prepared to use force – if the UN agreed. And the threat of nuclear destruction might have applied equally to the collective as well as to the individual use of force. For example, would a UN intervention to stop Russia in Hungary or Czechoslovakia have been safe from nuclear retaliation?

Logically, Bevan's argument implied complete pacifism. It gave a *carte blanche* to the blackmailer anywhere in the world. He would have been on much firmer ground had he argued that in this case there was no British interest at stake sufficiently vital to run the risk of nuclear war. But, as I have indicated earlier, the argument was never primarily conducted in terms of interests. Had it been so, a more realistic debate could have developed round this very question, giving both sides an opportunity to consider in concrete terms what Nasser's action actually involved. What *actual* difference would it make to Britain's position? Would it deprive her of oil supplies? Could alternative supplies or routes be developed? These questions were hardly considered. In the evolution of British world attitudes they had become secondary to the moral aim of preserving civilized standards wherever Britain had once exercised responsibility.

The real dilemma of the Labour Party was different. It had inherited the liberal ideal of orderly international behaviour, which it interpreted largely in terms of universalizing British values. In other words, it willed the *end* of bringing back the Suez Canal to international control. But it could not bring itself to accept the means. It had a deeply ingrained hostility to the use of force, partly pacifist, partly 'progressive'. It had a deep mistrust of the motives of a Conservative Government. For, as in the 1930s when it was a question of supplying the National Government with the armaments to oppose Hitler, the Labour Party half suspected that the 'civilized' designs of the Conservative leaders were a cover for more sinister intentions. Only a Labour Government, in other words, could be entrusted with the use of force. For a Labour Opposition, therefore, the appeal to the UN, like the earlier reliance on the League, provided an ideal escape from the world of painful choices. It enabled a fine flourish of moral indignation at the expense of Eden and Nasser – and of reality.

If Labour's position was in the end impervious to facts, so, for different reasons, was Eden's. Let us concede that Eden had a reasonable grievance against Nasser. That alone would not be sufficient to justify the use of force. The aim of war is to secure a change for the better. If the result of war is going to mean a change for the worse, either because one will not be able to win it, or because the price may be too high, there can be no justification in starting it, however strong one's moral position. As John Vincent put it: 'Had the Final Solution been German policy in 1939, its wickedness would have afforded no reason for war, unless we had reason to suppose that war would enable us favourably to change matters.'[21] This kind of consideration is clearly a decisive constraint on the pursuit of a 'moral' foreign policy. Many people in 1956 were horrified at Russian action in Hungary. But they judged, rightly or wrongly, that the price of intervention was too high. Eden can be criticized, then, for threatening and making war on two grounds: (1) that Britain lacked, even in conjunction with France, the military capability of mounting an action within the time-span necessary to secure immunity from wider adverse reactions; and (2) that even if the action had been militarily successful, there was no real possibility of gaining the political fruits of victory.

The military aspect of the Suez crisis has to be set in the context of the British decision of 1954 to withdraw from the Canal base; indeed Nasser nationalized the Canal about a month after the last British troops left. It is worth recalling the House of Commons debate in 1954. The chief strategic argument advanced by the Government was that the base had become untenable in the nuclear age; the chief political argument, that it was impossible to maintain a military base in a hostile environment. At that time everyone was obsessed by the Russian menace. This was the age of 'massive retaliation'. Dulles's strategy, to which the British Government subscribed, envisaged placing the whole of the non-Communist world under a gigantic nuclear umbrella. This had two basic weaknesses. It ignored the problem of what to do in circumstances when neither side would be prepared to risk nuclear war; and secondly, the Russian obsession blinded military planners to the possibility of disturbances which in themselves had little or nothing to do with the global Cold War situation. Perceptive critics of the Eden policy made this point in the 1954 debate; for example, Grimond said: 'surely what we are faced with very often is not a world war or a hydrogen bomb war, but local aggression . . . such as we may see in the Middle East. It is against that sort of attack that we have to provide defences, just as much as for a full-scale world war with hydrogen bombs.'[22] At the time, these opinions were ignored.

The main Labour charge in 1954 was that the withdrawal had left a vacuum in the Middle East, potentially dangerous for Israel. The Government's reply took two forms. It pointed out that the base could be reactivated under certain conditions; and secondly, it claimed as a benefit of its policy a great gain in strategic mobility. Eden, replying to Attlee, said: 'There is no vacuum because as a result of these arrangements we shall be able to redeploy our forces and make them mobile to an extent which they have not been hitherto.' This policy implied building up a highly mobile strategic reserve, capable of being moved rapidly to centres of disturbance – a policy which would have permitted a rapid military reaction to Nasser's moves in 1956. But no such preparations were made before 1956.

To preserve some kind of effective presence in the Middle East, a number of Labour and Conservative speakers, including Crossman and Wigg, made a surprising suggestion: to set up a British base, with Israeli agreement, at Haifa.[23] This would serve the dual purpose of enabling British troops to get back rapidly into the Canal Zone should the need arise, and perhaps, more importantly, of deterring or dissuading Nasser from doing anything rash, such as moving against Israel or taking over the Canal. This suggestion was not followed up. The doctrine of 'massive retaliation' was designed to deter the Soviet Union; but there was nothing in existence that could possibly deter Nasser.

Eden's inquiries at the end of July 1956 revealed that there was no chance of an immediate military riposte. There was no contingency plan for the reoccupation of the Canal Zone: parachutists had had no recent training; in any case there were no aircraft available to transport them. It was an axiom of British military planning that paratroops had to be supported within twenty-four hours. Yet the nearest feasible base, Cyprus, had no suitable harbours for naval ships; the naval expedition would have to sail from Malta, a thousand miles and six days' sailing time away. The shipping required had to be gathered together from all parts of the world; landing craft had to be got out of mothballs where they had lain since the Normandy landings of 1944. The French had similar difficulties. The fact was that the conventional military strategy of both powers was NATO-oriented; neither Britain nor France possessed an 'intervention' force, a commando group with its own aviation, shipping, amphibious vehicles, tanks and artillery held in constant readiness for swift independent action. Moreover, even within NATO there was an absence of the integration that could have facilitated a joint operation. The British and French used a different type of rifle, different shell calibres, different bolt threads and engines for vehicles, different petrol, oils and lubricants, different signals and battle orders, and of course spoke different languages. 'The British soldiers', the Brombergers observe, 'drink tea which makes the French soldiers throw up. French soldiers eat sardines in oil, which revolt the Tommies.'

Yet even when most of these difficulties had been overcome and the expedition stood ready to move by early September, the fundamental difficulty had not been resolved: namely, how to get the force into the Canal Zone quickly enough to forestall decisive political pressures at home and abroad. The military preparations, it seems, took no account of the international climate in which they would have to be conducted. The demands of each service escalated as each sought maximum security against real or imagined dangers. The expedition's scale, as one commentator remarks, 'was determined by prognosis of the very worst'. The result was that in the end a colossal armada was assembled: 80,000 troops, 150 warships, including 7 aircraft-carriers and 40 submarines; hundreds of landing craft, 80 merchant ships carrying stores; 20,000 vehicles. The French were more realistic. They wanted the emphasis placed on paratroop landings. The British remembered Arnhem and refused to contemplate using paratroops except as an advance guard of a much larger force. In vain, the French protested that it was the Suez Canal, not the Kiel Canal; that they were to fight Egyptians and not Germans. The British replied that as they had largely trained the Egyptian Army, it must be good.

In the event, the military and political difficulties were compounded by a double error. The first was the Anglo-French decision to use the Israeli attack as a pretext for their own intervention; the second was Eden's moral scruples about taking advantage of the foreknowledge he had of the Israeli attack to send the fleet from Malta in advance of the delivery of the ultimatum on 30 October. The less important consequence of the first mistake was to hold back the Anglo-French expedition for at least a fortnight while plans were co-ordinated with the Israelis. The more important consequence was to rob the Anglo-French intervention of any plausible connection with the initial action of Nasser to which it was intended as a riposte. Eden was forced to renounce the initial justification of force for the much weaker one of 'separating the combatants' – on terms manifestly to Egypt's disadvantage – a shift which largely destroyed Britain's moral position. The consequence of the second error was to delay the military operation for almost a week when every minute was vital to its success. As Elizabeth Monroe rightly observes, 'Deeds that stood a chance of taking the world's breath away if done quickly stood none by Day Six.' By the time the Anglo-French expedition was finally ready to go into action, Eden was in the process of being forced into a political capitulation.

Could he have resisted? Churchill is supposed to have said: 'I am not sure I should have dared to start, but I am sure I should not have dared to stop.' Dulles, after doing his best to sabotage the expedition, remarked to the British delegate at the UN: 'Why on earth didn't you go through with it?' Hugh Thomas has summed up as follows: 'Probably there would have been neither world war nor devaluation if we had continued for [twenty-four hours], and, having got so far, the morale of the Army and the Entente Cordiale, that incomparable friendship, would have been better served by going on at Suez. But the risk was imponderable . . .'[24] In the end it was the logic of the very internationalism for which Eden had gone to war that ruined him: he could not act in defiance of world opinion.

The cumbersome military preparations were not entirely the fault of the military planners. They were not given any clear indication of the political objective that force was meant to accomplish. The Government's instructions to them were of the vaguest kind: 'to mount joint operations against Egypt to restore the Suez Canal to international control'. What exactly did this involve? Would Egypt have to be reoccupied or not? Would a new Government be found for Cairo? These problems were never cleared up. The Army planners, having to divine government intentions, envisaged landings in Alexandria and Cairo leading to a temporary military occupation of Egypt; these were later altered to landings in the Canal Zone itself. The Government probably hoped it would not come to that; they seemed to assume that, with the appearance of Anglo-French forces in Egypt, Nasser would flee the country and the people would rally to the 'idol of the masses' General Neguib, or even more improbably to the discredited Nahas Pasha, the old Wafd leader. Some curiously inept leaflets were dropped over Egypt during the phase of 'psychological bombing' early in November to promote these ends. With the assumption of a friendly Government and a docile population, Eden did not have to think far beyond the military landings. But one of the chief reasons for the evacuation in 1954 was the belief that a base could not be maintained in a hostile country. And it seems clear that the British Government had given very little thought about what to do if the Egyptian people refused to accept their 'temporary occupation', but launched a guerrilla and sabotage campaign of the type common in other countries, and even then in progress in Cyprus. How, in particular, could the Canal be kept open in such circumstances? And how could there be any guarantee that oil from the other Arab countries would be kept flowing?

These were gigantic risks, and there is no evidence that they were weighed properly in considering the use of force. It may be that they would have turned out well. One cannot agree with Bevan's comment that 'the heroism of the civilian, as displayed in Hungary, makes nonsense of the power of tanks'.[25] In fact the power of tanks made nonsense of the heroism of the civilian. But Soviet Russia, in the maintenance of its interests in Hungary, was prepared to use force to a degree that would be considered unacceptable for a democratic and liberal power like England. By using force at Suez without having a realistic and realizable political objective, the Eden Government violated the fundamental maxim of war.

In the Suez débâcle, both Eden and Gaitskell were prisoners of an illusion – the illusion of Britain's special mission to preserve peace, law and stability in the world. It arose in the imperial era, when, with superb effrontery, the British tried to remake millions of Asians and Africans – not to mention Europeans – in their own image; tried to enforce on them, or persuade them into, a code of behaviour which, while in keeping with Britain's own interests, could be generalized as a solvent for the world's problems. The Labour Party inherited the idea, divested it of its imperialist trimmings, infused it with a moral fervour, and tried to apply it through such post-imperialist institutions as the League of Nations, the UN and the Commonwealth of Nations. It was the white man's burden all over again.

The Suez crisis exposed its hollowness. Britain had neither the power nor the will to make it work. For the old international order depended on the existence of powerful policemen, confident in their right to impose the law in the areas under their control, and able to do so. Eden dubbed the Suez intervention a 'police operation'. Yet the post-imperial British policeman not only lacked credibility, in view of the existence of more powerful policemen round him, hostile to his pretensions, but perhaps, more importantly, lacked the old faith in his mission. He no longer believed that he had right overwhelmingly on his side. He had been educated for years into the belief that imperialism, the fact of power that made possible all his illusions, was dirty, exploitative and ignoble. He could no longer believe that he was acting from the loftiest, disinterested motives. (Wasn't Suez really about preserving the oil companies, the Baghdad Pact, the client states, the whole system of influence, patronage and corruption which served Britain's Middle Eastern interests?)

The British spokesmen appealed to world opinion and received the biggest shock of all. The United States refused co-operate; the UN sided with the law-breaker, as did the Asian and African members of the Commonwealth; the white dominions extended lukewarm support; most of Europe remained indifferent; while France came in from much less worthy motives, motives that had to be smothered by a pillow of cloudy international rhetoric. With dawning horror, the British realized that they were totally out of touch with the sentiment and feelings of the rest of the world.

If anything the Labour Party's illusion ran deeper. The Tories' concept of their post-imperial responsibilities rested upon the illusion of power. Once that illusion was shattered, little remained of that concept; the way was opened to joining Europe. But the Labour Party's illusion rested on something that no mere harsh facts could dispose of. The old imperial idea had been transposed into a dream of world brotherhood. It rested on the repudiation of power, the repudiation, in fact, of everything that goes up to make the real world. It was an imperialism with all the pain, the injustice, the cruelty and the oppression conjured out of existence by magic. It was the imperialism of the intelligentsia, both an atonement for past sins and a guarantee of status without tears.

Yet it must not be this illusion that goes down in history as the lesson of Suez. For the fact was that the United Nations failed to redress the wrong which most British people felt had been perpetrated by Colonel Nasser; what is more, it never stood a real chance of doing so. In the desperation of failure, the Eden Government claimed that at least it had given teeth to the UN. But in reality the UN proved quite incapable of preserving peace in the Middle East. For the resolution setting up the

330

peace-keeping force accepted the original British contention that it was impossible to maintain a military position in a hostile country, and thus stipulated that it remain in Egypt only as long as Egypt wanted it to. In 1967 Egypt asked it to leave – and it did.

In the wake of Britain's final withdrawal from the role of a world power, and the increasing difficulties of the American position in Vietnam – difficulties which make it extremely unlikely that the United States will take on a similar commitment again – the collapse of a Western-sustained international order threatens to become complete. The world East of Suez at any rate is likely to undergo drastic and probably violent changes, over which the Western powers and the United Nations will have very little influence. These changes will not be understood with a simple model of the replacement of Western-style internationalism by Communist-style internationalism; that would be replacing one kind of illusion by another. The Communist bloc, it seems, is subject to very much the same fissiparous and centrifugal tendencies as the non-Communist bloc. The convulsions in Eastern Europe, and the Sino-Soviet conflict, point to the break-up of the Communist monolith; 'working-class' imperialism has had an even shorter history than 'capitalist' imperialism.

With the decay of Utopian dreams of internationalism, whether of the Western or Marxist variety, a new politics is coming to the fore – a politics of race and regionalism. We may expect an increasing tendency to regional power blocs based on a common culture, or common economic interests, or a common enemy, or a combination of all three; each pledged to defend its integrity against outside interference. Any such concentrations of regional power will probably be accompanied by the creation of nuclear armaments, common market trading patterns, and common institutions. The old internationalists will not welcome any of these developments; but they offer perhaps the best hope of stability in a world in which empire is obsolete, nationalism destructive, and internationalism further away then ever.

NOTES

1   For example Hugh Thomas, *The Suez Affair* (1967).
2   A. Moncrieff [ed.], *Suez Ten Years After* (1967), pp. 130, 139.
3   Earl of Avon, *The Eden Memoirs: Full Circle* (1960), p. 320.
4   *Hansard*, vol. 557, col. 1660.

5   Ibid., vol. 558, cols. 143–4.
6   L. Epstein, *British Politics in the Suez Crisis* (1964), p. 64.
7   *Hansard*, vol. 531, col. 760.
8   Ibid., col. 785.
9   Avon, *Full Circle*, p. 260.
10 *Hansard*, vol. 557, cols. 1616–17.
11 Ibid., vol. 558, col. 176.
12 Ibid., cols. 334–5.
13 Ibid., cols. 91, 93–4.
14 R. G. Menzies, *Afternoon Light* (1967), pp. 165–6.
15 *Hansard*, vol. 558, col. 181.
16 Ibid., cols. 40 f.
17 Ibid., col. 137.
18 Epstein, *British Politics in the Suez Crisis*, p. 67.
19 Department of State, *The Suez Canal Problem* (1957), 26 July–22 September 1956, p. 333.
20 *Hansard*, vol. 558, cols. 1708–9.
21 *Cambridge Review*, 1 May 1965.
22 *Hansard*, vol. 531, col. 785.
23 Ibid., cols. 760, 770, 791.
24 Thomas, *The Suez Affair*, p. 164.
25 Paul Johnson, *The Suez War* (1957), pp. xi–xii.

A CHRONOLOGY OF LEADING DATES

1956

26 July	Nasser nationalizes the Suez Canal Company.
16–23 Aug.	The 22-Power Conference in London proposes an International Board to run the Canal.
9 Sept.	Nasser rejects the proposal.
12 Sept.	Eden announces in Parliament the plan for a Canal-Users' Association.
23 Sept.	Britain and France appeal to the Security Council.
16–28 Oct.	Anglo-French-Israeli talks.
30 Oct.	Anglo-French ultimatum following Israeli invasion.
5 Nov.	Anglo-French paratroops land at Port Said.
6 Nov.	Seaborne invasion followed by cease-fire at midnight.
7 Nov.	General Assembly agrees to set up UN Police Force.
22 Dec.	Last British forces leave Suez.

CHAPTER FORTY-NINE

Anthony Eden

Robert Rhodes James, *Anthony Eden*
[Weidenfeld, 1985]

ALTHOUGH Anthony Eden died only in 1977, his world had already disappeared. He was born in 1897 at the zenith of an empire which spanned a quarter of the globe; when he died Britain was an impoverished and still-declining offshore island of Europe. This astonishing unravelling mostly took place in twenty years, from 1936 to 1956, when Eden was a dominating figure in British politics – as Foreign Secretary and, at the end, as Prime Minister. The country he led to defeat and humiliation at Suez was already broken as a world power. Eden was never much interested in domestic politics, but the liberal, even left-wing, Conservatism he espoused, was also in full retreat by the time he died.

There is obviously material here for a massive indictment, and it was made by David Carlton in his extremely acute biography of Eden, published in 1981, now reprinted as a paperback. Robert Rhodes James in his new 'authorized' life of Eden finds Carlton's hostility to Eden 'mystifying'. But there is no mystery about it. Carlton's Eden is not bad, but inadequate. His métier was foreign policy. But he lacked the ruthlessness to defend Britain's inheritance, or the imagination to rebuild it in Europe once it was gone. Above all, his policies resulted in a vast expansion of Soviet power. The Suez fiasco was the culmination of a career of unclarity, masked by a command of diplomatic detail. Carlton's thesis was foreshadowed by Winston Churchill when he remarked of his protégé: 'Anthony was totally incapable of differentiating great points from small points.'

Rhodes James does not directly confront this verdict. Rather, he switches the defence to a more human, and conventional, plane. His Anthony Eden is above all a *nice* man, dogged by tragedy, and finally ruined by ill-health. 'He brought honour and dignity, kindness and loyalty to the often grubby trade of politics'. With great artistry Rhodes James fashions a life of sunlight and shadows, of 'a man of sorrows, and acquainted with grief', a portrait which, when combined with robustly conventional judgments about Eden's political stands, undermines our critical faculties. It starts at the Eden home, Windlestone, Co. Durham, a classical mansion set in acres of beautiful parks and lakes. But from the beginning there were serpents in the garden, in the form of an explosively bad-tempered father, and a beautiful but alarmingly spend-thrift and amoral mother. Eden inherited his mother's beauty and his father's irritability, as well as his love of pictures. He had a fine war record and a mind good enough to get a first class honours degree at Oxford in Oriental Languages. But his attractive presence, exquisite manners, and affectionate nature were never backed up by a comparable self-confidence. His political career was built on the unstable foundations of a disintegrating marriage, neurotic work-habits, financial troubles, nervousness, and almost continual ill-health. (The medical incompetence to which he was subjected by English doctors is horrendous, culminating in an operation on his gall bladder in 1953, in which the surgeon's knife 'slipped' and accidentally severed his bile duct.) On top of all this, he lost an adored brother in the First World War, and his favourite son in the second.

So we have been emotionally well prepared for the climax of Rhodes James's story: an outstandingly dramatic and harrowing account of the Suez crisis, for which alone this book must be read and will endure. With the help of unusually full and vivid cabinet minutes, which the biographer received 'special permission' to reproduce for the first time in advance of their release next year under the Thirty Years Rule, Rhodes James has added new and exciting details to a familiar story. Historians will debate his judgments. Did Dulles really double-cross Eden by promising and then withdrawing American support? Did Gaitskell let him down after leading him to expect Labour's backing for military measures? Did the chiefs of staff bungle the military planning? Was Eden betrayed in his own cabinet by Macmillan and Butler?

However, we must not be led by the biographer's art into imagining that Suez was anything but a political disaster, for which Eden was mainly responsible. He was not up to the challenge. Rhodes James's skill in enlisting our feelings on behalf of a Prime Minister subject to intolerable pressures, piling mistake on mistake, and finally breaking under the strain, should not delude us into thinking that 'his policy over Suez deserved a more sympathetic understanding than it has usually received'. It did not, and does not. Everything about it was full of error and muddle, from the initial political judgment that Colonel Nasser was an 'evil brigand' who must be destroyed at all costs, down to the amazing decision to call off the military operation before the Canal had been seized.

This brings us back to David Carlton, whose theme is the mediocre quality of Eden's understanding and statesmanship throughout his career. Eden's problem was not that he was denied luck at crucial moments, as Rhodes James believes; but that for most of his life he had too much political good luck for his own good. His greatest stroke of luck was in escaping the discredit of Neville Chamberlain's appeasement policy by resigning as Foreign Secretary in February 1938. True enough, he did resign. But it was over a trivial issue (about the timing of a British approach to Mussolini) and without Eden offering any real alternative to appeasement. (He described his own policy as one of 'unheroic cunctation'.) But his youth, his looks and the timing of his departure made him a symbol of resistance to the dictators; a reputation sealed once Churchill – who loved Eden but was always troubled about his competence – anointed him as his successor. Even before Suez Eden's premiership had started to look ominously transient.

In Anthony Eden, Robert Rhodes James has found a subject perfectly suited to his talents, sympathies and biographical style. He is a natural courtier, which means he is perfectly happy with the implied contract usual in 'official' bigoraphies, by which the widow permits access to private papers in return for biographical discretion and a requisite, though not embarrassing, degree of adulation. This biography is discreet and Rhodes James loses few opportunities of drawing attention to the fact that he knows all, but tells only as much as he thinks 'appropriate'. The name of the 'lovely lady' with whom Eden fell in love (in the 1930s) is withheld; as is that of the surgeon whose knife slipped. While Rhodes James's language is generally vigorous, it can become courtly, not to say sickly, as when recording the Queen's 'gracious' permission to allow him to reproduce the letter she wrote Eden when he resigned.

As a former clerk of the House of Commons, and now Conservative MP for Cambridge, Rhodes James has a strong hold on political personality, the atmosphere of the House of Commons, and the interplay of personality and events so necessary to understand Eden. He captures perfectly the elements of mingled idealism and self-seeking, vanity and self-disgust, attachment and betrayal, which go to make up the political game. Eden's weakness was that people liked him too much and respected him too little which made him difficult to strike, but easy to wound.

Finally and most importantly, Rhodes James admires Eden's political position. A Tory wet himself, he endorses his subject's liberal Conservatism derived from Baldwin, and sympathizes with his high-minded liberal imperialism. Like all political biographers he is in the business of myth-making. Had Mrs Thatcher not been in power would he, one wonders, have written of Neville Chamberlain: 'Thus, one of the most third-rate of modern British governments was deliberately devoid of talent, intellect and independence, while on the back benches men of far greater ability viewed it, and its autocratic leader with increasing distaste which in many cases became personal detestation of the Prime Minister . . .'? The whole analysis of Britain's decline and the causes which brought it about – the background to Carlton's Eden – gives way in Rhodes James's story to a swelling duet between subject and biographer of commonplace opinions and conventional reflections which will delight the middlebrow and confirm them in their judgment that all is for the best, or would be if we had decent and honourable chaps like Anthony Eden running the show today. It is a powerful and persuasive essay in this genre; but the lesson is mislearnt.

CHAPTER FIFTY

Harold Macmillan

Alastair Horne, *Macmillan 1957–1986*, vol. 2 of the Official Biography
[Macmillan, 1989]

ALASTAIR HORNE has done Harold Macmillan proud. Last year's first volume of his official biography was excellent; the second is magnificent. Macmillan is now a star; and the biography has acquired star quality. Moreover, Macmillan is a star on the world stage. This was the last time that a British Prime Minister could aspire to reshape the affairs of the planet. Through biography we relive the great international events of the period – the death throes of empire in Africa, the hazardous passage to the beginnings of *détente*, the birth of the EC and the trauma of Britain's exclusion from it.

Horne's strengths lie in his vivid portrayal of personality, his sense of drama, above all his ability to shape narrative. He has wisely based himself on the more intimate side of the official record: on Macmillan's caustic, irreverent, often despairing diary, written up late at night in a shaky, war-wounded, hand; on his personal papers, including correspondence with world leaders; on the remarkable table-talk of his extreme old age. Resourceful interviewing and judicious use of American archives provide a useful counterpoint to Macmillan's own judgments. The result is political biography at its best. The interplay of personality, the atmospherics of summitry, the influence of personality on events are all superbly captured. But what Horne also makes clear is that Macmillan's statesmanship was projected from a rapidly crumbling British power base. This is what gives his story its special poignancy. The gap between ambitions and means, appearance and reality, had become massive. And this in turn prompts one to ask: How well did Macmillan play the hand which history had dealt him? Was there any other way to play it?

The case for Macmillan is that he bridged the gap by style: 'le style, c'est l'homme'. On this view, style created substance; it was a power resource. Macmillan's was a laid-back Edwardian style, projected with a showmanship suitable for an age of mass politics: a Balfour style built for television, delicately poised between seriousness and frivolity, languour and resolution, elegance and vulgarity, diffidence and disdain, banality and profundity. By the time Macmillan became Prime Minister, the unkempt gentleman-publisher had been cleaned up for power: the disarrayed teeth fixed, the commissar-like spectacles discarded, the Colonel Blimp moustache ruthlessly pruned, the hair stylishly cut, the baggy trousers replaced by spruce Savile Row suits. Yet never was effortless superiority so effortfully achieved. He would often throw up before a major speech, and, as Prime Minister, would take to his bed for days in deep depression (his 'Black Dog'). The shyness, insecurity, fear of intimacy had been masked, not conquered. They were to surface with disastrous results in the last fifteen months of his premiership, in the messy butchery of the 'night of the long knives' in July 1962, and his maladroit handling of the Profumo scandal a year later.

Unflappability defined the Macmillan style. As Horne makes clear, this was partly a reaction against Eden's manic frenzy. It emerged most famously on two occasions. 'These little local difficulties' he murmured as he left for a six-week Commonwealth tour in January 1958, having just lost his entire Treasury team. Even better was his put down of

337

Khrushchev in 1960. 'Perhaps we could have a translation,' he disdain-fully remarked as the Soviet leader banged his shoe on the table while Macmillan was addressing the General Assembly of the United Nations.

Macmillan's increasingly successful evocation of a classic British type not only fitted the mood of post-Suez Britain; it was also well calculated to succeed in Washington. Macmillan made no secret of the priority he attached to restoring the 'special relationship' damaged at Suez. To this aim he brought one of his sweeping historical analogies: Britain would play Greece to America's Rome. Surprisingly, the Ameri-cans played along. Macmillan's great success was his seduction of Kennedy. So cosy did their relationship become that during one working lunch on nuclear arms, the President suddenly said: 'I wonder how it is with you, Harold. If I don't have a woman for three days, I get a terrible headache.' The seduction got results. America accepted Britain as junior partner in the Middle East in 1958; shared its nuclear secrets and provided delivery systems for Britain's hydrogen bomb; allowed Mac-millan to make the running for the Test Ban Treaty of 1962. Macmillan was favoured with a daily transatlantic telephone call right through the Cuban missile crisis of 1962, Horne commenting, 'if it was not actually "consultation", then it was something very close to it'. Success with the Americans, in turn, limited the psychological damage of withdrawal from Africa – who now remembers the Central African Federation, that abortive, but not ignoble, experiment in multiracial government? – which Macmilian signposted in his famous 'wind of change' speech to the South African parliament in 1959.

But Alastair Horne is also alert to the case on the other side. Macmilian complained of having to keep too many balls in the air. The charge against him is that he juggled, or fiddled, too long. The stylist was a fantasist, not a realist; he wrapped decline in illusion. To Enoch Powell, he was always the old 'actor-manager' of the Edwardian melodrama. Macmillan, in turn, had Powell moved down the Cabinet table to where he could not see him: 'I can't bear those mad eyes staring at me a moment longer.' One can understand Powell's point. Macmillan thought too exclusively in terms of historical and literary analogies, which are by their nature imprecise. At the end of his life he accused Mrs Thatcher of 'selling off the family silver'. It was vintage Macmillan – in its vividness and inaccuracy.

The first charge is that he mismanaged Britain's sluggish economy. Like practically everyone of his generation he was a prisoner of the

1930s. He fitfully saw the dangers of inflation – 'we shall refuse to create more money to finance wage awards which are not covered by increased output' he wrote in his diary – but always ended by paying up. The reason is that he feared a slump above everything else. The way to avoid a slump was to keep up demand even at the cost of a small amount of inflation. This is what Keynes had taught him, and reinforcing the dead Keynes was the living Roy Harrod, Macmillan's economic guru. So inflationary expectations were gradually built into the system.

But there is something else. Communism was then regarded as a successful economic system – almost unimaginable today. Macmillan feared that any faltering of capitalism would tilt the ideological balance towards the Soviet Union. This is a possibility which Mrs Thatcher never had to worry about. Even so, it is surprising how little attention Macmillan, or anyone else, paid to the 'supply side' of the economy – the key to higher productivity. Anthony Eden had wanted to reform the trade unions in 1955, but Macmillan shrank from any such thought. The Conservatives must not be identified with either deflation or union bashing. Electorally, he was vindicated in 1959: 'most of our people have never had it so good'. The price would be paid later.

Secondly, it can be argued that Macmillan's mismanagement of Britain's relations with France and Germany led to it being excluded from the Common Market just when it was starting to lose influence in Washington. Dean Acheson spelt it out brutally in 1962: 'Great Britain has lost an empire and has not yet found a role.' It is easy to say in retrospect that that role was in the Common Market. But Horne's masterly analysis of this imbroglio shows that the choice between America and Europe was not clearly seen by anyone at the time, least of all by De Gaulle. Admittedly, the British, including Macmillan, treated the French abominably, ignoring the fact that it was the French they had let down so badly over Suez. Here again Macmillan was prisoner of his war experiences. He understood all De Gaulle's resentments – 'had Hitler danced in London we'd have had no trouble with De Gaulle . . .' he told Horne in 1978 – but forgot that he now had the power of a rapidly reviving France behind him.

But initially De Gaulle himself attached little importance to either the Common Market or the Paris–Bonn axis as a power base. What he wanted was a place for France in a Tripartite directorate of the Free World; specifically, access to American nuclear know-how to develop France's own 'force de frappe'. Neither Kennedy nor Macmillan would play – not least because the scheme implied the exclusion of Germany. But more importantly Macmillan *could* not play. He could not promise De Gaulle what Kennedy would not deliver. De Gaulle only turned to European hegemony once he had been excluded from Atlantic partnership. This implied keeping Britain out of Europe. It is hard to see what Macmillan could have done about it.

Ambiguity was Macmillan's mode for coping with a world which lacked clarity. His artistry kept the Black Dog at bay – his own and his country's. It is unfair to blame him for not thinking thoughts out of his time or not making choices which only became possible later. By placing him so ably in his context Alastair Horne has written a superb biography, and made a major contribution to history.

CHAPTER FIFTY-ONE

The Choice for Europe

[1970]

We warmly desire to improve the co-operation between European countries for the promotion of their common interests and will help to bring it about. We cnnot, however, help to create any political or economic group which could in any way be regarded as hostile to the American or any other continent, or which would weaken our political cooperation with the other members of the British Commonwealth.

ARE these the words of Mr Michael Stewart, Sir Alec Douglas-Home, or any other British Foreign Secretary over the last fifteen years? Not at all. This was the official Foreign Office response to the Briand Plan for the union of Europe put forward in 1930. To recall this and other pronouncements by British spokesmen in almost identical terms down to the present day is to understand something of the strength of the opposition to the European commitment which has existed, and continues to exist, at all levels of British society.

At the grass roots this expresses itself as fear of increased food prices and dislike of foreigners. Among economists of the Anglo-American orientation, there is a profound mistrust of customs union, derived from a commitment to free trade and a belief in a one-world economy. (The anti-European bias of one or two eminent émigré economists, who having escaped from Central Europe are determined never to go back there, reinforces this.) In Foreign Office circles, there still lingers the conviction that Britain's future lies in a wider grouping, or in overlapping groupings – for example, Mr Stewart's recent denial of any incompatibility between European integration with Britain taking part, and a Commonwealth 'growing in cooperation through its own unique nexus of consultative institutions' (*The Times*, 20 February 1970).

What is the common thread running through all these responses? Surely it is the fear of being boxed into a Continental system. Every major power seeks as far as possible to secure a world compatible with its own interests and needs: it universalizes its own aspirations. For modern Britain the 'ideal' world was one in which commercial connections were maximized (free trade), in which there was permanent peace (the corollary of the first) and in which power was divided up into large numbers of units (thus enabling Britain to exert a plitical leverage out of all proportion to its physical resources). This was, if you like, the liberal vision projected onto the world stage. It was unequivocally anti-integrationist, for integration implied not just a cession of sovereignty (which any country which seeks to join another has to face) but for Britain the abandonment of a unique posture: of being both independent *and* universal, of being committed to none, and yet having a hand (or at least a finger) in the shaping of all. What other country has had as much impact on the world in the last two hundred years? What continent exists which has not felt the profound influence of English ideas, language, commerce and institutions? The great European powers have seemed almost parochial by comparison and it is easy to understand the British feeling that to enter a purely European concern would be to betray the past and to cramp the future.

Yet such a choice is dictated, not just by present needs, but by past experience. Despite its far-flung possessions, its world-wide interests, England is, has been, and always will be, primarily a European power, for the simple reason that what happens just across the channel is bound to be more important to it than what happens several thousand miles away. This has been the single, consistent theme of British history, with the possible exception of the brief period of 'splendid isolation' in the middle of the nineteenth century, which also coincided with the triumph of the Cobdenite, universal, ideal. But already by the end of the nineteenth century this thinking was completely obsolete, and at no point has this been more dramatically illustrated than by England's involvement in the two major European wars of this century.

For what happened in 1939? Hitler, in effect, offered England the alternatives of falling back on the undisturbed enjoyment of Empire and embarking on a European war in which defeat was a real possibility: the choice between Commonwealth and Europe. England chose the latter, because in that moment of decision it realized that what might happen in India, Australia or Africa in the end mattered not a jot compared with what might happen in Paris, Rome, Prague, Berlin or Moscow. Churchill's quixotic offer of union with France in 1940 spelt out the same message. At that moment of supreme danger it was France that had to be preserved, not the Empire. Though it was not obvious at the time, England's participation from the start in both World Wars, in effect, foreclosed the imperial option, and signified its commitment to a European destiny.

The lesson was ignored in the immediate post-war era. England emerged from the war bound firmly to America and the Commonwealth. Its 'solution' to the European problem was to dissolve West Europe in a developing complex of Atlanticist institutions like NATO, OEEC, IMF, GATT, etc., which it and America jointly controlled. The British response to the growth of the European movement was therefore schizophrenic. On the one hand, it welcomed it, as a step towards transcending age-old European rivalries. On the other hand, it could not but reflect that its own traditional 'divide and rule' policy had depended precisely on the existence and perpetuation of these rivalries. The concentration of European power, the creation of a European economic bloc, even the minor resurgence of European nationalism (this time French, not German), therefore posed the same sort of challenge in the new context as did the efforts of Napoleon and Hitler earlier on: they threatened, not so much England's security, as its influence in the world. America might prefer to deal direct with a united Europe, bypassing the 'special relationship'; Britain would no longer be able to hold the balance of power in Western Europe; finally, all the Commonwealth preferences in the world would not compensate for exclusion from a growing European market. No wonder, as Macmillan told Washington in 1959, that Britain was 'deeply concerned at the political implications of a new independent power on the Continent'.

Britain's response to these developments might best be described as selective sabotage. The basic purpose of its European policy was to encourage the movement towards European free trade (from which the sluggish British economy would presumably benefit) while seeking to weaken the political impetus which lay at the heart of the European movement. At the same time it firmly resisted the notion that there might be any conflict of interests between Europe and the United States. The stages of this policy may be briefly described. In 1948 Britain tried to stop the discussion of tariffs and quotas on a regional, European basis. In the early 1950s it opposed EDC or the idea of a *European* (as opposed to a NATO) defence community. In 1955 it warned the Messina Powers not to proceed with the project for a Common Market. In 1956 it tried to fob them off with the European Free Trade Area Proposals. Common to all these schemes was an attempt to dilute the impulse to unity, to dissolve the European venture into some much wider and more nebulous grouping which would lack any political meaning: hence the repeated British injunction to Europe that it should be more 'outward-looking'.

It is at least arguable that the 1961 application to join the EEC was a continuation of the same policy by other means: since Britain could no longer stop the thrust to unity from the outside, it would try from the inside. Even such a strong supporter of entry as *The Economist* could not fail to notice that 'the swing of British policy coincided, within a few weeks in the summer of 1960 with General de Gaulle's proposal to the other common market members that they should form a political union . . .' (14 July 1962). By this time, too, America, alarmed at the turn in French foreign policy, was anxious for Britain to get inside to prevent de Gaulle, with the aged Adenauer in tow, from running away with the European movement. If Britain was to be America's Trojan Horse in Europe, Holland was Britain's. The Dutch insistence that de Gaulle's Fouchet Plan for confederation be held up till Britain joined finally killed it in the autumn of 1962 and, together with Macmillan's Nassau Agreement with President Kennedy, led directly to the French veto. This is all now old history. The point is that it is still an open question whether Britain in 1962 was trying to get onto the European bus with the intention of going on a real journey, or merely to drive it off to the nearest scrap-heap.

The significance of the story of Britain's post-war relations with Europe lies in the revelation of how continually and intimately concerned the British were with everything going on in Western Europe. In our opposition to the projects of the Continental powers, we were showing ourselves to be just as European as they were; in their desire to have Britain in, they acknowledged the simple fact that without Britain their efforts would be incomplete. The whole struggle was an entirely European affair. Once the Six had overcome Britain's efforts to thwart the impetus towards integration, then Britain, as a European power, had no real alternative but to align itself with it.

Surely this lesson has now been learnt? An encouraging sign is that British officials are now starting to think and talk much more seriously about a shared European future – as witness the interest in a European monetary union, the switch to a European defence policy, the support for stronger Community institutions. On the other hand, the opinion polls have turned decisively hostile to the idea of Britain's entry, and with the (temporary) recovery of economic well-being has come a regrettable recovery of delusions of grandeur. Having successfully gone it alone for just over twelve months, some people now think that there's no reason why we shouldn't go it alone, equally successfully, for ever.* Mr Wilson's firm commitment has become Mr Shore's 'option'. The White Paper spells out a gloomy tale of additional costs.

It is therefore worth emphasizing and restating at every opportunity the incontrovertible political argument. Britain has always been a European power. What happens on the other side of the Channel has, by the simple facts of geography and history, always mattered more to Britain than what happens elsewhere in the world. This remains as true today as it ever did. Today the European powers are coming together in political union. Britain can no longer stop it. To stand outside would be to cut itself off for the first time from the Continent of which it has always been a part. That would be the real betrayal of England's past, and the real guarantee that it would have no future.

* A reference to the floating of the pound in 1970.

CHAPTER FIFTY-TWO

Britain and Europe

[Written in 1991]

Introduction

BRITAIN is the only member of the European Community (EC) to have lost a Prime Minister to the 'new Europe'. This is because in Britain, uniquely, the geopolitical argument triggered by the end of bipolarity has been intertwined with the explosive issue of national sovereignty. On balance, most EC members have seen the partial disengagement of the United States and the Soviet Union from Europe as reinforcing the need for the political unification of the Twelve. By contrast, the British have favoured 'widening' the Community to include at least some of the newly independent countries of Eastern Europe, which means halting, or slowing down, political 'deepening'. There is a genuine issue here about how best to help the transition from communism and planned economies to democracy and capitalism in Eastern Europe. But Great Britain's predilection in favour of widening reflects a long-standing opposition to political unification. That is why the debate in Britain has been so damaging for the ruling Conservative Party. It would have been equally so for the Labour Party, had it been in power.

What the current British debate shows is that any attempt to increase the Community's political competence triggers in Britain a national sovereignty reflex that, with the partial exception of France, scarcely exists elsewhere in the EC. For historical, ideological and temperamental reasons, Margaret Thatcher embodied this reflex in her last two years in power, when the drive toward European unification accelerated. However, the resulting marginalization of Britain's influence over European developments was equally unacceptable to Britain's political, business, and financial élites. In November 1990, Mrs Thatcher was replaced by the more diplomatic John Major. This change of leadership occurred, however, without any real resolution of the basic tension between the British dislike of Europe's forward political momentum and the need, born of British self-interest, to retain influence over the direction and pace of the journey. Many in Britain have felt rather like the late President Ceausescu's architects – reluctant accomplices in a folly they can neither control nor disavow. But this tension has always been at the heart of Britain's relationship with the EC.

The fact is that no agreement exists in Britain for carrying the European project much further than it has already gone. The extent of Britain's participation in the new European order will therefore depend on the shape of that order and the demands it makes on Britain. The kind of Europe into which Britain is most likely to fit is one built on permanent association between overlapping groups of states, rather than one based on the political integration of the EC. If the dominant members of the EC – Germany and France – insist on going further, or faster, down the road of political unification than is acceptable to the British, a multitrack, or multispeed, European Community seems inevitable.

What is British?

There is, of course, no single British attitude toward 'Europe'. Political opinion ranges from the Liberal Democrats, who are ardent federalists, to the neo-Gaullist Bruges Group. But the weight of opinion is differently distributed from that on the Continent, with most Britons to be found on the minimalist side of the European project.

The two main political parties, Conservative and Labour, are split on Europe. A recent Market Research International poll of members of Parliament showed the Conservatives with a 60–40 per cent pro-European edge. In the general election of 1983, Labour was committed to withdrawing Britain from the Common Market and only accepted membership in 1987. Both parties, in government, have been 'awkward partners' in Europe.[1] In substance, there has been great continuity between the Harold Wilson–James Callaghan governments in the 1970s and the Thatcher government in the 1980s, although Thatcher's far-from-honeyed tone was unique to her. There have been two main causes of friction. Britain has never accepted some parts of the original EC design, notably the Common Agricultural Policy (CAP) and the external tariff. In addition, it has always suspected that a hidden agenda existed, designed to transform the EC into a new European state. Thus, 'pro-European' has always been a relative term in Britain. It has meant little more than a dogged determination to stay in the EC in order to turn the

346

Community's potential benefits Britain's way and prevent worse from happening. Euro-enthusiasm has been conspicuously absent.

This attitude runs through the policy-making and policy-advising élites. The economics establishment (including the Treasury) has been consistently more anti-European than the Foreign Office, in large part because the EC had institutional features like the CAP, the budget, and the common external tariff that hurt British interests. In the 1980s, economic views were highly influenced by the *laissez-faire* reorientation of the British economy under the Thatcher government. British economic vitality in the mid-1980s was contrasted with 'Euro-sclerosis' on the Continent. Resisting tax harmonization, the Treasury argued that market forces, not regulation, should determine sustainable tax differences. In monetary policy, however, the government split. Nigel Lawson, Chancellor of the Exchequer from 1983 to 1989, wanted Britain to join the Exchange Rate Mechanism (ERM) of the European Monetary System (EMS) in 1985; Thatcher vetoed it. There are strong doubts in Britain about the economic benefits of a single currency, and there is general hostility to its imposition by a majority decision. The 'basic' British model has remained economic integration through free trade, with a minimum of monetary, fiscal, and institutional infrastructure.

The Foreign Office is more European-minded. The political case for entry into the EC always seemed more powerful than the economic case. Once the Treaty of Rome was signed, the Foreign Office realized that the EC was the most important game in town and that Britain needed to join. The Foreign Office has always favoured European political co-operation as strengthening the second pillar of John F. Kennedy's two-pillar concept of the Atlantic Alliance, and felt it important to represent Atlanticism in the Community. However, the Foreign Office is no more federalist than the Treasury. Refusing to see the EC as the sole embodiment of European co-operation, it has reactivated parallel, but overlapping, institutions like the Western European Union (WEU) to prevent the European Community from taking on political – especially security and defence – functions. The Treasury and the Foreign Office both prefer 'widening' to 'deepening': the Treasury to avoid excessive harmonization, the Foreign Office to break up the Franco-German hegemony.

The British strategy, in short, has been to handle the different aspects of European integration – the single market, the social market,

347

European Monetary Union, European Political Union – separately, refusing to play the linkage/trade-off game among the four. Above all, Britain has refused to see them as part of a single process ending in a European 'superstate'. This has made the British bad players of the European 'game' and made many doubt their 'European vocation'.

Business is also divided. All sections favour that aspect of the EC denoted by the single market. Big business – represented by the Confederation of British Industry (CBI) – is at home in Brussels, attracted by the cartelization policies that the Commission has often favoured (e.g., in the steel industry) and also by the EC's protection-cum-subsidy for 'essential' European industries like automobiles and computers. The City of London also supports the single market, seeing a British comparative advantage in banking and financial services. There is less enthusiasm for monetary union, but a strong desire to influence the shape of future monetary arrangements. Small and medium-scale business is less concerned with monetary and high Brussels diplomacy in general. It prefers a free market, unencumbered by harmonization and the social dimension. Sir John Hoskyns, the retiring director-general of the Institute of Directors, voiced typical small business attitudes when he castigated the 'Brussels machine' for 'dreams of 1960s-style social engineering, administrative incompetence, bureaucratic dishonesty, and fraud'.[2]

The general context of British business also makes for 'awkwardness'. Two factors are important: the world-wide pattern of British economic relations, and the *laissez-faire* revival under Mrs Thatcher. Between 1978 and 1987, United Kingdom investment in the United States went up from 18.6 per cent to 35.5 per cent, and to the EC from 25.8 per cent to 27.7 per cent. Restructuring of the British economy in the 1980s took place along US lines, emphasizing curbs on trade union powers, abrogation of minimum wage legislation, decentralization of pay bargaining, deregulation and privatization. This was part of a world-wide trend, but the British commitment to internal and external free trade was more fervent, with Brussels being perceived as the home of old fashioned *dirigisme* and corporatism.

Britain's culture is more hostile to the EC than that of any other member. At the élite level, there is a strong pro-Europeanism, but it is not expressed as support for the EC. Historian Hugh Thomas said: 'The language of Brussels is definitely not the language of Goethe.'[3] This cultural pro-Europeanism has been balanced – many would say overbalanced – by the continuing special relationship with the United States. The so-called brain drain has been to the United States, not Europe. In the 'culture' of Thatcherism, the United States, not Europe, is the favoured model for British regeneration. All this will change as the wartime generation dies off, British politicians and administrators become more comfortable working in Europe, and the appeal of Thatcherite and Reaganite economics fades.

Popular attitudes toward Europe, as measured by the Euro-barometer, have been consistently more hostile than the European 'norm'. In 1973, slightly more than 30 per cent of the British thought membership in the EC a 'good thing'; by 1990, this had risen to slightly more than 50 per cent. The EC average in the same period went from slightly less than 60 per cent to 67 per cent. However, the British trend disguises a very sharp dip from 1975 to 1981. In her neo-Gaullism and rejection of 'social market economy', Mrs Thatcher had been increasingly out of step with the trend of mass opinion. On the other hand, she managed to tap a vein of anti-European nationalism, crassly manifested in soccer hooliganism, which seems to have no real counterpart on the Continent.

Despite the range of British opinion, four generalizations about Britain's recent relationship with Europe seem valid. They are as follows:

- Britain rejects the goal of political unification;
- Britain favours a model of economic integration based on free trade;
- Britain prefers foreign policy, security, and defence co-ordination outside the EC framework;
- Britain has rarely maximized its influence with the EC.

What is Europe?

In talking about a 'new European order', the main problem is to understand what is happening. 'Europe' is a process, not a thing. Unfinished business was built into the Treaty of Rome. Political unification was the end, economic integration the historically available means. For some, political unification was Europe's destiny, the next stage in the dialectical progress of the Hegelian spirit. For others, less fanciful or philosophically inclined, unification was the means of overcoming specific historical problems: the warlike Franco-German rivalry, the

349

'dwarfing' of Europe by the United States and the Soviet Union, and the problem of rescuing Europeans' cultural inheritance from the twin snares of US capitalism and Soviet communism. Despite some initial post-war rhetoric, the British have never been inspired by European visions. For British policy-makers, 'Europe' was a factor that had to be taken into account, but only as one part of a larger mosaic in which Britain had its place – and by no means the most attractive part. What drives the process that is Europe? Earlier neo-functionalist theories, replete with spillover effects, which inspired some of the founding fathers and greatly influenced academic work, are now largely discredited. The launches and relaunches of Europe – what the British see as the federalist creep – have always been driven much more by high politics than by low economics. The German problem in its various post-war manifestations, international monetary disorder, and the insecurities created by the collapse of bipolarity have given the crucial impetus to bouts of Euro-construction. The neo-functionalist view retains some explanatory power, however.

Two further sources of dynamism are evident. The first is suggested by public choice theory. Create transnational institutions like the Brussels Commission and the Strasbourg Parliament and, like any group of bureaucrats or politicians, they will try to expand their power and budgets. Second, 'Europe' can be seen as a public good for its members, unblocking frozen national societies or, alternatively, entrenching economic inefficiencies transnationally. Free trade and the Exchange Rate Mechanism are examples of the former; harmonization policies are arguably examples of the latter. Both its institutions and its functions drive Europe forward.

At what point does the process become a thing, and how is the thing to be labelled? No one can say whether it will lead to a new political entity, clothed in state-like attributes. The European bus has no settled nor pre-ordained destination. The probability is that, despite many hopes, Europe will not become a state in the modern sense. Strong states are products of insecurity. Far from requiring a political capping stone, the renunciation of war implied by the very process of post-war European state-building might seem to make a capping stone unnecessary. In addition, war between Europe, the United States, and probably Japan has become unthinkable. That is to say, a large part of the world is reverting to the cosmopolitanism of the nineteenth century when security issues took a back seat.

In the long run, Europe may have to square up to the challenge of Islamic fundamentalism. For the foreseeable future, however, 'threats' such as 'crises' in East Europe and the Middle East, mass migration, world poverty, and threats against the environment hardly seem sufficient to force Europe to unite in the sense that Germany and Italy were 'united' in the nineteenth century, although they may impel greater co-ordination of national policy.[4] Thus, much of the logic that drove the Europeans toward union earlier in this century has disappeared, and new logics are constantly having to be invented.

The British worry more than most about labels; the lack of clear design in the European architecture is a source of anxiety, rather than reassurance. The alternatives as the British see them are either federalism, based on a president and European executive, or a community of independent nations, based on intergovernmental co-operation. Britons cannot live easily with something that lies between these two. They suspect that federalism is inherent in the process, and they are torn among the choices of getting off the federalist bus, trying to slow it down, trying to stop it, or trying to divert it to a less dangerous route. The British fear that 'Europe' will destroy national independence seems exaggerated. What is developing seems more like the medieval order, shorn of its warlike character, in which authority is fragmented, jurisdictions multilayered, and diversity contained in a unity that never acquires coherent political form. Such a political order has no label at present, but it should be one with which Britain can live and to which it can contribute in accord with its own traditions: on the mimimalist, rather than the maximalist, side of political integration; on the liberal, rather than the *dirigiste*, side of economic integration; and pushing Europe outward, rather than inward. This role is dictated by its history.

The Basic Axioms

Nations' policies are based on principles considered so axiomatic they are hardly worth stating. These axioms trigger reflexes. Britain's axioms derive ultimately from its geographical location as an island narrowly divided from the mainland by the English Channel. This location produced historical experiences, and reflections on these are not always accurate. The British experience, of being tethered to the mainland but not part of it, can be contrasted with Japan's. Isolation was never an option. Today, geography is less important, but the attitudes created by it survive.

The following experiences are particularly important to the British viewpoint:

- Britain was not a European conqueror, nor was it conquered (1066 notwithstanding). As a result, the British have never had a constructive political project in Europe, although they have intervened to prevent someone else's project – usually of uniting Europe through conquest.
- Britain's independence from Europe served as a springboard for maritime and commercial supremacy.
- Britain experienced a unique continuity of political history and developed a unique regard for its inherited political forms as a guarantee of its independence. Continental Europe has its long-standing nation-states, too – especially France and Spain. But all European constitutions have been provisional. As Walter Hallstein has noted, many post-war constitutions have written into them provisions for transferring powers to supranational institutions.[5] Britain has never bothered to write down its constitution. But the inherited doctrines of untrammelled parliamentary sovereignty and the unique accountability of the executive to Parliament are hard to reconcile with European constitution-building.

The axioms that resulted are as follows:

- preservation of the European balance of power, defined as preventing the concentration of economic and political power on the European continent;
- maintenance of a liberal world trading system;
- acceptance of US leadership (after the Second World War).

The prevention of concentrated power on the mainland, capable of bridging the Channel, became the corner-stone of British foreign policy during the reign of Elizabeth I. Its instruments were a *persistent* British diplomacy aimed at stopping the forcible unification of Europe, naval supremacy, and the willingness to deploy ground forces in support of this aim if necessary. Winston Churchill recalled this tradition in an address to the Conservative Members Committee on Foreign Affairs in March 1936:

> For four hundred years the foreign policy of England has been to oppose the strongest, most aggressive, most dominating Power on the Continent, and particularly to prevent the Low Countries [from] falling into the hands of such a Power. Viewed in the light of history, these four centuries of consistent purpose . . . must rank as one of the most remarkable episodes which the records of any race, nation, State, or people can show. Moreover, on all occasions England took the more difficult course. Faced by Philip II of Spain, against Louis XIV under William III and Marlborough, against Napoleon, against William II of Germany, it would have been easy and must have been very tempting to join with the stronger and share the fruits of his conquest. However, we always . . . joined with the less strong Powers, made a combination among them, and thus defeated and frustrated the Continental military tyrant, whoever he was, whatever nation he led. Thus we preserved the liberties of Europe, protected the growth of its vivacious and varied society, and emerged after four struggles with an ever-growing fame and widening Empire. . . . Here is the wonderful unconscious tradition of British Foreign Policy.[6]

The instruments by which Continental tyranny was frustrated were precisely those that promoted Britain's commercial supremacy, the foundation of its world role. Preserving the European balance and promoting Britain's prosperity became axiomatically the same thing. From the mercantile period date two features of British economic life that have persisted to this day, and whose persistence in the mind is even greater. The first is the worldwide nature of Britain's trading and financial relations. The second is the free trade basis of its commercial and, later, industrial policy. In both respects, the continental experience diverged from the British in degree, although not absolutely. Even before the free trade era, Britain's mercantile system, as its name suggests, was merchant-led, not state-led: the product of a constitutional system that forced monarchs to trade commercial privileges for revenue. The transition to free trade did not involve a transformation of the system's internal logic, but acceptance of the fact that the exuberant growth of commerce had far outstripped the administrative machinery available to control and channel it. By contrast, eighteenth-century Continental – Spanish and French – commercial practice was state-led. Continental industrialization, which came later than Britain's, was planned and partly financed by the state and extremely well protected from foreign (mainly British) competition. These contrasting images have not lost their resonance.

Britain has its own tradition of state intervention, represented in the twentieth century by John Maynard Keynes (macroeconomic stabilization), William Beveridge (welfare state) and the Fabians (public ownership). But these interventions were justified on technical grounds, as adjustments to *laissez-faire*, and not rooted in a social and political philosophy hostile to *laissez-faire*, as in Catholic social theory ('corporatism') or the dominant continental tradition of state-building through economic integration (Jean-Baptiste Colbert, the *Zollverein*). So when the technical arguments for state intervention started to be challenged in the 1970s and 1980s, the British naturally reverted to free trade and parliamentary sovereignty: weapons used by Mrs Thatcher against the Eurocrats.

The 'Three Circles' doctrine of Churchill was a mid-twentieth-century adaptation of the axioms to the reality of British decline and the experience of two World Wars. Britain was to rely on a 'special relationship' with the United States to underwrite its imperial and European policy. But Britain was also to use its imperial and European position to influence the United States. The special relationship has been rather like the Cheshire Cat – here one minute, gone the next. But the British keep conjuring it up, no one more so than Mrs Thatcher in the 1980s. To use a different image, the British are rather like the faithful wife, who is convinced the husband will come home, however much he plays around. From this can be inferred that Britain was the more ardent wooer. The United States has often tired of British attention. Occasionally, however, the faithful wife can take on a new aspect of allure, as when Margaret Thatcher went courting Ronald Reagan. Born in war, the special relationship still thrives in military matters, as the Gulf crisis demonstrated, though it has long since vanished in regard to money.

The proximate cause of the special relationship was the Second World War, when continental Europe was united under Adolf Hitler and the United States joined with Britain to liberate it. This laid the basis of the post-war order – the Bretton Woods system, the General Agreement on Tariffs and Trade (GATT), and the insertion of the United States into Europe through the North Atlantic Treaty Organization (NATO) to balance the Soviet Union and control Germany. The actual historical process, of course, defies any such neat summary. In the late 1940s, France was just as keen as Britain to secure a US commitment to Western Europe. But the British systematically exploited the special relationship to this end and have continued to do so. The prevention of a US return to economic and political isolation became a central axiom of British foreign policy.

Britain emerged from the long European civil war (1914–45) without the continental sense that the old balance of power game needed to be transcended. The French, too, wanted to balance Germany, but between the wars already had started to follow the alternative tack of trying to lock Germany into industrial partnership – vitiated, however, by their use of reparations to dismember or weaken the Weimar Republic. There were more idealistic schemes for federal union promoted by writers like Coudenhove-Kalergi. The British response in 1930 to the Briand Plan might have been delivered by any foreign secretary throughout the next forty years in identical language:

> We warmly desire to improve the cooperation between European countries for the promotion of their common interests and will help bring it about. . . . We cannot, however, help to create any political or economic group which could in any way be regarded as hostile to the American or any other continent, or which would weaken our political cooperation with the other members of the British Commonwealth.[7]

The post-1945 British idea of intergovernmental co-operation for limited purposes – the Marshall Plan, common defence – was soon challenged by the much more powerful idea of Europe as a 'third force' between the United States and the Soviet Union. France suggested a customs union in the late 1940s, which Britain opposed on the grounds that the need for markets was global. Konrad Adenauer suggested a political union between France and Germany in 1951. Charles de Gaulle commented:

> If one were not constrained to look at matters coolly, one would be dazzled by the prospect of what could be achieved by a

combination of German and French strength. . . . Altogether, it would mean giving modern economic, social, strategic, and cultural shape to the work of the Emperor Charlemagne.[8]

To this historical vision, the British were immune. The only British politician who urged such a combination, with Britain taking a leading part in constructing it, was the pre-war Fascist leader Sir Oswald Mosley.

Three conclusions can be drawn from these British experiences, still relevant, *mutatis mutandis*, to current British attitudes toward Europe. First, there is the fear of an undue concentration of continental power: the fear, as Mrs Thatcher noted it at Bruges in 1988, of a 'European superstate exercising a new dominance from Brussls'.[9] Second, the British reject the idea of Europe as an economic superpower, organized to do battle against the Americans and the Japanese. Third, there is a determination to keep the United States involved in Europe. Inherent in the first two attitudes is latent nationalism. This came increasingly to the fore in the 1970s as Britain's world role declined. If Britain could not orchestrate the international order, it could retreat to an island position, from which, as Enoch Powell liked to say, the great adventure started. One of the problems in the 1980s was the strong link in Mrs Thatcher's mind between 'rolling back the state' in Britain and the recovery of national pride. This resurgence of nationalism, linked to renewed economic vitality, unfortunately coincided with the 'relaunch' of the European drive to political integration. An evocative historical image to both Left and Right was 1940, when Britain stood alone against Europe and without the United States. Thus, globalism and nationalism can be seen as twin poles of Britain's relationship with the European Community. European regionalism was Britain's aim only in the context of the Atlantic Alliance.

Britain and the EC

When de Gaulle vetoed Britain's first application for entry to the EC in 1963, the ostensible reason was his fear that Britain would neuter Europe at the behest of the United States. British Prime Minister Harold Macmillan ascribed the veto to national pique: 'If Hitler had danced in London, we'd have had no trouble with de Gaulle,' he later told his biographer Alistair Horne.[10] Equally, had Hitler danced in London,

356

de Gaulle would have had no trouble with Macmillan. Both were right. Ten years later, Britain's power to 'neuter' Europe – if that is what it wanted to do – was much reduced. In 1963, Britain still saw itself as Western Europe's arbiter; in 1974, it entered as a suppliant; shrunk economically and politically. Europe, meanwhile, had grown. But so had British resentment.

Since 1974, Britain has been a largely ineffective player in the European Community. It failed to balance the Franco-German axis. It showed a tendency to assert its national interest against the EC, not through it. However, its role was by no means entirely obstructive. In the mid-1980s, Britain developed a constructive European programme designed to deepen the market and political co-operation. Although Mrs Thatcher's hostility to centralization was one of the things that brought her government down in 1990, she was the first to see that the collapse of communism and Eastern Europe's liberation called into question the logic of unification. Soviet disintegration may strengthen her cause further. In short, on this point she may still be vindicated. Much of the reason for Britain's awkwardness derived from its not being party to the original deals that established the EC. So Britain entered the Community on unsatisfactory terms. The quarrel over these terms took up the first ten years of British membership and, at times, overshadowed all other British and EC business. Four phases in Britain's relationship with the EC can be discerned.

I   THE BUDGET CONTRIBUTION DISPUTE

Called by Sir Geoffrey Howe Britain's 'tiresome hobby horse', Britain's quarrel over its contribution to the EC budget only became active when the transitional period ended in 1979. Mrs Thatcher appeared in Dublin in 1979 saying 'I want my money back.' The dispute was finally settled by a rebate formula agreed upon at Stuttgart in 1983, confirmed at Fontainebleau in 1984. Throughout the dispute, Mrs Thatcher used the Gaullist tactic of blocking EC business until Britain was accommodated.

British intransigence derived not just from the accession terms, which forced it to pay a large net contribution to the Community budget, but also from intense dislike of the Common Agricultural Policy, for which it was being taxed. The CAP was as abhorrent to *dirigistes* on the Left and paternalists on the Right who both preferred the previous British system of deficiency payments to farmers, as to free traders who rejected any need for agricultural subsidies. John Silkin, Labour's Minister of Agriculture in the 1970s, used to say that the CAP proved that crime paid. The quarrel was embittered by Mrs Thatcher's view that the Community did not need a budget at all (apart from one to support its staff) because no continuous cross-border transfers were required. Therefore, she concluded, the main function of the budget was political – to provide revenue for a European state.

II MONETARY NATIONALISM VERSUS MONETARY UNION

Britain was a currency floater in the 1970s and 1980s, when Germany first organized the 'snake' as a 'zone of stability' in the early 1970s, and then France and Germany promoted the European Monetary System. Callaghan's decision to stay out of the Exchange Rate Mechanism of the EMS in 1978 was crucial: entry, he said, would place obligations on Britain that might result in unnecessary deflation and unemployment.[11] Callaghan's decision set the scene for Mrs Thatcher's monetarist experiment from 1979 to 1983. Mrs Thatcher needed monetary nationalism for the purposes of national monetarism. By 1985, with inflation under control, Nigel Lawson wanted Britain in the ERM, but Mrs Thatcher clung to monetary nationalism. She rejected Bundesbank control of British monetary policy. 'Who needs the Bundesbank if you have me?' she is reported to have said.

Mrs Thatcher's position was untenable for two reasons: Monetarism, à la Milton Friedman, was predicated not on a political *tour de force*, but on fixed rules governing the rate of growth of the money supply. Monetarism, Thatcher-style, ignored such rules, once the original monetary targets were overshot. Second, the liberalization of capital movements and financial deregulation aggravated the problem of both defining and controlling the money supply, which was now divorced from national money income. The two halves of British policy, financial deregulation and national monetarism, were inconsistent. National monetarism, which involved floating the pound, was also inconsistent with the City of London's aspiration to expand its European business. It was also in opposition to the world-wide movement toward stable exchange rates, signified in the Plaza Agreement (1985) and Louvre Accord (1987). The seeds of Mrs Thatcher's downfall were thus sown when she resisted Lawson's ideas in 1985, at the behest of her special adviser, Sir Alan Walters, now a professor at Johns Hopkins University in Baltimore.

III THE CONSTRUCTIVE PERIOD 1984–1986

The '1992' project to complete the European internal market, launched at Stuttgart in 1983 and embodied in the Single European Act of 1986, was largely shaped by Britain, although an important impetus was the failure of Mitterrandism in France and Chancellor Helmut Kohl's accession to power in Germany. As David Allen writes: 'In calling for the completion of a truly free market, the British in 1984 made their first major contribution to setting the Community's agenda. . . .'[12] The British proposals, first outlined by Foreign Secretary Sir Geoffrey Howe in his Chatham House lecture of December 1983, largely influenced the proposals adopted by the European summit in Luxembourg in December 1985; Britain's Trade Commissioner in Brussels, Lord Cockfield, worked out the details. To escape the paralysing national veto, the 'single market' was to be achieved by qualified majority voting by the Council of Ministers. 'The revolutionary British suggestion', said Howe with heavy irony, 'is that the Community should establish a *common market*.'[13]

Howe also urged 'European political cooperation' and suggested reviving the Western European Union for this purpose.[14] By the mid-1980s, Mrs Thatcher had carved out an important niche for Britian as go-between, often on behalf of Europe, between the United States and the Soviet Union. Her credibility in both Washington and Moscow enabled her to play this role, despite her being on generally bad terms with François Mitterrand and Helmut Kohl. This period may turn out to be the last heroic period of British diplomacy. Personal chemistry between Mrs Thatcher and Ronald Reagan, and Mrs Thatcher and Mikhail Gorbachev, played its part; in addition, Mrs Thatcher was determined to be the United States' one completely loyal ally. Reagan 'owed her' for having deployed US cruise missiles and for having allowed US fighters to bomb Libya from Britain in 1986, and Mrs Thatcher successfully called in the debt after the Reykjavik Summit, when Reagan had seemed prepared to bargain away the British and French deterrents. By 1987, the Conservative election manifesto could proclaim with some truth: 'This government has taken Britain from the sidelines into the mainstream of Europe.'

IV DESTRUCTIVE CONFLICT 1987–1990

Britain's economic and political proposals were designed to head off less desirable reforms. In this it failed, for in the late 1980s the subtext of the Single European Act became increasingly explicit: monetary union, tax harmonization, and 'a social common market'. The French and Germans, already committed to monetary union, saw a single currency as a logical consequence of completing the internal market; Mrs Thatcher countercharged in the House of Commons on 9 March 1988, that 'the necessary corollary of a European central bank was a central European government.'[15] But she could not prevent the organization of the Delors Committee of central bankers and financial experts in June 1988, which in April 1989 published a three-stage plan for achieving monetary union (a single currency and a European Central Bank) by 1996. The British responded with their proposal for a parallel currency immune from devaluation, the so-called 'hard ecu', that has found little favour.

Britain's conflict with its EC partners was presented by sections of the British press as a personal duel between the Iron Lady and Jacques Delors, the Commission president. Delors told the European Parliament in July 1988 that the freeing of the internal market would necessarily involve the transfer of sovereignty to the Community. 'In ten years,' he predicted, '80 per cent of economic, perhaps even social and tax legislation, will be of community origin.'[16] He compounded his offence by appearing at the annual conference of the Trades Union Congress in Bournemouth in September 1988, saying that market reforms must be accompanied by 'guaranteed social rights' and worker participation in company management. It was 'impossible to build Europe on only deregulation.'[17] Mrs Thatcher responded at the Tory party conference in Brighton in October by accusing Delors of perverting the Treaty of Rome to spread socialism: 'We haven't worked all these years to free Britain from the paralysis of socialism only to see it creep back through the back door of central control and bureaucracy at Brussels.'[18] This was echoed by a headline in the populist *Sun* newspaper: 'Up your Delors.' At her last conference as leader in October 1990, Mrs Thatcher again rejected socialism 'by the back Delors'.

Mrs Thatcher's main counter-attack came at Bruges in September 1988. She started well by remarking that her invitation to speak there must seem like 'inviting Genghis Khan to speak on the virtues of peaceful coexistence', but then produced an alarmingly bleak vision of the

Community's *institutional* future. The Prime Minister reminded her audience that the special British contribution to Europe's diversity was to 'prevent Europe from falling under the dominance of a single power'. She pointed out that the EC was only one manifestation of Europe's identity: 'We shall always look on Warsaw, Prague, and Budapest as great European cities.' The United States was part of 'European values' too. She rejected any Brussels-imposed view of Europe's development: 'The EC belongs to *all* its members' and must reflect all their traditions. She then restated the well-worn British themes. The political basis of Europe was 'willing cooperation between sovereign states', its economic basis was the market, including a free market in agricultural goods: 'action to *free* markets, action to *widen* choice, action to *reduce* government intervention'. The 'social market' was rejected on cost-raising grounds. On defence and foreign policy, Kennedy's Two Pillar concept was stoutly upheld. Repeatedly, Mrs Thatcher rejected building Europe through institutions: 'We have not successfully rolled back the frontiers of the state in Britain only to see them reimposed at a European level, with a European superstate exercising a new dominance from Brussels.'[19] The clear signal the Bruges speech conveyed to the rest of the EC was that Mrs Thatcher had decided to play the anti-European card to rescue herself from mounting political difficulties at home. From that moment, she ceased to count in Europe.

A French newspaper commented: 'Mrs Thatcher has rediscovered Gaullism as a means of defending not nationalism but her particular vision of the free enterprise society.'[20] Mrs Thatcher's invocation of de Gaulle failed to persuade for two reasons. First, de Gaulle had played the national card, rhetorically at least, on behalf of Europe, not against it. Second, the game had changed with the problem of imminent German reunification. François Mitterrand was no more enthusiastic about this than was Mrs Thatcher. But whereas the British strategy was to deal with the problem through traditional balance of power methods and enlargement – which also served the British purpose of arresting the federalist creep – France and Germany, after a sour interlude in 1989, relaunched the federalist project through the intergovernmental conferences on political and monetary union. Britain thus failed to dent the Paris–Bonn axis. In addition, Mrs Thatcher's position in Washington weakened with the change of presidency.

British Community policy had been ruined by inept diplomacy. By treating the Community as a single entity that was opposed to British values, Mrs Thatcher failed to exploit the possibility of coalition-building. She ignored the fact that Germany and The Netherlands shared her suspicion of Delors' *dirigiste* tendencies, that France had no love for the European Parliament, that Germany wanted 'convergence' to precede monetary union, that Spain opposed environmental regulations, that the Dutch opposed giving the EC a defence competence, and other facts. It seemed impossible to restart a European policy as long as Mrs Thatcher or a Thatcher-style government remained in power. The failure of her European policy thus played a crucial part in bringing about her downfall in November 1990.

Present Issues

John Major's style has been very different from Mrs Thatcher's, on both European and domestic issues. He wants to reinsert Britain into the 'heart of Europe'; at home Major uses a rhetoric of 'classlessness' and 'social market economy' – distancing himself from the social policy of his predecessor and Reagan's United States. Whereas Mrs Thatcher and Kohl disliked each other, Major has apparently established a good relationship with the German Chancellor. British Conservative parliamentarians have started to co-operate again with their Christian Democrat counterparts at Strasbourg. There is, in short, a determined British effort under way to become an active player once more in the European game. This does not mean commitment to federalism, but the predisposition toward viewing every European initiative as a stalking horse for federalism is much less than it had been in Mrs Thatcher's last years. It is still difficult, however, to discern the difference between style and substance with Major. Style is very important, but an accumulated thirty years of squabbling remain to be overcome.

It seems necessary to conclude this essay by first sketching briefly the present balance of political forces in Britain and then summarizing the key issues for the 1990s as the British see them. The Conservative Party is split three ways on Europe. On 21 May 1991, 105 Conservative MPs signed a motion calling on John Major to reject moves toward a monetary union, yet probably only forty to fifty MPs would regard themselves as hard-line Thatcherites. The Thatcherite position on Europe (and much else) is represented by the Bruges Group, of which the former Prime Minister is honorary president. Set up in January 1989 to support the Thatcher thesis of 'a Europe based on willing and active co-operation between independent sovereign states', its active membership consists of academics and politicians hostile to a federal Europe; Lord Harris of High Cross, its chairman, was formerly head of the influential free market think tank, the Institute of Economic Affairs. Its importance lies in its articulating, for the first time in Britain, an ideological opposition to the dominant version of the European project. An attempt has been made to orchestrate this opposition on a European-wide basis. A French 'Committee for a Europe of Nations' was unveiled in 1989 under portraits of Mrs Thatcher and General de Gaulle. Twenty-six German liberal economists signed a manifesto in Frankfurt demanding that the internal market not become a pretext for 'unrelated transfers of powers and international standardization by decree'.[21] The Group's policy is free trade guaranteed by national sovereignty. The tension between the two is covered up by a reading of British history that makes them correlative terms in the British tradition. It is a reading that, as already noted, has some basis.

At the opposite end of the spectrum of Conservative attitudes are the old Common Marketeers led by Edward Heath. Heath's line has always been that Europe must be able to 'compete with the two economic superpowers on equal terms'.[22] The chief spokesman of this position in the government is Michael Heseltine. Restored to the cabinet by Major after resigning from Thatcher's government over the Westland helicopter affair, Heseltine's vision is one of a Europe of business consortia united to do battle against US and Japanese multinationals on the technological 'leading edge'. He repudiates Thatcher's Europe of *laissez-faire*.[23] This is music to many European ears. Heseltine, however, is not a federalist. He stands for big business Toryism rather than market liberalism – a tradition that goes back to the Chamberlain dynasty. However, he was decisively defeated for the Conservative Party leadership, and speaks for no more than forty or fifty MPs. The two hundred or so 'Majorettes' in the middle are pragmatists rather than ideologists, but it is not clear what their sticking point is, or whether they have one. If federalism were the explicit choice, they would reject it, but prudence would probably cause them not to recognize it.

The Labour Party is the most recent convert to Europe, its 'instinctive dislike of the Community . . . tempered by M. Delors's revelation that it would be a useful vehicle for socialism.'[24] But the Labour Party leadership (and particularly its Treasury team) also advocated ERM entry in 1988 to establish the party's anti-inflation credibility. Labour's conversion illustrates the attractiveness of Europe as an extranational court of appeal. Whether Labour's new-found Europeanism would survive office is another matter. Old Labour anti-Marketeers like Peter Shore and Austin Mitchell have suggested that there is incompatibility between ERM membership and full employment. Overall, there is probably less intrinsic support for the European project in any of its forms in the Labour Party than in the Conservative Party, which took Britain into Europe against majority Labour opposition. The position of the Liberal-Democrats could be pivotal if a general election, which has to take place by June 1992, produces a hung parliament. As things stand, the Conservatives are not doing well enough to win comfortably, nor is the Labour Party doing badly enough to lose by much, so the result could be a lot closer than in 1979, 1983 or 1987. In such a situation, the Liberal-Democrats could exert a decisive influence on the pro-European, and even pro-federal, side of the debate.

To sum up, the John Major–Douglas Hurd axis, big business, and the City of London make it virtually inconceivable that Britain will allow itself to become as isolated in Europe as it was in Mrs Thatcher's last phase. That means Britain will be prepared to negotiate constructively and imaginatively on all the issues that the British regard as important. Five such issues seem central.

I   ERM VERSUS A SINGLE CURRENCY

Britain's decision to join the Exchange Rate Mechanism of the EMS in October 1990 brought to an end the long debate between Margaret Thatcher and Nigel Lawson, her Chancellor until 1989, on how best to control domestic inflation. Accepted Thatcherite orthodoxy is that Lawson lost control of the money supply by shadowing the Deutschmark between February 1987 and February 1988. Mrs Thatcher's prolonged resistance to ERM membership was dictated not just by her belief in the national control of money – which ironically goes back to the Keynesian revolution that she repudiated in every other respect – but also by the fact that under the Delors proposals 'to enter upon the first stage [of monetary union] should be a decision to enter upon the entire process.' For Mrs Thatcher, this raised an issue not just of policy, but of sovereignty. The political dilemma was, and is, that although

Britain could block any move by the EC toward a single currency, it could not stop members of the EC from establishing one outside the EC framework. The Major government is no more disposed than the Thatcher government to sign up for a single currency, but it seems to have accepted the latest compromise, which allows each member country to decide to take the final step in its own time. The likeliest outcome will be a multitrack EMU, with a smaller currency union developing within the ERM system and a British decision on participation deferred for a newly elected parliament. (There is a precedent in the Latin Monetary Union, which kept the franc and lira at parity before 1914 within the gold standard system.) The other issue relevant to sovereignty is whether Britain or any other country would retain the right to leave a currency union it had once joined. This would depend on the constitutional rules that establish the union. The politics of the matter are also unclear: British reservations are strongly shared by the Bundesbank itself, so the British have some leverage for slowing down Delors' Stage III. What is slowed may not come to pass.

Politics aside, there are technical economic issues of benefits and costs. In Tim Congdon's summary: 'The steady-state benefits [of a single currency] need to be weighed against the substantial costs involved in the transition to the new system.' Against the steady-state benefits of price stability, elimination of transaction costs, and transparency of investment decisions need to be set the risks of 'high and persistent' unemployment and real contractual costs in the transition to a new regime. Congdon also makes the point that price stability is more likely under a fixed exchange system underpinned by the Bundesbank than in a single currency system presided over by a Euro-Fed diluted by France and Italy or even Britain. (In theory, there is no reason why a paper ecu should keep its value any better than any national paper currency.) Opponents of a single currency point out that the regional transfers needed to bail out uncompetitive areas deprived of the right to devalue would require a Community budget two or three times as large as the existing one and, thus, reinforce the federalist creep. Against this stands a strong credibility argument: a single currency will make national devaluation impossible, although not, of course, the devaluation of the single currency (ecu) against the dollar or the yen.[25]

II CONSTITUTIONAL ISSUES AND THE 'DEMOCRATIC DEFICIT'

An important debate in Britain is between those who wish to make Community actions more accountable to the European Parliament and those who want to keep them under the control of national parliaments. British critics of federalism argue that national sovereignty is the only way of making the Community democratic: No 'general will' can emerge from Strasbourg.[26] They have at last started to pay serious attention to constitutional mechanisms for safeguarding national sovereignty, rather than just resisting any amendment to the Treaty of Rome. The proposals by Frank Vibert, deputy director of the Institute of Economic Affairs, seem to be close to current government thinking. Vibert wants the vague notion of 'subsidiarity', conceded by Delors at Bruges in September 1989, to be much more carefully defined, with an 'articulation of demarcation procedures' for assigning tasks to different levels. Vibert proposes a treaty, to be underwritten by the Court of Justice, affirming that Community bodies act only on transferred powers. He also calls for a 'full array of decision rules', ranging from unanimity to qualified majority voting, with the rules drawn up on 'veil of ignorance' assumptions to satisfy the interests of all Community members. The retention of the power of veto in specified cases might be combined with a procedure to opt out that allows others to proceed if they so wished. Second, Vibert wants Community enlargement through more flexible membership qualification rules. Third, the exclusive right of the Commission to initiate legislation would be terminated, and all proposals to the Council would be subject to a 'pre-legislative review' by national parliaments. The result would be a 'larger Community whose members can cooperate on different topics at different speeds'.[27] The Bruges Group has also put forward constitutional proposals that call for, among other things, a referendum on the principle of political unification.[28]

Arguments about how to overcome the 'democratic deficit' miss an important aspect of the European process, which has involved setting up institutions designed to bypass democratic road-blocks. The great example has been Germany's Bundesbank, whose anti-inflationary virtue stems from its independence from political control. According to the 'public choice' school of political science, inflation is the result of a surplus – not a deficiency – of democracy. A strong case can certainly be made for saying that the more democratic Europe is, either in its national and subnational parts or at the Community level, the less it will be able to function as a public good for all its members.

III ECONOMIC STRUCTURE

A third important area of debate will be economic structure. Opponents of the Community in its present form argue that it is seriously protectionist and *dirigiste* in practice, aiming to back 'European winners' through harmonization, merger policies and subsidies. As Patrick Minford writes: 'True winners need no backing other than a stable economic framework, low taxes, and the absence of political roadblocks.'[29] Harmonization merely entrenches average practice and destroys important ingredients of comparative advantage: what it meant, one Thatcherite complained, was 'cross-frontier subsidization'.[30] According to the Bruges Group, the Social Charter, with its references to 'a decent wage', 'maximum working hours', 'worker participation', and the 'right to vocational training', sought to impose an 'outdated social regime' on the European Community.[31]

With the collapse of state socialism, four economic ideologies can be identified: *dirigisme*, corporatism, the 'social market', and economic liberalism. (The Pope's recent encyclical, *Centesimus Annus*, issued on the one hundredth anniversary of Leo XIII's attack on Marxism in *Rerum Novarum*, attempts to combine all four.) One reason for the current British enthusiasm for 'widening' the Community is that economic liberalism is likely to receive powerful reinforcement from Poland, Czechoslovakia and Hungary. Two contradictory pulls can be identified. On the one hand, the Major government has retreated from the purity of Thatcherite economics, and a Labour government is likely to converge even closer to European social democratic norms. On the other hand, the general decrease in global insecurity is likely to lessen the pressures for government control over the economy. The need to protect 'essential' industries for 'strategic' purposes is obviously likely to be less felt in a peaceful world. So the classic British position might command more support.

IV THE GERMAN PROBLEM

The threat of a renewed German take-over of Europe following reunification was a fundamental concern of Margaret Thatcher at the end of

367

her premiership: she lost her Secretary for Trade and Industry, Nicholas Ridley, when he voiced this fear too openly shortly before her own departure. If the French aimed at 'balancing Germany through institutionalization', Mrs Thatcher argued that federal institutions would simply be a fig leaf for German dominance, a view somewhat inconsistent with her fear of a new 'superstate' run from Brussels.[32] The basic British policy is to keep the United States in Europe to balance Germany, as well as to widen the Community to recreate a balance of power. The so-called German problem thus gives the widening versus deepening argument a new salience. Perhaps, though, this is an area of concern more dominated by historical reflex than current reality. A great deal of Euro-construction still inclines toward prevention of the last war.

V EUROPEAN SECURITY

Connected with the last issue is the future shape of the European security order. This question overshadows Britain's parochial concerns. The basic problem for the British is not 'Europe's desire to carry its Euro-integration into foreign policy, security policy, and ultimately defense policy', but the British conviction that any European security pillar must be part of an Atlantic defence community, based on national decision making.[33] In the British view, the Gulf War showed that the Community could not substitute for the decision-making capacity of nations in the security and military sphere and that any attempt to make it do so would produce not a firm, but a crumbling, pillar. Thus, the British aim is to ensure that any European defence 'identity' remains linked to the United States through NATO and controlled by its leading states (through a strengthened WEU), rather than being integrated into the EC.[34] This conflicts with the French desire to have a European force completely independent of NATO, linked to the EC. The recent NATO decision to create a European-dominated Rapid Reaction Force, commanded by a British general, represents a victory for the British point of view.[35] But the problem of who is to control the 'identity', and how the British and French nuclear deterrents fit into this identity, remains. The WEU probably offers the best framework for relinking France to NATO's military alliance and retaining the US 'pillar' of Europe's defence.[36] On this issue, unlike some others, Britain is not really at loggerheads with 'Europe', but stands for a reasonable compromise between the conflicting

368

European positions. However, the salience of this issue will depend on international developments.

These are the questions that will dominate Britain's relations with the Continent in the 1990s. If it plays the European game effectively, there is no reason for Britain to be in a perpetual minority of one. Britain has formidable intellectual, political, economic and cultural assets to bring to the European project. Its best service to Europe, as Charles Moore, the *Spectator*'s editor, recently suggested, will be Britain's ability to act as a 'bridge', bringing to the Community the Anglo-Saxon 'cultural preference for competition, free markets, and parliamentary accountability', while carrying a disproportionate share of the traffic between the EC, the United States, NATO, and GATT.[37] It is a role dictated by its historical tradition, itself part of Europe's tangled skein.

NOTES

1   See Stephen George, *An Awkward Partner: Britain in the European Community* (1990), for the most succinct account of the relationship.

2   Sir Ralf Dahrendorf, *Whose Europe: Competing Visions for 1992* (1989), p. 13.

3   Hugh Thomas, *A History of Diversity* (1989), p. 5.

4   Uffe Elleman-Jensen, Danish Foreign Minister, writing in the *Financial Times*, 25 April 1991.

5   Walter Hallstein, *Europe in the Making* (1972), p. 22.

6   Winston S. Churchill, *The Second World War* (1948).

7   D. Carlton, *MacDonald versus Henderson: The Foreign Policy of the Second Labour Government* (1970), p. 85.

8   Jean Monnet, *Memoirs* (1978), p. 287.

9   See *Financial Times*, 21 September 1988.

10   Alistair Horne, *Macmillan 1957–1986*, vol. 2 (1989), p. 91.

11   George, *An Awkward Partner*, pp. 129–30.

12   David Allen, 'British Foreign Policy and West European Cooperation' in Peter Byrd (ed.), *British Foreign Policy under Mrs Thatcher* (1988), p. 42.

13   Ibid., same page.

14   Sir Geoffrey Howe, 'The Future of the European Community: Britain's Approach to the Negotiations', *International Affairs*, 60:2 (1984), pp. 190–92.

15   George, *An Awkward Partner*, p. 193.

16   See the *Financial Times*, 7 July 1988.

17   George, *An Awkward Partner*, p. 191.

18   *Financial Times*, 21 September 1988.

19   'Britain and Europe': text of the speech delivered in Bruges by the Prime

Minister, Margaret Thatcher, on 20 September 1988 (London, Conservative Political Centre, 1988).

20   From *Le Soir*, as quoted in the *Sunday Times*, 25 September 1988.

21   See reports in *The Times*, 21 March 1989, *Le Figaro*, 19 April 1989, and the *Daily Telegraph*, 30 May 1989. The Bruges Group was started by Patrick Robertson, a twenty-year-old history undergraduate at Keble College, Oxford.

22   *Daily Telegraph*, 9 February 1989.

23   Michael Heseltine's European programme is described in his book *The Challenge of Europe: Can Britain Win?* 1989).

24   Ronald Butt in *The Times*, 3 April 1989.

25   Tim Congdon, 'EMU Now?: The Leap to European Money Assessed' (1990). For a defence of monetary union, see Samuel Brittan and Michael Artis, *Europe without Currency Barriers* (1989).

26   Kenneth Minogue, *Independent*, 20 September 1989.

27   Frank Vibert, 'Constitutional Change and Political Union in the European Community', *IEA Inquiry* (December 1990).

28   Alan Sked, *A Prospect for European Union*, Bruges Group, Occasional Paper no. 9 (May 1990).

29   Patrick Minford, *Daily Telegraph*, 8 February 1989.

30   R. Harris, *Sunday Telegraph*, 16 April 1989.

31   Bruges Group, Press Release, 24 October 1989.

32   Barry Buzan et al., *The European Security Order Recast* (1990), p. 210.

33   *The Economist*, 25–31 May 1991.

34   See Douglas Hurd in the *Financial Times*, 15 April 1991. See also the interview with Manfred Woerner, Secretary-General of NATO, in the *Financial Times*, 7 May 1991. Woerner rejects Delors' view that Europe should have its own independent defence policy.

35   See the *Financial Times*, 1–2 June 1991.

36   See the discussion in *The Economist*, 1–8 June 1991, p. 48.

37   Charles Moore, *Daily Telegraph*, 7 June 1991.

The Uses of History

CHAPTER FIFTY-THREE

The Economic Decline of Britain

[1985]

I

THE Decline of Britain is the longest-running saga in modern history. It used to be rivalled by the German Problem. Both started about the same time – in the 1870s or thereabouts. But the German Problem came to an end in 1945, to be succeeded by the German Miracle, whereas the British Problem is still running strongly into its second century, without any apparent diminution in audience appeal or scholarly attention.

Indeed, Britain presents a historical spectacle of undoubted attraction to students of the paradoxical. What could be more puzzling for scholars brought up on 'stages of development' than a pioneer capitalist society smothered by the monarchical and aristocratic embrace, than a pioneer industrial society whose decreasing aptitude for business was matched only by its capacity for waging victorious wars, than a nation which combined a passion for utility with intense outpourings of religious piety? No one has yet denied that Britain *had* an Industrial Revolution. But it has become fashionable to deny that it ever had a 'bourgeois' revolution – that it ever developed a true entrepreneurial class, detached from the values of the land and its supporting professions. As the American historian Martin Weiner sees it, commercial gain was forever being transferred back into landed proprietorship, commercial values into visions of Arcadia regained.[1] On a different tack, the economist Mancur Olson has recently found Britain a perfect confirmation of his theory of an ageing process brought about by the accumulation of interest groups and coalitions which prevent the market from doing its job.[2]

Britain's decline has served as an awful political warning. A pioneer of industrial society, Britain has given the industrial world a new nightmare: de-industrialization. Once upon a time (*circa* 1830) reforming rulers tried to make their countries as like Britain as possible. Today their efforts are directed to eradicating any symptoms of the British disease they detect in their own societies. Britain has taken the Ottoman Empire's place as the sick man of Europe, but with this difference. The Ottoman Empire's disease was the failure to modernize. The British disease is the failure to stay modern. Britain is the first modern nation to suffer from the distempers of senility. Mrs Thatcher is the latest in a long line of British leaders who have staked their claim to power on their ability to find a cure for it.

We must define our terms. By 'decline of Britain' I don't mean the 'decline and fall of the British Empire'. This is a profoundly interesting topic, much exploited by the nostalgia industry, which has barely begun to be tackled by historians. But it is obviously part of a much larger story which has to do with the political decline of Western Europe *vis-à-vis* the rest of the world – a decline which was partly inevitable, and was certainly speeded up by the two World Wars. I shall take the decline of Britain to mean its decline relative to its peers – the countries with which we have been accustomed to compare ourselves. At the turn of the century the British were comparing themselves to the Germans and the Americans and finding the comparison increasingly disturbing: both countries had just overtaken Britain in the production of coal and steel. We were fearful of our future in a club of great powers which had, by 1945, come to include Russia and Japan. The measures of decline at this stage were political and military: economic failure was relevant chiefly as diminishing the resource base needed to sustain a 'world' position. By the 1960s, and particularly following the Suez fiasco, when great power ambitions were finally abandoned, we started to measure ourselves against Western Europe. The ranking by this time was purely or largely in terms of economic performance. Once more the comparison was deeply disturbing.

Almost any economic league table we choose to construct, made up of ourselves and the twenty or so nations closest to us in economic, social and political systems would show the same progression over the century: we start at or near the top and end at or near the bottom. On trend, our relegation to a second division of 'middle income' countries is only a matter of time. What is more, we will have the honour of being the first industrialized country to be so demoted. All comparisons of 'growth' or 'standards of living' between countries and over time are notoriously tricky, but a couple of examples will show the trend. In the 1860s and 1870s Britain had the fastest annual rate of growth of output and of output per man in the world. Between 1950 and 1973 it had the slowest annual rate of growth of output and of output per man of the sixteen leading developed countries. In 1950 it had the fifth highest income per head of the same group. By 1984 it had the lowest. Only

Spain and Ireland of the developed countries are now poorer than we are.[3]

There are two arguments usually advanced against taking such comparisons too tragically. The first is that though Britain is sinking in the league table, the league as a whole, including Britain, is much better off than it was in 1870, or for that matter 1950. This is true. The British standard of living has just about doubled between 1950 and today. As long as it keeps rising why should we worry unduly that others' are rising even faster? The first answer is that we do in fact worry and this worry has tangible effects. One of them is the 'brain drain' which diminishes our ability to produce wealth in the future. Secondly, relative decline can lead to absolute decline. A relative decline in living standards is an effect of a relatively slow rate of growth, which in turn usually reflects a declining ability to compete in world markets. If there is plenty of growth in the system as a whole, even inefficient economies can get some of it. If the general growth slows down, it stops first in the least efficient economies. And the least efficient economies get less and less able to compete, so that eventually they may be shrinking even as the rest of the world is growing.

The second argument is that league tables of this kind don't measure what we mean by living standards. This is true. An individual's standard of living is made up not just of things money can buy but of all the things which make a particular place, society or way of life agreeable: the 'quality of life' in so far as that is independent of material goods. To that extent attempts to measure living standards by money values are wrong. But the argument is not conclusive. In the 1970s it was commonly argued that low income growth was the price we paid for preserving the 'British way of life' – with the strong implication that this way of life was far superior to that of the workaholic Americans, Germans, and Japanese. That the British way of life produces low income growth is certainly true. But that it compensates for, and thus in a way justifies, low income growth would be tenable only if the British 'quality of life' defined above was *in fact* superior to that of more dynamic societies or if the British got more intense pleasure out of their quality of life than did the Americans, Germans, Japanese, etc. It would be hard to know how to prove the first proposition; and the second is intuitively implausible: indeed, our way of life seems to bring us less obvious pleasure than that of places where the sun shines more and it rains less. Thus it is reasonable to use real income levels as proxies for living standards, and as a matter of fact we do.

375

There is another reason for trusting them as proxies which may not have existed to the same extent before. The satisfactions which people may have got in the past from non-material goods and services have been drying up. Religious beliefs are on the wane and anyway are not so intensely felt. Nationalistic fervour is frowned on. Empire, which offered patriotic and racial satisfactions, is gone. Twentieth-century wars, horrible though they were, undoubtedly provided peculiarly intense satisfactions for those who lived through them. But few people today want to bring back these kinds of compensation for poverty, even if it were possible. A capitalist environment – even a British one – tends in the long run to be hostile to them. Societies which are geared to the increase of wealth tend to produce character-types less suited to martial or religious callings. The pursuit of contentment through wealth is no doubt an illusion in itself; but it seems to be the least damaging one available.

The conclusion is that we are locked into a system in which growth in wealth has overtaken all other objects of human striving. Individuals may opt out: many do. But societies cannot safely do so without offering something else. There are many candidates, but few takers. In the competition to produce more wealth Britain has been doing increasingly badly. If 'standard of living' is defined in terms of what the contemporary world has to offer, the British are getting a decreasing share of it. This is the only meaning of decline which makes sense in our world: but it does make sense.

II

The 'long decline' of the British economy has been attributed to a complex of causes collectively known as the British disease. This disease was first diagnosed about a hundred years ago. The patient was so illustrious, that doctors from all over the world crowded round his bedside. Nor have their diagnoses varied much over time, though medical language has changed: literary and anecdotal observations are now expressed in sociological and economic jargon. Despite greater precision in diagnosis, no cure has yet been found. Perhaps there is none. Perhaps they are dealing with one of those cases where the patient recovers spontaneously, or not at all.

Before turning to the invalid, it is worth recalling how he struck observers in his period of rude health. Voltaire, who lived in England in

1726–9, found the distinguishing mark of English society to be its combination of liberty and commercial enterprise. He particularly noted the openness of the aristocracy to trade – 'A peer's brother does not think trade beneath him' – and went on to contrast this with the disdain for trade prevalent in similar French circles: 'I need not say which is most useful to a nation; a lord, powdered in the tip of the mode, who knows exactly at what o'clock the king rises and goes to bed ... or a merchant, who enriches his country, dispatches orders from his counting-house to Surat and Grand Cairo, and contributes to the well-being of the world.'[4] Voltaire was contrasting the useful with the decorative: a comparison which was to be turned against England later on.

The most penetrating account of England in its heyday was left by the American Ralph Waldo Emerson, who visited the country in 1833, and again in 1847, when he delivered lectures to Mechanics' Institutes in Lancashire and Yorkshire. His *English Traits*, first published in 1865, thus reflects his (somewhat out-of-date) experience of the Industrial North as well as a London circle of writers and artists. Believing that 'if there be one successful country in the universe for the last millenium, that country is England', Emerson set out to discover the secret of England's greatness. He found his first clue in the 'tough, acrid, animal' nature of its people, expressed by delight in bloodthirsty sports, public executions, and fisticuffs. This delight was shared by all classes: 'the difference of rank does not divide the national heart ... the language of the noble is the language of the poor ... The laborer is a possible lord. The lord is a possible basketmaker ... In politics and war they hold together as by hooks of steel.' Emerson was one of the long line of visitors who have admired England civic culture, while disliking its people. He noted the English tradition of public courtesy to foreigners and political exiles which, however, 'puts no sweetness into their unaccommodating manners, no check on that puissant nationalism which makes their existence incompatible with all that is not English'.

Superimposed on these unaccommodating manners was a genius for practical logic and detail which had made England the workshop of the world. The passion for efficient means was channelled towards a single end: creating wealth. Echoing Voltaire, Emerson wrote:

> There is no country in which so absolute a homage is paid to wealth. In America there is a touch of shame when a man exhibits the evidences of a large property, as if after all it needed

377

apology. But the Englishman has pride in his wealth, and esteems it a final certificate ... The last term of insult is, 'a beggar'. The natural fruit of this homage to wealth is a brutal political economy ... The Englishman believes that every man must take care of himself, and has himself to thank if he do not mend his condition. To pay their debts is their national point of honour ... Solvency is in the ideas and mechanism of an Englishman. The Crystal Palace is not considered honest until it pays; no matter how much convenience, beauty or *éclat*, it must be self-supporting ... Every household exhibits an exact economy ... If they cannot pay, they do not buy ... An Englishman ... labors three times as many hours in the course of a year as another European ... He works fast. Everything in England is at a quick pace. They have reinforced their own productivity by the creation of that marvellous machinery which differences this age from any other age ... Whatever surly sweetness possession can give, is tasted in England to the dregs.

But in the very virtues of the English, Emerson saw harbingers of decay. The counterpart of their practicality, of their insular self-assurance, was a mistrust of abstract reasoning, a deadly parochialism. 'They have difficulty', he wrote, 'in bringing their reason to act, and on all occasions use their memory first. As soon as they have got rid of some grievance and settled the better practice, they make haste to fix it as a finality, and never wish to hear of alteration more', even if circumstances change: Emerson gave free trade as an example. English thought was 'wise and rich' but it lived off its own capital. 'Their mind is in a state of arrested development – a divine cripple like Vulcan ... There is a drag of inertia which resists reform in every shape.' Emerson could not help feeling that America, not England, was destined to be 'the seat and centre of the British race ... and that England, an old and exhausted island, must one day be contented, like other parents, to be strong only in her children'.[5]

Emerson identified two ingredients of English greatness which later Conservative revivalists have usually tried to run in harness: a sense of social cohesion built round tribal tastes and loyalties and an individualist approach to wealth-creation, based on the Protestant ethic, which sees 'wealth' as a certificate of grace, and 'possession' as a 'surly sweetener'. The thought that emerges from his account is not that the Industrial

Revolution made Britain, but that Britain made the Industrial Revolution; its economic success caused it and did not long outlast it, because, by dividing Britain into 'two nations', the Industrial Revolution undermined the successful formula.

Little more than a quarter of a century after Emerson published, the image of a British industry resting on its laurels, while the more energetic (and less civilized) foreigners – who were beginning to include 'backward races' like the Japanese – crept up and stole the business, was firmly established in both the British and foreign consciousness. As early as 1885 it was clear to the Cambridge philosopher Henry Sidgwick 'that we are past all culmination, relatively speaking'. The only question which troubled him was: would the decline be violent or painless?[6] His colleague, the economist Alfred Marshall, was more optimistic: he thought that a combination of continuing free trade and technical education might yet keep manufacturers and artisans on their toes. What increasingly worried him was the power of the unions. 'I want these people beaten at all costs: the complete destruction of unionism would be . . . not too high a price,' he wrote to the Master of Balliol in 1897 when the Engineers struck against proposals for the dilution of labour. It was about the last time a thought like that could be expressed quite so robustly.[7] The symptoms of the disease were starting to take familiar shape. The American historian Brook Adams has a chapter called 'The Decay of England' in a book, *America's Economic Supremacy*, published in 1900. During the first portion of the nineteenth century, he wrote, 'the Englishman stood forth as the personification of energy' in war, commerce, intellectual activity, industry, invention. But recently things had changed. 'For example, for more than two decades contractors have complained, with growing vehemence, that English firms were dilatory, and that Englishmen seldom leave their dinners or their sport for business.' Shops open late and close early, nothing is done on Saturdays, and on Mondays workers turn up after a weekend of boozing in a 'demoralized' state. English agriculture has been ruined because of the obsolete railway system. 'Strangest of all', Adams continued, practically repeating what Emerson had said, 'is the mental inertia which prevents the Englishman from comprehending the world about him. He still looks on American competition as an accident, he still regards his railways as the best, he is still pleased with the results attained at his universities, he is satisfied with the place he holds; he does not care to change. He fails to perceive that beyond the boundaries of Great Britain the methods of organization and administration have altered throughout the world, while within they tend to fixity'.[8]

My next witness, the American economist Thorstein Veblen, tried to explain what Brooks Adams described. In a book published in 1915 comparing Britain and Germany,[9] Veblen argued that Britain's industrial stagnation was due to the fact that it was the first in the field and that, in consequence, it suffered from institutional obsolescence: 'Towns, roadways, factories, harbors, habitations, were placed and constructed to meet the exigencies of what is now an obsolete state of the industrial arts, and they are, all and several, "irrelevant, incompetent, and impertinent".' Veblen failed to state exactly what it was about these things that was irrelevant. But undoubtedly his most telling, and idiosyncratic, insight is that a society which first breaks through to a higher standard of living will be the first to decline, because it will be the first to develop playful and decorative at the expense of useful social habits. In Veblenesque language, the higher the standard of living the higher the proportion of income that goes on conspicuous waste: to Veblen a rising standing of living *means* 'cumulative growth of wasteful expenditures'. A conspicuous example of conspicuous waste is the cost of production of an English gentleman – 'several-fold the cost of a German gentleman of conventionally equal standing' and a proportionately larger charge on productive resources. 'Doubtless', Veblen wrote, 'the English today lead the Christian world both in the volume of their gentility and in its cost per unit of output'; but the Germans were quickly catching up 'in the decent waste of time and substance'.

Societies decline not only because savings are squandered or misdirected – Veblen regarded the financial operations of the City not so much useful as a game played for amusement – but because the affluent businessman and worker become frivolous, no longer take work seriously. Veblen regarded the British addiction to sport as a serious 'abatement' on industrial efficiency, failing to realize, perhaps, that it long antedated industrialism. 'Sports', he wrote, 'have been a very substantial resource in this gradually maturing British scheme of conspicuous waste ... all this superfluity of inanities has in the course of time been worked into the British conception of what is right, good and necessary to civilised life.' Energies which German businessmen and workers devote to their business are in England squandered on hunting, shooting and football.[10]

380

Veblen was the first writer, I think, to offer an analytical account of relative decline in terms of how and why relatively rich societies turn from the efficient production of things to 'conspicuous waste', such waste being regarded as the mark of civilization. He provides a plausible explanation of many of the agreed symptoms of British decline: amateurism, conservative attitudes to change, the 'long weekend', refinements of class distinctions, the educational attention devoted to the 'production of gentlemen', complacency and ignorance. The French journalist André Siegfried was to take up many of these points in his book *England's Crisis*. Although it was published in 1931, in the depth of the Great Depression, Siegfried's concern was not so much with the short-term problem as with 'the slow but persistent leakage' of Britain's position. The description is familiar: 'Although almost one-third of the present century has passed, Great Britain still depends on an economic structure and methods which often definitely belong to the last century.' Time does not seem to flow in England as quickly as elsewhere – this is one of the secrets of its 'extraordinary charm'. The 'entire economic structure is frozen'; much of the economy is 'isolated . . . from economic laws'. The Englishman, Siefried exhorted, 'must modify his way of working, of thinking, and even of living'. He must stop blaming others for his misfortunes. Above all, businessmen must pull up their socks. They must abandon 'the old British idea that discipline and practical experience are better than technique', that they will 'muddle through' in the end. Siegfried echoes Emerson when he remarks that British managers are not in general men of 'general culture' or 'wide education', but rather have the outlook of 'superior foremen who have risen in the world'.

At the same time there were other possible causes of industrial 'retardation' which did not figure prominently in the early literature on decline, but which were to be stressed much more later. One was that, with captive and dispersed imperial markets, British businessmen had no real incentive to innovate more than they did. Another laid stress on the increasingly 'sclerotic' condition of the labour and other markets, which Olson was later to explain by his theory of the accumulation of special interest groups exerting market power in their favour either through direct action or through legislative patronage. A third explanation to hand was government policy. British businessmen characteristically blamed their difficulties on free trade policy and growing social expenditures which burdened them with extra rates and taxes: their political spokesman was Joseph Chamberlain. Keynes, of course, vehemently attacked the policy of returning to the gold standard in 1925 at the pre-war parity. Finally there was the class system, created by the Industrial Revolution itself, in much more uncompromising form in England than elsewhere, and surviving with a unique tenacity. Clearly Britain would have needed a massive jolt to shake it out of its entrenched habits, which the two World Wars in the end failed to deliver. Owing to the inherent strength of its defensive position, it never suffered the 'creative destruction' of equipment and institutions which Allied bombers, armies and occupation regimes were able to inflict on Germany, but which the Germans were unable to reciprocate. In a playful, but puzzled, memorandum to the Cabinet of 18 March 1945 Keynes wrote that 'If by some sad geographical slip the American Air Force (it is too late now to hope for much from the enemy) were to destroy every factory on the North-East coast and in Lancashire (at an hour when the directors were sitting there and no one else), we should have nothing to fear. How else we are to regain the exuberant inexperience which is necessary, it seems, for success I cannot surmise.'[11]

The literature of decline starts up again in the 1960s, after it became clear that the Labour 'renewal' of 1945–51, inherited and managed by the Conservatives during their 'thirteen wasted years', had failed to produce the expected improvement in relative economic performance. Britain was growing a bit faster than before, but since the other countries in the 'league' had improved on their growth rates in the same proportion, it failed to reverse the 'long decline'. A new panel of expert diagnosticians appeared; as well as a new sense of urgency, even desperation. The magazine *Encounter* ran a symposium in its issue of June 1963 called *Suicide of a Nation?* British government, civil service, political parties and their ideas, the educational system, employers, trade unions, and even sexual habits were all comprehensively castigated for their contribution to the national malaise. Michael Shanks, author of *The Stagnant Society*, summed up the main thrust of the new criticism when he wrote:

> A working class whose horizons are limited to the currently-fashionable consumer durable; a middle-class intent on refining the caste marks distinguishing it from those below; industries concerned to limit competition; a trade union movement seeking only to shield its members from the impact of change; a civil service dedicated to avoiding the awkward parliamentary ques-

tion. These are the hallmarks of a society which has embraced stagnation as a way of life.[12]

Most of it could have been said, and was, sixty years before.

III

Every British government this century has promised, and to some extent implemented, reforms designed to improve efficiency. Indeed, to judge from their rhetoric, and even their actions, politicians of all parties have been inspired by a passion to bring Britain up to date. Balfour, Macmillan, Heath and Mrs Thatcher, harnessed Conservatism, Asquith and Lloyd George Liberalism, Attlee, Morrison, Dalton, and Harold Wilson Socialism, to the cause of efficiency. The quest for national efficiency has provided the consensual basis for British politics in the twentieth century. Nor has there been nearly as much disagreement about *means* as party rhetoric – especially the rhetoric of Capitalism versus Socialism – would indicate. The general tendency of reform has been interventionist and collectivist, since there was a general disposition, running across the whole political spectrum, to blame the private sector, whether seen as markets to be superseded by planning, or monopolies to be regulated or nationalized, or a system which needed stabilizing, for the failure of Britain to grow at the required rate. The last strenuous effort at institutional renewal was undertaken by the Wilson Government in the 1960s: socialism was to be the means by which advanced technology and modern management technique came to Britain. The fact remains that, despite all those efforts, national efficiency has hardly been improved at all relative to trend. Britain's national income was growing at just under 2 per cent a year in the forty years before the First World War and just over 2 per cent in the forty years after the Second World War. The regimes, the policies, the institutions have varied very considerably over the whole period. We start with a small public sector, weak unions, pre-Keynesian monetary and fiscal policy; we end with a large public sector, strong unions, a huge Treasury model of the economy serviced by dozens of top economists, and the economic performance is almost exactly the same. A first suspicion may be that this immense apparatus of sophistication and control has increased the living standards of the country by not one jot from what they would have been in its absence. A further suspicion may be that it has served to prevent any chance of the patient curing himself; or even worse heresy, may even have aggravated the disease.

Plainly there is strong resistance by the British to the attempts of their politicians to cure them of their vices. Reforms designed to improve the efficiency of the British way of life do not seem to have their intended effect, but seem merely to perpetuate the old habits in new settings. Notable examples are the failure of comprehensive education to raise working-class expectations and achievements, and of the new universities and polytechnics to increase the supply of technologists. As Thorstein Veblen remarked in his own inimitable style, 'wasteful conventions spread with great facility through the body of the population by force of emulative imitation of upper-class usage by the lower pecuniary classes'.[13] The anti-utilitarian bias of the ancient universities, seats of the gentlemanly tradition of learning, was sedulously aped by the new institutions, their teachers and their students; so that today the government is still trying (for the second time in its period of office) to switch teacher and student intake towards the applied sciences.

In considering why government policies over the 'long decline' have failed to reverse it, two explanations are possible. The first is that policies were misconceived. The wrong policies were adopted at the wrong time. This was the traditional view: the next time the right government, with the right policies, would reverse the mistakes of its predecessors. Or the failures of policy were due to the amateurish and incompetent civil servants who gave the wrong advice: the answer was to reform the Civil Service. The optimism of the 1960s shines through in Michael Shanks's horrified discovery that there were only two dozen economists in the Treasury; the implication being how much better for the country if the numbers were doubled or even trebled (as, of course, they have been). Repeated failure has been disillusioning. Many people are wondering today whether governments should be in the revival business at all. It may be that the task is beyond conscious collective effort, and that as a society we are doomed to many more years of invalidism. If this is so it may be that the first duty of government is not to make matters worse than they would otherwise have been by inflicting costs in a vain effort to secure revivalist gains.

If we accept that we are in for a long period of invalidism what are dynamic and restless persons to do who don't want to spend the rest of their lives in a social hospital? One answer, of course, is to get out of those occupations and activities in which the odour of decay has become too palpable. Not everything in Britain works badly: much of the society and economy continues to work extremely well and there are plenty of jobs where rewards are high and the tasks challenging. But emigration remains a final possibility. Alfred Hirschman wrote that one can respond to dissatisfaction with the service being offered either by 'voice' (complaint) or by 'exit' (transferring one's custom elsewhere – at the extreme, to another country). This most individualist of solutions has always had a powerful attraction for the British – more so than for any other European people – which makes one wonder whether the traditional British way of life has ever been quite so attractive to the British as Establishment mythology would have it. Twenty million people left these shores in the century 1815 to 1914 – only a quarter from famine-ravaged Ireland. It has always struck me as odd that families notoriously reluctant to move a few miles in search of a job should be ready to travel thousands in search of a new home. But perhaps they are rational to believe that a move to a neighbouring town would change nothing but that a whole new life would open up for them in a new continent. Emigration, as millions of emigrants at all times have understood, is an answer to decline, not for the society they leave behind, but for themselves, their families and their children; and one very much in the British tradition.

Admittedly such a solution only touches the fringe of the problem: the disease is cured for those who leave, but remains for the majority who stay. The more comforting thought is that no decline goes on for ever. Little though we understand them, long declines have systemic causes which, sooner or later, disappear, not through soothing therapy, or deliberately planted shocks, but through changing circumstances. Declines have to do with dominant institutions and interests which have stakes in the old ways, and which are too powerful to be shifted by frontal assault. But subterranean forces of technology, competition, the slow attrition of new ideas, may be at work which gradually empty them of life. Suddenly they are a push-over. Here governments *can* play a part by permitting some things to happen, previously forbidden, and forbidding other things, previously allowed; not going against public opinion, but perhaps a little ahead of it. Mrs Thatcher may have sensed some of these subterranean movements; and if her government can create a legal framework in which they can grow and prosper she will have given the British not a cure but a chance to cure themselves.

NOTES

1   Martin J. Weiner, *English Culture and the Decline of the Industrial Spirit* (1982).
2   Mancur Olson, *The Rise and Decline of Nations* (1982), p. 78.
3   Sources: Angus Maddison, *Pioneers of Capitalist Development* (1982), pp. 45, 96; World Bank *World Tables*, vol. 1; and *World Development Report* (1985).
4   D. Flower (ed.), *Voltaire's England* (1950).
5   Ralph Waldo Emerson, *English Traits* (1883); quotations from pp. 38, 99, 285, 142–9, 109, 233, 288, 261.
6   H. Sidgwick, Diary, 26 January 1885; quoted in A. and E. M. Sidgwick, *Henry Sidgwick: A Memoir* (1906).
7   Alfred Marshall, *Memorials* (1925), pp. 298–300.
8   Brooks Adams, *America's Economic Supremacy* (1900), pp. 146–52.
9   Thorstein Veblen, *Imperial Germany and the Industrial Revolution* (1915),
10   Quotations from pp. 131, 209, 141, 200, 148, 246, 199.
11   J. M. Keynes, *Collected Writings*, xxiv, p. 261.
12   *Encounter* (June 1963), p. 38.
13   Veblen, *Imperial Germany*, p. 147.

CHAPTER FIFTY-FOUR

Rhodes James's British Revolution

Robert Rhodes James, *The British Revolution: British Politics 1880–1939. Vol. 1. From Gladstone to Asquith 1880–1914*
[Hamish Hamilton, 1976]

THE MAIN puzzle about Mr Robert Rhodes James's new book is its title. Admittedly this is only the first of two volumes. The second will take the story up to 1939. Even so, after almost 300 pages, one should have some inkling of what, in the author's view, the British Revolution consisted. It was clearly not the 'complete overthrow of the established government' which is one of the two definitions of 'revolution' in the Shorter Oxford English Dictionary. So it must be 'an instance of a great change in affairs'.

There are a number of candidates in this period. Democracy arrived and the State grew. Industrial Britain became more organized and less dynamic. Consumption rose and religion declined. One can expatiate on the New Wealth, the New Philosophy, the New Theatre, the New Writing, the New Education and last, but not least, the New Woman. Perhaps all these things amounted to a British Revolution; perhaps not. But they are not what this book is about. Mr Rhodes James is interested in the world that was dying, not the world that was being born. Of course, he provides some obligatory background. Every seventy pages or so he tells us firmly that Britain's economic position was 'causing concern' and provides a paragraph of not very illuminating statistics. Clearly it was not causing Mr Rhodes James much concern. Yet here is an excellent example of coming events casting their shadows before. From the 1880s the British economy started to run down. Even contemporaries felt a loss of energy in comparison with America and Germany, and it filled them with foreboding. Some attempt to explain why this was happening might have been expected. One might argue that a country which starts first is thereafter always at a disadvantage in renewing its machinery. One might put the blame on the empire and its captive markets. Or one might go further and ask whether Britain ever experienced a true bourgeois revolution; whether, in fact, the formation of a bourgeoisie was blocked by the ease of assimilation into aristocracy and gentry, and the profoundly anti-industrial (not anti-commercial) values of the latter. One might; but Mr Rhodes James does not. This is evidently an uncongenial area of history for him.

Then there was the emergence of mass democracy. What effect did it have on politics? Mr Rhodes James mentions one: county councils were elected after 1887. There were others, more important. In 1900 the Labour Party was formed. By 1906 it had thirty MPs. It was the start of class politics in Britain. Perhaps it happened because the Tories and Liberals, like Mr Rhodes James himself, were more interested in Ireland than in working-class issues. More likely, the formation of a working class with its own organization and consciousness was inherent in industrial society. Its effect, though, was to bring industrial and social demands from the periphery into the centre. This really did change the political life of this country. It affected the character of the Liberal government of 1906–14. Together with the business clamour for Protection, it marked the beginning of the end of Victorian *laissez-faire*. Henceforth the government would intervene ever more actively in social and economic affairs. The rise of Labour was also beginning to pose an immense survival problem for the Liberals. Between 1906 and 1914, the

Liberal Party started to disintegrate at the local level. Lloyd George, with his usual sensitivity to history's hoofbeat, was already seeking a way out. His flirtations with both the Labour Party and the Conservatives from 1910 onwards have to be set in the context of Liberalism's decline as an independent political force. But here again Mr Rhodes James is strangely uninterested in this new political horizon.

Another instance of the same indifference is his antipathy to Joseph Chamberlain. Chamberlain was not very likeable. Mr Rhodes James finds him 'cold', which is fair enough. But he is incomparably the most significant British politician of this era. He is right at the heart of the transition from the Victorian to the modern world. He originates practically every modernizing impulse in late Victorian politics: municipal socialism, the party caucus, Radicalism, populism, the cult of efficiency. He was the first to challenge free trade, and indiscriminate capital exports, with a producer's policy based on Protection and Imperial Preference. Even his 'retrograde' stand on Ireland which, it should be remembered, opposed Home Rule but offered devolution all round, now looks positively futuristic compared with a policy which so obstinately ignored the reality of Ulster. But, of course, Chamberlain's modernism is precisely what Mr Rhodes James dislikes about him. Chamberlain recognized Britain's predicaments and applied himself to finding remedies for them. He was an intellectual, perhaps not by habit, but by circumstance. Mr Rhodes James likes intellectual politicians only if their intellectual activity is divorced from their political actions. The idea of a politician applying his mind to the solution of problems plainly fills him with acute apprehension.

This leads him to a serious misjudgment of Chamberlain. His mind, he says, 'ranged neither wide nor deep'. This fits the younger son, Neville, but is a very odd thing to say about the father, whose whole career is so impregnated with a sense of the future. What really annoys Mr Rhodes James about Chamberlain is that he had plans – unlike Salisbury, Balfour and Rosebery, who were above that sort of thing. Mr Rhodes James dislikes plans. Plans, ideas, are things that break up parties. Chamberlain broke up two. In particular, he didn't understand that the great strength of the Tory Party was being wholly devoid of ideas, except of the most nebulous character. (Mr Heath fails Mr Rhodes James's test for the same reason.) Yet Chamberlain's political importance is surely to have triggered off the process of party realignment which was destined to replace the Victorian by the modern party system: part of that British 'revolution' which Mr Rhodes James is supposed to be chronicling with sympathy.

Mr Rhodes James reveals his approach to his craft when he comments on the Irish Home Rule crisis of 1885–6: 'the historian must be careful not to impose order and coherence ... upon a human and confused business'. This is a peculiar doctrine. What function has the historian but to impose 'order and coherence' on a mass of raw data? Mr Rhodes James's choice of words betrays another oddity. He identifies human with 'confused'; in other passages also with 'ambitious', 'self-interested', 'irrational'. But prominent among the specific *human* attributes are rationality, imagination, and altruism. The tendency of many historians to admire politicians who display none of these qualities, on the ground that this somehow makes them more 'human', is one of the stranger aberrations of the profession.

This book has nothing to do with a British Revolution, in any of its possible forms. Instead we get traditional political history, very well done. The focus is on Parliament – the alternation of governments, the succession of 'great' issues and dramatic incidents, the clash of personalities and ambitions. There are interludes of 'background' and biography. The latter are never less than gripping. When Mr Rhodes James sympathizes enough to understand, he produces memorable writing in his sketches of Salisbury, Lord Randolph Churchill and Rosebery. The style, too, is pleasing; the book's production, with Mr Rhodes James's face gazing benevolently from the back jacket, almost impeccable. But at this time, with the problems now confronting British society for which one turns to the past for understanding and illumination, this is not the kind of book I would have thought of writing.

CHAPTER FIFTY-FIVE

Our Finest Hour?

Corelli Barnett, *The Audit of War: The Illusion
and Reality of Britain as a Great Nation*
[Macmillan, 1986]

CORELLI BARNETT is a military historian, who has written various military histories. This book is not another one, although it is set in the Second World War. Rather, it is a continuation of a wide-ranging enquiry, which he started in his *The Collapse of British Power* (1972), into the causes of Britain's decline. This is a topic that has attracted historians, sociologists and economists. In the last few years the volume of this literature has swelled enormously, and not surprisingly, since Mrs Thatcher has made the attempt to reverse that decline the central issue in British politics. The chief interest in Barnett's attempt is the perspective a military historian brings to the problem; though it is important to add the caution that not all the contributors to this literature are talking about the same thing.

Barnett's main theses will be familiar to readers of his earlier book. There he attributes the 'collapse of British power' to the rot in the national character which set in during the nineteenth century, under the influence of evangelicalism. The evangelical revival produced the Arnold-ian model of the 'Christian gentleman' which dominated the Victorian public school. It turned a ruling class of hard-willed, hard-minded pragmatists into one of woolly-minded moralists, despising science and technology and all those activities which derogated from the gentlemanly vocation. This class sacrificed the true requisites of national power – the ruthless pursuit of the national interest (by war if necessary), backed by a war capacity rooted in science-based industry – to a 'romantic internationalism' in foreign policy and a *laissez-faire* attitude to the domestic economy.

Such attitudes, buttressed by Britain's temporary post-Napoleonic supremacy, were challenged in the late nineteenth century by a hard-headed school of imperial statesmen. They wanted to organize the empire as a strategic and economic unit to counter the rise of Germany. But 'within a few days' of Britain's entry into the First World War, the moralizing internationalists had 'psychologically taken over the war they had previously condemned, moralized it, turned it into a crusade, and given it a characteristically romantic set of characteristically impractical but inspiringly idealistic aims'. In the inter-war years, the Christian gentlemen were in control. The upshot was the appeasement of practically everyone, partly made necessary by the neglect of the 'very heart of British power, her own industrial machine', which beat feebly 'within the vast body of British world involvement'. Britain entered the Second World War as industrially unprepared as it had been for the First World War.

Running through this polemic is the contrast between the 'Elizabethan and Cromwellian conception of the nation-state as a single strategic and commercial enterprise' and the high value attached to individualistic muddling-through which succeeded it. 'Whereas the British solved the problem of the inefficiency of the State by abolishing the State as far as possible, European countries like Prussia instead modernised the State and made it efficient.' *The Collapse of British Power* is the tract of an unregenerate mercantilist for whom the international arena is a Hobbesian jungle, and a nation's industry a power resource which enables it to fight off the other predators. We shall return to this argument later. For the moment, it is merely necessary to note that Barnett applies it virtually unchanged to the story he has to tell in his new book. The 'audit of war' is an excellent title. Barnett aims to capture the performance of British industry at a particular moment of stress and show why the dreadful inefficiencies which the audit reveals were not remedied. The explanation, in turn, involves those cultural attitudes he had described in his previous book, which dictated the response to the war experience, ensured its real lessons were not learnt, and pushed us further down the slope.

Barnett's project involves a systematic attempt to destroy the myth of Britain's finest hour – at least on its industrial side. Far from humming to the new tunes of common purpose and productive zeal, the British war effort was a thing of shreds and patches, exhibiting all the familiar signs of the 'British disease'. Indeed, man for man, German industry performed far better than Britain's. Only Hitler's 'faulty steering' plus American help saved us from defeat. Our performance gave no grounds for optimism about the future. As Barnett puts it: 'German shortcomings in production derived essentially from the nature of the Nazi regime and ceased with its demise: Britain's shortcomings belonged to Britain's industrial system itself.' But the true 'audit of war' remained hidden by 'the outward facade of victory, the propaganda about the scale of the national effort, and the deceptive inflow of American aid under Lend-Lease'. As a result, the British started the peace blind to the true extent of their weakness, and the steps required to remedy it. Instead of re-equipping their industries, reforming their trade unions, and educating their work-force to compete in world markets, they set out to build a New Jerusalem, burdening an already weak economy with vast additional costs. The upshot was protracted industrial decline, which culminated in the debacles of the last ten years.

Barnett's three dense chapters on the coal, steel, and shipbuilding industries make up a depressing catalogue of inefficiencies culled from hundreds of investigative reports and enquiries. Britain entered the war with a coal industry fit only to ride 'with little competitive effort on the crest of fast-swelling demand'. Production was spread over 1700 mines; productivity was between a half and two-thirds of Germany's, largely reflecting the much lower percentage of coal mechanically cut, conveyed, and loaded; the managers were badly trained; the alienated miners more interested in raising wages than coal. National reorganization in 1942 instead of concentrating production on the efficient pits supported the unfit at the expense of the fit by means of a levy to average out costs. The story of steel is the same: 'plant already mostly obsolescent or even obsolete in date or design, organisation of production and marketing fragmented, leadership outmoded in outlook and often technically ignorant, research and development neglected and underfunded, work-force wedded to traditional methods of demarcations'. Cecil Bentham's technical survey of shipbuilding workshops 'evokes a traveller's account of the craftsmen's booths in an Arab *soukh*'. Despite an ambitious programme of capital re-equipment undertaken in 1942–4, 'the charac-ter of British shipbuilding, with its historical flaws, still remained . . . as it was; and especially the human flaws'.

Even the more successful new-technology industries, directly related to combat performance, found it hard to make their way in face of inherited defects. The Spitfire was as good as the Messerschmitt BF 109 but took two-thirds more man-hours to build; the progress of the jet-engined aircraft from the drawing board to the squadron 'evokes the turkey rather than the jet'. The rise in aircraft production (one of the war's success stories) was achieved not by a 'revolution in productivity, but simply by deploying 115,500 extra machine tools and over 1 million extra workers'. British tanks until late in the war 'were mechanical abortions that foreshadowed the disastrous car models launched into world markets by the British automobile industry in the postwar era'. Even with radar a familiar disharmony appeared 'between scientific genius and industrial backwardness. For while Britain could devise all these technological wonders, she could not make them quickly enough or in large enough quantities.' The electronics industry 'suffered from a galloping attack of the British disease – fragmentation of resources and effort, overlaps in production design, batch production virtually by hand, utter want of standardisation of parts and components'. Only one industry emerges unscathed from Barnett's audit – the chemical industry. It had been started by a German, Ludwig Mond.

The story is certainly a grim one; but the audit is only half done. Barnett has not tried to provide a true balance sheet of the performance of the British economy under wartime conditions, but only an audit of the state of Britain's industrial efficiency, which boded ill for the coming battles for world markets. He provides an important corrective, therefore, to the traditional emphasis on the success of macroeconomic management and of allocating resources. But this side of the balance must be kept in mind if one is to understand the way the British responded to the war record. For example, Britain managed to mobilize a far higher proportion of its manpower (and womanpower) for war production than Germany did. That output was raised mainly by the cavalry charge method – hurling resources at industry regardless of cost or efficiency – was probably inevitable in wartime. Civilian leadership was far better than Germany's – as Barnett acknowledges. Here is a puzzle which Barnett does not solve: how was it that all those products of the Arnoldian public school system, supposedly ignorant of modern life, managed to rise to the challenge of modern war? There is another point which Barnett ignores. Promises of a better life were not the result of a mistaken audit of war; they were integral to the war effort itself. Politicians knew that they reneged on them at their peril.

There are other 'inefficiencies' which emerge from Barnett's audit which are less convincing. Barnett emphasizes that Germany was more self-sufficient as a war economy than Britain; that Britain was constantly having to buy, beg or borrow vital parts from the United States (especially machine tools) to keep its war effort going. This is true, but the lesson which Barnett seeks to draw is not valid. American help was not a stroke of luck. Expectation that such help would be forthcoming was a vital element in Britain's strategic calculations – as it had been since the turn of the century. And it was not disappointed in either war. The British accumulation of overseas assets, whatever its effect on the domestic economy, also makes sense from this point of view: it was an emergency war chest. One can go further. All that British moralizing rhetoric which Barnett so despises was expertly attuned to American susceptibilities; so perhaps our ruling class was not so feather-brained as it appeared. In any case, it is a strange doctrine for a military historian that one should expect to fight a war without allies, or that subsidies have no place in alliance policy. Of course, the condition for British success was Anglo-American control of the Atlantic, which was maintained in both World Wars, though only just. But even if Barnett is right in his belief that reliance on America for vital war parts was a weakness for a war economy, its relevance to peacetime competitive prospects is not clear. Self-sufficiency may be a sound strategic doctrine, but it is a poor economic one.

I point these things out in order to show that the plans of the planners were not so illusory as Barnett supposes. Barnett's few pages of dismissive comment on the illusions bred by wartime macroeconomic management reflect the currently fashionable obsession with supply-side economics rather than serious economic analysis. They leave out two important points. First, planning for full employment after 1945 assumed a continuously higher level of *world* demand than had existed in the 1930s, to be achieved by a combination of national full-employment policies and the reformed international monetary system established at Bretton Woods in 1944. Secondly, it assumed American aid or loans to Europe during the reconstruction period. Both of these assumptions were more or less proved correct (though Marshall Aid may more plausibly be regarded as a 'stroke of luck' for the British economy than was Lend-Lease). Barnett remarks that the failure of wartime full employment to boost the productivity of labour was 'hardly encouraging' for its prospects for doing so in peacetime. This ignores the fact that the bulk of savings which fuller wartime employment brought were consumed by the war itself; something which would obviously not happen in peacetime.

Nevertheless, Barnett is right in thinking that post-war planning had in it an element of myopia. Whitehall was certainly alive to the dire balance of payments position which Britain would face after the war; some of the apostles of the New Jerusalem were not. Also people were blinded by a too seductive analogy between what could be done in war and what could be done in peace. The argument: we made the shells, why can't we build the houses? ignores the fact that we had to pay for the houses by exports while the shells were paid for by Lend-Lease. Undoubtedly, macroeconomic policy was too readily assumed to be the panacea for all structural problems of the British economy: an illusion, though, that owes more to the success of the Attlee government in 1945–51 than to wartime thinking.

For what the audit of war should have shown, according to Barnett, was that British industry was badly led, badly equipped, and had an appalling badly-trained labour force wedded to restrictive practices which even the war had been unable to dislodge: in short, was in no position to compete successfully either with its late enemies or the United States. All the best brains of the country and all available resources should have been directed to remedy this state of affairs as quickly as possible. Instead energies and projected resources were largely taken up in New Jerusalem projects: establishing the Welfare State, rehousing the working class, bringing new industries to decayed areas for social reasons, and reconstructing the educational system with humanist rather than practical intent. Thus was the great opportunity lost.

Barnett's special scorn in a book not short of it is reserved for the New Jerusalemers – 'latter-day White Knights riding out in wartime Britain to combat evil with the flashing sword of moral indignation, and questing in simple faith for the grail of human harmony and happiness'. His thesis, in essence, is that the 'enlightened' Establishment of his previous book turned their appeasing touch from the unrewarding task of trying to moralize Hitler to the job of moralizing the British working class – moralizing, not educating, them. They troop into view, Tories, Liberals, Socialists, Christians, Jews, atheists – Barnett does not bother with fine distinctions – to be mown down by his machine-gun prose. At their head are the two Williams – William Beveridge (ex-Toynbee Hall) and William Temple, Archbishop of Canterbury ('I shall regret the day when we become efficient at the cost of our spirit') – followed by a motley army of do-gooders. Victorious in wartime over intermittent realists like Churchill and more persistent ones like Sir Kingsley Wood, Chancellor of the Exchequer from 1940 to 1943 (one of our less likely unsung heroes), they finally get their come-uppance from Barnett.

The key point in Barnett's alternative programme would have been mass education for capability in the Cruel Real World, not in the Brave

New World. Barnett views the condition of the workers not from the moral standpoint but 'as a military historian might evaluate the rank and file of an unvictorious army'. In his earlier work the rot in the national character stopped with the ruling class: indeed Barnett was disposed to see the 'crude nationalism and hatred of foreigners of urban masses' untouched by the evangelical revival as a powerful support for a vigorous foreign policy. But it is now their lack of technical skills, erosion of personal capacity, alienation, truculence, slackness and 'coolie' mentality which most impresses him. 'Had a malevolent conqueror wished to pursue a long-term policy of degrading the British industrial population into a physically, intellectually and technologically inferior race of "natives" posing little competitive threat, he could hardly have succeeded better than the unwitting effects of *laissez-faire* dogma, shortsighted exploitation of cheap resources by "practical-man" capitalists and sheer want of effective public administration in the Britain of 1780–1840.'

His fundamental criticism of the wartime New Jerusalemers is not that they burdened an enfeebled economy with additional costs for social services, but that they promulgated and imposed a system of mass education which not only bored most of its pupils but systematically deprived British workers of the technical skills they needed to break out of their underdevelopment and the nation out of its. His most deadly darts are aimed at the churchmen and classicists who dictated the philosophy of the 1944 Education Act. He shows that practically the whole of the time of R. A. Butler and his officials at the Board of Education was spent in negotiating with church bodies on the place of Christian instruction in the curriculum and the future of the church schools. 'As a consequence', he writes, 'the crucial question of providing the nation with an education for capability from primary school up to technical university equal to that of her competitors was squeezed away to the sidelines.' Compulsory continuation education till eighteen, promised in the 1944 Act, remains a dead letter to this day.

Barnett's two books are part of a single enterprise. In the earlier one the emphasis was on the incapacity of Britain's ruling class in foreign policy; here the focus is on Britain's 'business' failure. What ideas does a military historian bring to such an enterprise? The most important thing to say is that for Barnett 'political' and 'economic' decline are part of the same problem. As he sees it a nation's primary task is to preserve or increase its power in a Hobbesian world. Industry is both a war resource and a method of waging war by other means. He sees industries defending and conquering markets like armies defend and conquer territories; and believes that the same values, the same principles of organization, are valid for both kinds of operation. Failure in one department is likely to go hand in hand with failure in the other. To Barnett, therefore, the decline and fall of British industry is part and parcel of the story of the decline and fall of the British empire, with a single set of explanations for both.

This kind of thinking used to be commonplace; it is less usual today. Since the nineteenth century, in the Anglo-Saxon world at least, war and business have usually been seen as appealing to different motives, politics and economics as separate realms. Typically economic life is seen as a matter of individuals or households pursuing their private ends through markets, not of disciplined national armies fighting each other for resources. The cultures spawned by war and business – aristocratic and bourgeois – are usually viewed as antithetical. Thus an influential strand in the literature on Britain's economic decline stresses the growing incapacity of the business class for business, owing to its capture by aristocratic (i.e. pre-industrial) values. Barnett will have none of this. To him the captain of industry and the military commander are the same types, pursuing victory by the same methods. The requirements for success in both activities are a General Staff to devise strategy; well-led, well-trained, well-equipped disciplined formations to carry it out. Against this he has erected ideal types of failure which he considers characteristically British: the Bishop and *laissez-faire*. For too long, he says, Britain has been run by lay bishops; industrial organization sacrificed to individualism. That is why we have gone downhill.

What light does such a perspective throw on our economic decline? It obviously distances Barnett from much, but not all, of the current debate. It separates him from that wing of Thatcherism which blames our malaise on increasing state intervention which has reduced the efficiency of markets. But it is quite compatible with Mrs Thatcher's determination to break the power of the trade unions, her attempt to reduce the social overhead represented by welfare, her emphasis on technical education, and her essays in the 'creative destruction' of obsolete plant and technology. (Barnett has nothing but scorn for Dalton's policy – enacted into law by the Coalition government in 1945 – of attracting new industry to decaying areas. 'New species', he tartly observes, 'emerge and thrive better in new habitats'.) Similarly Barnett's position has no point of connection with Marxist explanations of British decline in terms of the intensity of the class war. To Barnett the truculent and defensive attitude of the British working class is a function of its educational level, not of its position in the productive process. On the other hand, he might sympathize with the argument that British industry was sacrificed to the financial interests of the City of London. He shares with the Left the belief that 'Industry' is a good thing. Nigel Lawson's view that we should all earn our living by selling services would fill him with horror.

Like a good strategist, Barnett would prefer to occupy what Andrew Gamble calls the 'centre' ground of the current debate, which is concerned not with the question of ownership of industry or state intervention as such but with 'the way in which government interacts with industry' (*New Society*, 28 February 1986). Successful economies seem to have developed successful patterns of interaction. The way Japanese corporations and government jointly plan, years ahead, the conquest of foreign markets by strategically selected products evokes Schlieffen rather than Adam Smith or Karl Marx. That this is the road to success is the main message of Barnett's pungent, angry polemic. But I doubt if Britain will take it. It goes against the grain. It is too Prussian. And anyway look what happened to the Schlieffen Plan!

CHAPTER FIFTY-SIX

A Critique of the Ageing Hypothesis *

I

WHEN economic life is going badly, economists call on history, sociology and political science to explain why. When it is going well, they regard these subjects as scarcely worthy of notice. This may seem unfair, but it is as it should be. When things are going well, economists can feel that their models fit the current institutional setting in which economic activity takes place. (Whether, or to what extent, economics actually

---

* I would like to thank Professor Ian Little for his helpful comments on the first draft of this essay.

makes economies work better is another question.) When things are going badly, they begin to feel that their theories no longer fit reality. They call on outside help to discover in what ways the real world has been changing, so that they can choose better models. I am interested in the kind of help history can give macroeconomics. Macroeconomists suffer most when the economy falters, since their livelihood and reputations depend on equipping governments with policies which produce economic success as popularly understood. The current 'crisis in economics' is almost wholly a crisis in macroeconomics. History may be able to help. But historians have their own research programmes and methods of enquiry which may not fit the needs of economists. When economists are driven to study or write history on their own account they usually do it badly. They cannot abandon their deductive habits of mind even when they think they are being most historical. If history is to help macroeconomics it must be done by properly trained historians prepared to turn their knowledge of the past into useful knowledge. And economists may find historical facts more liberating than historical fictions.

The problem faced by economists in doing history arises, I think, from the fact that they are not trained to think about phenomena over time. Any strict deductive system depends on the elimination of time. Nevertheless time, which brings continuous change, threatens to wreak havoc with any logical system for thinking about the human condition. There are two strategies for dealing with this threat. The first is to base one's reasoning on a few constants which are held to exert a preponderant influence on behaviour. Changes wrought by the passage of time can then be ignored as transient or subsidiary. The second strategy is to assume that change itself is subject to laws which, if they can be discovered, will tell us what 'stage of development' we have reached. The first strategy enables our model to *resist* time; the second offers the hope of being able to *adjust* it to the appropriate stage of development. One should perhaps mention a third strategy, which is to *plan* time itself so that only those changes occur which are planned to occur: the totalitarian dream.

Strategies I and III require no history. But the third is still, fortunately, unfeasible, while the first is likely to be unsatisfactory to any economist who aims at an adequate degree of realism. So the macroeconomist is likely to become dependent on some version of the second strategy. And it is at this point that the historian comes in with his objections. Historians tend to see events as unique. They may detect patterns; they rarely discover laws. Economics tends to see the phenomena it deals with as law-governed; and if time is part of the problem, time itself must be subjected to laws. The historian's main objection to any law-governed historical scheme is that it will be grossly over-determined, and therefore will be bad history. The objection that it is bound to produce bad macroeconomics is worth pursuing a little further. Seductive though the prospect is, the imagination is apt to play a nasty trick on those who try to think of societies moving through time according to some discoverable pattern. Societies undoubtedly move forward: England in 1982 is a hundred years 'older' than it was in 1882. Yet our words for describing such movement are derived chiefly from the life cycle of the individual: we instinctively think in terms of youth, maturity, and old age. As a result it is difficult to avoid thinking of social movement through time as other than an ageing process. Even when the conclusion – death – is rejected, the metaphor remains: people talk about 'rejuvenating' industry or 'reviving' the economy.

Of course, societies with a historical sense have, at times, managed to escape from this particular metaphor. The favourite escape route has been through the notion of Progress. At various times, for reasons associated with a vast expansion of material possibilities, societies or clusters of societies have felt sufficiently optimistic to develop a different language for dealing with time. They have thought of the future as better than the past, not older. But such moments have generally been fairly brief. The nineteenth century was one: yet before it ended the metaphor of decay had reasserted itself; and has, on balance, dominated the way people have tried to think systematically about the future this century: as witness the cyclical schemes of Spengler, Toynbee, and Sorokin. Mention of these names reminds us that it is by no means only economists who have succumbed to the attractions of the metaphor of ageing. Economists are immune to the extent that they do not think much about history in any case. It is when they are forced to do so by unexplained and unanticipated changes in conditions that the danger arises.

Macroeconomics, I think, is of all branches of economic theory most likely to draw on the metaphor of ageing, for the very concept of a 'macroeconomic problem' might seem to imply some such thing. Buried deep in the assumptions of macroeconomic reasoning, so deep as to be almost invisible, is the notion that at one time our industrial societies were young and they have now become old. The older societies become, the more rigid they get. Collective forms of life replace individual forms. A conclusion frequently drawn is that older societies require more governing than younger ones. Government, it is felt, is bound to expand as a simple function of social longevity – to compensate for rigidities which have accumulated elsewhere in the social system. Eventually it too becomes part of the 'macroeconomic problem'. In old age the market economy evolves into corporatism or even socialism. Schumpeter and Galbraith are two well-known examples of economists whose historical speculations have yielded conclusions of this kind. A historical critique of such views cannot be expected to give comfort to any particular school of macroeconomics. It cannot, for example, support those who claim that nothing has changed since Ricardo's day. On the other hand, it gives no support to the ageing hypothesis either. Societies change. They may even progress. They do not age. This thought is liberating.

II

A persuasive recent argument that social 'sclerosis' is at the root of the 'macroeconomic problem' has been put forward by the economist Mancur Olson in his plea for an 'evolutionary approach to macroeconomics'. He writes:

> Obviously something is accumulating or progressing over time such as changing policies, or structures or institutions, which is changing the character of the economic problem. We know, both from the tendency of real output to vary more with changes in aggregate demand and from direct observation of the prices themselves, that stickier prices and wages are crucial to the change that is taking place. But we do not *explain* the change by referring to sticky prices, any more than we explain anything by referring to *ad hoc* assumptions like 'rigid wages' or merely descriptive concepts like Phillips curves. The *cause* of the fact that most wages and prices were less flexible in the interwar years than in the nineteenth century, and still less flexible in these stagflationary times, must be found. That cause, in turn, must play a leading role in our macroeconomic theory.[1]

From this quotation we may infer that Olson believes that the 'macroeconomic problem' has passed through at least three historical stages.

These may be described as follows – though I am not sure that Professor Olson would do so. In the first, which lasted through the nineteenth century, there was, strictly speaking, no macroeconomic *problem*. Insufficiency of demand did not occur, because changes in demand brought price adjustments, leaving the volume of output unchanged, or subject only to temporary fluctuations. The second stage – the inter-war years – may be characterized as one exhibiting downward rigidity in *money wages* as well as a reduced mobility of labour. Changes in relative prices no longer brought about the required adjustments in costs or shifts between occupations – or at any rate not quickly enough to prevent general unemployment from developing and persisting. This is the stage of the macroeconomic problem that called forth the Keynesian revolution. In the third (and contemporary) stage of the macroeconomic problem it is *real wages* which are inflexible downwards. At this stage attempts by government to maintain full employment by monetary expansion are defeated by workers' insistence on being compensated in full for every rise in the price level. The failure of Keynesian policy to secure the employment-maximizing condition that wages must not exceed the marginal productivity of labour leads naturally to 'stagflation' and the 'crisis of Keynesian economics'. Each stage, it will be noticed, is marked by an extra rigidity, to which macroeconomic policy must adjust if it is to be serviceable. Today, it is often said, macroeconomic policy can work only if it is buttressed by 'incomes policy'.

How would a historian set about criticizing the notion of 'accumulating' rigidities in an industrial society? The fundamental objection is philosophical. Sclerosis, he might want to say, is the norm of any settled society. It is inherent not in longevity but in social organization itself. Societies appear to the historian 'old' at the dawn of history, in the sense that they are rigidly bound by custom and tradition. The task is not to explain why societies become rigid, but to consider the means by which they escape from the consequences of rigidity from time to time – without which, of course, no 'progress' is possible. Three such mechanisms have a long ancestry: migration, war, and revolution. A fourth which has operated since the eighteenth century is the application of science to the arts of production and to the art of governing.

No one who accepts this position would, I think, make the mistake of suggesting that European societies were in some sense young or unsclerotic at the start of the commercial and industrial age. Market economy had emerged and was to grow in importance. But it was deeply embedded in feudal substance. This was not true of North America. But in the nineteenth century much of the New World was not a society, or collection of societies, so much as an outlet for migrants from Europe. It provided an external solution for Europe's Malthusian problem, of a type familiar throughout history.

This perspective opens up what I would call a historical approach to the macroeconomic problem. Olson's argument is that in the 'youth' of capitalism the adjustment to changes in economic conditions was effected by prices not by quantities. There is obviously some truth in this, but I doubt whether it can carry the whole burden of explanation for the relatively satisfactory levels of economic activity achieved in this period. For one thing it assumes that the price of labour was at this time much like the price of other commodities – that is, mechanically subject to the laws of supply and demand. This may seem plausible to the theorists of 'ageing', and may even have been true to some extent in America, but it could not have been true in European societies where the relative price of different catagories of labour was protected by long-standing custom long before the emergence of effective trade unionism. Nor did nineteenth-century economists, contrary to myth, believe that the price of labour was like other prices. Take the careful evidence of J. N. Keynes, Maynard Keynes's father, to the *Royal Commission on the Depression of Trade and Industry in 1886*:

A general fall in prices will, unless under very exceptional circumstances, be accompanied in the long run by a fall in wages. But the fall in prices and the fall in wages may not go on *pari passu*. Generally speaking, prices are more easily acted upon than wages, a tendency to a fall in the former does not meet with the same resistance as a tendency to a fall in the latter. It is not, of course, intended to lay down an absolute rule. But it may be said that the effect of a contraction of the metallic standard is likely to be manifested first in the prices of commodities and only subsequently in wages. This, at any rate, seems to be the case in the present instance. Profits ncessarily suffer temporarily, and again the effect is loss of confidence and a feeling of depression, in consequence of which the working classes themselves ultimately suffer.[2]

This is a far cry from a modern statement of the problem: but it does show that nineteenth-century economists were at least aware that output adjustments could go together with price adjustments. What needs to be explained is why such output adjustments did not lead to longlasting depression as occurred in the inter-war years. It might be argued that the time-lag between the fall in prices and the fall in costs lengthened as a result of the increasing organization of labour. But it is hard to believe that on its own it was sufficiently shorter in the nineteenth century to have prevented a Keynesian deficiency of demand from persisting. The reason it did not seems to lie in the existence of a third adjustment mechanism which had largely disappeared by the inter-war years: emigration. It was emigration of surplus labour combined with the export of capital, not the rapid adjustment of labour costs to falling prices, which overcame depression of domestic demand in the nineteenth century: falling prices produced emigration rather than wage cuts. Thus it was the existence of a quasi-permanent *shortage* of labour in the New World balancing a quasi-permanent *excess* of labour in the Old World which solved the macroeconomic problem in the nineteenth century. The world came out of the Depression of the 1880s and 1890s through a massive redistribution of labour and capital not between occupations in the same country but between countries and continents.

Of course, it is very difficult to *prove* the above interpretation. It may still be argued that the crucial change relevant to the macroeconomic problem between 1880 and 1930 was the growth of trade union organization, not the 'closing of the frontier'. Unfortunately this is the kind of argument that is very difficult to settle by purely historical enquiry, which may, indeed, supply evidence to support both positions. The reason is that it is virtually impossible to apply to historical investigation the logical method of difference – i.e., the method of comparing two instances which resemble each other in all but one respect. Any comparison between two periods or two societies throws up too much that is different and too little the same for the crucial differences to be isolated with assurance. Thus Olson's own 'law' that in two societies 'in other ways equal' the one which has been stable will be more sclerotic because it has had more time to accumulate 'distributional coalitions' cannot be tested historically in the way he seems to want because the *ceteris paribus* condition cannot be satisfied. Nevertheless, faced with a choice between two explanations, one of which relies on an ageing process and the other of which provides an *ad hoc* reason of the kind outlined above, most historians would, I think, intuitively prefer the second to the first.

III

The insidious fascination of the ageing hypothesis emerges in another context of interest to macroeconomics: the role and scope of government. It is fairly widely accepted that the size of the public sector has some connection with the contemporary problem of 'stagflation', though the causal connection is unclear. It may be argued that beyond a certain point the growth of the public sector outstrips the revenues available to support it, leaving it dependent on inflationary finance. Or it may be claimed that the larger the public sector the greater the ability of trade unions to impose inflation on society, since the public employer is more concerned to avoid political rather than financial losses. (Both arguments apply only to a 'mixed' economy which enjoys full political and industrial rights.) The way one thinks about the macroeconomic problem will inevitably be affected by whether one thinks there is or is not some necessity for the state to *grow* in a 'developed' society. Those who think there is often tend to see the macroeconomic policy of the future in terms of a restriction of hitherto accepted freedoms, not because they necessarily welcome the prospect (though some of them do) but because they think it the only means by which the present 'macroeconomic problem' can be overcome.

No proposition is more firmly established in the mythology of social ageing than that the tendency of government to grow is palpable and irreversible: this growth being connected with the wants of a mature or 'rheumatic' society. First stated as a 'law' (the so-called Law of Increasing State Expenditure) by the German economist Adolf Wagner at the end of the nineteenth century it helped create a mood in which every increment of public relative to private activity tended to be accepted as inescapably in the nature of mature social life. At the same time nothing has proved more difficult to establish analytically than this particular law. In trying to understand the 'growth of the state', the historian faces, on the one hand, the undoubted fact that, by whatever test is applied (spending, employment, regulation, ownership), public activities have expanded relative to private ones over the course of this century in the developed democracies: and, on the other hand, the fact that there is no reputable ground for the belief that this was inevitable.

Naturally, he is driven to look for *ad hoc* explanations, which are not difficult to discover.

The thesis that the growth of the state is a function of social ageing is supported by a number of arguments of which I pick out the two most familiar: the technological imperative and the growth of democracy.

It is often argued that technology causes the size of the firm to grow and, as a consequence, production to concentrate in fewer units. The growth of the state can be seen as a function of both developments. The larger the firm the more it needs the state to guarantee it a market, to underwrite its costs of development, to control the trade unions, etc. Indeed, according to Galbraith, the growth of macroeconomic intervention by government is itself the direct result of the needs of large, inflexible corporations. Left-wing economists then proceed to argue that once government subsidizes big business it has the right to tell it how to spend the money it provides. On the other side, the growth of the state can be seen as a response to the growth of private monopoly. The argument seems to be that advanced technology causes private monopoly to develop, which the state has to convert into public monopoly as the only way of reconciling the claims of welfare and stability. Thus there is a direct correlation between technical progress and the growth of the state.

The faults in this complex of arguments have been pointed out many times without making much dent in their popularity. Technological progress may favour bigness in some phases, smallness in others. Smaller firms may be readier to innovate than larger ones, being less sclerotic. Industrial concentration in a single country may be offset by the growth of international competition; in any case, there is little evidence that it has increased in the United States (the main home of these theories) over the last eighty years. Moreover, a great part (though by no means all) of the explanation of the growth in size of firms and of private monopoly is to be found not in a supposed technological imperative but in state policy itself. The state has actively promoted these tendencies, either as a by-product of strategic or political objectives or (especially in Britain in the 1960s) in the (probably mistaken) belief that bigger always means more efficient. Thus government policy has done much to create the giant businesses whose power and lack of commercial viability then provide a standing invitation for further extension of public ownership or control.

After a careful survey of Wagner's Law, Robert A. Musgrave concluded that, 'The driving force in the rise of civilian state expenditure to GNP ratio has been the growing importance of social services, pointing to change in social and political climate as a decisive causal factor in expenditure development.'[3] From this point of view the crucial difference between the nineteenth century and the twentieth has been the emergence of universal suffrage. And indeed no historian would wish to deny its importance in causing the state to grow relative to the rest of society. Yet the view that democracy *itself* causes a growing proportion of GNP to be spent by public authorities is a priori implausible. It must depend, in part at least, on the nature of the electorate being considered, particularly its level of affluence, the degree of inequality in the distribution of income, and the way the tax burden is distributed. As a matter of historic fact democracy came into existence in Europe at a time when the vast majority of the voters had no property and very low wages, and when it was natural for them to look to the state to supply desired services which they could not supply out of their own incomes. Moreover, the electorate was enlarged in most European countries without a corresponding enlargement in their obligation to pay direct taxes. As Peacock and Wiseman have put it, '. . . the widening of the franchise increases the political importance of the groups most likely to believe that public expenditures should be increased for their benefit, but that the necessary revenues should be raised from the . . . richer by such means as progressive taxation.'[4] John Stuart Mill was more direct. 'Those who pay no taxes,' he wrote, 'disposing by their votes of other people's money, have every motive to be lavish, and none to economise'. If every voter was directly taxed, the poor were more likely to identify their interests with 'a low scale of public expenditure.'

This may have been naive. Nevertheless, the degree of affluence of a given electorate as well as the arrangement of the tax liability must have some influence in determining the 'democratic' preference for different levels of public expenditure. It is perfectly plausible to expect that an affluent democracy, the majority of whose citizens pays for the full cost of social services which the state provides for it, may be inclined to vote for lower taxes and fewer social services. And history provides at least partial confirmation of this view in the American experience, where a democratic electorate which antedated Europe's but which was much more affluent, has never supported anything like the European scale of social provision.

407

The conclusion of this argument is that while democracy has been an important cause of the growth of the state in the last hundred years, there is no compelling reason to suppose that the demand for constantly enlarging state expenditures is inherent in democracy; and some reason to suppose that in the next period we will see a shift in democratic demands towards a relatively reduced level of public provision. The weakness of the 'democratic imperative' argument is the failure to specify the conditions under which one might expect one reaction rather than the other.

To the historian there is one extremely important cause of the twentieth-century growth of the state which is normally ignored by theorists of growing state expenditures precisely because it cannot be made subject to any plausible law of social development. That is the impact of the two World Wars, separately and cumulatively. The importance of war for the size of the state has long been recognized by historians. The fact that Western nations emerged from each of the World Wars with the scope of their governments much enlarged is well established. The interesting question is why the role of the state failed to contract in either 1918 or 1945 to what it had been before. There was some contraction in both cases but not to the previous level. This is in great contrast to the decades which followed the Napoleonic wars. There seem to be two main reasons. The first is that in neither 1918 nor 1945 did the conclusion of hostilities restore the expectation of permanent peace which the nineteenth century had had. As a result the legal status of peace became far more costly than most previous wars had been. The second reason is that in both wars governments were compelled to demand a degree of civilian involvement in the war effort unprecedented in modern times. Civilian conscription could be secured only by promising a better life for the majority after the war. Since the material requisites of a better life could no longer be seized from the defeated enemy, as in ancient times, the only way they could be rapidly provided was through the tax system.

There is a further point. Both World Wars, but especially the First, had a great effect on the 'macroeconomic problem' as it developed and as it was perceived. By disorganizing the machinery of international transfers – of goods, capital, and labour – the First World War made macroeconomic problems less capable of external solution. In that sense, twentieth-century war itself has contributed to the closing of the frontier – for capital and labour – not just by creating barriers to exchange within the capitalist world, but by closing off a large socialist bloc from international commerce. Yet unless we think war is endemic to the twentieth century, there is no reason for these frontiers to stay closed, and for governments to have to go on compensating for their closure. We are driven to the conclusion that a large part of the current expectation about the role government is bound to play in economic life derives from events whose influence will diminish the further we move away from them.

IV

Release from the ageing hypothesis could have both a sobering and liberating effect on economics. Sobering is the realization that the normal condition of societies is to be *more or less* old. No model based on the assumption that society is, or could be made like, a market is likely to be an adequate guide to policy. Economies can be more or less flexible, not perfectly so. Liberating is release from the tyranny of the trend. We are not bound by historical laws, only by facts. Some of these facts may change spontaneously; others can *be* changed by governments acting differently. The most liberating thing of all that a knowledge of history can bring is to enable us to ignore the past when it suits us.

NOTES

1   Quoted in 'The Crisis in Economic Theory', *The Public Interest*, Special Issue (1980), p. 79n.
2   *Third Report of the Royal Commission on the Depression of Trade and Industry* (1886), Appendix C, pp. 415–17.
3   R. A. Musgrave, *Fiscal Systems* (1969), p. 123.
4   A. T. Peacock and J. Wiseman, *The Growth of Public Expenditure in the United Kingdom* (1961), p. 67.

CHAPTER FIFTY-SEVEN

Psychohistory

A Speech to the South Place Ethical Society, 12 February 1977

[James] had always kept this old symbol of taking a knife and striking his father to the heart. Only now, as he grew older, and sat staring at his father in an impotent rage, it was not him, that old man reading, whom he wanted to kill, but it was the thing that descended on him – without his knowing it perhaps: that fierce sudden black-winged harpy, with its talons and its beak all cold and hard, that struck and struck at you (he could feel the beak on his bare legs, where it had struck when he was a child) and then made off, and there he was again, an old man, very sad, reading his book. That he would kill, that he would strike to the heart. Whatever he did – (and he might do anything, he felt, looking at the Lighthouse and the distant shore) whether he was in a business, in a bank, a barrister, a man at the head of some enterprise, that he would fight, that he would track and stamp out – tyranny, despotism, he called it – making people do what they did not want to do, cutting off their right to speak.

THIS passage, from Virginia Woolf's *To the Lighthouse*, in which we are led to see how James's unconscious urge to kill his father, Mr Ramsay, will be transmuted into a passion to stamp out 'tyranny, despotism', is a fit introduction to the central idea of what is called psychohistory. Virginia Woolf was herself heavily influenced by Freud. The main purpose of psychohistory is to show how the Oedipal conflict, which Freud postulated as central to the development of adult sexuality, can act as an independent generator of social, religious, political, and artistic change.

Let me start, by way of contrast, with conventional history, the kind practised by most unreflecting British historians. The historian's subject-matter is public events. He selects an event, or happening, which seems sufficiently important and problematic to write about. He will embark on his job with three main questions in mind. What happened? How did it happen? Why did it happen? To answer these questions he uses evidence – state papers, newspapers, private letters, diaries, statistics, artefacts, and so on. Out of these he constructs his story and explanation.

Take as an example the origins of the Second World War. The historian would talk about grievances felt by Germans about the Treaty of Versailles. He would talk about Hitler's plans. He would discuss public opinion in Britain and France. He would try to make sense of Chamberlain's policy. On these and other matters he would bring evidence to bear. If he wants to explain Churchill's conduct he will quote from speeches and letters, in which Churchill explains his attitude. That isn't to say he will take Churchill's own explanations at their face value. Any good historian will ask questions about his documents. Are they authentic? Are they relevant to the problem at hand? Who is the writer writing for, or the speaker speaking to? What is his purpose? Who is he hoping to persuade? He will be suspicious. He will question motives. The evidence may give rise to different interpretations. He may weigh some evidence higher than other. The debate between Alan Taylor and Trevor-Roper about Hitler's intentions turns wholly on the value as evidence which they attach to different documents. But the important point is that the questioning will be mainly in the sphere of *conscious* motives, or intentions, the kind that one can find evidence for.

Such is normal history as it was and still is generally practised, with lesser or greater degrees of skill and sophistication. It is derived from the standard Western view of the nature of the mind. In this view, people's instincts get transformed by environment and ever increasing knowledge into a system of preferences. As Anthony Quinton has written: 'It is not doubted that man always has a clear idea of what he wants and of what motivates him to act as he does.'[1] To be sure he may be mistaken about what gives him pleasure or pain, or about the best means to pursue his aims. But his behaviour is voluntary, conscious; or at least, it is treated as such for the purpose of historical explanation.

Then came the revolutionary challenge of Marx and Freud. What they did, essentially, was to shift historical explanation from intentions to situations, the first economic, the second psychic. Marxists see historical change in terms of a class struggle derived from feudal, later capitalist, 'relations of production'. Freudians emphasize generational aspects of change, derived from the Oedipal conflict between father and son. Marx, unlike Freud, remained in the rationalist tradition. Historians have always accepted the existence of causes for events which it is not

411

particularly useful to discuss in terms of individual intention or preference. When, following an earthquake, people flee their homes, it seems a
sensible shorthand to say the earthquake caused their flight. It also seems
sensible to say that in traditional societies harvest failures cause death
from starvation. Technical change is another such 'cause'. We say that
climate, geography, or technique causes people to behave in certain
ways, because we notice that certain climatic or geographical or technical
circumstances or events are associated with certain kinds of behaviour;
although, on a philosophical view, only people can cause themselves to
behave in the way they do.

Marx took this idea a step further. To him the class struggle,
derived from exploitative 'relations of production', was the dynamic
force behind domestic and international conflict. But since a key point in
his analysis was that the ruling class ruled by deception, evidences of its
exploitative intentions were not to be found in its documents, which
would be typically expressed in a language of law and order, harmony
of interests, national security, or patriotism. (Whether rulers were
deceiving themselves as well as the ruled was left ambiguous.) Setting up
an 'objective' standard of rationality which could not *in principle* be
subjected to the test of documentary evidence deprived historians of
their main tool: the archive. This cut off Marxist historiography from
the mainstream.

I should mention a third thinker in the assault on conventional
historiography, the sociologist Vilfred Pareto. An Italian contemporary
of Freud, an engineer and economist by training, he saw in his own
lifetime a massive revolt against what he considered reasonable economic
and social arrangements, culminating in the most destructive war and
revolution in history. He became convinced of the power of the irrational
in human affairs. The youths who sacrificed their lives for their country
or for 'scientific socialism' were moved by faith, not reason. 'The
diffusion of a doctrine', he wrote, 'depends hardly at all on its logical
value.' Historical studies had failed to grasp the irrational sources of
behaviour because human beings have an incurable tendency to give
reasons for their actions. They invent logical theories to justify behaviour
which is instinctive to the human species. From his own study of human
behaviour, Pareto was led to analyse action in terms of residues and
derivations. Residues are the stable, instinctive elements in human
behaviour; derivations, the assertions, principles, and verbal proofs in
terms of which they are justified and explained. From these principles he

412

developed a remarkably cynical view of human history as the 'circulation of élites' in which principles and ideals dignify an elemental and continuing struggle for power. From this point of view Marxism was simply the ideology of the counter-élite.

Marx, Freud and Pareto faced historical writing with a revolutionary challenge. They attacked it at its fundamental point. The type of evidence on which historians relied was inadequate, they claimed, to explain what was really happening, and why it was happening. Wars had to be explained by underlying economic or instinctive forces; or, early Freudians were wont to say, by the unconscious urges of the war-makers. What is more, Marxists and Freudians claimed, one could detect these forces only if one was trained in Marxist or psychoanalytic technique, because it was only then that one could know *where to look*.

However, I leave Marx and Pareto to one side. Psychohistory is the application of psychoanalysis to the problem of historical explanation. As a conscious form of historical writing it is associated particularly with the work of Erik Erikson, whose books on Luther and Gandhi exhibit the method applied to its most obvious subject, biography, in a genuinely illuminating way. Bruce Mazlish's recent book on James and John Stuart Mill is a less successful example of the approach.* It is still largely an American enthusiasm.

Psychohistory makes three claims. The first is that since men and women act for reasons largely unknown to them, the explanation for their actions cannot be revealed by the unmediated study of their beliefs, intentions, interests and calculations. The second claim is that there exists a science of the mind – psychoanalysis – which can enable historians to arrive at the true explanations of human conduct. Thirdly, psychohistory argues that the Oedipal conflict, the clash between father and son, is the primary mechanism of social change, the mechanism which ensures the progress of the species. One should add that Erikson has shifted the focus of psycholanalysis from early childhood to adolescence. His central concept is the 'identity crisis' by means of which, between puberty and adulthood, a new person is created 'and with the new person, a new generation, and with that a new era'.²

Let us examine these three claims in turn. Psychohistorians have

---

* The two books by Erik Erikson are *Young Man Luther* (1959), and *Gandhi's Truth* (1970); Bruce Mazlish's is *James and John Stuart Mill: Father and Son in the Nineteenth Century* (1975).

put their finger on a genuine problem, especially in biographical writing. Most historians are not equipped to tackle the basic biographical questions: how to explain a person's opinions, behaviour, success or failure. All historians feel this poverty of explanatory power. We are all aware of a certain demonic quality in Enoch Powell. He seems to be driven by emotions of which he is not fully aware or of which he is not fully in control. In fact, we also know that it is precisely this part of him that brings passion to his utterances and through which he establishes a political rapport with sections of the electorate which is unique in contemporary politics. Yet we have no approved language for talking about these things other than one of interest, calculation, belief. This was brought home to me when I was at Nuffield College. Powell came to a seminar run by the political scientist, David Butler – this would have been in 1966 or 1967. Butler could not understand why Powell was making these extraordinary speeches up and down the country. Was he hoping to form a new party? he asked him. Was he trying to overthrow Edward Heath? Surely he would be doing better to toe the line? After Butler had gone on for some moments with these speculations, Powell interrupted him with the icy remark: 'Dr Butler, has it ever occurred to you that I enjoy making speeches?'

Psychohistory, then, has emphasized the crudeness and inadequacy of standard historical explanations of human motive. This charge is justified. However, its own efforts to remedy history's failures are so seriously flawed that one wonders how much of value it has to offer the practising historian. The most general problem arises from the status of Freudian theory itself. To what extent is it a true 'science of the mind' as its proponents claim – as opposed to a set of imaginative insights, daring, but entirely unproved and unprovable, speculations? The usual test for a scientific theory is whether it can be falsified. What conceivable event or circumstance would prove Freudian theory wrong? I can think of none, because, like Marxism, it has an endless number of escape routes. Let me mention just two. Hostile criticism is discounted as being nothing more than the reflection of emotional resistance on the part of the critic. The second is more interesting. Freud originally held that the traumatic events in infancy experienced by his neurotic patients were actual seductions. When this was attacked, he replaced it by the hypothesis of sexual fantasies, with the rival parent as object. This replaces a hypothesis which in principle is falsifiable, by one which is not. For how does one justify an assertion about a state of mind for which no known evidence exists? Unconscious states of mind are apparently 'recalled' in the course of psychoanalysis, e.g., through dreams. The recalled matter is then interpreted to provide evidence of the existence of an Oedipus conflict in early childhood or adolescence. But such evidence can be interpreted in different ways. The 'data', in other words, can be made consistent with different hypotheses.

So, of course, can much historical data. But although a historian's story is constructed from the data, the existence of the data is not itself the point at issue in most historical disputes, merely whether it tends to establish the contention being advanced. In all such disputes the assumption is that there is some data which might in principle settle the matter. If I say that Anthony Eden went to war with Nasser because Nasser had slept with Eden's mother, and you point out that this did not, and could not, have happened, that is the end of the story. If, however, I replied that this is what Eden believed to be the case, and on your asking for evidence of this belief, I said that the evidence is to be found in certain remarks Eden made which, while ostensibly about other topics, 'unconsciously' let the cat out of the bag, argument would become interminable. Every genuine historical hypothesis can be refuted by contrary evidence. If this were not so, there would be no distinction between history and fiction.

The reliance of Freudian hypotheses on evidence which is not ostensibly relevant to the problem under discussion is a serious matter for a historian. Good therapeutic results can be achieved on the basis of magic – if, for example, the patient believes the psychoanalyst can help him. But psychohistory's object, like that of any history, is to find out the truth about a historical event. The psychohistorian is putting a historical figure on the couch, not to help him, but to find out what really happened. He has both more and less contact with his subject than is available to a clinician. On the one hand, he cannot get at his subject's unconscious mind through free association. On the other hand, he may have a mass of autobiographical and other material from which to extract meaning. When therapy is not the object, the status of the theory according to which something counts as evidence for something else is of key importance. Psychohistory, like psychoanalysis, starts out by looking for evidence of an Oedipal conflict; and finds that the material can always be made to show evidence of such a conflict.

Take Bruce Mazlish's account of the relationship between John Stuart Mill and his father. When the young Mill was sixteen, he lost his watch, which had been given to him by his father. An accident, one may feel. But there are no accidents in psychohistory: the loss was unconsciously intended. The watch, writes Mazlish, was a symbol of the 'mechanical aspect of life'; its loss symbolized 'John's desire to stop being accountable to his father for every moment of his life . . . In "losing" his watch John was unconsciously rebelling against his father's rigid control.'[3] 'From such evidence', Mazlish wisely notes in another connection, 'one can build castles in the air.' Yet most of the evidence for the existence of an Oedipal conflict in the book is of this character. It is convincing if one accepts the system of thought which sees it as evidence of John Stuart Mill's resistance to his father's will. It has no power to convince independently, a characteristic it shares with religious belief. Yet I have an uncomfortable feeling that there is *something* in what Mazlish is saying.

Erikson seems to be well aware of the dangers of the psychoanalytic method. He writes '. . . when a devotional denial of the face, and a systematic mistrust of all surface are used as tools . . . they can lead to an almost obsessional preoccupation with "the unconscious", a dogmatic emphasis on inner processes as the only true essence of things human, and an overestimation of verbal meanings in human life.'[4] Yet in his study of Martin Luther he does not altogether escape these traps. Here are three statements. 'But a clinician's training permits, and in fact forces him, to recognise major trends even where the facts are not available.' Translation: it must have happened this way even if there is no supporting evidence. Again, 'we must view the scant data on Luther's upbringing, surer of the forces than the facts'. Finally, 'I said Luther could not hate his father openly. This statement presumes that he did hate him underneath. Do we have any proof of this? Only the proof which lies in action delayed, and delayed so long that the final explosion hits the non-participants.'[5] Since Erikson's whole interpretation of Luther hinges on his unconscious hatred of his father, a hatred which he consciously turned, after many spiritual crises, against the Pope, it is disconcerting to find so little of what a historian would call evidence for this emotion.

Luther's rejection of the Catholic doctrine of salvation through works in favour of salvation through faith was, it is clear, a gradual process taking place over a number of years. Erikson admits this, though he has to extend Luther's 'identity crisis' till he was thirty and over to fit his scheme. However, his style of writing and method of analysis commit him to place great weight on certain traumatic moments which he portrays as decisive turning points. There are a number of famous ones in Luther's life – the fit in the choir, the thunderstorm, the panic at the first Mass, the 'revelation in the tower'. Erikson does not question the historical authenticity of these moments, or their actual historical place in Luther's life. He accepts Luther's own retrospective view of them, and contents himself with interpreting Luther's own psychological truth to the reader.

Sometimes it is his own psychological truth which seems more important. A casual remark of Luther's table talk reported in 1532, i.e., eighteen or nineteen years after his new theology had been worked out, suggests that some of Luther's insights came to him on the lavatory. This is by no means the only interpretation one can put on the text; it is not clear that Luther was referring to a lavatory at all; and certainly he did not attach weight to it, the remark being recorded just once in his life. But this launches Erikson into a long discussion, based on the Freudian theory of anality, on the connection between Luther's moralism and his lifelong constipation and water retention. The discovery of faith was accompanied by a distinct improvement in these functions. Luther's religious liberation occurs in the closet and is associated with the release of his bowels, or as Erikson puts it, 'he changed from a highly restrained and retentive individual into an explosive person'.[6] Erikson is being true to his credo. He follows the forces rather than the facts; or rather his theory tells him that the facts must be so. In John Osborne's play on Luther, constipation plays a major role in the foundation of Protestantism.

Similarly with Gandhi: the doctrine of non-violent resistance is derived from the 'feminine' way in which Gandhi nursed his sick father in order to 'deny the boyish wish to replace the (ageing) father in the possession of the (young) mother . . .' Thus 'the pattern would be set for a style of leadership which can defeat a superior adversary only non violently and with the express intent of saving him as well as those whom he oppressed'.[7] This interpretation hinges completely on the assumption of an Oedipal conflict, for which no evidence is adduced.

The problem of evidence is thus one major barrier to the acceptance of the scientific status of psychohistory. A second is the assumption that the psychoanalytic categories are equally valid in all places and at all times. In his study of Gandhi, Erikson, to be sure, acknowledges the 'difficulty of applying to the Indian scene any interpretation derived from the Western family', specifically the irrelevance of the Oedipal conflict in India owing to the 'diffusion of the mother in the joint family' and therefore the lack of salience of her relationship with the father.[8] Yet, as I have just shown, the analysis develops in terms of the Oedipal conflict just the same. Of Luther's relationship with his father, Erikson writes, 'I know this kind of parent–child relationship all too well from my young patients.'[9] How can one apply evidence, even if valid, from mid-twentieth-century America to fifteenth-century Germany, especially in the light of studies, such as Eric Shorter's,* which emphasize how radically different from our own were family relationships in pre-capitalist rural societies? Confidence in Erikson's interpretative scheme is undermined by his statement that religion 'will occupy our attention primarily as a source of ideologies for those who seek identities'.[10] Erikson writes, with specific reference to the Oedipal conflict, 'I will not discuss here the cultural relativity of Freud's observations nor the dated origin of his terms, but I assume that those who wish to quibble about all this will feel the obligation to advance specific propositions about family, childhood and society which come closer to the core, rather than go back to the periphery of the riddle which Freud was the first to penetrate.'[11] Apart from Erikson's unfortunate condemnation of his critics in advance as 'mere quibblers', the passage is seriously objection-ble. It is Erikson's responsibility, not that of his quibbling critics, to advance specific arguments which come closer to the core. The raw application of timeless ideas about identity crises and Oedipal conflicts, unmediated by changes in family structure, child-rearing practices, and sundry other conditions, from twentieth-century America (or Vienna) to fifteenth-century Germany is a disconcerting aspect of Erikson's work.

The third objection to psychohistory as a science of the mind adequate for historical use arises from its treatment of greatness. Erikson explicitly describes his book on Luther as an attempt to 'understand better the origin of greatness'.[12] And surely this is a most challenging and necessary task. But I doubt whether Freudian theory offers a persuasive psychology of greatness. Any analysis of greatness should surely aim, one feels, to understand those attributes which *distinguish* great people from others such as cleverness or imagination or courage or determination. Psychohistory, by contrast, bases explanations of great-

---

* Edward Shorter, *The Making of the Modern Family* (1975).

ness on psychic conditions supposedly common to all. What we need to know is why people are exceptional, normal, or neurotic. The explanation cannot be something they all share, like premature potty training. Erikson admits that an essential element of Luther's greatness was what Luther himself brought to experiences which were common enough to German boys of that age at that time. He was 'observant and imaginative'. He had 'one of the most powerful minds of his age'. Luther's life work, Erikson writes, was produced by a combination of his 'personal needs and superlative gifts'.[13] This is unexceptionable. But all we hear about are the former, nothing about the latter. Similarly, he recognizes that Gandhi 'harboured an early sense of originality and, in fact, superiority', and that what distinguishes a great man is his capacity to 'manage' the complexes which destroy or constrict others.[14] But the aspects of Gandhi which he singles out for attention are precisely those aspects derived from Freud's study of neurotic patients.

What we need is a psychological map of greatness which brings motives and qualities out of the region of 'instincts' or 'drives' to that state of consciousness where they are capable of being discussed by historians. A start on this has been made by the psychologist Abraham Maslow. What he says – which common sense has always known – is that in any given motivational pattern, conscious and unconscious motives coexist and interact. Neither the conscious nor unconscious mind should be understood as a prior state.*

The final claim of psychohistory is to link social changes to the Oedipal conflict and ensuing generation war. As Erikson writes, 'For if some youths did not feel estranged from the compromise patterns into which their societies had settled down … societies would lose an essential avenue to rejuvenation and to [the] rebellious expansion of human consciousness which alone can keep pace with the technological and social change.'[15] Social change and identity crisis are seen as interacting with each other. Erikson argues that situations of fluidity, such as existed in sixteenth-century Germany at the dawn of capitalism, increase generational tension, which in turn produces rebels who bring about appropriate changes in consciousness. Generational conflict is society's way of generating new ideas when it needs them, the need being determined by the state of the productive arts.

This is an interesting thought, worth further investigation. It might

---

* A. H. Maslow, *The Further Reaches of Human Nature* (1975).

be applied with profit to early as well as late nineteenth-century Europe, and more recently to the changes of the 1960s.* It is a useful way of exploring the relationship between individual and social strains. Specifically, it offers a valuable justification of biography as a way of doing history. But there is something puzzling in Erikson's statement: 'There is an optimum ego synthesis to which the individual aspires; and there is an optimum social metabolism for which societies and cultures strive. In describing the interdependence of individual aspiration and of social striving, we describe something indispensable to life.'[16] Here we have an infelicitous mingling of Freudian and Marxist ideas which take us outside the realm of history into teleology.

The verdict on psychohistory has to be mixed. It offers historians a valuable tool for exploring motive, but its rightful sphere has to be more carefully delineated. Specifically, history's evidence-based nature precludes it from becoming a central method for investigating historical problems. It is particularly useful where the historian has reason to suspect self-deception. Brutus gives as his reason for murdering Caesar the wish to preserve the Roman Republic, but we suspect that he was consumed with envy. In that sense, historians have always been open to pathological explanations of action. What triggers off such explanations is a feeling of disproportion or mismatch between what would be reasonable for someone to do in the circumstances, or a person's stated reason for doing something, and the nature of the act. The historian assumes rational motives, that is, unless he has reason (evidence) to suppose otherwise. This brings out the point that Freudianism is only one of a family of languages for dealing with the instinctive, non-rational elements in human activity, and is very far from having established a privileged claim to consideration. Unconscious sexual jealousy of the father is not the only possible explanation of non-rational behaviour. Both Jung and Adler, and of course Pareto, challenged Freud on this point.

Psychohistory links generational struggle to social change in ways which historians have traditionally ignored. As we have seen, it furnishes a strong justification for biography; in the hands of a sensitive practitioner like Erikson it can yield powerful historical poetry. But its explanatory power, as Erikson recognizes, is much stronger in fluid than in static epochs; and historians without special psychological skill will no

* See my review of Noel Annan's *Our Age* in this volume.

doubt continue to concentrate on the external determinants of change, leaving the psychic panorama to be explored by novelists and poets.

We can agree with Erikson that psychohistory offers an example of the 'compost heap of today's interdisciplinary efforts, which may help to fertilize new fields, and to produce future flowers of new methodological clarity'.[17] Alas that day is not yet.

NOTES

1   Anthony Quinton, 'Freud and Philosophy' in Jonathan Miller (ed.), *Freud, The Man, his World, his Influence* (1972), p. 74.

2   Erik Erikson, *Young Man Luther* (1959), p. 17.

3   Bruce Mazlish, *James and John Stuart Mill: Father and Son in the Nineteenth Century* (1975), pp. 224–5.

4   Erikson, *Luther*, p. 147.

5   Ibid., pp. 47, 51, 62.

6   Ibid., p. 199.

7   Erik Erikson, *Gandhi's Truth* (1970).

8   Ibid., p. 43.

9   Erikson, *Luther*, p. 61.

10   Ibid., p. 19.

11   Erikson, *Gandhi*.

12   Erikson, *Luther*, p. 145.

13   Ibid., pp. 59, 141, 189.

14   Erikson, *Gandhi*, p. 113.

15   Erikson, *Luther*, p. 145.

16   Ibid., p. 247.

17   Ibid., p. 13.

CHAPTER FIFTY-EIGHT

Hugh Dalton

Hugh Dalton
[Jonathan Cape, 1985]

IN TRYING to create the character and explain the achievement of Hugh Dalton, Ben Pimlott rightly rejects the distinction between 'public facts and private facts'. 'It is surely apparent', he writes, 'that in politics every publicly-expressed passion – of patriotism, class, sentiment, concern for the poor or whatever – has a private dimension; and that "political character" is always a package in which "public" and "private" traits are intertwined.' Quite so: and it is the achievement of this thoughtful and thought-provoking book that it does reveal, and reveal convincingly, the private dimension of Dalton's political personality. Pimlott has had the enormous benefit of Dalton's own diary – 'an Aladdin's cave for historians' – but he has also done the rest of his homework thoroughly. The result is a professional job. The effects are the product of much industry, much attention to 'connections', much artistry.

The tension in the book arises quite simply from the fact that Dalton was a 'shit' who was also, in many ways, an admirable public man. The avalanche of denigration starts with Queen Victoria ('what a horrid little boy') and rarely falters. Dalton was quite exceptionally unlovable. His appalling mannerisms – the booming, hectoring voice, the rolling eyes, the false bonhomie – were physical expressions of insecurities so deep that he could never sustain a personal relationship. Most of the officials who served under him loathed him; his political equals despised him. He was both bully and coward; vain, self-pitying and insensitive; a shameless fixer who usually ended up by being fixed himself. The cumulative effect of the indictment is to make him a figure of pathos. As Chancellor of the Exchequer in 1947 he thrashed around like a 'wounded beast', his features disfigured by boils. He died alone in a public geriatric ward, booming away till the end. Monsters like Beaverbrook had friends who loved them; Dalton was no monster, yet he was almost completely friendless. Nevertheless, Pimlott considers him a high-principled socialist and successful Labour politician, the chief architect of Labour's post-war governmental philosophy, the creator almost singlehanded of Labour's post-Attlee leadership. He was driven, in Pimlott's view, by a wholly admirable passion for equality, fortified by a clear-sighted policy for attaining it. The problem is: how does the 'shit' Pimlott conjures up relate to the public man he clearly admires?

What Pimlott would like to say is that hatred of Dalton was the perfectly understandable hatred of the upper classes against a 'class traitor' who threatened to despoil them of their ill-gotten wealth. If the biography has a thesis, this is it. But the story he tells is rather different. The son of a remote mother and a grotesque, snobbish Canon of Windsor, who much preferred the memory of his royal pupils Eddy and

George (later George V) to the actuality of the unlovable Hugh, Dalton lacked the looks, the charm and the brains to succeed in the Eton and Cambridge circles to which he aspired. Personal rejection by his parents and by his own class led him to identify with the workers against the royal family, the aristocracy and the rich. Trained as an economist, by Keynes among others, he developed powerful economic arguments, for disinheriting the wealthy through a massive capital levy. But, Pimlott writes, 'Tories felt, and they may have been right, that for all the intellectual sophistication of Dalton's utilitarianism, he was emotionally less interested in helping the poor than hurting the rich.' Pimlott is, of course, right to say that Dalton was disliked by Tories and capitalists because he wanted to reduce inequality. But he was just as much disliked by his own side. He could easily have survived his pre-budget indiscretion as Chancellor in 1947 had Labour's Big Four not seen it as a welcome excuse to get rid of him. The economist and temporary civil servant, James Meade, a liberal-socialist redistributor himself, found Dalton a 'paranoid bully'.

Pimlott as a historian, and particularly as a Labour historian, shrinks from the implications of what he is saying as a biographer. He prefers to think of political conflict in terms of ideology, not personality. One can sympathize with this – especially against the background of the standard Tory view that social conscience must be the expression of character deficiency. As he tells it, Dalton takes his place as one of the sacrificial victims of the Labour leadership's endless compromise with capitalism. I am more impressed by the illiberal character of Dalton's attempt in the 1940s to institutionalize the wartime state; and its emotional roots in his desire to revenge past humiliations. It was not just Tories who felt that there was something wrong with Dalton's thinking because there was something wrong with his feeling.

This brings us to a large subsidiary theme. Like his father, Dalton was what Pimlott calls 'homoerotic'. Nicholas Davenport wrote that he 'adored good-looking and gallant young men . . . His first great love was Rupert Brooke; his last was Anthony Crosland, though Tony was greatly embarrassed by his attention . . . When Rupert Brooke died in the First World War . . . Dalton never forgave the Germans.' Here again personal tensions had political effects. Dalton's hatred of the Germans played an important part in swinging the Labour Party into belated support for rearmament in the 1930s. For this Dalton was highly praised. It also helped delay Labour's acceptance of German rearmament in the 1950s.

Pathological hatred is not, after all, the best preparation for statesmanship, even though it may occasionally point policy in the right direction; and George VI was right to object to Dalton as Foreign Secretary in 1945.

On the other hand, I agree with Pimlott that Dalton's discerning love for young men was a vital factor in renewing Labour's leadership – and the party – in the 1950s. As Pimlott notes, Harold Wilson's administrations were staffed by 'Dalton's poodles'. I suspect that the Labour Party would have started dying on its feet much earlier had this chapter-house politician not been so energetically pulling strings to get able young men into Parliament, government and leadership. This was Dalton's greatest service to the left; and it was inspired by love, not hate. The grimmer legacy of his homoeroticism was a largely loveless marriage. Pimlott makes it clear that the instability of Dalton's political behaviour had much to do with the gaping hole in his private life. Whether Ruth Dalton was by nature frigid or made that way by Hugh's indifference is not clear. But together they made an awful pair; and try as he may, Pimlott cannot altogether absolve them of responsibility for the death of their four year old daughter from meningitis: a victim, if ever there was one, of parental neglect. Home provided Dalton with no relief from political tensions. His private frustrations were channelled not into political ideals but into political neuroses.

The disturbing thought which comes out of this story concerns the relationship between politicians and the societies they rule. Both history and political science treat the activity of politics, and of politicians, as deriving from necessities and forces in the public domain. This is one way of holding on to the comforting belief that politicians are basically in the business of damage-limitation. But this is clearly not the case with many politicians. They are damaged goods themselves, and they amplify rather than dampen down social conflict. Political biography is best placed to bring this out; and it is a tribute to Pimlott that he has done so, despite his own deepest feelings. Contemporaries sensed in Dalton surplus hostility; this rightly alerted them to a disagreeable personality dimension to his public causes; that is why they were suspicious of him. The private dimension which Pimlott reveals makes Dalton a less admirable public man than he believes him to be.

CHAPTER FIFTY-NINE

Nye Bevan

John Campbell, *Nye Bevan and the Mirage of British Socialism*
[Weidenfeld & Nicolson, 1987]

THE BRITISH tradition of political biography is courtly rather than debunking. One thinks of those admiring Victorian-style edifices: Moneypenny and Buckle on Disraeli, Garvin on Chamberlain, Morley on Gladstone. In our own day we have had Blake on Disraeli, Michael Foot on Bevan, Marquand on MacDonald, Williams on Gaitskell, Pimlott on Dalton, Rhodes James on Eden: all written by political admirers of their subjects. Without sympathy, the biographical cliché goes, there can be no understanding. And it has always seemed ungentlemanly to stick the knife into a dead man.

John Campbell, author of good books on Lloyd George and F. E. Smith, has broken with this tradition in a most interesting way. He admires Bevan as a person, but hates his ideas. It is this mix of attitudes which gives the biography its plot and strength. Bevan is portrayed as a man of brilliant gifts who was doomed to sterility because he was trapped in Marxist dogma. His greatest achievement, the National Health Service of 1948, was intended as a first instalment of the socialist advance. In fact it was its culmination. In the 1950s the Conservatives were back in power; Bevan was stranded in the affluent society. Long before he died in 1960, at the early age of sixty two, he was politically irrelevant; his socialism somewhat embarrassing.

There is a great deal in this. All his life Bevan talked much more nonsense than a man as clever as he is entitled to. The nonsense was strikingly, even passionately, phrased: like other great Welshmen Bevan had the gift of tongues. But it remained nonsense. He took the fixed view that capitalism could not improve the condition of the people; that only socialism, defined as public ownership, could do this; and that the coming of socialism was guaranteed by history, because the exploited masses were in the majority. In his weekly columns in *Tribune*, on the public platform, Bevan analysed every twist and turn of the political game in terms of this rigid scheme. One can understand how he came to it. It was the view from Tredegar, rationalized by a course of study at

London's Central Labour College. As John Campbell puts it: 'In South Wales in 1900 there were only two classes that mattered. On the one hand were the coal owners and their managers . . . on the other were the miners . . . Here was, on paper, an almost perfect Marxist situation, ripe for class conflict . . .' But Bevan was never a revolutionary. The other lesson he took from Tredegar was that property would have to yield to democracy.

Bevan thought the socialist dawn had arrived in 1945. He wanted, and expected, Labour to stay in power for at least twenty-five years, to achieve the 'complete extinction of the Tory party' (Mrs Thatcher's aims seem rather modest by comparison); he sought, in 1943, to inaugurate the Socialist Utopia by the 'immediate nationalisation of all the basic industries of the country and their administration by a Supreme Council of "able men"', leaving the free market 'to operate only in minor areas of economic activity'. To his great credit, Anthony Crosland realized that this Marxist fundamentalism made no sense by the 1950s, if it ever had. But Nye was too old and too mentally lazy to bring his ideas up to date. *In Place of Fear*, his manifesto for the 1950s, was, in Campbell's words, 'the wordy last gasp of a dying political tradition, not the herald of its rebirth. The very flaccidity of the book's conclusion suggests that Bevan in his heart knew it as well as anyone.' Like so many socialists of his generation he swung between denying that affluence had arrived and chiding the working class for selling out its historic mission for a 'candyfloss' culture.

However, John Campbell also provides the evidence for telling the story another way. In the alternative version it is personality defects, not history, which defeat Bevan and the causes he espoused. As a young Labour MP Bevan flirted with Oswald Mosley in 1930–31. He was always seen by his opponents in the Labour Party as suffering from a 'Mosley complex'; the complex consisting, essentially, of refusing to play the game except on his own terms; and generally breaking things up when thwarted. The comparison with Mosley is certainly suggestive. Bevan felt himself to be a natural aristocrat born into the wrong class and forced by circumstances to spend his life with dullards. Much of his resentment against the established order, as well as his delight in the company of mavericks and adventurers can be traced to this feeling: it was *unmerited* privilege that he really hated. In the Labour Party he suffered from terrible frustration and boredom which comes out in semi-

426

public outbursts: 'Why should I have to bother with these people!'; 'He's nothing, nothing, nothing' (this about Gaitskell); 'Aren't I worth £13 million pounds?'; 'I won't have it. I won't have it'. In a way Bevan was less loyal to the Labour Party than middle-class dons like Gaitskell and Crosland, who actually had no roots in it. They at least felt they had to work their passage; whereeas he felt he had already worked his by spending nine years down the mines in Tredegar. But, unlike Mosley, Bevan had nowhere to go outside the Labour Party – the penalty for not being born with a silver spoon in his mouth. Also, unlike Mosley, Bevan was given a proper job to do, as Minister of Health between 1945 and 1951. So while he flounced out of a Labour Government, he never left the Labour Party. He always managed to land just on the right side of disloyalty.

Nevertheless, with such behaviour patterns he was always an extremely turbulent presence. Campbell provides a gripping account of Bevan in Attlee's Cabinet. Put in as a sop to the Left after five years spent sniping at Churchill in the war, he showed, like John Wheatley in 1924, that he was no empty phrase-maker, but an outstanding man of government. Campbell tells how he outmanoeuvred the British Medical Association to get his National Health Service; and reminds us that Bevan's council houses, while fewer, were bigger and better than Macmillan's ('nothing but the best for the working-class'). He also redresses Philip Williams's account (in his biography of Gaitskell) of Bevan's quarrel with Gaitskell over prescription charges and rearmament which led, in 1951, to Bevan's defeat and resignation, and ushered in years of fratricidal strife. Campbell's verdict: Bevan had the better of the argument with the Chancellor, but ruined his case by abominable, egocentric behaviour.

This brings us back to the role of personality in history. 'Finally,' Campbell writes of Bevan's resignation, 'there is the consequence: the Labour Party riven in two, doomed to waste itself in fractious opposition for half a generation, until both principal protagonists were dead. Bevan's defeat was scarcely Gaitskell's victory. Between them they practically destroyed the thing that in their different ways they loved.' Here we have a broad hint of an alternative ending. Had Attlee handled Bevan better in the closing stages of his government (by making him, say, Foreign Secretary); had the resignations and recriminations been avoided; had Labour clung to office long enough to take advantage of the start of the long post war boom, would not everything have been different? Would Labour have not then got something close to the twenty-five years Bevan wanted to establish socialism?

The answer is no. Certainly there was a chance for a party of the Left in the early 1950s. But not for that Labour Government created by that Labour Party. Socialism was not on the agenda of government in the 1950s. But the party was intellectually and spiritually unprepared to face any other future. The debate between the Gaitskellites and the Bevanites could not, in the end, be resolved within the Labour Party itself. The Gaitskellites – those middle-class dons – point to the SDP. Bevanism pointed nowhere. But Campbell is right not to write Bevan off; in fact, to give him the generous, searching appraisal he deserves. Gaitskell was in tune with the future. But Bevan was a hero.

CHAPTER SIXTY

The Misuse of History

Paul Johnson, *Enemies of Society*
[Weidenfeld & Nicolson, 1977]

SINCE the late 1960s we have all become aware that our civilization is dangerously insecure. To explain how that insecurity has come about is the ambitious aim of Paul Johnson's new book. Johnson's argument is as follows. Progress only takes place under conditions of political freedom. Freedom makes possible the pursuit of truth. It is also associated, as cause and effect, with urban, middle-class capitalism, which in turn promotes economic growth and prosperity. This can be demonstrated historically, and Johnson attempts to do so in a rapid survey of two thousand years which takes us up to the 'permanent miracle' which capitalism and science seemingly secured in the nineteenth century. Then came the early twentieth-century shocks of war and depression. Keynes re-established capitalist democracy on an even stronger footing. But now has come a setback which may prove more serious. The economic disturbances of the early 1970s, which should have been an 'invitation to enlarge our understanding and refine our armour of weapons', has produced a crisis of confidence. The reason lies in the *trahison des clercs*. The intelligentsia has undermined faith in freedom and reason and therefore in Western man's capacity, and even obligation, to save his civilization. Language has become escapist. Philosophers spend their time splitting hairs, instead of discussing issues. Pseudo-sciences and freak religions proclaim their apocalyptic visions. The universities have yielded to the 'new student Fascist Left'. Johnson castigates the psychological relativism that refuses to distinguish madness from sanity; the disappearance of representation in art and tonality in music; the spurious justifications of violence. His villains are predictable: Marcuse, Tillich, Sartre, Lévi-Strauss. So are his heroes: Popper and Medawar. The disintegrating forces battle with the optimist legacy of scientific humanism. The prize is our future. In this struggle, Johnson enjoins us to take our firm stand with him on the absolute values which have created Western civilization.

This is not a crude summary of a subtle argument. It is a crude summary of a crude argument. Johnson is vigorous, clever, self-assured, incisive, but not subtle. His mind is stocked with certainties. There is no hint here of Iris Murdoch's 'tragic discovery . . . that rational men can . . . see the world with a radical difference'. Reason is defined in the Popperian sense of falsifiable propositions; deviations from it are attributed to the Marxist–Freudian conspiracy. There is little sympathy for other points of view. Does Johnson protest too much? So often this type of rigidity comes from the repression of extremely powerful contrary emotions, the imposition of iron discipline on a disobedient nature. Only through the certainty of doctrine can evil be held at bay: a position which, in the end, is little different from that of the pseudo-sciences Johnson seeks to controvert. Johnson knows a great deal of history, but not enough for the task he has set himself; and lacks the sense of history to make up for the absence of detailed scholarship. He has no feel for the uniqueness of different cultures and epochs. No historian would, I think, write of Antiquity as 'to a great extent the history of lost opportunities', or think of previous ages as trial runs for successful capitalism. A strong dose of Moses Finley is recommended for this particular disease.

There are many mistakes of fact and interpretation. Johnson says that the initiative for trade and colonization in ancient Greece 'came not from the state or the community but from individuals'. But trade and colonization were the specific things promoted by the tyrants Periander of Corinth and Peisistratus of Athens: it was the much maligned tyrants who laid the economic and political foundations of Greek civilization; as did the Etruscan monarchy those of ancient Rome. Similarly, it was vigorous state activity, whether in the form of the mercantile wars waged by the Dutch and English in the sixteenth, seventeenth and eighteenth centuries, or the 'enlightened despotism' of the eighteenth-century continental monarchies, which produced important preconditions for industrial take-off. Johnson follows Adam Smith in his misinterpretation of mercantilism. Sophisticated mercantilists did *not* believe that specie *is* wealth. They saw it as a means to wealth, e.g., Sir Josiah Child who thought that a plentiful money supply would stimulate business by lowering interest rates. Again, is it true that it was over-taxation which prevented Holland from being the first country to industrialize? In 1785, the British and Dutch paid about the same taxes: 35 shillings annually per head of population. In the period of its industrial take-off, Britain was a (comparatively) highly-taxed, warlike state, with a growing national debt; far from the *laissez-faire* Arcadia revealed by Johnson. I have two final quibbles. Johnson's view that freedom is a bourgeois invention ignores the roots of freedom in aristocracy: Montesquieu and Tocqueville would have been relevant here. Finally, it is odd to find the late Roman and early medieval loss of realism in art and sculpture treated in the context of the growth of the state – certainly not something one would deduce from the 'social realist' art of modern Communist states. What it surely denoted was a flight from this world during the terrible time of troubles which came in the third century AD, from which Antiquity never recovered, and which continued till the eleventh century.

I dwell on such details because they are symptoms of a systematic misinterpretation based on a deceptively plausible formula: economic progress is caused by the growth of the middle classes; decay by the growth of the state. In fact, the role of the state in the pattern of progress and decline, dynamism and stagnation, is much more complicated than that. I would substitute an alternative formula: the role of the state is a function of the level of difficulty a society experiences in earning its livelihood and defending itself against its enemies. Asiatic despotism, for example, which I would agree with Johnson restricted economic development, was itself partly a response to the impossibility of supporting economic life in the great river civilizations without collective effort. By contrast, Mediterranean cultivation did not require a complex social and

430

political organization. The growth of the Roman bureaucracy reflected growing economic and security problems in the third century AD, which, of course, it aggravated. As George Orwell noted, 'an effect can become a cause, reinforcing the original cause and producing the same effect in intensified form, and so on indefinitely'. It is this sense of the interaction of different causes to produce a particular result that is absent from Johnson's historical vision.

This is a serious defect when he comes to analyse the dangers besetting out own societies. In Johnson's view, the doctrines of unreason, which he often attacks cogently and well, spring purely from the minds of individual philosophers, though usually those with German connections. They can be overcome by contrary affirmations. Occasionally, of course, Johnson does note, in passing, that the appearance and growing acceptance of these doctrines at this particular time is itself something which needs to be explained. Thus he agrees that the growth of the philosophy of violence is caused by lack of space, as well as the teachings of Fanon; there is a brief homage to Stephen Spender's view that artistic dislocation might reflect 'the physical dislocation of the twentieth century caused by wars, the mingling of cultures, social and scientific change and the increased mobility of man'. Also when Johnson talks of the 'restless dynamism of Western culture', with its constant urge to transcend its past, he comes close to recognizing its self-destructive character.

However, this part of the book could have been greatly strengthened by sociological insights. No one who seeks to understand why our system of values and beliefs is subject to revolutionary transformation can do without Marx, Tocqueville, Weber and Schumpeter. Johnson never confronts Marx's picture of a self-destructive bourgeoisie, the levelling and centralizing trends discerned, though for different reasons, by Tocqueville and Weber, Schumpeter's claim that capitalism gives rise to a subversive intelligentsia, or for that matter Polanyi's view that the market system which Johnson, the erstwhile socialist, so vigorously defends, forces society to take protective measures against it to avoid being reduced to a heap of ruins. In short, Johnson's analysis of our intellectual crisis lacks any dynamic theory of change.

It would be wrong to end on a negative note. There are many good insights. I was very struck by Johnson's view of contemporary doctrines of violence as providing intellectual camouflage for a reversion to barbarism. I, too, believe that the assertion of basic values is necessary

431

for their survival. Commitment to freedom can direct attention and energy to those solutions to problems which do least damage to it. As a defender of freedom I welcome this book. As a historian I wish the defence rested on solider historical foundations than it does.

CHAPTER SIXTY-ONE

A. J. P. Taylor

[1990]

ALAN JOHN Percivale Taylor was the best-known historian of his generation. Much of his fame rested on his public, and popularizing, activities – as journalist, television star, and leading light in CND. But he was also a technically outstanding historian, with two special qualities: intuition – what he himself called his 'green fingers' – and a unique gift for making ordinary language carry extraordinary thoughts. His individuality proved too much for the historical etablishment. Taylor made his reputation by debunking Establishments of all kinds. That is why the highest academic and public honours eluded him.

Like Bismarck, of whom he made the remark, Taylor could be 'made to sparkle whichever way you look at him'. But his autobiography, *A Personal History*, published in 1983, revealed, beneath the glitter, an insecure, contradictory person and a life of some distress. He was born on 25 March 1906 in Southport, Lancashire, from Dissenting stock on both sides of the family. The cussedness of radical Nonconformity clung to him all his life. His father, a wealthy cotton merchant, sent him to Bootham, the Quaker school in Yorkshire, where he lost his religious belief, but acquired a Quaker training in evasiveness. This stuck to him as a historian. His best ideas were asides, discussed by thousands, but rarely by Taylor himself. I have heard him make startling statements; when challenged he would usually retreat into meditation. He once described himself as 'a man of extreme opinions weakly held'.

In 1924 he went to Oriel College, Oxford, on a history scholarship. During the General Strike he flirted briefly with Communism, but 'common sense kept breaking through'. He became a lifelong, though latterly disillusioned, Labour supporter. After obtaining a First in

History, he schooled himself in the austerities of research at Vienna's *Staatsarchiv*. It was somehow typical of him that he became a diplomatic historian by accident, not because he had any wish to improve the world. Fate, rather than Design, also plays the leading role in his histories. After Vienna, Taylor spent eight years teaching at Manchester University, where his head of department was the formidable Lewis Namier, before returning to Oxford as Fellow and Tutor in Modern History at Magdalen College in 1938. It was at Manchester that Taylor first developed his journalistic and platform skills. Lecturing without notes became his trade mark. Later on, in his television lectures, he would talk direct to camera, without teleprompter or props. His earliest books, *The Italian Problem in European Diplomacy 1847–49*, and *Germany's First Bid for Colonies 1884–85*, are detailed accounts of particular episodes, meticulously built up from the daily exchange of diplomatic messages. His marriage in 1931 to Margaret Adams, a girl from a Roman Catholic, upper-middle-class background, gave him 'nine years of great happiness and four children who were for long my mainstay in life. Thereafter it gave me a decade of intense, almost indescribable misery, which left me crippled and stunted emotionally, a person useless to god or man.'

For a political radical, Taylor wrote unexpectedly old-fashioned history. He supported the poor, but rarely wrote about them. Most of his history was about Courts and Chancelleries, diplomats and soldiers and outstanding men. They move like sleep-walkers in a world ultimately shaped by the facts of power, geography, nationality. Ideas, plans, purposes, good or bad, play little independent part in Taylor's history. He had little time for social history. Perhaps he simply recognized that history is the story of the rich and powerful.

In the Second World War, morals and history seemed for once to pull the same way. Taylor never doubted that the war against Hitler was a 'just' war, as well as a classic 'balance of power' war, with the flanks uniting against an exploding centre. Taylor served in the Home Guard and lectured and broadcast on war aims. Five of his next six books, *The Course of German History* (1945), *The Hapsburg Monarchy, 1809–1918* (1948), *The Struggle for Mastery in Europe 1848–1918* (1954), *Bismarck: The Man and the Statesman* (1955), and *The Origins of the Second World War* (1961) revolved round the German Problem. Germany, he wrote, had had no natural frontiers and therefore no natural restraints. In *The Struggle for Mastery*, he wrote: 'Where most of Europe felt overshadowed by Germany, she saw the more distant

Russian shadow; and many Germans thought of anticipating the Russian danger almost as genuinely as others thought of combining against the weight of Germany.' The historic achievement of the Red Army was to 'solve' the German problem as well as getting rid of Eastern Europe's landlords and capitalists. This judgment shows that historians are no better at predicting the future than anyone else. After the war he blamed America rather than Russia for the Cold War and refused to visit the United States on principle. Writing in *The Times* to support the release of Rudolf Hess from Spandau, he perpetrated a classic Taylorism when he suggested that Hess's only crime was to have been 'a premature supporter of NATO'.

In the 1950s Taylor's professional and public career reached its zenith. His *Struggle for Mastery* was recognized as a classic of technical virtuosity. His Monday morning lectures in the Oxford Examination Schools attracted audiences of hundreds. He was the first 'telly' don, appearing on such long-running chat shows as *In The News* and *Face the Press*. He wrote regular columns for the *Daily Herald* and *Sunday Express*. Moreover, in the afterglow of the Second World War it was still possible to feel that history was moving the right way. In 1955–6 he gave the Ford Lectures at Oxford on the Dissenting tradition in British foreign policy, published in 1956 as *The Troublemakers*. Its contemporary message was clear: Britain was locked in the wrong alliance system. 1956 was the year of the Suez crisis, and Taylor could imagine himself leading a crusade against a new Boer War. In 1957 he found a more durable moral cause when Britain started to manufacture the hydrogen bomb. Taylor became a founder-member of the Campaign for Nuclear Disarmament, serving on its Executive Committee. He saw himself as a modern Bright. His passion and demagogic skills made a great impact on audiences. It was in this heroic mood that he embarked on his *English History, 1914–1945*, published in 1965. It ended 'Few now sang Land of Hope and Glory. Few even sang England Arise. England had risen all the same.'

These illusions soon faded. CND had a few inspiring years, then collapsed. Taylor's personal and professional life also started to disintegrate. In 1953 he had married, as his second wife, Eve Crosland, sister of Tony Crosland. They had two sons. But this marriage failed as well, in circumstances so painful that Taylor had to omit from his memoirs any mention of his second wife. In 1957, to general surprise, Harold Macmillan passed him over for the Regius Professorship in Modern History in favour of Hugh Trevor-Roper. Taylor's popularity as a lecturer, journalist, and television personality had clearly aroused great jealousy. Lewis Namier, who advised the Prime Minister on the appointment, said he would support Taylor if he gave up writing for the *Sunday Express*. Taylor refused, and never spoke to Namier again. (He also claimed he would never have accepted the Chair from 'hands stained with the blood of Suez'.) Then, in 1961, at the height of the CND campaign, he published his *Origins of the Second World War*. Its denial that Hitler brought any special malevolent intent to the conduct of German foreign policy – 'In international affairs', Taylor wrote, 'there was nothing wrong with Hitler except that he was a German' – attracted widespread criticism from historians and public alike. Trevor-Roper (now Lord Dacre) led a furious onslaught against the book: Taylor's historical reputation, he said, was 'irreparably harmed'. Although Taylor overstated his case, it is his critics who look foolish today. In particular, they failed to grasp the relationship between Taylor's assessment of Hitler and his view of the German problem through time. As a result of this row, Taylor's special lectureship in international history was terminated in 1963. This brought his Oxford life effectively to an end, though he remained a non-teaching Fellow of Magdalen College till his retirement in 1976.

He went on working in London. Disappointed in his Oxford colleagues, Taylor had developed an unexpectedly warm friendship with Lord Beaverbrook, who had a soft spot for maverick men of the Left. Beaverbrook said of one Taylor speech that 'for clarity, wit and polish [it] was equal to the matured orations of Churchill, and with the fire and enthusiasm of Lloyd George at the height of his powers'. When Beaverbrook died, Taylor repaid his debt with an adoring, 700-page life of the press magnate, published in 1972. As Director of the Beaverbrook Library, housing the Beaverbrook and Lloyd George Papers, and at a regular weekly seminar, he kept in touch with the younger generation of researchers. His televised lectures on war and peace created a new audience for history; slim volumes of these lectures, essays, and book reviews appeared regularly. In 1975 came his last important work, *The Second World War*, in which he linked up the European and Far Eastern Wars into a single whole. A charming collection of occasional pieces, *An Old Man's Diary* (1984), was his last published work.

I only got to know Alan Taylor in the last fifteen years of his life. He was about to embark on his third marriage, to the Hungarian historian Eva Haraszti, in which he at last found the happiness which had eluded him earlier. (Her account of the marriage, *A Life with Alan*, was published in 1987.) I had persuaded him to give a couple of lectures in Bologna where I was teaching at the European graduate school of the Johns Hopkins University. We flew out together and spent the day visiting cathedrals – church architecture was a lifelong passion with him. I remember him bounding up to the top of the Romanesque cathedral at Modena, two steps at a time. 'Lloyd George always used to do that in old age to show he wasn't gaga,' Taylor informed me. At six o'clock precisely he walked into the packed auditorium having apparently not given the matter a thought all day, and concluded exactly on the stroke of seven that the only demonstrable cause of the First World War was that the Archduke Franz Ferdinand's chauffeur had taken the wrong turning at Sarajevo. At dinner that evening he alarmed my American students by saying that Nixon was a better President than Kennedy.

Physically Taylor was a small, somewhat unshapely, man, slightly stooped. His most prominent features were hooded eyes, encased in thick-lensed glasses, and a mobile mouth which often assumed a mischievous grin. He always wore a bow-tie. He was the most amiable of companions. He loved jokes and gossip, others' as well as his own. He had a wonderful speaking voice, but did not dominate conversations, often responding to some tendentious remark with a quizzical raising of the eyebrows as if to say: 'Do you really believe that?'. When I knew him he was deeply alarmed by inflation, obsessed by the threat of nuclear destruction, and despondent about the future of Britain. As the years passed and he fell victim to Parkinson's disease he fell increasingly silent in company. He was a shy man who found personal gestures difficult, but after one supper at our house at which he had hardly spoken, he said to me as he was leaving: 'I'm sorry I couldn't contribute much, but I did enjoy myself.' His greatest sadness was not being able to write any more. He once told me proudly how he used to polish off book reviews for the *Observer* in an hour; now he could no longer gather his thoughts.

His chief personal fault was vanity; as a historian he sometimes sacrificed truth to showmanship, being a prisoner, as well as a master, of style. But his influence has been overwhelmingly positive. Too old-fashioned in method, too eclectic in judgment, to found a school, he has been a liberating force in the study of modern history. His genius was to seize the neglected or unsuspected part of the truth, express it artistically, and add a pinch of mischief. Historians have been emboldened to pursue a heretical line of thought because they have the authority of Alan

Taylor. Students have been stimulated to historical thought itself by such sentences as 'Great events do not necessarily have great causes'; 'Bismarck fought "necessary" wars and killed thousands; the idealists of the twentieth century fought "just" wars and killed millions'; 'Which was better to be: a betrayed Czech or a saved Pole?' And many thousands of non-historians the world over have caught something at least of the spirit of history from the words and example of Alan Taylor.

Index